The Scottish Tradition in Literature

The Scottish Tradition in Literature

Kurt Wittig

GREENWOOD PRESS, PUBLISHERS
WESTPORT, CONNECTICUT

The Library of Congress has catalogued this publication as follows:

Library of Congress Cataloging in Publication Data

Wittig, Kurt, 1914-
The Scottish tradition in literature.

Bibliography: p.
1. Scottish literature--History and criticism.
I. Title.
[PR8511.W5 1972] 820'.9'941 72-6926
ISBN 0-8371-6504-0

First published in 1958 by Oliver and Boyd, Edinburgh

Reprinted with the permission of Kurt Wittig

Reprinted in 1972 by Greenwood Press, Inc.
51 Riverside Avenue, Westport, Conn. 06880

Library of Congress catalog card number 72-6926
ISBN 0-8371-6504-0

Printed in the United States of America

10 9 8 7 6 5 4 3 2

Preface

IN QUOTATIONS from Scottish authors of the fourteenth, fifteenth and sixteenth centuries, I have (very occasionally) altered the punctuation, have modernised the capitalisation, and (substantially in accordance with modern Scottish practice), have freely interchanged *i*, *j*, and *y*, and *u*, *v*, and *w* : but except in these respects I have reproduced the text as printed in the edition cited. If, in glossing the quotations, I have erred on the side of liberality, it is because I hope that among my readers there will be many who have no previous knowledge of Scots.

I am greatly indebted to the British Council for the grants without which this book could not have been written, and for the courteous consideration with which the staff of its offices in London, Aberdeen, and Düsseldorf studied all my various wishes.

I am also beholden to all Departments and offices of the University of Aberdeen with which I came in contact for the full co-operation which I enjoyed ; and am especially grateful to Mr James Michie, Lecturer in Scottish Literature ; to Mr Walter R. Humphries, Lecturer in Scottish History ; to Mr John Macdonald and Dr Annie Mackenzie, both of the Celtic Department ; and to Dr Douglas Simpson, the Librarian, and his staff.

Finally, I owe special thanks to Messrs Oliver and Boyd Ltd., and, above all, to Mr R. L. C. Lorimer, their editor, for the extreme care which he and his colleagues have devoted to this book. My correspondence with Mr Lorimer has been highly stimulating, and it has been a great advantage that he is both a Gaelic-reader and an expert on classical Highland pipe-music. In improving the form of this book, in checking (and finding) quotations, and in revising the footnotes, he has been indefatigable ; and but for his help I do not know how, far from Scotland, I could have seen this book through the press.

Lastly, acknowledgments are due to Dr C. M. Grieve, Mr Sydney Goodsir Smith, Mr Douglas Young, Mr George Bruce, and Mr Sorley Maclean, for permission to quote from their published poems ; to Mr John Soutar, for permission to quote from those of the late William Soutar ; to Messrs Faber & Faber Limited, for permission to quote from Dr Edwin Muir's published poems and from the novels of Neil Gunn ; and to Messrs Jarrolds (London) for permission to quote from *A Scots Quair*, by the late Leslie Mitchell.

K. W.

FREIBURG
December 1957

Contents

Part III

Another Spring?

Ane Exclamatioun

Aganis Detractouris and oncurtas Redaris that bene owr studius, but occasioun, to note and spy out Faltis or Offencis in this Volum, or ony othir crafty Warkis

Now throw the deip fast to the port I mark,
For heir is endit the lang desparit wark. . . .

Bot quhat danger is ocht to compile, allace !
Herand thir detractouris intill every place,
Or evir thai reid the wark, byddis byrn the buike.
Sum beyn sa frawart in malice and wangrace,
Quhat is weill said thai love nocht worth an ace,
Bot castis thame over to spy out falt and cruik :
All that thai fynd in hidlis, hyrn or nyuk
Thai blaw out, sayand in every manis face,
Lo, heir he failzeis, se thar he leis, luik ! . . .

Far eythar is, quha list syt doun to mote,
Ane othir sayaris faltis to spy and note,
Than but offence or falt thame self to wryte :
Bot for to chyde sum bene so brym and hoit,
Hald thai thar peax, the word wald scald thar throte ;
And has sik custum to jangill and bakbyte,
That, bot thai schent sum, thai suld bryst for syte.
I say na mayr, quhen all thar rerd is roung,
That wicht mon speke that can nocht hald his toung.

Quod Gawinus Douglas.

Introduction

BEFORE WE BEGIN, may I assure my readers that in speaking of a Scottish tradition in literature I have no subversive aims, no reactionary or revolutionary intentions? Scottish literature is part of our European heritage; and though the perspective in which I am going to expound some of its inherent moral and æsthetic values is perhaps an unfamiliar one, I am not surreptitiously attempting to separate things that are better joined, or to erect an invisible barrier that would isolate Scottish literature itself from the larger world to which it inseparably belongs.

In the study of literature, we can concentrate on single writers and their work, or we can view literature itself in relation to the whole cultural trend, the thought, the moral, æsthetic and intellectual climate of the particular period to which it belongs. The first of these two ways of studying literature may throw light on the creative process and of the work of art as such; the second may give us a better understanding of literature as an expression of its own day and age.

Though I recognise the advantages of both these methods of study, I set out from the somewhat different premise that literature is not written in a vacuum, but grows out of the life of the community, and must therefore be studied as a product of that particular community in which it originated. From one country to another, the climate differs as much intellectually as meteorologically: terms like, for example, "romantic" and "classical," "realism" and "symbolism," "wit," "irony," "humour," and "satire," have different connotations, if not actually different denotations, in Italy, France, Germany, England and Scotland. To the horizontal dimension of contemporary moral, æsthetic and intellectual climate we must add, therefore, the vertical dimension of place and heritage, and must do the literature that we are studying the honour of recognising that it has both "a local habitation and a name."

Now, in writing a history of English or even of British literature it would only be fit and proper to take London as the point at which our vertical and horizontal intersect. But from London—as shown by the usual resultant caricature of Dunbar as a Chaucerian—the work of Scottish writers is seen in a false perspective ; not because London is four hundred miles from Edinburgh, but because in Scotland a different set of traditions has created a society which in many respects (though not in all) is very different from that which exists in England. Scotland was for many centuries an independent country, and had a self-centred culture of its own. This ought surely to be our starting-point. Whether we ourselves *want* Scotland to go on having different traditions is neither here nor there ; for as long as even a few Scottish writers are conscious of having inherited a Scottish tradition we shall not do justice to their work unless we study it in relation to that Scottish tradition which they themselves are conscious of having inherited. This approach does not supersede the study of single writers and their work, or of literature considered as an expression of the spirit of its age ; it complements it by adding a vertical dimension.

Nor is this book meant to be a history of Scottish literature. Rather, as already said, it is an attempt to expound some of the moral, æsthetic and intellectual values inherent in the Scottish literary tradition. In expounding these values I have picked out the ones which to me seem to be specifically Scottish, and have largely ignored the rest. And—though I trust that in dealing with individual writers whose work I have had occasion to discuss, I have not distorted my account so as to suit my own purposes—completeness has not been my aim. I know that I have thus laid myself wide open to the reproach " You ought at least to have included Robert Wrangeneuch—he isn't at all a bad poet, really." With such strong local loyalties as there are in Scotland, this is inevitable. In dealing with contemporary Scottish literature, I have had to exclude a few whom some of my readers, and perhaps posterity too, may well regard as major Scottish writers ; and to my own deep regret, I have also had to exclude all Scottish criticism, devotional literature (for centuries the staple literary diet), and Latin writings.

Let me emphasise, too, that in speaking of a tradition I am not postulating any inherited racial characteristics. Some well-known architectural motifs—such as crowstepped gabling, open spires and crowns, and stone-slabbed roofing—are often said to be characteristically Scottish. Does that imply that none of them can be found elsewhere? Or does it mean that they all express a Scottish spirit? The implication is, I take it, that they reflect an underlying, essentially Scottish conception of beauty, and that the same essentially Scottish conception of it is to some extent reflected in certain other Scottish arts. In fact one can detect a certain affinity between the carved archways of Dryburgh, St Oran's Chapel, Melrose and Elgin Cathedral and the intricate ornamentation of much Scottish poetry, especially the sonnets; and in expounding the Scottish tradition in literature I have occasionally hinted at parallels in other arts.

It may be that none of the characteristics of the Scottish tradition in literature, as I have presented it, is peculiar to it: all of them could perhaps be identified in a writer here, a poem there, in the literature of many other countries. But, as I see it, the really decisive consideration is that they are so much more pronounced in Scottish than in other literature; and for some of them—with my limited knowledge—I have *not* found parallels elsewhere. For all I know, some of these traits *may* be a racial inheritance. Many of them are collectively a spontaneous expression of the national character as shaped, *inter alia*, by geography, climate, history, social conditions, education, religious beliefs, and various conventional Scottish attitudes, opinions, and prejudices. And some certainly are nothing more than literary conventions that have come to be widely accepted in the Scottish society—or, on a higher level, conceptions of what literature, and art in general, should be.

One fundamental fact about Scottish culture is that it has for centuries possessed two languages, and now possesses a third: for to Scottish Gaelic and Lowland Scots, we must now add standard Southern English. Gaelic and Scots each had its own associated oral and literary traditions; and how surprising it would have been if these two streams of tradition had been able to remain coolly apart from each other! But here we must be cautious, for only the outer edges of this particular field have yet been ploughed.

Gael and Sassenach, Highlander and Lowlander, have not always seen eye to eye with one another: but for better or worse they have been thrown together in one unitary national society. Though he is largely unaware of it, the staunch Lowlander carries on his back a Gaelic biological and linguistic heritage. It is by no means the only one, but it is there. Today, "quhilk to consider is ane pane," the number of Gaelic-speakers has dwindled to less than 100,000: in the time of Walter Scott, though only a minority of the total population spoke Gaelic, the greater part of the country was Gaelic-speaking territory. In the time of King Robert I, who himself came from a Gaelic-speaking district, parliamentary business was transacted in Gaelic ; and before Malcolm III brought Margaret to the throne, English, such as it then was, had not yet established itself outside a small corner in the south-east. So, at one time or another, as far as they were of the old stock, the ancestors of today's Lowlanders took up Scots as a second, a foreign language—but for centuries there must have been a large number of more or less bilingual people, who still continued to think in Gaelic.

All this has left its traces on either of the two languages, and on the ideas which they are used to express. Perhaps it is only a coincidence that Scots retained the fricative in *nicht*, *thocht*, etc.—a fricative that Gaelic has kept, too. But is it purely coincidental that Scots *toun* and Gaelic *baile* both mean " farm, homestead," as well as *town* ? That Scots *foot* and Gaelic *bun* can both mean the " mouth of a river," as in Galafoot, Leaderfoot, Footdee, Bunessan, Bun Neabhais ? That the *-ing*—form, various modal forms of the verb, and substantival expressions are used much more frequently in Scots and Gaelic than in English ? And that when she goes shopping a Scots housewife will say, " I was wanting a cauliflower " ; or when " a ring comes to the door," " who will that be now, I'm wondering ? "

In trying to assess the influence of Gaelic literature on Scots we must bear it in mind that to a much greater extent than elsewhere, the " literature " of the Highlands and Islands was transmitted orally. Even in the eighteenth century such outstanding poets as Duncan McIntyre and John MacCodrum were (literally) illiterate and carried both the poetry of the past and their own in their heads. In the Highlands and Islands, till quite recently, the one great forum was the *ceilidh*, the fireside gathering, at which there was much telling of traditional tales, singing of songs, reciting of poems, and instancing of proverbs and other ancient lore. The language of poetry *may* thus have influenced the language of everyday life : it *must* have fostered a taste for this kind of poetry in a widely scattered public which first gradually become bilingual and sooner or later went finally over to Scots. Usually there is no literary " source " in which we can point to chapter and verse. But through such devious channels as these, Gaelic conceptions of poetry must subtly but powerfully have influenced Lowland Scots literary taste.

How powerfully the stream of Scottish literary tradition still flows through such subterranean channels may be shown by one curious example. In the Bannatyne Manuscript, written in 1568, there is an anonymous poem which tells " How the first Helandman of God was maid of ane horss turd." For centuries, not one word further of this obscure poem. Then, today, an equally anonymous children's version not only is sung in the streets, but is so popular that an Edinburgh restaurant thinks fit to quote the first stanza as an advertisement on the front page of *The Scotsman* for 9th April 1955 ! And perhaps the modern popular version of Alexander MacDonald's Gaelic song to Morag is related to it in the same kind of way.

I have not Gaelic enough to speak authoritatively about Gaelic poetry. But, for the reasons that I have indicated, I felt that I could not totally exclude it, that to maintain a true perspective I must at least keep it always in the corner of my eye. If I have made mistakes in my comparisons of Scots with Gaelic, I shall be the first to welcome any that are more competent.

Lastly, what business is it of a foreigner's to evaluate, or try to evaluate, so inherently Scottish a concern as the Scottish tradition in literature ? That is indeed a delicate question, for even to speak of it as *Scottish* literature may involve the Scot himself, consciously or unconsciously, in many an agonising conflict of loyalties. Surely there can be such a thing as Scottish literature without prejudice to the Union, perhaps even to the Crown ? Though some Scots will be capable of giving you a rational answer, others will react almost as if you had touched them on a naked nerve. What is, what should be, Scotland's literary language ? The " true language " or " *beurla chruaidh* " ? Lallans ? Synthetic Scots ? What was the date at which the decline of Scottish literary tradition began ? 1745 ? 1707 ? 1603 ? 1560 ? 1513 ? Or perhaps even in 1314, which postponed the Union for nearly four hundred years ? Try putting a few of these straightforward questions and in some company you may be startled at the violence of the contradictory responses that you provoke, for deep down in the heart and mind of many Scotsmen there is a kind of schism arising out of the clash of his conflicting loyalties, and today in Scotland cultural and political life provides abundant evidence that these questions are not merely academic ones.

Here somebody from outside enjoys a happy detachment. He has the advantage of seeing things from both outside and inside, so that he can distinguish between the typical (often, from inside, taken for granted) and the specific. And finally there is a better guarantee that he will be impartial, no matter how much he loves the country and its people.

Part I

Spring Tide

I

First Stirrings: John Barbour

THE Scottish tradition in literature begins relatively late. The first work of any size that can with certainty be assigned a definite date is *The Bruce*, by JOHN BARBOUR, archdeacon of St Machar's, Aberdeen, on which (as he informs us [1]) the poet was at work in 1375. As regards earlier works,[2] Barbour himself mentions ballads that the girls were singing about Sir John de Soulis (XVI.519), and quotes the fable of the fisher and the fox (XIX.649 ff.). The lament for Alexander III (d. 1285-6) of which eight lines are quoted by Andrew of Wyntoun [3] may well have been a contemporary tribute. But apart from these pieces of indirect evidence, we are in the realm of surmise.[4] The frequent sacking of archives in a country ravaged by war is one reason for the paucity of early Scots literary documents; the fact that the "Inglis" spoken in Scotland was only just beginning to be distinguishable from Northern English, another. Moreover, we must not overlook the fact that English or Scots was only the language of a minority in a Gaelic-speaking nation.

In John Barbour, however, we have at the root of the tradition no mere legendary figure, but a man of considerable substance, and his poem is without parallel in the Middle Ages.[5] Therefore the way

[1] XIII.699 ff.

[2] Cp. *The Buik of Alexander*, ed. R. L. Græme Ritchie, Scottish Text Society (hereafter cited as S.T.S.), 4 vols., 1921-9, VOL. I, pp. xcix ff., and Friedrich Brie, *Die nationale Literatur Schottlands von den Anfängen bis zur Renaissance*, Halle 1937, chs. I and II.5.

[3] *The original Chronicle of Andrew of Wyntoun* (*c.* 1420), ed. F. J. Amours, S.T.S., 6 vols., 1903-14, BK. VII.3261 ff.

[4] See below, pp. 103 ff.

[5] I am not here concerned with Barbour's possible authorship of the *Buik of Alexander* (above, n. 2), of "The Ballet of the nine Nobles," of the legends of St Machor and St Ninian (Nos. XXVII and XL in *Legends of the Saints*, ed. W. M. Metcalfe, S.T.S., 3 vols., 1896), and of the *Troy* fragments in Camb. U.L. MS. Kk.v.30 (*The Bruce*, ed. W. W. SKEAT, S.T.S., 2 vols., 1894, pp. xlvi ff.); or with Wyntoun's ref. to a *Brut* (II.767) and a Stewart genealogy (II.131, III.621). These questions have received undue prominence in criticism: cp. Albert Hermann, *Untersuchungen über des schottische Alexanderbuch*, Halle 1893; G. Neilson, *John Barbour, Poet and Translator*, London 1900; J. T. T. Brown, "*The Wallace*" *and* "*The Bruce*" *restudied*, Bonn 1900; E. Koeppel in *Englische Studien*, X (1887), 373 ff., and P. Buss in *Anglia*, IX (1886), 493 ff.

in which *The Bruce* is neglected today is truly astonishing : not only has there been no reprint since the edition by W. M. Mackenzie in 1909,[6] but not even a selection is available, and surveys of the Scottish tradition frequently begin a century later.[7]

Yet *The Bruce*, written before Chaucer's great poems, is a remarkable work. Here, in the second half of the fourteenth century, when, under the shameful reign of David II (*regn.* 1329-71), Scotland's national existence was in jeopardy, a poet sets out to commemorate the heroism of the Scottish nation, so as to preserve it from oblivion and at the same time to inspire patriotism. Barbour is not concerned with chivalry or with personal loyalty, with knightly prowess or with individual bravery ; nor (as some critics would have us believe [8]) is patriotism merely, in his poem, an incidental theme. In order to assure ourselves of this, we have only to glance through the proem (I.1-444) : Barbour first (1-36) straightforwardly announces his purpose, which is to compile a " suthfast " narrative of the achievements of " King Robert of Scotland " and of " gud Schyr James off Douglas." Then (37-179) he sketches in the political background of the story, with reference especially to the dispute concerning the succession which had arisen in Scotland after the death of Alexander III. Speaking as a patriot, he deplores (113 ff.) the folly of the Scots barons in submitting the dispute to Edward I of England for arbitration—

Had yhe [a]tane kep quhat was [b]thrillag... — [a] *taken heed* [b] *thraldom*
Yhe suld, [a]for-owtyn his [b]demyng, — [a] *without* [b] *judgment*
Haiff chosyn yhow a king, that mycht
Have haldyn [a]weyle the land in rycht. — [a] *well*

—thus providing a pretext for English aggression, and opening the way for the destruction of Scottish national independence. This leads to a further section (180-224) in which the poet dwells on the misery and injustice suffered by the Scots under foreign rule ; and

[6] John Barbour, *The Bruce*, ed. W. M. Mackenzie, London 1909 ; this edn. is used here in preference to Skeat (above, n. 5), whose preface, etc., are, however, indispensable. For nationalist ideas in Barbour, see Brie (above, n. 2), whose fine criticism is unfortunately marred by political tendencies and terminology of his time, and *The Buik of Alexander*, ed. Ritchie (*ibid.*).

[7] *E.g.* John Speirs, *The Scots Literary Tradition*, London 1940 (presumably because Scots was not yet fully differentiated from English).

[8] *E.g.* Mackenzie, Leatham (*John Barbour, Father of English Poetry*, 1933, an insignificant lecture), and Ritchie (in *B. of Alex.*, vol. I, p. ccviii, as against p. ccxxv).

the underlying theme, already foreshadowed in the previous section, is then boldly and triumphantly proclaimed in the famous apostrophe (225 ff.) :

> A ! fredome is a noble thing !

The proem ends with the introduction (275-444) of the " good Sir James " as a man who has himself suffered shameful injustice. The poem proper begins (445 ff.) at the words

> Lordingis, quha likis for [a]till her, *[a] to hear*
> The romanys now begynnys her.

And here again (468 ff.) Barbour stresses the twin themes of " fredome " and " richt " by comparing the Scots with the Maccabees, of whom we read in the Bible that they

> Fawcht in-to mony stalwart [a]stour, *[a] battle*
> For to delyvir thar countre
> Fra folk that, throw iniquite,
> Held thaim and thairis in thrillage.

Barbour's theme is, fundamentally, the moral and political conception that the conventional knightly virtues—prowess, chivalry, loyalty, patriotism itself—are of no account unless they are supported by the ideals of " fredome " and " richt " ; and in this respect, at any rate, his " romance " is quite without parallel in the Middle Ages.

Barbour's conviction that his cause is also the cause of " fredome " and " richt " is the basis of a remarkable quality that can perhaps best be described as " poise " : he need not hotly assert his patriotism, but can afford to be objective in judging his enemies. He flares up at their injustice and oppression, but even in Englishmen he praises courage and probity wherever they appear. On occasion (*e.g.* XVI.565 ff., 645 ff.), he does not hesitate to represent the English in a more advantageous light than his own countrymen ; and in his account of Bannockburn he hails Sir Giles de Argentine, an Englishman, as the third knight in his time after the Emperor Henry and Robert the Bruce, thus placing him above even Sir James Douglas. This poise, as I have called it, is no mere reflex of political caution in a time of political vacillation (Brie, p. 102), or of a conventionally chivalrous outlook ; it is based on faith in the justice of a cause, and is essentially a moral attitude. Barbour regarded the war with

England, not as a civil or dynastic struggle, but as a war for freedom and independence, and his own patriotism was neither aggressive nor sentimental, spiteful or provincial.[9]

It is essential to grasp the fact that the conviction on which Barbour's poise was based had itself a religious basis. It is astonishing that a critic of Brie's insight disputes this and always seeks to represent Barbour's religious utterances as purely conventional (pp. 75, 77). Of course Barbour sometimes refers to God in set forms of words (I.34 ff., 157). Yet it is instructive to consider Bruce's reply (I.157 ff.) when Edward I offers him the Kingdom of Scotland on condition that Bruce will recognise him as overlord :

' Schyr,' said he, ' sa God me save,
The kynryk [a]yharn I nocht to have, — [a] *yearn*
Bot gyff it fall of *rycht* to me :
And gyff *God* will that it sa be,
I sall als *frely* in all thing
Hald it, as it [a]afferis to king.' — [a] *befits*

" Fredome " and " richt " are here represented as things that God alone can give. This is a conception that runs like a red thread through the whole poem. Douglas waits for God's help to regain his right (I.312, 328). In the thematic passage beginning the romance proper (I.445 ff.) God is mentioned thrice within ten lines, as he who gives force, irresistible help, and almighty protection even against superior forces (450, 456, 459). It might be objected that this is one of the few Biblical allusions in the whole poem, and that in referring to the Maccabees it was only natural for Barbour to mention God's name several times. But why *does* Barbour refer to the Maccabees? Is not the fact that he compares the Scots, especially in such a context, to a small nation defending their God-given right and God-given freedom, with God's active help, against vastly superior forces, in itself highly significant? In this connexion, it should be observed that the Declaration of Arbroath (1320),[10] surely the most remarkable

[9] Barbour had been to Oxford and Paris, and had seen the world.

[10] From the Barons of Scotland (who assembled at Arbroath on 6 April 1320) to Pope John XXII. In translation, the relevant paragraph (about a fifth of the whole) reads as follows : " From these innumerable evils, with the aid of Him who heals and sains the wounded, we have been delivered by our most valiant prince, king and lord, the Lord Robert, who, to set free his people and his heritage, cheerfully, like another Maccabaeus or Joshua, endured toil and weariness, hardships and dangers. He it is that God's Providence and, in accordance with our laws and customs, which we shall defend even with our lives, the rightful succession and the due consent and agreement of us all, have made our prince

political document of the Middle Ages, expresses the same ideas of freedom and right and God's help, and also compares Bruce to Maccabaeus : the crucial passage reads like a synopsis of Barbour's poem.

Elsewhere, Bruce is rescued from critical dangers by God's hand (v.533 ff., 577 ff. ; VII.291, 488, 519), or help is implored from God (v.583 ff. ; VIII.261 ff., 309 ff. ; XI.203, etc.), and before Bannockburn the Scots kneel in prayer to the jeers of the English. Barbour proceeds from the conviction (I.128 ff.) that every thing lies with God :

> For in this warld, that is sa wyde
> Is nane determynat that sall
> Knaw thingis that ar for to fall :
> But God, that is [a]off maist poweste, — [a] *of most power*
> Reservyt till his majeste
> For to knaw, in his prescience,
> Off [a]alkyn tyme the [b]mowence. — [a] *every kind of* [b] *change*

These passages, it is true, are short in themselves ; but before drawing conclusions from this it would surely be prudent to form some estimate of Barbour's artistic methods, and in particular to notice one point entirely ignored by Brie—namely the fact that Barbour frequently makes use of understatement. We shall see later that despite his habitual prolixity Barbour just hints at the deepest emotions, as if almost ashamed to say too much. The fervent hymn to freedom and

---

and king : and to him, as having wrought the salvation of his people, we, for the safeguarding of our liberty, are bound as much by his rights as by his merits, and shall in all things adhere. But were he to desist from the task that he has begun, or show himself willing to subject us and our realm to the King of England or to the English, we should instantly strive to expel him as our enemy and subverter of his rights and ours, and should make another our King who would be equal to the task of our defence. For so long as one hundred of us shall be left alive, we shall never in any degree submit to the domination of the English. For it is not for glory, riches or honour that we fight, but for FREEDOM alone, which no good man surrenders but with his life." Further on, there is also a remarkable sentence in which the Scots lords argue with the Pope as Scottish Presbyterians were later to argue with God : " But if, lending too credulous an ear to the allegations of the English, Your Holiness does not act sincerely, but continues to favour them to our discomfiture, we believe that the destruction of bodies, the perdition of souls, and all other consequent evils which they shall do to us and we to them, shall be charged to your account by the Most High." The Declaration of Arbroath has been printed (in Latin and English) by Sir George Mackenzie, *Causae forenses* (in *Works*, I.145) ; in a pamphlet, *United Scotland*, 1943 (2nd edn., 1951) ; and by the late Lord Cooper of Culross, Lord President of the Court of Session (who shows that it was probably drafted by Bernard of Linton), in *Supra crepidam* (Edinburgh 1951 : reprinted in *Selected Papers*, Edinburgh 1956, pp. 324 ff.). There is also a translation by the late Dr Agnes Mure Mackenzie (Saltire Society 1951).

the above quotation are perhaps the longest passages in which Barbour reveals any of his deepest convictions ; otherwise our poet does not make the movements of his heart the small change of everyday.

Brie is on firmer ground when he expresses astonishment that Barbour, the archdeacon, has so little to say about the part played by the clergy in the War of Independence (cp., however, Barbour's account of the Bishop of St Andrews in Book I), and nothing at all about the ecclesiastical conditions of the time, about the Pope's attitude, about the excommunication of Bruce and the clergy of the country, or about Bruce's own religious convictions or his donations to the Church. There is very little Biblical language, and none of the heroes resembles the ideal of a martyr. Barbour introduces neither angels nor saints,[11] nor anything of the supernatural apparatus so important in other medieval epics. Once he mentions a rumour of miracles, but here (xvii.877 ff.) he shows himself a realist :

> Bot [a]quhethir he [b]haly wes or [c]nane, — [a] *whether* [b] *holy* [c] lit. *none*
> At Pomfret [a]thusgat was he slane. — [a] *in this way*

Only one event is explained as a miracle, namely the occasion on which the women and children carrying arrows to the defenders of Berwick escape uninjured ; but that was rather (xvii.824 f.)

> The myrakill of God Almychty,
> And *to* [a]*nocht ellis* it set can I. — [a] *nothing else*

Some of these facts are really astonishing. Fordun, too, in his *Chronicle*, is careful not to touch the hot iron of Church politics. But if the archdeacon left no traces, no more did the lawyer, the clerk of audit, the auditor of exchequer. Barbour knew life at court, but there is no courtly element. The attitude shown by Barbour in dealing with historical events is decidedly realistic, yet it does not clash with the religious presuppositions of his own patriotism. Though he was no great artist, Barbour realised that selection and unity of purpose were essential principles in an epic poem. He cut out everything that had no bearing on his theme : such as the wavering and far from blameless early career of Bruce, and even the deeds of William Wallace, a more disinterested and in many ways a greater figure than Robert the Bruce and one whose memory has perhaps always appealed more to the heart of the people. Ritchie (pp. ccvi ff.)

[11] Except St Margaret (d. 1093, wife of Malcolm III), whose prophecy regarding Edinburgh Castle is mentioned at x.736 ff.

thinks that this omission is to be explained by Barbour's desire to glorify royalty, but royal dignity or symbols do not enter into the poem at all. For Barbour, Robert the Bruce was the man in whom the " richt " of Scotland was vested, and who, when urged to make an end of English iniquity and oppression and to take his right into his own hands, said (I.507 ff.) :

' [a]Sen yhe will it be [b]swa, — [a] *since you* [b] *so*
I will blythly apon me [a]ta — [a] *take*
The state, for I [a]wate I have rycht ; — [a] *know*
And rycht [a]mays oft the feble [b]wycht.' — [a] *makes* [b] *strong*

Of all the other efforts to achieve independence, only that of James Douglas is given a certain prominence here, no doubt because he was so closely connected with Bruce and carried his heart against the Infidel. Thus, in spite of the numerous details and the occasionally tangled threads of the action, Barbour achieves a certain artistic unity of interest by means of his moral theme and its religious foundation. Tension spans the poem from beginning to end : from Bruce's murder of his rival John the Red Comyn before the altar of the Church of the Grey Friars in Dumfries to Bruce's testament and the carrying of his heart against the Saracens. The former sounds (II.45 ff.) a note of fate—

Tharfor sa hard myscheiff him [a]fell, — [a] *befell*
That Ik herd nevir in romanys tell
Off man sa hard [a]frayit as wes he, — [a] *beset with terrors*
That eftirwart [a]com to [b]sic bounte ; — [a] *came* [b] *such bounty*

with the latter, the " richt " returns to God's hands, the " good Sir James " is killed, and the poem as a whole is brought neatly and effectively to a conclusion.[12]

Still, Barbour's religious attitude is astonishing in a child of the fourteenth century. He has a profound faith in God, yet nowhere does he refer to the Church as a mediator, mention its rituals, invoke its saints, or himself employ its symbolism, its allegories, its dogmas. A century and a half before the Reformation, he converses with God face to face. We shall find other instances of this in Scottish poetry—

[12] The unity inspired by the theme of " fredome " and " richt " fades somewhat after the detailed account of Bannockburn ; here Barbour inserts a kind of colophon (XIII.703 ff.) which may originally have been meant to form the conclusion of the poem. If, as has been suggested, the sequel was written under biographical and historical necessity, Barbour at least achieved a skilful interpretation of the end.

for example, in Henryson. Barbour is only the first of a long series of Scottish writers who seem not only to be on terms of an informal intimacy with God (or the Devil), but even to be disposed, on occasion, to argue with Him.

No wonder that the Scottish people were later to find the spirit of the Reformation so congenial. For Barbour, no less than Henryson, was evidently expressing the popular attitude; and it may be no accident that the Gaelic proverbs (which were only collected in the late eighteenth and nineteenth centuries,[13] but doubtless reflect the attitude of a much earlier period) embody a similar conception: God, just and almighty, is the ruler of Destiny, but Christ is little mentioned, and no *specifically* Christian ideas are expressed.

Barbour uses many proverbs and proverbial expressions[14]; his language is popular and full of mother-wit, it is the kind of language that coins proverbs. His religious utterances are not made as detached moral comments in the style (say) of Thackeray. They are frequently in the form of a fervent prayer of the poet's, for help in a crisis (v.583 f.; VII.578; VIII.309 ff.): the poet cannot sit still, his own personality is in the tale. His comments often break in on the narrative; impatient, ironical, irate, in the same grim humour that we shall find in Carlyle, and also in Henryson. Anger at the short-sightedness of the Scottish nobles (I.91 ff.); a curse against a traitor (IV.25):

In hell condampnyt mot he be!

a shrewd peasant's chuckle at a plan that miscarried (XI.151):

... but, [a]nocht-for-thi, — [a] *nevertheless*
[a]Or thai cum all to thair [b]entent, — [a] *before* [b] *intent*
[a]Howis in [b]haill clath sall be rent. — [a] *holes* [b] *whole cloth*

This, however, takes us from a study of the basic ideas to that of the style.

* * *

John Barbour aimed at a true and authentic account. Efforts at verisimilitude occur repeatedly in the fourteenth century,[15] but no-where is precision sought so persistently as it is here. Barbour was

[13] 1785, ed. Donald Mackintosh; standard edition by Alexander Nicolson 1881. Cp. Magnus Maclean, *The Literature of the Highlands*, 2nd edn., 1925, pp.137 ff. The Scots proverbs have a more universal character.

[14] The list in Skeat (see Index IV, *s.v.* Proverbs) could easily be enlarged.

[15] Cp. Brie, pp. 44 f.

born some six years after Bannockburn, during Robert the Bruce's reign, and within his own circle of acquaintances he must have known men whose fathers had fought in the great war. He makes great efforts at authenticity. Occasional phrases such as " sum men sayis," " as men said me," " as I herd say," etc., may be just a way of speaking ; but occasionally the poet stresses that he has his knowledge from an eye-witness, gives the name of his informant (IX.575), states expressly that he does not know a name or detail (V.537, 541 ff. ; IV.110 ff. ; XV.206 ff. ; VI.493 ff.), reports two different versions (I ; II.40 ff. ; VII.53 ff. ; XVII.46), or presents something as a rumour the truth of which he cannot check (XVII.877). Barbour habitually stresses details that were tactically important or helped to decide the outcome of a battle : details of an ambush where a superior force was vanquished (VI.373 ff.) ; exactly how a sleuth-hound loses the trail at the brook (VII.1 ff.) ; the precise configuration of a moor, pass, shaw, ford which the Scots exploit to compensate their small numbers (VIII.32 ff., 94 ff. ; IX.384 ff. ; X.17 ff. ; XVI.377 ff.) ; the close personal reconnaissance that Bruce invariably makes before selecting his battlefield or deciding his tactics (VIII.164 ff. ; IX.264), etc.[16] No essential detail is overlooked. The accounts of the taking of the walled towns and castles (Perth, IX.384 ff. ; Linlithgow, X.131 ff. ; Roxburgh, X.332 ff. ; Edinburgh, X.584 ff. ; and especially Berwick, XVII) contain a wealth of accurate information. Sometimes the details are of greater picturesque than historical value, but they help to make the description vivid : for example, a fleeing man is caught by the sheath of his sword, but his steed starts so impetuously that the belt breaks (VIII.80 ff.) ; the King is the second to climb the walls of Perth (IX.412), and Thomas Randolph the third to mount the ramparts of Edinburgh Castle (X.645).[17] We feel the gusto of the story-teller when the Scots approach Roxburgh Castle in the dusk of Shrove Tuesday, on all fours, and (X.386 ff.) one of the sentries takes them for cattle, exclaiming :

> ' This man thinkis to mak gude chere,'
> (And [a]nemmyt ane husband thar-by neir) — [a] *named*
> ' That has left all his oxyne out.'

[16] Again this is the historical truth, for skilful exploitation of terrain *was* one of the major reasons for the success of the Scots.

[17] It is interesting to compare what Dr James Ritchie has to say of the Scottish scientist : " The natural genius of these men and the genius of Scottish science bears a characteristic stamp—it is a faculty for minute detailed observation, for accuracy in small things. . . . " (*Scotland*, ed. H. W. Meikle, Edinburgh 1947, p. 138).

In his passion for giving as full and as exact an account as possible, Barbour borders, at times, on the pedestrian, as in his story of the captain in this siege (x.487 ff.)—but an obsession with facts is something that the English often cast up against the Scots. Many of the details given in his narrative look as if taken over from some older ballad on the event (xiii.662).

While in his details Barbour is very accurate, down to the date and the weather (ix.127 f. ; xi.352), he is rather high-handed in his manipulation of the sequence of events : a battle of 1313 may be found in the midst of the account of 1307[18] ; and a defeat in Ireland is hidden (xvi.263) behind the bland statement :

Bot to gif battale nane thai fand.

Sometimes Barbour's material may have been defective, but sometimes he arranges it, consciously or not, according to subject-matter. Thus *all* the castles recaptured by the Scots are listed in Bk. X. During the siege of Berwick by the English, several attacks from the sea are telescoped into one, which is then described in very vivid pictures, especially of the fire (xvii.465 ff.).

Barbour has collected all that he could—some of it from eye-witnesses—and he seems to have felt that as much of it as possible must be written down, that no detail, however trivial, must be allowed to pass into oblivion. In order to show that Bruce and his companions were second to none, Barbour also inserts, especially in the earlier books, many digressions concerning the heroes of antiquity ; and the king himself tells similar stories as a moral or example to his fellow-sufferers. As a result of all this, the poem totals 13,550 lines—a length that is remarkable in Scottish literature, which excels rather in short concentrated works of art than in longer pieces.

Though this suggests, at first sight, a comparison with the prolixity of the *Orrmulum* or of Sir David Lyndsay, it is due principally to the author's unspoken conviction that (as another Scottish poet put it) " facts are chiels that winna ding," and to the resultant inclusion of so much detail ; yet each of the series of the individual events which form the core of Barbour's narrative is drawn in with quick, suggestive strokes, with a delight in action and movement recalling the Scottish ballads. This is more marked in the earlier parts (*e.g.* the siege and

[18] Much has been made of the confusion of Robert Bruce the Elder and the Younger in the poem, but nobody with the least knowledge of the background will be confused. For Ritchie's opinion of the historical details see below, n. 20.

fire of Kildrummy, IV.80 ff.) ; after Bannockburn the poem tends to be encyclopædic. The dialogues—which are as, under the circumstances, they could only have been—are splendidly concise and terse. Just compare the endless declamations of Emenidus and his knights in *Li Fuerres di Gadres* when an urgent message is to be sent to Alexander [19] with the precise dialogue, quick and to the point, in *Bruce*, VII.9 ff., 122 ff., 137 ff., 179 ff., 241 ff.—to mention only a single book. Here there is quick dramatic movement, especially in the last of these five passages, giving it vivid life, even though it may not be relevant. Elsewhere, the dramatist in Barbour breaks out in many places : his accounts of the dispute over the succession (I.37 ff.), and of the conflict between Edward I and Douglas (I.415 ff.) are tautly and pungently dramatic. With sharp insight, Barbour enables us to enter into the minds of the participants—we *feel* Edward's ire as well as Douglas's sense of grievance—and does not allow his narrative to be encumbered with legal or chronological complexities. The issue between Edward, Bruce, and Balliol (I.153 ff.) is presented in the form of dramatic exchange ; the laconic and popular language of this scene has something of the drama of a cattle-market. Other remarkably dramatic scenes are that under the walls of Edinburgh Castle (x.620 ff.), or when Edward haughtily refuses the advice to retreat at Bannockburn and then to counter-attack when the Scots would be looting the abandoned camp (XII.450 ff.). These scenes owe their dramatic character not only to Barbour's fine handling of dialogue, but also to his quick penetration into the minds of the participants ; quick changes of scene heighten the effect.

Many passages of laconic brevity are thus incorporated in the broad descriptive sweep of Barbour's narrative. Everything static or merely ceremonial is quickly swept aside : having dealt with Bruce's coronation in four lines (II.178 ff.), Barbour adds :

> Bot of [a]thar nobleis gret affer, — [a] *their*
> Thar service, [a]na thar [b]realte, — [a] *nor* [b] *royalty*
> Yhe sall [a]her na thing now for me. — [a] *hear nothing*

But our poet is specially tightlipped when he comes close to emotion : here he practises the Scottish art of understatement. Where another poet of his time would indulge in praises of a magnificent gift, Barbour will call it " fair eneuch." The despondency of the English army

[19] *Li Fuerres di Gadres*, 8.24-21.13 (= *Forray of Gadderis*, 209-814), in *B. of Alex.*, ed. Ritchie, VOL. I, pp. 7-26.

before Bannockburn is expressed (xii.386 f.) in a half-negative fashion :

> Bot nocht-for-thi I [a]trow thai sall — [a] *believe*
> [a]In-till thair hertis [b]dredande be. — [a] *in* [b] *afraid*

The annihilation of an army, Barbour says (x.96), " till Johne of Lorne it suld displese." Barbour fights shy of pathos and sentimentality ; where another poet would exult, he confines himself to grim humour or caustic irony. The arrows fall so thick (xiii.45 ff.) that they

> ... left eftir thame [a]taknyng — [a] *tokening*
> That sall neid, as I trow, [b]lechyng. — [a] *leeching*

Elsewhere (ix.645 ff.), the enemy is beaten so severely that

> I trow he sall nocht mony day
> Have will to [a]warra that cuntre, — [a] *make war on*
> [a]With-thi Schir Edward tharin be ! — [a] *while*

—one example among many. This ironical twist, which arises from a juxtaposition of high emotion and commonplace reality, is frequent in Scottish poetry, and also in Scottish prose and speech. Barbour, for one, was well aware of the intensifying power of contrast : his hymn to freedom is followed (i.241) by the proverbial saying :

> Thus contrar thingis [a]evir-mar — [a] *always*
> Discoveryngis [a]off the tothir ar. — [a] *of each other*

There is grim satisfaction when the poet says, with reference to the enemy's plans, " bot othir wayis than yheid the gle " (went the affair ; ix.701, and frequently). This irony is a typical folk element. We seem to hear the dry, realistic voice of the canny Scots crofter, and we are never far from a proverb (cp. quotations, xi.24 f., 151 ff.) : Edward " of othir mennis landis large wes he " (xi.148) ; " quha had gud hors gat best away ! " (ix.279) ; etc. This humour to hide the emotion is equally grim, and just as heartfelt, when the poet's own people have the tables turned on them ; as when, in Ireland, Edward Bruce has walked into a trap, and the enemy opens the sluices (xiv.363 ff.) to flood his camp :

> He maid thame [a]na gud fest, perfay, — [a] *no good feast, in truth*
> And nocht-for-thi [a]yneuch had thai. — [a] *enough*
> For [a]thouch thame failit of the met, — [a] *tho' they had no meat*
> I warne yhow weill thai [a]war weill wet. — [a] *were*

It must however be emphasised that this laconic brevity and understatement applies predominantly to emotions, not to the number of men present at a battle, to the magnitude of their achievement, collective or individual, or to frailties in human behaviour. On these points Barbour does speak up and is given to grotesque exaggeration, as when Edward " owt off his wyt he went weill ner " (II.199), or when the Scots are scarcely " half-deill ane dyner " (XIV.187 ; an Irishman is speaking !). Some of the passages already quoted would illustrate the same tendency.

The Bruce is an epic of 13,550 lines, but we gather already that it lacks real epic development, continuity of action, and grasp of different threads. Barbour is brilliant in small pictures of intense action or a closely watched scene, but in the transitions he is as clumsy as Orrm, repeats himself, and often has us guessing which of his characters " he " or " thai " denote. It takes him thirty lines to tell us that Sir William of Keith learns of Douglas's death (XX.491-520). The action is not continuous ; it lingers at one focus and then jumps to the next. Frequently, Barbour inserts a stage-direction in which he informs us which thread of his action he is now letting go and which he is taking up, and the relative independence of the various episodes is increased by an exposition repeating part of what we know already (VII.189 ; IX.328 f. = 308 f. ; XVI.345 f. ; XVII.729 ff.) ; these seem to be the devices of a poet who meant his poem to be read aloud. The leaps and bounds are made easy by his literary model, the romance with its quick four-beat metre, whose sharp scansion is stressed by rich alliteration ; but they also recall the ballads. The highlights of the poem are quick dramatic scenes of movement and action, but these stones of the mosaic are embedded in a jumble of transitions, meditations, reflexions, comparisons, recapitulations, exhortations ; no doubt Barbour's contemporaries were looking for something like this.

Barbour's treatment of individual episodes shows that he possessed not only a sceptical sense of reality, but also a keen enjoyment of sense-impressions, which he registers with the same accuracy that he shows in compiling historic detail. What the poet can visualise as a strictly limited, concrete scene comes to life in our own eye : spellbound we stare at the burning of Kildrummy, forgetful that we are only seeing it through Barbour's verse (IV.80 ff.). Barbour is fascinated by sensuous impressions—especially by light effects ; the reflexion of sunlight by helmets, armour and weapons is mentioned several times (*e.g.* VIII.216-34; XI.188 ff., 460 ff.[20]) with such epithets as "schynand, glemand"; Barbour "paints like an artist." [21] Relevant descriptions of nature come in to make a scene live; an engagement is fought at Martinmas when snow covered the ground (IX.127 ff.); morning fog favours a surprise attack (IX.572 ff.). The trick of a crofter to smuggle Scots soldiers into Linlithgow Castle under a load of hay demands a background of harvest-fields (X.185 ff.). We visualise the trap, already mentioned, into which Edward Bruce walks because so many perceptions of nature help our eye (XIV.317 ff.; similarly VI.67 ff.). In two places we have the conventional seasonal opening with a picture of spring or May (V.1 ff.; XVI.63 ff.)—but how much of a convention was it before Chaucer? And even here a realistic background is given, not a dream, and the memory of the grim winter storms or the budding leaves are at least personal observations.

The poet's delight in sensuous impressions is matched by his shrewd and sceptical sense of reality. He has no room for the legends and miracles in circulation about his hero, nor for the idealistic conventions of the romances where the knights fight to enhance their

[20] Ritchie gives these among the passages influenced by the French *Roman d'Alixandre*. But the latter only has clichés such as any historian might use of an army ("li soleus s'esbrandist qui en lor armes raie," "cler au soleil resplendir," quoted by Ritchie, VOL. I, pp. lxxxvi-vii) while the Scottish *Buik of Alexander* and *The Bruce* both contain a wealth of impressionistic detail far surpassing this. Where a French knight refuses to leave before the battle ("S' ainçois ne vois au branc conmencer .i. note," 10.8), the Scots version (*Forray of Gadderis*, 26. 280) has

> I sall se first the grete bargane
> Begin with brandis that are *bricht*.

Where *Li Fuerres di Gadres* (11.3) speaks merely of a large number, *The Forray of Gadderis* (311-2) gives a vivid picture:

> As in gret wynd dois *haill and snaw*,
> Sa come thay on but dreid or aw.

The "parallels" between the French romance and *The Bruce* are all conventional formulas such as are typical of any battle-piece, perhaps the only exception being the description of Douglas (*Bruce*, I.381 ff.). There is a specific coincidence between the Scottish *Buik of Alexander* and *The Bruce*—but then who borrowed from whom? There are signs that the corresponding passages in the *B. of Alex.* were derived from those in *Bruce*; alternatively, Barbour may have written both. Consequently there is no need to doubt the accuracy and reliability of Barbour's details. Alexander, too, appeals to his knights to put honour before gain, as he is doing; but Bruce's exhortation to his men to refrain from looting till the battle is over, and then to take all "at yhour liking" is based on sound strategic principles, and seems to reflect precise knowledge of circumstances. Where the French romance has conventional generalities, Barbour's *Bruce* gives particular concrete details.

[21] Cosmo Innes, preface to edn. of 1856, p. xxv (quoted by Skeat, VOL. I, p. lxvii); cp. also XI.614 ff., XIII.34 ff.

own glory and the honour of their ladies (cp. Brie, pp. 87 ff.). This is not the least of the differences between Barbour's *Bruce* and other romances of the Middle Ages. The battles of *The Bruce* are real, tough battles, they are the hard and bitter way to Scotland's freedom. In describing them, Barbour displays qualities often attributed to the Scots : he is shrewd, canny, and hard-headed. In sober narrative, there is no room for knightly pomp or tournament-like engagements ; and how remote we seem to be from chivalrous pageantry when Barbour explains (v.419 ff.) that Douglas burnt down his own castle

For he [a]na hop had of reskewyng : — [a] *no hope*
And it is [a]to perelous thing — [a] *too risky*
In castell [a]till assegit be, — [a] *to be besieged*
[a]Quhair that ane wantis of [b]thir thre, — [a] *where* [b] *these*
Vittale, or men with thair armyng,
[a]Or than gud hop of reskewing. — [a] *or else*

This applies to all castles taken by the Scots. Only Berwick, then the most important of Scotland's towns, makes an exception. Otherwise the Scots fight with " slicht and hardiment," in moor and hill, where small numbers can be turned to an advantage. Not that they are not chivalrous, but their end is to drive out the enemy. Mere bravado, fighting for the love of fighting or for glory, are not virtues in Barbour's eyes.[22] If Neil Flemyng and the sixty with him fight till death, their sacrifice is justified by the strategic purpose of protecting an unarmed army (xv.139 ff.). Edward Bruce sometimes exhibits a daring recklessness ; but his brother takes him to task for his chivalrous gesture of giving Stirling a year's respite (xi.37 ff.) and reads him a lesson in tactics when Edward's vanguard proceeds too impetuously (xvi.246 ff.). When Edward Bruce dies in Ireland recklessly defying a superior force, this is " wilfulness " and " syn " (xviii.175 ff.). What matters is not personal glory or a code of honour, but the freedom of the country. Therefore Barbour is not afraid to show his King fleeing, chased by sleuth-hounds, or breaking off a battle when the hour is against him (ii.433 ff.).

Barbour does not close his eyes to the ugly side of war, hunger, cold, misery, suffering, looting, breaches of discipline. Booty is mentioned frequently, as well as the subsequent " mery cher." There is no reason to think that looting was commoner in Bruce's army

[22] Brie's remarks about " altgermanisches Heldentum " (85 f.) are a curious aberration due to the political prejudice of his time.

than in other armies of the Middle Ages (or of later periods) ; but Barbour, with characteristic hard-headedness, takes more account of war in its less chivalrous aspects than other medieval romance-writers and chroniclers. He does not *glamourise* the toughness of war, and censures the Scots for looting against orders, after the capture of Berwick (XVII.101 ff. ; cf. also quotation XII.303 ff., 450 ff.) ; [23] such lack of discipline, Barbour feels, could not but jeopardise Bruce's tactics.

Like most Scots, Barbour was a keen moralist, and the shrewdness with which he appraised the realities of life seems also to have played an important part in determining his scale of virtues. Barbour's account of moral excellence has, of course, various points of contact with that which is embodied in so many medieval allegories (*e.g.* honour, etc.) : but we shall search his pages in vain for references to the earthly pilgrimage, chastity, the code of love ; true, he mentions the Wheel of Fortune (XIII.631 ff.), but his account of it is somewhat anomalous, and is not borne out by the narrative which it purports to illustrate. The virtues on which, throughout, he lays the greatest emphasis are, on the whole, social and political—leadership, justice, tenacity of purpose, foresight, prudence, responsibility—and the psychological insight displayed in his presentation of them is much deeper than we might have expected at that date. The value of a good captain is stressed in a number of other romances ; for example, in the *Voeux du Paon*, where it is said that he can make a small army strong by giving presents and by imploring his followers to fight. How much more realistic is Barbour's good captain (IX.36 ff.), who dares fearlessly to seize the God-given hour, and sets an inspiring example of tenacity, courage and foresight—whereas the " wrechyt-ness " of the " wikkit chiftane " quickly infects his followers, with disastrous effects on their morale. This is no chivalrous code of honour, but true leadership drawing its strength from the ethical forces of the people. At first sight, Barbour's account (VI.25-320) of Bruce's single-handed defence against " wele twa hundir men, and ma," reads like a legend intended to elevate Bruce to the level of Tydeus. But in the light of his subsequent disquisition (VI.325 ff.) on " worschip " (true valour), which he carefully distinguishes from " fule-hardyment " on the one hand, and from " cowardis " on the other, it becomes clear that Barbour's real reason for giving such a

[23] The amount of booty after Bannockburn is stressed so highly (XIII.443-502), but this is historically correct.

wealth of circumstantial detail is that he wants to show how fully Bruce embodied the qualities of the good captain. The King and his small troop have escaped to a marsh beyond a river. As always, Bruce's first concern is for his men's welfare : with only two companions, he himself takes the watch to allow his tired followers to rest. As always, he makes, in person, a careful reconnaissance, and finds that the only access is by the ford they waded, which can only be waded by one at a time ; so he tells his two comrades to sleep. After a time, he hears distant barking, but thinks it unnecessary, " for ane hundis questionying ", to alert his men. But it is a sleuth-hound bringing the enemy straight to the ford. When the noise comes closer the King sends his two companions to call his men.[24] Realising that this was an error of judgment—for, like all good leaders, he recognises his own mistakes—he carefully considers the risk of either abandoning the ford or fighting the enemy single-handed. His armour protects him from arrows ; the enemy can only wade the ford and climb the bank one at a time : so he stays. Barbour himself points out (VI.126) that this decision showed " stark wtrageous curage "; but he is at least equally concerned (VI.359 ff.) to stress the fact that before arriving at it Bruce made a careful appreciation of the situation ; and (VI.333) that

> [a]Thar may no man haf [b]worthyhed, — *[a] there [b] worthiness*
> Bot he haf wit to steir his dede,
> And [a]se quhat is to [b]leif or [c]ta; — *[a] see what [b] leave [c] take*

for, in Barbour's view, it is foresight—this calm appraisal of all relevant factors—that alone distinguishes " worschip " from recklessness, and makes it a political virtue, capable of serving higher ends.

Another of Bruce's traits on which Barbour lays great stress is his constant preoccupation with the state of morale. On taking command before Bannockburn, his first act is to inspect his troops, mingling freely with them as they arrive and assuring himself that they are in good spirits ; later he forbids Douglas and Keith, on returning from their reconnaissance, to put it about that the enemy's morale is high ; and before the first encounter takes place he enjoins any who have " hart nocht sekyr " to go while the going is good. Barbour's *Bruce* is, in some respects, a handbook of leadership, and it is severely practical. His portrait of the good captain has little in

[24] The only illogical point is that he sends both. In C, the Cambridge MS (ll. 85-92) he had previously dismissed them to the camp.

common with the various representations of vice and virtue found in other medieval romances.

In this connexion let us briefly examine Barbour's attack on astrology and necromancy (IV.668-774). In the late Middle Ages, it was widely believed that the study of the course of the stars might reveal a knowledge of God's purposes. As Chaucer's Franklin shows, Barbour was by no means alone in adopting a sceptical attitude: but the arguments on which he takes his stand against the teaching of the Church are striking. The prophets of the Old Testament, he says, had the gift of looking into the future; but to-day any clerk believes he can prophesy from the conjunction of the stars. But, he continues, even if a man made a lifelong study of astrology, so "that on sternys his hewyd he brak," yet he would not, "the wyss man sayis," achieve certainty in his predictions three times in all his life: "than is that," he comments, with an irony that almost anticipates David Hume's, "na certane demyng." Secondly, even if all the necessary astrological data were available, astrologers are not able to predict with certainty, because (whether naturally virtuous or wicked) a man *can* "refrenyhe [bridle] his will": by sheer force of will and intellect he can change the destiny mapped out by the constellations. Will-power counts high with Barbour (cp. III.269 ff.). He accepts the proverbial wisdom of Thomas the Rhymer's prophecies (II.86), or St Margaret's (X.736 ff.), or that concerning ships crossing the isthmus of Tarbert (XV.292 ff.).[25] But to have one's future foretold is an act of abject folly that paralyses a man's will-power, if nothing worse (IV.205 ff.).

Barbour knows, too, how close good and evil motives can be to one another: Bruce praises a man for bringing the plan to take Berwick directly to himself, as such a prize might have created ill-will between Thomas Randolph and James Douglas (XVII.52 ff.; similarly XII.110 ff.). His thrilling account of the capture of Edinburgh Castle by Thomas Randolph (X.605 ff.) shows not merely that he is able to create dramatic tension, but also that he knows the psychology of men exposed to danger, and understands the different reaction to nervous strain of friend and foe, besieger and besieged. And Barbour even succeeds in creating the psychological spell of a hallucination: the King waits for a fire-signal from the mainland; he is watching

[25] Magnus, King of Norway, had an agreement with Edgar of Scotland (1102) that he was to be owner of all land round which he could sail; he had a ship drawn across the isthmus of Tarbert in Argyll, cutting off Kintyre.

so intently that he thinks he sees one, and when he points it out to others, they believe so too (IV.612 ff.).[26]

Barbour's psychological insight is also his main instrument in characterisation. For his heroes are not the stereotypes of the romances: in them strength is combined with weakness, and they have profiles of a clearcut sharpness not matched before Chaucer. One could not be mistaken for another: Edward Bruce, the impetuous; James Douglas, originally of more courtly disposition and a favourite with the ladies (II.570 ff.)—he had spent his youth in Paris—, but grown defiant, resourceful, almost a fox, under his fate. Thomas Randolph, Earl of Moray, the King's nephew, can at times be a hot-headed youth (IX.739 ff.; XIX.635 ff.), but he has a background of training in statecraft (X.259 ff., 302 ff.). We even see a certain development of character, and some of them are different men in the end from what we knew them in the beginning. Robert the Bruce, at first a dashing young nobleman sensitive to any personal affront, has grown into a mature, wise king whom destiny has forged into an experienced leader of men—circumspect, far-sighted, and compassionate. A study of his character is very illuminating, both for Barbour's ideals and for the Scottish literary tradition.

We have had some glimpses already of Robert the Bruce's character: level-headed, no nonsense, prudent, canny, almost suspicious of opportunity, but quick to seize it. In his early years, the conventions of warfare may have led him into traps (II.257 ff.), but later his uncanny resourcefulness is a match for anybody (X.17 ff.; XVI.99 ff.). He leaves nothing to chance; with foresight, wisdom, will-power, careful planning and shrewd calculation, he weighs the risks and forces the hand of destiny (VIII.151 ff.; XI.284 ff., 360 ff.). Action is better than waiting, yet he has no use for mere adventurous recklessness: his punishment of a knight who against his orders attacks and kills two enemy archers almost foreshadows the problem of Kleist's *Prinz von Homburg* (XVI.99 ff.). Fighting as he does for a higher cause, Bruce is lenient towards those of his countrymen who dare not rise for him, he usually spares his Scottish enemies, and takes great pains to convince his nephew, Thomas Randolph, of the justice of the Scottish cause (IX.73 ff.; X.259 ff.).

Barbour's Bruce is a great leader, a great ruler, and a great

[26] The text here (" hym thoucht weill . . . , ilk man thoucht weill . . . ") apparently contradicts V.25 ff., according to which there *was* a fire, but not the one that they were looking for.

general ; but he is good as well as great. We have seen the seriousness with which he undertakes his task, and he reveals to his nephew how his heavy responsibility forces him to act cannily, even should this be against chivalrous tradition (IX.739 ff.). Realistically he also takes account of the weaknesses of human nature, the lust to plunder or secret envy. We have seen, too, his qualities as a good captain, and his example at the ford of Perth (IX.384 ff.) provokes a spontaneous outburst of praise from a French knight, who contrasts this with the life of luxury of the French barons. Above all, Bruce is always concerned with morale (above, p. 27), and knows the real secret of inspiring confidence in times of despair (III.187 ff.) ; he will even conceal a fact that might discourage his men, and bids the messenger (XI.487 ff.) be silent about the huge number of the English army marching towards Bannockburn,

> For [a]oftsis of ane word may [b]ris — [a] *often* [b] *rise*
> Discomfort and [a]tynsall with-all. — [a] *loss*
> And throu a word, [a]als weill may fall, — [a] *as*
> Comfort may ris and hardiment,
> That [a]gerris men cum to their entent. — [a] *causes . . . to*

Above all, he knows the real secret of leadership, that of making his men believe not in him, but in themselves. Before expressing his own opinions he asks others to express theirs ; this makes them feel that they have participated in the final decisions. It is not a question of *ordering* and being followed ; before Bannockburn, Bruce carefully prepares his soldiers' minds by painting the effect which the defeat of a small English force on the day before the great battle must have had on the whole enemy army—and then leaves the decision to his men. Only after their decision to fight does he make his famous address, perhaps the climax of the whole poem [27] : they fight for a right bestowed by God ; they are in the stronger position as Edward has come to their own country and brought his riches with him (!) ; they fight for their lives, their children, their wives, the freedom of their country. Though Bruce as a rule shuns pathos, he can appeal

[27] As we are here concerned with *Barbour's* ideals, the literary sources or models really do not matter. There is no connexion of substance with the speech Alexander makes (cp. above, n. 20). The echoes of 1 *Maccabees* (I.17-21, IV.17-18), and of the Declaration of Arbroath, are fully characteristic of Barbour's style. A speech on similar lines by Bruce before Bannockburn is given in a Latin poem by Bernard of Linton, Abbot of Arbroath and Bruce's Chancellor (Mackenzie, pp. 497 ff.).

to ideals at the given time and inspire his followers with his own sense of responsibility.

These are not the conventional attributes of a feudal lord, and Barbour attaches great importance to this difference between feudal, class-conscious England and—as we would say—democratic Scotland. The proud pomp of the English army before Bannockburn contrasts with the " homely, hardy, stalwart " aspect of the Scots (xi.240 ff.) :

Our all the host than [a]yheid the kyng,	[a] *went*
And beheld to thair [a]contanyng,	[a] *demeanour*
And saw thame of full fair [a]effer ;	[a] *appearance*
Of hardy [a]contynans thai wer,	[a] *countenance*
Be [a]liklynes the mast [b]cowart	[a] *likelihood* [b] *cowardly*
Semyt till do richt weill his part.	
The King has seyn all thair [a]having,	[a] *manner* (lit. *having*)
That knew hym weill in-to sic thing,	
And saw thame all comonly	
Of [a]sekyr contynans and hardy,	[a] *safe, firm*
[a]Forouten [b]effray or [c]abaysyng.	[a] *without* [b] *fear* [c] *abasement, dismay*
In his hert had he gret liking,	
And thoucht that men of sa gret will,	
Gif thai wald set thair mycht [a]thair-till,	[a] *thereto*
Suld be full hard [a]till wyn, [b]perfay.	[a] *to defeat* [b] *by my faith, verily*
Ay as he met thame in the way,	
He welcummyt thame with gladsum fair,	
Spekand gud wordis heir and thair.	
And thai, that thar lord so mekly	
Saw welcum thame and so [a]hamly,	[a] *homely*
Joyful thai war, and thoucht [a]'at thai	[a] *that*
Micht weill put thame in-till assay	
Of hard fechting in stalwart [a]stour,	[a] *battle*
For till maynteyn weill his honour.	

Amazed, the English see that a yeoman in Scotland counts as much as a knight in England (xix.165 ff.) ; on the whole there appears to be much less social stratification on the Scottish side.[28] The King lives in close contact with his people and shares their sufferings, even taking the heaviest part. With delight Barbour relates how

[28] Some ten years after *The Bruce*, in Barbour's lifetime, a contingent of French knights in Scotland complained indignantly of the impertinence of the Scots peasants. The churls would not stand aside to let them ride through standing corn and even demanded compensation : what next ? G. M. Thomson, *A Short History of Scotland*, 1930, p. 56.

Bruce personally took care of a pregnant washerwoman (XVI.270 ff.). On the other hand, his people feel *their* share in his responsibility, and spontaneously make his cause their own: the farmer whose initiative conquers Linlithgow (X.148 ff.); the burgher who develops the plan to take Berwick (XVII.11 ff.); the help from the people that is instrumental in climbing the walls of Roxburgh and Edinburgh (X.358 ff., 530 ff.), or the camp-followers joining in the attack at Bannockburn (XIII.225 ff.).[29] This co-operation is an essential element in the theme of "fredome" and "richt."

There is no doubt that Barbour is very far from the poetic and verbal art of the French romances which he took as his model, but it is equally true that his seriousness, his moral or psychological depth, and the high aim of his poem have created a work of greater weight than all the romances. Up north in Aberdeen Barbour was living on the fringe of the literary conventions of his time, but he left a poem whose message still carries weight, if only as the first literary document concerning self-determination and the rights of small nations, as well as the right of the individual to participate in all decisions by which he himself is vitally affected.

[29] The success of Wallace and Bruce was largely due to the support by the common people and the tenants. They even began to fight, with Wallace, without their "natural" leaders, the barons. Edward I came to terms with the Scots lords, but failed to recognise that the Scottish people had a will of their own.

II

Full Tide: The Makars

1. Robert Henryson

OVER A GENERATION AGO Neilson and Webster called ROBERT HENRYSON perhaps the most striking case of neglected genius in the whole of "English" literature.[1] Much has since been done for a better recognition of the "scolmaister of Dumfermling," both by new editions and criticism.[2] Tillyard's chapter on Henryson's *Testament of Cresseid* is the finest study so far of Henryson as a poetic artist and as a child of his time. Stearns's fact-finding study is a meticulous reconstruction of the social conditions of the age, but it sometimes reads too much into the text and is too much concerned with externals; the chapter on "Religion," for example, only speaks of ecclesiastical politics, law, and abuse—not a word of Henryson's own religious attitude. Any study of Henryson is hampered by the paucity of our knowledge of the poet's life: he is connected with Dunfermline, seems to have been a schoolmaster, flourished *c.* 1480-90, and was dead by 1508, when Dunbar mentions him in his "Lament for the Makars." The numerous prints of his works, however, testify to Henryson's popularity. He was writing from the centre of the

[1] *Chief British Poets of the fourteenth and fifteenth Centuries*, edd. W. A. Neilson and K. G. T. Webster, New York 1916, pref. and p. 434 n.

[2] See esp. *The Poems and Fables of Robert Henryson*, ed. H. HARVEY WOOD, Edinburgh 1933. Based on recently available material, this is now the best edition, and all our quotations are from it (*T. Cr.* = *Testament of Cresseid*; *F.* = *Fabillis*; *O.* = *Orpheus and Eurydice*).

See also *The Poems and Fables of Robert Henryson*, ed. D. LAING, Edinburgh 1865; *The Poems of Robert Henryson*, ed. G. GREGORY SMITH, S.T.S., 3 vols., 1906-14; *The Testament of Cresseid*, edd. (1) Bruce Dickins, 1925, and (2) R. K. Gordon, in *The Story of Troilus*, 1934, pp. 351-67; and *Selections from the Poems of Robert Henryson*, ed. D. Murison, Saltire Classics, Edinburgh 1952.

For studies, see Marshall W. Stearns, *Robert Henryson*, Columbia U.P. 1949; E. M. W. Tillyard, "The Testament of Cresseid," in *Five Poems 1470-1870*, 1948; Edwin Muir, *Essays in Literature and Society*, 1949, ch. 1; H. Harvey Wood, in *Edinburgh Essays in Scots Literature*, Edinburgh 1933; J. Kinsley, in *Scottish Poetry*, ed. Kinsley, London 1955; and C. S. Lewis, in *The Allegory of Love*, Oxford 1936.

thought of his age, but his work is also a keystone in the Scottish tradition, an aspect all too neglected hitherto.

It has hitherto been customary to call Henryson, together with James I, Dunbar and Gavin Douglas, a "Scottish Chaucerian." True, they introduced into Scots literature Chaucer's example and his handling of themes derived from European literature, and recognised him as their master. But they are far from imitating Chaucer in the same way as Lydgate and Occleve; they have so much besides Chaucerian matter that I prefer to call them by their Scots name of "makars." James I alone—if he was the author of the *Kingis Quair* [3] —is a real imitator of Chaucer, but even he shows more originality in doing so than Chaucer's English disciples. Instead of a dream allegory the poet presents us with a real event, his own personal love, with a wealth of perception and an eye alert to the fleeting impressions of fire, reflexions, colour, running water, jumping fish.[4] There is moral seriousness of purpose in his glorification of matrimonial instead of courtly love, and in his essentially Christian outlook (142). Not unlike Barbour, the poet stresses (147) the autonomy of the will, even against Fortune:

> Bot othir clerkis halden, that the man
> Has in himself the [a]chose and libertee — [a] *choice*
> To cause his [a]awin fortune, how or quhan — [a] *own*
> That him best [a]lest, and no necessitee — [a] *(may) please*
> Was in the [a]hevin at his nativitee... — [a] *heaven*

All these traits have their special weight in the Scottish tradition.

Robert Henryson's debt to Chaucer is great, and he is the first to acknowledge it (*T.Cr.*, ll. 41 ff.). But he does not imitate. He

[3] Edd. W. W. Skeat, S.T.S., revised edn. 1911, and W. Mackay Mackenzie, 1939 (here quoted: nos. denote stanzas). Cp. E. W. M. Balfour Melville, *James I, King of Scots*, 1936, and Sir W. Craigie, "The Language of *The Kingis Quair*," in *Essays and Studies*, xxv (1939). *Christis Kirk on the Grene* and *Peblis to the Play* (for which see below, pp. 114, 120) are sometimes attributed to James I also.

[4] *E.g.* the wealth of concrete sensuous detail in the poet's description (46-9) of the jewels; in the expression (136) of abstract ideas; and in his account (152 ff.) of the "lusty plane." Chaucer had of course described fish in *The Parlement of Foules* (188); but whereas his description is static and highly conventional, that in *The Kingis Quair* (153) is full of quick movement, flashing reflexions, and momentaneous sense-impressions. As we have seen, similar impressions occur here and there in Barbour's *Bruce*, and jumping fish have always had a special fascination for Scottish poets: cp. Gavin Douglas, *Eneados*, Prol. xii (ed. Small, vol. iv, p. 81, ll. 31 ff.); in Gaelic (see below, pp. 189-94), Alexander MacDonald, "Oran a' gheamhraidh," and Duncan McIntyre, "Oran Coire a' Cheathaich."

assimilates Chaucer's conception of poetry and creates from this artistic centre. In a more limited field he achieves (as Tillyard observes) the same artistic level as his master, and there are even passages where Henryson surpasses Chaucer, as in the introduction to the *Testament* or the meeting of the lovers. He fertilises Chaucer's heritage with his own native tradition and achieves a new subtlety which is totally his own.

This is obvious from his verse. Henryson writes practically all his poems in the Chaucerian stanza and he is sensitive to its melody and harmony. But he superimposes native alliteration, a common feature of Scots poetry before and after the Renaissance. This gives his rhythm a stronger stress arising from his Scots speech. Henryson uses alliteration, not formally, but as a poetic device to vary the intensity of his expression. In his description of the planets, harsh, icy Saturn is portrayed (*T. Cr.*, ll. 151 ff.) in rough verse with heavy alliteration of *tch*, *f*(*r*), and such plosives as *p*, *t*, *k* : fourfold alliteration is the rule, run-on alliteration or two alliterative patterns in one line frequent. Moreover, massed consonants, heavy stresses, and many shortly ejaculated vowels help (ll. 155 ff.) to suggest a picture of wild, harsh force :

His face [a]fronsit, his [b]lyre was lyke the [c]leid, — [a] *knotted* [b] *skin* [c] *lead*
His teith chatterit, and [a]cheverit with the chin. . . . — [a] *shivered*

[a]Atour his belt his [b]lyart lokkis lay — [a] *out over* [b] *gray*
[a]Felterit unfair, [b]ouirfret with froistis hoir,... — [a] *matted* [b] *over-fretted*
Under his girdill ane [a]flasche of felloun flanis, — [a] *sheaf of deadly arrows*
[a]Fedderit with ice, and [b]heidit with hailstanis. — [a] *feathered* [b] *headed, tipped*

Jupiter, " richt fair and amiabill," is portrayed (ll. 169 ff.) in gentler rhythms with many tripping dactyls ; the vowels are longer, the consonants no longer massed ; alliteration is used more economically and does not fall so heavily (ll. 176 f.) on consecutive words :

His voice was [a]cleir, as cristall wer his [b]ene, — [a] *clear* [b] *eyes*
As goldin wyre sa glitterand was his hair.

With Mars (ll. 183 ff.) a more metallic note is struck, with many monosyllables and richer alliteration, often on fricatives such as *f* and *h* ; but there are neither the harshness of accent and alliteration nor (ll. 185 ff.) the knotted consonants of Saturn's picture :

> To chide and [a]fecht, als [b]feirs as ony fyre ; — [a] *fight* [b] *fierce*
> In hard harnes, [a]hewmond and [b]habirgeoun, — [a] *helmet* [b] *coat of mail*
> And on his hanche ane roustie [a]fell fachioun... — [a] *dire falchion*

In such passages as these, the melody, sound harmony and poetic inspiration of Chaucer, and the greater substance, harsher force, and more rugged rhythm of the native metre are welded into a new artistic expressiveness and suggestiveness, which enables Henryson to achieve a subtler modulation even than Chaucer. Henryson's feeling for contrasting rhythms shows in such a line as that (*T.Cr.*, l. 225) on Venus,

> Under smyling [a]scho was dissimulait, — [a] *she*

where the façade of the first half is torn to shreds by the whispering of the second, with its painting of disgust by sibilants and short *i* s. The Complaints of Cresseid (*T. Cr.*, ll. 407 ff.) and also of Orpheus (*O.*, ll. 134 ff.) are considered metrical masterpieces ; but Henryson also knows the effects to be produced by the common metre of the ballads (" Robene and Makyne," " The Bludy Serk "). In contrast, however, to Dunbar's enormously richer variety of metres, Henryson's verse always serves the poetic expression and never inclines to virtuosity.

Though no less flexible than Chaucer's, Henryson's verse has a greater austerity. This is simply a characteristic of the Scots language as he wrote it. It is also a national characteristic, and the poet's outlook has the same austere quality as his verses. In his *Troilus and Criseyde*, Chaucer is an observer of the human comedy : whereas Henryson's *Testament of Cresseid* has the tragic intensity of a ballad. Even the slightest of Henryson's deviations from Chaucer go to heighten the effect of the " swordstroke tragedy." In the *Testament*, Calchas is a priest of Venus (not Apollo) and very fond of his daughter Cresseid. This makes Cresseid's fate all the more pathetic when she is punished for her blaspheming of Venus and Cupid. In his *Fabillis*, Henryson is even more independent, digesting his sources rather than following them, and combining elements from different fables to create a new meaning. For " Robene and Makyne " no real source or model is known,[5] and Makyne seems to have been his own creation. His creative genius assimilates popular or traditional material so well that his tales read as though they had never been told before (HARVEY WOOD). His handling of the plot of " The Wolf and the Lamb " is a good example of the manner in which he takes only a general

[5] Despite W. Powell Jones, in *Modern Language Notes*, XLVI (1931), p. 457 ; cp. HARVEY WOOD, p. 266.

idea, and of the originality he shows in developing it in his own way: though the wolf has his victim in his power he tries to prove legally that the lamb has fouled his water. His legalistic subtleties tear the disguise of allegory, and out comes a sharp satire on the abuse of law against the innocent. The morality—in this case almost half of the whole *Fable*—is even less medieval. Across three centuries we seem to hear the voice of Burns in the fervent indictment of the wolves in human shape, the perverters of right and the oppressors of the common people. The animal has been lost sight of; we get a detailed picture of social conditions, and the poet's whole sympathy is with the sturdy peasants suffering under bondage.

Henryson rarely is imitative or conventional. The description of summer and autumn in "The Preiching of the Swallow" (*F.*, ll. 1678 ff.) follows a traditional pattern, with Bacchus, classical gods, and Mediterranean landscape; but those of winter (ll. 1692 ff.) and spring (ll. 1706 ff.) are based on genuine observation of the Lowland scene. The bleak picture of winter, with the wild animals (ll. 1703 ff.) creeping together for warmth in sheltered places, is wonderfully suggestive: so, too, the glimpses of the country folk (ll. 1721 ff.) mending their dykes in spring. With the poet we seem to smell (ll. 1718 f.) the promise of pregnant spring in the soil:

To se the soill that wes richt sessonabill,
Sappie, and to [a]resave all [b]seidis abill. — [a] *receive* [b] *seeds*

At first sight, the opening of "The Taill of the Lyonn and the Mous" looks like the conventional dream allegory, but this introduction of the dream of Æsop, who also pronounces the moral, is due to political caution in a fable that makes dangerous allusion to the weak king James III, and to treason (Stearns). And even in this dream there is much more individual realism, specific local colour and sharp observation than in Chaucer—or any English poet before the pre-romantics:

His [a]bonat round, and off the [b]auld fassoun. — [a] *bonnet* [b] *old fashion*

'Displeis you not, my gude maister, [a]thocht I — [a] *though*
Demand your birth, your [a]facultye, and name, — [a] *profession*
Quhy ye come heir, or quhair ye dwell at hame? [6]

The beginning of *The Testament of Cresseid* is the best evidence of Henryson's sovereign mastery in handling Chaucer's conventions. We

[6] *F.*, ll. 1353, 1366 ff.

have a seasonal opening, but without a trace of conventionality. The action is real, not a dream ; it is very specific and highly personal. Instead of the traditional May, we have winter—which has always had a fascination for the Scots poets—with closely observed Scottish characteristics. The cold of winter, and the cold of old age in the poet create the bleak tragic atmosphere necessary for his tale. This use of setting and atmosphere (*T. Cr.*, ll. 1 ff.) to heighten intensity has no precise equivalent in Chaucer's poetry :

> Ane [a]doolie sessoun to ane [b]cairfull dyte — *[a] gloomy [b] sorrowful poem*
> Suld correspond, and be equivalent.
> Richt sa it wes quhen I began to wryte
> This tragedie, the [a]wedder richt fervent, — *[a] weather*
> Quhen Aries, in middis of the Lent,
> Schouris of haill [a]can fra the north [b]discend, — *[a] did [b] send down*
> That [a]scantlie fra the cauld I micht defend. — *[a] scarcely*

Looking through the window of his " oratur," the poet sees Venus rising in opposition to the setting sun, and notices that a north wind has dispersed the clouds : but then (ll. 19 ff.) :

> The froist freisit, the blastis bitterly
> Fra Pole Artick come quhisling loud and [a]schill — *[a] shrill*
> And causit me [a]remufe aganis my will. — *[a] remove*
>
> For I [a]traistit that Venus, [b]Luifis Quene, — *[a] trusted [b] Love's*
> To [a]quhome sum tyme I [b]hecht obedience, — *[a] whom [b] vowed*
> My faidit hart of lufe scho wald mak grene,
> And therupon with humbill reverence,
> I thocht to pray hir [a]hie Magnificence ; — *[a] high*
> Bot for greit cald as than I [a]lattit was, — *[a] hindered*
> And in my [a]chalmer to the fyre [b]can pas. — *[a] chamber [b] did*

In old age, love no longer fires the blood, and " the fyre outward is the best remeid " : therefore, he goes on (ll. 36 ff.),

> I mend the fyre and [a]beikit me about, — *[a] warmed*
> Than tuik ane drink my [a]spreitis to comfort, — *[a] spirits*
> And armit me weill fra the cauld thairout.

To shorten the winter night, he reads Chaucer's *Troylus and Criseyde*, but then takes up another book, which tells (ll. 62 ff.) [7]

[7] On the possible source of Henryson's sequel, see J. Kinsley in *The Times Literary Supplement* for 14 Nov. 1952, and in *Scottish Poetry*, ed. Kinsley, 1955, p. 289, n. 34.

the fatall destenie
Of fair Cresseid, that endit wretchitlie.

"Quha wait [knows]," he reflects (l. 64), "gif all that Chauceir wrait was trew?" And in narrating the "wofull end of this lustie Creisseid," he shows the same consummate mastery. Deserted by Diomeid, Cresseid, "sum men sayis" (l. 77), walked the "Court commoun," but finally returned repentant to her father. In her despair, she curses Venus and Cupid (ll. 126 ff.): but for her blasphemy the Gods, sitting in judgment, strike her (ll. 302 ff.) with leprosy. At the leper-house Troilus (ll. 495 ff.) rides past. Cresseid and he do not recognise each other, but her look suddenly calls up the picture of his Cresseid, and he leaves a rich gift. She inquires (ll. 533 ff.) who it is that has done the lepers "so greit humanitie"—but when she is told it was "Schir Troylus,"

Stiffer than [a]steill, thair stert ane bitter [b]stound *[a] steel [b] pang*
Throwout hir hart, and fell doun to the ground.

She acknowledges her own unfaithfulness, makes her testament and dies. Troilus erects a marble tomb where golden letters proclaim (ll. 607 ff.):

Lo, fair ladyis, Crisseid, of Troyis toun,
Symtyme countit the [a]flour of womanheid, *[a] flower of womanhood*
Under this [a]stane [b]lait lipper lyis [c]deid. *[a] stone [b] late leper [c] dead*

The pace is quick and relentless, the whole poem completed in eighty-six stanzas. It is knit still more closely and dramatically by certain recurring themes, such as that of Esperus and Saturn [8]: this note of fate and of cold makes the tragedy inescapable.

If the *Testament* is Henryson's tragic masterpiece, the thirteen *Morall Fabillis of Esope the Phrygian* are its serene counterpart. Fables were very popular in the Middle Ages; they express the medieval conception of the unity of the world and of all life (Muir). Projecting human situations on to a lower and simpler level they facilitate a moral—and allow us to laugh at human weaknesses. Usually, the animal disguise is rather threadbare, a mere allegory. But Henryson's peculiarity is the close observation of *both* the human and the animal detail. He watches his animals intensely: the fox (*F.*, 2294)

Lowrence come [a]lourand, for he [b]lufit never licht. *[a] lurking [b] loved*

[8] *T. Cr.*, stanzas 2, 7, 20, 46, and esp. 58, where no evening star shines on Cresseid as she enters the leper-house.

The difference can perhaps best be summed up as follows : in most fables the animals are simply human beings in disguise, but Henryson's animals are closely observed, and they are real animals. True, he endows them with human emotions and human motives, but this is largely in order to make it possible to answer the question how the *animal* would feel in such a situation—if it had human faculties. The animals in Henryson's *Fabillis* are thus both creatures and symbols. He has intense sympathy with them, and almost succeeds in entering into their minds—much like Liam O'Flaherty in his animal tales, or Robert Burns in mock-heroic form.[9]

The poet sinks his whole personality in his tale, and " The Taill of the Uponlandis Mous and the Burges Mous " is a masterpiece ; " The Preiching of the Swallow " and " The Taill of the Wolf, the Foxe and the Cadgear [hawker] " also deserve mention. His fables usually have a twofold moral : one—highly humanitarian and sociological—implicit in the tale ; the other, the conventional *moralitas*, at the end. The latter sometimes comes as a surprise : in " The Taill of the Cok and the Jasp [precious stone] " we sympathise with the cock to whom the jewel, swept carelessly on to the midden by wanton damsels, is of no interest—corn or draff would be more useful. Yet in the *moralitas* the cock is represented as a fool scorning science, the jewel as the love of learning, now lost because men are satisfied with riches and have no patience to seek it. It seems almost as if the poet has allowed his own colourful fable to run away with him, and is now returning to his duty ; for it is only the morality that justifies the " fenyeit taill " (*F.*, ll. 1 ff., 1384 ff.). The moralities of " The Wolf and the Lamb " (see above) or of " The Scheip and the Doig [dog] " are a certain exception in their close integration with the tale.

It may come as a surprise that a poet who did not essay a single Scottish subject should hold a key-position in Scotland's literary tradition. But the fact that Henryson gave all his tales a specifically Scottish setting shows how successfully he has digested and assimilated his foreign material. In addition to the native Scottish pictures already mentioned, we have, in *Orpheus and Eurydice* (ll. 289 f.),

> [a]Syne owr a mure, with thornis thick and scherp, — [a] *then over a moor*
> [a]Wepand alone, a [b]wilsum way he went... — [a] *weeping* [b] *wild*

[9] It is interesting to compare Henryson's *Fabillis* with the animal poems of Gaelic literature (see below, pp. 186, 191.).

And on finding a dead fox, the cadger (*F.*, ll. 2061 f.) dances with joy,

> And all the [a]trace he trippit on his [b]tais ; — [a] *track* [b] *toes*
> As he had [a]hard ane pyper play, he [b]gais ; [10] — [a] *heard* [b] *goes*

he will make mittens from its pelt, and not send it to Flanders (l. 2074) to which Scottish fur and wool was shipped. But the fox has only tricked the cadger, who now leaps over a dyke to cut (ll. 2103 f.) a stick of " holyne [holly] grene "—a fine Scottish picture.

Henryson's details are so accurate that they give us a picture of contemporary social conditions : for example, his descriptions (*F.*, ll. 1825 ff.) of the flax industry—whose centre in Scotland was Dunfermline—of ploughing (*F.*, ll. 2231 ff.), and of the leper-house outside the gates of the town (*T. Cr.*, ll. 381 ff.).[11] Henryson's imagery is so concrete that his description of Cresseid's symptoms enabled Sir J. Y. Simpson (the inventor of chloroform) to diagnose Greek elephantiasis, the most incurable variety of leprosis.[12] Whatever he is dealing with—social conditions, astrological medicine, ecclesiastical affairs, contemporary legal abuses—Henryson is truly representative of his time. That is why Stearns could reconstruct a picture of Henryson's age from his poems, and Tillyard took the *Testament* as representative of the moral background of the fifteenth century. Henryson has the same keen interest in matters of fact as Barbour, but in rendering account of them he is at once more selective and more concrete. Above all, he is never pedestrian, and is always a consummate artist. His account of the system of the planets (*T. Cr.*, ll. 141 ff.) and their astronomical, mythological, medical, moral characteristics according to the thinking of his time could have been a dull encyclopædic tract, like Lydgate's in the *Assembly of the Gods*. In fact, it is one of the finest jewels in the treasure-house of Henryson's poetry. With the sure instinct of an artist Henryson selects those traits which best serve his purpose. Individually they lend themselves to the creation of a concrete picture, collectively they symbolise fate, thus heightening the dramatic tension : for the stars reveal the will of God ; [13] and in the light of astrology, Cresseid's sin in blaspheming

[10] In this connexion, it is a curious fact that the Scottish country dances are danced on the toes, not, like most English folk dances, on the whole foot, or on the heels.

[11] Cp. Stearns's chapter on " Health and Sanitation."

[12] See *T. Cr.*, ll. 337 ff., and Sir J. Y. Simpson, in *Edinburgh Medical and Surgical Journal*, LVI-II (1841-2) ; cp. Stearns, and HARVEY WOOD, p. 257.

[13] See Tillyard, pp. 15 f., and Stearns, p. 72.

Venus, her trial under Saturn, and her leprosy, form an absolutely natural sequence, and not a single thread could be cut without impairing the intricate weaving of the tragic texture of the poem as a whole.

The condensation of Henryson's stories is largely achieved by his intense power of visualisation. He is never vague or general ; he makes us *see* a specific picture, complete in itself. Henryson does not simply report that the husbandman and the wolf take an oath, he makes us see how (*F.*, ll. 2313 f.)

> The wolff [a]braid furth his fute, the man his hand, *[a] thrust*
> And on the [a]toddis taill sworne thay ar to stand ; *[a] fox's*

he does not merely state that the flax has grown, but visualises (*F.*, ll. 1777 ff.) a specific scene :

> And [a]seidis that wer [b]sawin off beforne *[a] seeds [b] sown*
> Wer growin hie, that [a]hairis mycht thame hyde, *[a] hares*
> And [a]als the [b]quailye [c]craikand in the corne. *[a] also [b] quail [c] croaking*

Often, too, he tells us (*F.*, ll. 1743, 1792) where to look :

> ' Se ye yone churll ' (quod scho) ' beyond [a]yone *[a] that plough*
> pleuch... '
>
> ' Lift up your sicht, and tak gude [a]advertence... ' *[a] heed*

Nothing in this fable of " The Preiching of the Swallow " is statement devoid of setting : we watch the crofter work his flax, see a sharply visualised winter scene when he sets his nets, hear the death-song of the birds, and witness the exact movements of the fowler who slays some with a stick, wrings the necks of others, and puts them in his bag.[14]

The reader recreates Henryson's world with his eye, ear, nose.[15] Henryson is keenly alive to the sense of colour.[16] But he does not create static pictures ; his quickly moving poetry teems with impressions of motion : the crouching of the fox,[17] the cat playing with the mouse.[18] The latter passage, and " The Taill of the Paddok and the Mous," are, as it were, cinematic masterpieces. Above all, Henryson is fascinated by the manifold, ever-changing effects of light : light

[14] *F.*, ll. 1825 ff.
[15] *F.*, ll. 1653 ff., 1781, 1874 ff., 1979, 1982 ; *O.*, ll. 219 ff., 303 ff.
[16] *T. Cr.*, ll. 407 ff. ; *O.*, ll. 352 ff.
[17] *F.*, ll. 1979 ff., 2294 ff.
[18] *F.*, ll. 330 ff.

shining, shimmering, flashing ; again and again these create, in Henryson's eye, a vivid, specific, momentaneous impression.[19] If an imagined scene is not in itself sufficiently concrete, Henryson makes it more completely specific by means of a picturesque comparison. The coining of striking phrases and metaphors in which an image of immediate interest is presented with another suggested by it is one of the chief elements of style in all Scottish literature ; and Henryson is a master of the art. Usually, an abstract idea is projected (*F.*, ll. 344 f., 2311 f.) into the vivid world of the senses :

> ' Thy [a]mangerie is [b]mingit all with cair, — [a] *feast* [b] *mixed*
> Thy guse is gude, thy [a]gansell sour as gall.' — [a] *garlic sauce*

> ' Ye sall be sworne to stand at my [a]decreit, — [a] *decree*
> Quhether heirefter ye think it soure or sweit.'

The objects on which Henryson's senses concentrate are those of his immediate surroundings. There is no horizon, no distance, no far-off noise, no general survey of a landscape ; the sky (*T. Cr.*, ll. 1-28, 401 ; *F.*, ll. 1657-63) is only mentioned in connexion with the weather, or as a source of astrological data. Henryson presents *genre* pictures of country life with the pictorial sense of the Dutch painters. But in watching the objects around him he is so intent and goes so close to them that the perspective is lost and, as it were, he enters into them himself. The fox and the wolf, in the fable of the cadger, are not really *described* ; by numerous intimate observations the poet takes us so close that we enter into, and *feel*, their being, and they assume a life of their own. The picture resulting from such intensity of detail is not an objective one : the poet's own personality permeates the tale, we see with his eyes, hear with his ears, feel his emotions. If Henryson ejaculates (as he often does) an angry comment or a grimly humorous remark, these are almost our own reactions, as when (*F.*, ll. 694 ff.) he does not want to intrude on the confession of the fox ; or when (l. 295) looking through the corner of his eye, he says sardonically,

> Thay taryit not to [a]wesche, as I suppose. — [a] *wash*

These quick flashes of the poet's personality establish relations of intimacy : the action suddenly concerns us, and the initially objective

[19] *F.*, ll. 120 ff., 2385 ff. ; *O.*, ll. 317 ff., 324 ff., 338 ff.

picture is shot through with subjective feeling. The action becomes life.

Henryson apprehends the world by his senses, not by his reason. In the prologue of " The Preiching of the Swallow " the poet tells us (*F.*, ll. 1642 ff.) to " lat all ressoun be " if we want " to comprehend Him that contenis all " :

> Yit nevertheles we may have knawlegeing
> Off God almychtie, [a]be his creatouris, — [a] *by*
> That he is gude, ffair, wyis and [a]bening ; — [a] *benign*
> Exempill tak be [a]thir jolie flouris, — [b] *these*
> Rycht sweit of smell, and plesant off colouris.
> Sum grene, sum blew, sum purpour, quhyte, and
> reid,
> Thus distribute [a]be gift off his Godheid. — [a] *by*

This explains his innocent delight in the world of the senses. It also shows the strength and the limitation of his vision. Where, in *Orpheus and Eurydice*, Henryson gives a survey, a report, he is trite and pale ; but where he can intently visualise, *vivify*, a scene, down to the details of his own environment, there he is grand : as in Euridice's flight (*O.*, ll. 103 ff.), the memories of the Complaint (ll. 134 ff.), the music of the spheres (ll. 219 ff.), the scenes of the search (ll. 247-309). Henryson's strength lies in the reality of his setting, which betrays quite as pronounced a realism of outlook as Barbour's. The presentation of love in *The Testament of Cresseid* is realistic, not courtly ; the *Fabillis* are rich in realism—look at Sprutok's conception of love as compared with Pertok's courtly ideal in " Schir Chantecleir and the Foxe " (*F.*, ll. 509 ff.). " Robene and Makyne " is built up on such a conception, and *Orpheus and Eurydice* is one of the very few poems of the Middle Ages that tells a classical tale for its own sake, with no allegorical trappings.

The sharp clarity of Henryson's pictures lies partly in the fact that he practises the utmost economy of expression. There is no padding, not a stanza too much, and should the poet digress, he quickly returns to his theme. This concision gives his poems an enormous impact on our mind. Henryson satisfies Edgar Allan Poe's requirement that from the first sentence the writer of a short story must work towards a total effect. Henryson's economy of expression is most remarkable where he deals with deep emotions or with the sublime. Little of the intense feeling or the horror crosses his lips, but there is often immense suggestion in his understatement (*F.*, l. 2296 ; *T. Cr.*, ll. 71 ff.):

The man [a]leuch [b]na thing, quhen he saw that sicht. *[a] laughed [b] no*

Quhen Diomeid had all his appetyte,
And mair, fulfillit of this fair ladie,
Upon ane uther he set his [a]haill delyte *[a] whole*
And send to hir ane [a]lybell of [b]repudie, *[a] writ [b] repudiation, divorce*
And hir excludit fra his companie.
Than desolait scho walkit up and doun,
And sum men sayis into the court commoun.

... I have pietie thou suld fall sic mischance.

Cresseid prays in the temple " with baill aneuch [sorrow enough] in breist " (l. 110) ; after the hideous deformation of her beauty by the sentence of the gods she looks (ll. 349-50) into a mirror,

And quhen scho saw hir face sa deformait
[a]Gif scho in hart was [b]wa aneuch God [c]wait. *[a] if [b] woeful [c] knows*

Mute pain reaches its greatest depth when (*T. Cr.*, ll. 372 ff.) Calchas sees his daughter :

He luikit on hir uglye [a]lipper face, *[a] leper*
The [a]quhilk befor was quhyte as [b]lillie flour, *[a] which [b] lily flower*
Wringand his handis oftymes he said allace
That he had [a]levit to se that wofull hour, *[a] lived*
For he knew weill that thair was na succour
To hir [a]seikness, and that dowblit his pane. *[a] sickness*
Thus was thair cair aneuch betwix thame twane.

This is a specifically Scottish mode of expression.[20] The greatest emotion falls in the pause between two stanzas, and Henryson is a master of the art of making a pause speak. Most of the examples here are final lines, and it is also a final line (*T. Cr.*, l. 126) that conveys the shock of Cresseid's blasphemy :

' Allace that ever I [a]maid you sacrifice.' *[a] made*

[20] Our italics. Cp. Barbour's " landis fair aneuch," and, in *The Kingis Quair* (st. 47), " Beautee aneuch to mak a world to dote." We can trace this suspicious understatement right down through Scottish literature, and it is still a conspicuous feature of Scots speech, in which " no bad," or " no sae bad," is high praise, and " nae waur [no worse] " is often the nearest that the speaker will go to admitting that in fact he is doing splendidly (and cp. Scott's note in *The Antiquary*). Fear of the fairies often lay behind it : if you praised a child, they would become jealous and " take " it, leaving a " changeling " instead of it. Scottish Gaelic has the same trick of stating less than the whole it wishes to express : thus, " *gu leòir* " means " enough," but often implies " plenty " (cp. " whisky galore ") ; and understatement by negation is very common. This is where the Scot is really " canny," but not in his convictions, or in giving his personality.

The finest example, however, is during the luxurious banquet of "The Uponlandis Mous and the Burges Mous"; they have reached the blissful state of singing "haill yule, haill!" when (*F.*, ll. 293-4)

The [a]spenser come with keyis in his hand, [a] *steward*
Oppinnit the [a]dure, and thame at denner [b]fand. [b] *door* [c] *found*

We feel the petrifying shock in the pause before the next stanza;[21] the subsequent frantic haste is expressed (l. 295) in a sardonic negative understatement:

Thay taryit not to [a]wesche, as I suppose. [a] *wash*

This technique of using a pause to intensify dramatic tension closely resembles the ballads, as does the quick shifting of the scene (which one might call "montage").

This tightlipped reticence is partly achieved by Henryson's use of contrast. When pathos seems to rise to the highest pitch, the poet looks abruptly away and sees the common reality of every day. Thus Cresseid has just learnt her fate, and is still dazed with the horror of it, when a child comes from the hall to tell her that supper is ready and that her father (*T. Cr.*, ll. 362 ff.)

'... hes mervell [a]sa lang [b]on grouf ye ly, [a] *so long* [b] *grovelling*
And sayis your prayers bene [a]to lang [b]sum deill: [a] *too long* [b] *somewhat*
The goddis [a]wait all your intent full weill.' [a] *know*

The contrast of tone is heightened by a similar contrast of rhythm: the grating accents of Saturn's sentence, the soft cadences of Cresseid's first soliloquy, and the simplicity of the child bringing the father's message. From the high elegiac note and soft rhythms of her great complaint Cresseid is grimly brought back to earth by a fellow-leper, who says (*T. Cr.*, ll. 475 ff.):

... 'Quhy spurnis thow aganis the wall,
To [a]sla thy self, and mend nathing at all?' [a] *slay*

'[a]Sen thy weiping [b]dowbillis bot thy wo, [a] *since* [b] *doubles*
I counsall [a]the mak vertew of ane neid. [a] *thee*
To [a]leir to clap thy [b]clapper to and fro, [a] *learn* [b] *leper's clapper*
And leir efter the law of lipper [a]leid.' [a] *folk*

[21] Burns, another master of the pause, uses the opposite technique in *Tam o' Shanter*: Tam has *no* time for a pause, or the witches will get him. They are upon him instantly ("*And* in an instant all was dark . . ."), and the chase is up in the last three lines before the next pause.

From the opening contrast between bleak cold and ardent love to the epitaph " lait lipper lyis deid " written in letters of gold, sustained thematic contrast is the source from which the immense tension of the *Testament* arises. It is (as Tillyard points out) a contrast between knowledge and ignorance that underlies the tragic irony of the sublime scene that occurs when the lovers meet for the last time. What a world of difference there is between this chance encounter (*T. Cr.*, ll. 498-525) and their former meetings as lovers ! When Troilus, in splendid array, passes the deformed Cresseid at the leper-house :

> [a]Than upon him scho [b]kest up baith hir [c]ene, — [a] *then* [b] *cast* [c] *eyes*
> And with ane [a]blenk it come into his [b]thocht, — [a] *glance* [b] *thought*
> That he sumtime hir face befoir had sene.
> Bot scho was in [a]sic plye he knew hir nocht, — [a] *such plight*
> Yit [a]than hir luik into his mynd it brocht — [a] *then*
> The sweit visage and amorous blenking
> Of fair Cresseid sumtyme his awin darling.
>
> ... The [a]idole of ane thing, [b]in cace may be — [a] *image* [b] *perchance*
> Sa deip imprentit in the fantasy
> That it deludis the wittis outwardly,
> And sa appeiris in forme and lyke estait,
> Within the mynd as it was figurait.
>
> Ane spark of lufe than till his hart [a]culd spring... — [a] *did*
> Within ane quhyle he changit mony hew,
> And nevertheless not ane ane uther knew.

Has this passage, with its intense psychology and intimate penetration into the mind, any parallel in medieval literature ?

In the *Fabillis*, the contrast is not tragic but humorous, as in the opening (*F.*, ll. 2777 ff.) of " The Paddok [frog] and the Mous " :

> Upon ane tyme (as Esope [a]culd report) — [a] *did*
> Ane lytill mous come till ane [a]rever syde ; — [a] *river*
> Scho micht not waid, hir schankis were sa schort,
> Scho culd not swym, scho had na hors to ryde :
> [a]Of verray force behovit hir to byde, — [a] *of sheer necessity*
> And to and ffra besyde that revir deip
> Scho ran, cryand with mony pietuous peip.

This is wonderfully observed animal life—but like a flash comes the phrase " scho had na hors to ryde." From this intrusion of the human world and the resulting contrast of tall and small arises the tender and pervasive humour, the compassion which subtly points to the human in the animal, or the beast in man. Thus the " uponlandis mous " has (*F.*, l. 360) her " but and ben," [22] and her town-dwelling sister was (ll. 171 ff.) " gild brother " and " fre burges,"

And fredome had to [a]ga quhair ever scho list, — *[a] go [b] cheese*
Amang the [b]cheis in [c]ark, and [d]meill in [e]kist. — *[c] box [d] meal [e] chest*

In her pantry, the burgess mouse has (l. 265) " flesche and fische aneuch, baith [both] fresche and salt," and when (l. 180) her poor sister comes " bairfute, allone, with pykestaf in hir hand," they feast (ll. 267 ff.) like lords,

Except ane thing, thay drank the watter cleir.

Much of this is grotesque exaggeration, and the juxtaposition of understatement and overstatement is a characteristic phenomenon in Scottish literature : genuine emotions of the soul are rather suggested than expressed, but the airs that men give themselves are heightened to grotesquerie. This is all the more rollicking here because it is a tiny mouse that lives in a world of pretence. Who does not recognise the hysterics of that other mouse (*F.*, ll. 2798 ff.) dancing round the paddock [frog], or (ll. 218 ff.) our burgess mouse, indignant at the simple fare her sister offers :

' My fair sister ' (quod scho), ' have me excusit.
This rude dyat and I can not accord.
To tender meit my stomok is ay usit,
For [a]quhylis I [b]fair alsweill as ony lord. — *[a] sometimes [b] fare as well*
[a]Thir wydderit peis, and nuttis, [b]or thay be [c]bord, — *[a] these [b] ere [c] bored*
Wil brek my teith, and mak my [a]wame fful sklender, — *[a] belly*
[a]Quhilk wes before usit to meitis tender.' — *[a] which*

Equally authentic is her taunt (l. 249) :

' My dische [a]likingis is worth your haill expence.' — *[a] lickings*

The grotesqueness often lies in a comparison, as when the fox (*F.*, ll. 1051 ff.) answers the inquiries as to the success of a mission by pointing at the bloody head of his companion, the wolf :

Than Lowrence said : ' My lord, [a]speir not at me ! — *[a] ask*
Speir at your Doctour off Divinitie,
With his reid cap can tell yow weill aneuch.[23]

[22] A house with an outer and an inner room ; see *S.N.D.*
[23] For the fox, cp. also *F.*, ll. 747 ff., 768 ff.

How closely understatement and grotesque exaggeration may combine is shown when despite cheerful invitations by her sister the burgess mouse remains adamant (*F.*, ll. 239 f.) in her indignation :

> For all hir mery exhortatioun,
> This burges mous had littill will to sing [!].

★ ★ ★

Henryson's philosophy is rooted in deep religious and moral feeling, and is conspicuously humanitarian, democratic, and independent. Henryson does not speak much about his religion, but it is implicit everywhere. *The Testament of Cresseid* does not, as some critics think, reflect the sternness (as compared with Chaucer's humanity) of a puritanical Scottish schoolmaster : [24] rather it holds out a promise of Christian redemption for Cresseid. At the end of Chaucer's *Troilus and Criseyde*, she is a hated outcast and a bad example held up for the cruel scorn of posterity.[25] Henryson says (*T. Cr.*, ll. 87 f.) :

> I sall excuse, as far furth as I may,
> Thy womanheid...

She has violated the laws of love, and revolts against the planets as set on their courses by God. Even her punishment at first only leads to self-pity : she laments (ll. 351 ff.) *that* she spoke, not *what* she spoke. Only when, as a result of her new meeting with Troilus, she recognises his faithfulness and her own treason, does she *repent* (ll. 542 ff.) and accuse herself : she is saved by her love.[26] Now her *soul* is redeemed—Cresseid leaves it to chaste Diane—even though her body is the prey of toads and worms.

Henryson's creed is summed up (*F.*, ll. 1647 ff.) in " The Preiching of the Swallow " :

> Nane suld presume, [a]be ressoun naturall, *[a] by*
> To seirche the secreitis off the Trinitie,
> Bot [a]trow fermelie, and lat all ressoun be. *[a] believe*

He has the firm faith of his time in the divine order of God's creation, where man, animal, and planet all have their appointed place in

[24] Thus Sir H. J. C. Grierson, in *The Modern Scot,* IV (1934), and HARVEY WOOD ; but cp. Muir, and esp. Tillyard.

[25] Cp. l. 1681 : " Who shal now trowe on any oothes mo ? "

[26] This is a point missed by Tillyard in his otherwise excellent analysis.

one and the same universe, and all bear witness that God is "gude, ffair, wyis, and bening." Hence arises Henryson's own innocent delight in nature, of which we have already seen so many examples; hence, too, the righteous indignation with which he observes the failure of the mighty of this world to play the parts that God has allotted to them. For if God is good, he is also just, and those who exploit the poor should dread (*F.*, l. 2760) "the rychteous Goddis blame":

> O thow grit lord, that riches hes and rent,
> Be nocht ane wolf, thus to [a]devoir the [b]pure; *[a] devour [b] poor*
> Think that na thing cruell nor violent
> May in this warld perpetuallie indure.[27]

Henryson's sharp social and religious satire contains much that is commonplace: the burgess mouse does not say grace; Orpheus finds popes, cardinals, bishops, abbots, in hell; the abuses of the civil as well as the ecclesiastical courts are castigated; in "The Fox and the Wolf" there is a hint of abuse of the confession. But there are, however, some remarkable passages. In "The Wolf and the Lamb," the lamb (ll. 2663 ff.) protests against being judged for its father's guilt, while the wolf (ll. 2671 ff.) demands punishment down to the twentieth degree. Like Barbour before him, Henryson does not mention the intercession of the Church or her guardian angels and saints. He, and his creatures, address God directly. The lamb quotes Scripture. In "The Taill of the Scheip and the Doig," the sheep (ll. 1295 f.) reproaches its maker:

> And said, 'Lord God, quhy sleipis thow sa lang?
> [a]Walk, and [b]discerne my cause, groundit on richt,' *[a] wake [b] decide my case*

and the poet himself exclaims (ll. 1307 f.):

> Seis thow not (Lord) this warld owerturnit is,
> As quha wald change gude gold in leid or tyn?

In addressing God, Henryson uses a tone of intimacy that clearly foreshadows the Presbyterians and their daily reckoning with God. He does not share the Presbyterian tendency to mistrust happiness as such, but he does show a shrewdness that is characteristic of the peasant in all ages, and is very suspicious of all happiness not built

[27] *F.*, ll. 2763 ff.

up by one's own work—as when (*F.*, l. 278) the country mouse sees her sister's full larder :

> 'Ye, dame' (quod scho), 'how lang will this lest ?'

The swallow warns the birds that they will live to rue their easy-going carelessness ; they will pay with their own lives what they ate from the fowler (*F.*, ll. 1839 ff.). This, however, has already taken us to the secular side of Henryson's philosophy.

Henryson is a countryman ; and his philosophy is as firmly rooted in rustic folk wisdom as in religious faith. This gives him poise and the sturdy independence of the peasant who does his work but is too stiff to bow. In the fable—essentially democratic in its appeal—this independence finds an appropriate means of expression. Henryson puts all his love into two of the longest, "The Taill of the Uponlandis Mous and the Burges Mous" and "The Preiching of the Swallow" ; both express the same attitude, the instinctive prudence of the peasant who wants to have both feet on the ground and is suspicious of gambling. Turning her back on "ffeistis delicate" given (*F.*, ll. 232-3) with "ane glowmand [gloomy] brow," the country mouse returns (ll. 358 ff.)

> ... to hir den,
> [a]Als warme as [b]woll, [c]suppose it wes not gret ; [a] *as* [b] *wool* [c] *even though*

though modest, her own way of life is not lacking in happiness and dignity. This is not a cheap common-place, but an almost defiantly, yet unsentimentally, democratic attitude, such as we see also in "The Cok and the Jasp" or "The Wolf and the Lamb." It is almost the same as that seen in "A Man's a Man for a' that." Never before in medieval literature had the dignity and the rights of the peasant and the common people been proclaimed in such tones.[28] Henryson sees the crofter realistically, in his life and in his work ; the simplicity of his outlook and his few fundamental moral principles ; his uprightness, his obstinacy, his shrewdness, his homeliness, his suspicion of newfangled things, his gift of making the best of what he finds. This enables him to draw quick character studies of his countrymen, such as the calculating cadger (*F.*, ll. 2070 ff., 2091 ff.), the fowler (ll. 1839 ff.), the leper lady (*T. Cr.*, ll. 474 ff.) with no nonsense about her.

[28] In *Piers Plowman*, the peasant is quoted for moral and theological reasons : Barbour praises some men of the people for their doings in the War of Independence.

With his roots in the people, Henryson shares the old wisdom of the folk, their poetry, proverbs, and lore. His language is popular, his humour that of the people, his quick dialogues colloquial. But at the same time his art is of Chaucer's brilliancy, and his freshness makes even a proverb sound as if we had never heard it, as when (" Robene and Makyne," ll. 91 f.) Makyne tartly refuses Robene, who had previously scorned her advances :

The man that will nocht quhen he may
Sall haif nocht quhen he wald.

The closeness of Henryson to folk poetry is most evident in his many points of contact with the ballads ; the stark tragedy, the use of contrast, the montage, the grim humour, the drama. For Henryson is rarely the scenic artist (as in the pageant of the planets in the *Testament*), but presents, without transitions, speech and answer, picture beside picture, resolution and deed, as in " The Lyonn and the Mous," " The Wolf and the Lamb," the " Ressoning... " poems, or " Robene and Makyne," that remarkable precursor of pastoral drama.[29] Henryson writes art poetry, not folk poetry, but his work contains elements of folk poetry and is based partly on folk tradition. In his assimilation of European subject matter, of Chaucer's conception of poetic art, and of Scottish characteristics, Robert Henryson is one of the greatest poets of the whole of Scottish literature, perhaps the greatest of all, and certainly the one with the most marked personality.

[29] Tasso and Guarini wrote almost a century later.

2. William Dunbar

WILLIAM DUNBAR (?1460-?1521) is generally regarded as the main representative of Scots poetry during the Golden Age under James IV, and his works have attracted more attention than those of other Makars.[1] He is about one generation younger than Henryson, but the difference between the two is less one of age than of *milieu* and of temperament. Henryson's roots in the soil and in the people gave him an upright bearing and an inner poise. Dunbar is a town-dweller, and of his own choice a courtier ; and with him we enter a totally different atmosphere. Henryson's outlook was founded on self-respect. He was the first poet in Britain—or, for that matter, in Europe—who emphasised the *dignity* of the common man ; it angered him to see popular rights trampled underfoot by the mighty of the earth. Dunbar, too, was easily provoked. In one poem (67. " Of Covetyce," ll. 29 ff.) he reviles those lairds who wear silks for which their tenants have had to sell their summer corn ; in another (21. " None may Assure in this Warld," ll. 16 ff.), he complains that

> Nane heir bot rich men hes renown,
> And [a]pure men ar [b]plukit doun. *[a] poor [b] plucked*

This, however, is nothing but a formula by which he expresses his own sense of insecurity in the aftermath of Flodden. Frequently,

[1] All quotations are taken from *The Poems of William Dunbar*, ed. W. MACKAY MACKENZIE, Edinburgh 1932 (reprinted 1950) ; numbers preceding titles are those given them in his text. This is the latest and most reliable edition, and the preface is a very helpful introduction (see also W. M. Mackenzie in *Edinburgh Essays in Scots Literature*, 1933).

Earlier edns. by DAVID LAING, 2 vols., 1834 (suppl. 1865) ; by J. SMALL and W. GREGOR (with " Life " by J. G. Mackay), S.T.S., 3 vols., 1884-93 ; by JULIUS SCHIPPER (who had already written a monograph on Dunbar in 1884), Vienna 1894 ; and by H. B. BAILDON, 1907.

Though he has little to say about Dunbar as a poet, J. W. Baxter, *William Dunbar : A biographical Study*, Edinburgh 1952, is worth consulting ; see also the critical notice in *Scottish Historical Review*, XXXIII (1954), pp. 46-52, by M. P. McDiarmid, who adduces evidence that Dunbar may have been a chaplain to the Queen. Rachel Annand Taylor, *Dunbar, the Poet and his Period*, The Poets on the Poets, 1931, is prejudiced and somewhat unscholarly ; but as a poet, Miss Taylor has some fine remarks on Dunbar's artistic achievement. No writer, however, has shown so much understanding of Dunbar's art as C. S. Lewis in *English Literature in the sixteenth Century, excluding Drama* (VOL. III in Oxford Hists. of Eng. Lit.), 1954. See also Edwin Morgan, " Dunbar and the Language of Poetry," in *Essays in Criticism*, 1952, II.ii.

too, he bitterly denounces contemporary ecclesiastical abuses. But except in so far as they coincide with his own frustration Dunbar is not interested in the sufferings of the common people. In his poems, the " pure man " is nearly always Dunbar himself; and the burden of his complaint is invariably that the benefices so freely conferred on others are not conferred on him :

> I knaw nocht how the kirk is gydit,
> Bot beneficis ar nocht [a]leill devydit ; — [a] *loyal(ly)*
> Sum men hes sevin, and I nocht ane ;
> [a]Quhilk to considder is ane pane.[2] — [a] *which*

Again and again, Dunbar's grotesque ribaldry is directed against his social inferiors—soutars, tailors, merchants. There is real venom in his denunciation [3] of an upstart whom Nature had meant to muck the stable, but who, at table, now sits far above the " lerit sone [learned son] "—doubtless Dunbar himself—" off erl or lord," and as he rises in society dares more and more to despise " nobles off bluid." Henryson would never have spoken of " chuff-midding [chaff-dung-heap] churllis, cumin off cart-fillaris," with the contempt that Dunbar heaps on them in this poem ; and the gusto with which Dunbar enumerates the upstart's plebeian personal characteristics—" his wavill [twisted] feit and wirrok tais [corny toes] . . . and bausy [coarse] handis," and, last but not least, his

> ... [a]lut schulderis and [b]luttard bak, — [a] *bent* (cp. *lout*) [b] *stooping*
> Quhilk natur maid to [a]beir a pak, — [a] *bear*

—shows how far *he* was from believing, with Burns, that " a man's a man for a' that." [4]

The bitterness of many of Dunbar's poems is, in its own way, characteristically Scottish. Dunbar probably came of good family, but was evidently a younger son, or born on the wrong side of the blanket, with little or no patrimony. Under James IV, much favour was bestowed on *novi homines*, and it was to Dunbar a bitter disappointment that the ecclesiastical preferment which he had been brought up to regard as his birthright always somehow eluded him :

[2] 13. " Of the Warldis Instabilitie," ll. 45 ff.
[3] 19. " Complaint to the King," ll. 39 ff.
[4] Cp. also Dunbar's gusto in detailing the loutish appearance of Kennedy, his opponent in the " Flyting," passim.

I wes in youthe, on [a]nureice kne, [a] *nurse's*
Cald dandillie, bischop, dandillie,
And [a]quhone that age now dois me greif, [a] *when*
A sempill vicar I can not be....

Unfortunately for him, his own poetic gift had no market value, and this provokes the touchy haughtiness of the intellectual :

Jok, that wes wont to keip the [a]stirkis, [a] *steers (cattle)*
Can now draw him ane [a]cleik of kirkis, [a] *catch, clutch*
With ane fals [a]cairt in to his sleif, [a] *card*
Worthe all my ballattis under the [a]byrkis : [a] *birches*
Exces of thocht dois me mischeif.

Hence arose the gnawing sense of insecurity which provides one of Dunbar's most frequent themes :

How suld I [a]leif and I not landit, [a] *live*
Nor yit withe benefice am [a]blandit ? [5] [a] *blended, united ;* or (?) *soothed*

These small details betray an egocentric attitude and a lack of inner balance, a snatching at fleeting opportunities, and a feeling that he has no firm ground under his feet. Owing to these special circumstances, Dunbar's characteristically Scottish pride of birth made it impossible for him to be " contentit wi' little and cantie wi' mair," and found expression in numerous petitions to the King. It must at times have been deeply humiliating for a man of Dunbar's birth and temperament to be reduced to begging the King's favours :

As [a]saule in to purgatorie, [a] *soul*
Leifand in pane with [b]hoip of glorie, [a] *hope*
So is my selffe ye may beleiff
In hoip, sir, of your [a]adjutorie : [a] *assistance*
Exces of thocht dois me mischeif.[6]

But these petitions are shot through with so many flashes of savage humour, and such is their individual freshness, such the fervour with which the poet caricatures all the flatterers and job-hunters to be seen about the Court, that they escape the stale taste of subservience.

The religious attitude, too, of this chaplain-to-be lacks poise. The calm acceptance of God's will that figures so conspicuously in Barbour's

[5] This and the two previous quotations are from 20. " To the King," ll. 61 ff., 66 ff., and 76 ff.

[6] *Op. cit.*, ll. 81 ff.

Bruce does not reappear in Dunbar's poems, nor does Dunbar's own relationship with God have that intimacy which we remarked in Henryson's *Fabillis* and *Testament.* On occasion (for example in 83. " The Tabill of Confession ") Dunbar is genuinely, if conventionally, devout ; but far more frequently (as in 13. " Of the Warldis Instabilitie," 66. " Of the Changes of Life," 71. " All erdly Joy returnis in Pane," 74. " Of Manis Mortality," 75. " Of the Warldis Vanitie," etc.) the keynote of his religious poetry is *fear*—fear of change, fear of death—fear, too, of instability, that fear so widespread at the end of the Middle Ages. In Dunbar's treatment of this recurrent theme, there is, moreover, nothing specifically Christian. In the " Lament ' Quhen he wes sek ' "—usually, though perhaps rather misleadingly, referred to as the " Lament for the Makaris "—Dunbar's masterly use of the refrain " *Timor mortis conturbat me* " irresistibly evokes the sound of the death-knell, and his fear of death is voiced with telling simplicity. Despite the purely conventional assertion of Christian hope in the final stanza—

> [a]Sen for the [b]deid [c]remeid is none, — [a] *since* [b] *death* [c] *remedy*
> Best is that we for [a]dede dispone, — [a] *death*
> Eftir our [a]deid that [b]lif may we ; — [a] *death* [b] *live*
> *Timor mortis conturbat me.*[7]

—the poem as a whole is profoundly pessimistic : in death, all are simply obliterated, apparently without hope of redemption and resurrection.

The refrain " *Timor mortis conturbat me* " is borrowed from the Office for the Dead, and the " Lament ' Quhen he wes sek ' " is not the only religious poem in which Dunbar echoes the responses of the liturgical offices. Indeed it might be said that the spirit of his religious poetry is essentially liturgical and expresses the formula of religion (78. " Ane Orisoun "). When it is possible for him to visualise a concrete scene—as in 80. " The Passioun of Christ," [8] in which there is an almost morbid obsession with every detail of the Crucifixion that is highly characteristic of the late Middle Ages, and in " The Resurrection," which seems to re-echo the thunderous jubilation of the universe—Dunbar is not incapable of genuine religious feeling, and at times (*e.g.* in 84. " The Maner of Passing to Confession ")

[7] 7. " Lament ' Quhen he wes sek '," ll. 97 ff.

[8] Except in the allegorical *moralitas* (ll. 97 ff.), with its new refrains, which again suggests religion in its ritual aspect.

we may detect in Dunbar a sense of his priestly responsibilities : but he is concerned chiefly with outward observances, and the music of his religious poetry is unmistakably liturgical. In 79. " Of the Nativitie of Christ," for example, the conception of redemption that he expresses is somewhat mechanical, and the pageant of angels, " hevinly operationis," and so forth, perhaps unduly theatrical ; but we do hear the exultation of the heavenly choirs, especially in the last stanza [9] ; while in 82. " Ane Ballat of our Lady " Dunbar's exuberant rhyming—though perhaps *too* exuberant for our ears—is like a peal of bells, and, in listening to it, we can abandon ourselves to a purely sensuous delight, without bothering too much about the meaning of the words.

On occasion, Dunbar uses the same set of bells for an extremely secular melody, as in 40, the hilarious " Testament of Mr Andro Kennedy," and in 30, the blasphemous " Drege [Dirge] of Dunbar," in which Edinburgh and Stirling are identified with Heaven and Purgatory respectively, and the holy Office for the Dead is parodied, down to the very Paternoster. Such parodies are not infrequent in the late Middle Ages, but Dunbar's gusto in them is quite unsurpassed —and, at the same time, characteristically Scottish.

The differences between Dunbar and Henryson are so striking that there could scarcely be a better example of the diversity of which Scottish poetry is capable : yet they both belong to the same specifically Scottish tradition, and both spring from the same soil, now made " sessonabill, sappie, and to resave all seidis abill " by the genial influence of Chaucer. The influence of the English master is less apparent, at first sight, in Henryson's work than in Dunbar's : how frequently, for example, Dunbar falls asleep and dreams an allegory, as in 55. " The Thrissil and the Rois," 54. " Bewty and the Presoneir," 56. " The Goldyn Targe," to name a few ceremonial examples, and in such extravaganzas as 42. " The Devillis Inquest " and 57. " The Dance of the sevin deidly Synnis." Yet Dunbar's relationship with Chaucer is much looser than Henryson's ; he only appropriates Chaucer's apparatus of allegorical figures and technical method of introducing a poem, but nothing of his art of narrative, creation of character, human comedy, or closeness of insight. And he adds so many elements of a poetic art so peculiarly his own that in its total effect his work is very different from Chaucer's.

[9] The poem has been set to music by Francis George Scott, who has captured all its glorious exultation.

C. S. Lewis has acutely remarked that whereas Chaucer used and recognised one language and one poetic tradition only, the Scots makars not only developed a new kind of poetry, but also continued and carried on the various strands of native tradition.[10] (These strands perhaps reach back further in time than C. S. Lewis in his somewhat formal division indicates.) Each of these traditions—the vernacular ones and the aureate Chaucerian—belongs, socially and psychologically, to a different plane of experience, and each has its own appropriate style. Owing to their own awareness of all this, the Scots Makars have an air of professionalism and virtuosity totally lacking in Chaucer and his English imitators ; and of all the Makars, Dunbar is the most accomplished virtuoso, and flits most easily from one different plane to another.

Henryson makes language and rhythm subservient to expression ; Dunbar is a virtuoso whose command of an almost inexhaustible variety of metrical forms is such as no English poet possessed until the nineteenth century. In playing on all these instruments—often, apparently, for the sole pleasure of playing on them—he shows a master's touch. One need only compare the stately heraldic march of the Chaucerian stanzas in 55. " The Thrissil and the Rois " with the sumptuous but delicate embroidery of 56. " The goldyn Targe," or the over-rich peal of bells in 82." Ane Ballat of our Lady " (ll. 1 ff.) :

Hale, [a]sterne superne ! Hale, in eterne, — [a] *star*
  In Godis sicht to schyne !
[a]Lucerne in [b]derne for to discerne — [a] *lantern* [b] *darkness*
  Be glory and grace devyne

—which again we may contrast with the linguistic sobriety and metrical restraint of 7. " Lament ' Quhen he wes sek '," which has none of this brilliant rhythmical splendour, but irresistibly suggests (9 ff., 17 ff.) a ghostly procession of hooded figures :

The stait of man dois change and vary,
Now sound, now [a]seik, now blith, now [b]sary, — [a] *sick* [b] *sorry*
Now dansand mery, now like to dee ;
  Timor mortis conturbat me....

On to the [a]ded gois all Estatis, — [a] *death*
Princis, Prelotis, and Potestatis,
Baith riche and pur of al degre ;
  Timor mortis conturbat me.

[10] See below, pp. 103-26.

Dunbar's stanzas can suggest the murmuring of the brook as in 56. "The goldyn Targe" (ll. 28 ff.), where the long vowels and recurrent *l*s, especially when alliterating, evoke in our ears the lapping of waves on the bank,[11] or the furioso and whirling of a reel as in 36. "Epitaphe for Donald Owre," with its many hissing sounds and *i*s—the stanza is, quite appropriately, a form of the bob and wheel—or in 57. "The Dance of the sevin deidly Synnis." The special effect is often achieved by alliteration, which the poet adds in calculated doses to end-rhyme and internal rhyme "like an inexhaustible sound of spinning" (Taylor); in his astonishing extravaganza 47. "The Tretis of the twa mariit Wemen and the Wedo" he uses the alliterative long line without rhyme with the mocking intention of giving the realistic frankness of his three inimitable women the appearance of staunch heroism that the alliterative long line itself evokes. Whether in French models like *triolets* or *ballades* or in native ones like the tail-rhyme stanza, Dunbar utilises all traditions and shows a master's instinctive power of judging which metre will best suit his mood, and best display or decorate his subject. His skill in evoking moods by the very metre is revealed by a comparison of the tail-rhyme in 35. "Of Sir Thomas Norny," used with the same effect as in Chaucer's *Sir Topas*, with another tail-rhyme, the tripartite septenarius of 48. "Of the Ladyis Solistaris at Court," in which the short lines with their quickly recurring rhymes mimic to perfection the tripping gait of the ladies as (ll. 1 ff.) they go coquettishly about their business in the law courts:

> Thir ladyis fair, That makis repair
> And in the court ar [a]kend, — [a] *known*
> Thre dayis thair Thay will do mair
> Ane mater for till end,
> Than thair [a]gud men Will do in ten, — [a] *husbands*
> For ony craft thay can,
> So weill thay ken Quhat tyme and quhen
> [a]Thair menes thay [b]sowld mak [c]than. — [a] *their complaints* [b] *should* [c] *then*

With some of Dunbar's stanzas I cannot help feeling that they were meant for singing or musical accompaniment, especially the "dances," or 18. "That the King war Johne Thomsounis Man," with its pattern of folk-song rhythms. What as a poem sounds rather clumsy and

[11] Cp. "I hear lake water lapping with low sound by the shore" (W. B. Yeats, "The Lake Isle of Innisfree").

tactless—the poet longs for the King to become a complaisant husband, for then the Queen might cajole him into giving a benefice to Dunbar —could be rather witty and appropriate as a pert little song ; the idea is all the more tempting since the refrain is a proverb.[12]

Dunbar understands the effect to be gained from a refrain and its variations. In 2. " Ane his awin Ennemy," just listen to the poet's diabolical laughter when for the expected refrain " He wirkis sorrow to him sell," he substitutes (l. 25) " I gif him to the Devill of hell "—a surprise effect for which the listener is subtly prepared, both by the independence of this last stanza, and by the slight modification of rhythm which precedes the final stroke.[13] The same predilection for an effective and unexpected ending reveals itself in " How Dumbar was desyrd to be ane Freir," where the apparent St Francis turns out to be the Devil in disguise ; and in the " Amends to the Telyouris and Sowtaris ", in the last stanza of which the promised amends are adroitly converted into a slap in the face.

All these features reveal Dunbar as a conscious and dedicated artist ; his lines against one who had mangled his verses (5. " Complaint to the King aganis Mure ") express this self-confidence. The whole of Middle English poetry will not produce another such example of conscious artistry and virtuosity, but it is closely paralleled in the rigorous technical training of the Gaelic *fili* or trained bard. Dunbar would himself have been the first to " flyte " me for attributing to him " sic eloquence as thay in Erschry use "[14] whereby (57. " The Dance of the sevin deidly Synnis," ll. 118 ff.) the Devil himself

... sa [a]devit wes with thair yell, *[a] deafened*
That in the depest pot of hell
He [a]smorit thame with [b]smuke. *[a] smothered [b] smoke*

I do not wish to suggest that Dunbar was deeply versed in traditional

[12] See *Fergusson's Scottish Proverbs*, ed. Erskine Beveridge, S.T.S., 1924, No. A 459.

[13] Among the many poems with refrains, cp. 1, 9, 13, 28, 46. (In 13. " Of the Warldis Instabilitie," only recorded in the Maitland MS, the metrical structure and the train of thought lead me to believe that the second and third stanzas from the end have been transposed, and that the original sequence was : " I do not want more than a small church —but I despair of the treacherous and fickle world—yet my King will not allow my soul to perish for its deserts—my greatest hope is in your bounty." This sounds more convincing than if the order of the second and third phrases is reversed, and would also do full justice to the twofold variation of the refrain : " Quhilk to considder is ane pane "—" Na for sic syn to suffer pane "—" Quhilk is ane lessing of my pane.")

[14] 6. " The Flyting of Dunbar and Kennedie," l. 107.

Gaelic literature, or that he deliberately modelled his poetry on it. There is no evidence of anything like that. But the fact remains that Dunbar evidently had Celtic blood in his veins, with not a little of the Gaelic temperament; and his own genius has a recognisable affinity with the spirit of Celtic poetry. Even if Dunbar knew little or no Gaelic—and as to that the evidence is inconclusive[15]—he must certainly have been accustomed to the *sound* of Gaelic poetry, for during his time at Court payments for poetry-recitals were frequently made to Gaelic bards; and in a country where Gaelic was still dominant in the larger area and spoken by the King, where only two centuries before the official languages had been Gaelic and Latin, a mutual (though perhaps unconscious) influence was only to be expected. The predominantly strophic character, the elaborate technique, the combination of internal and end-rhyme with alliteration, the cultivation of specific forms for specific types of poems, the sheer virtuosity, all these are metrical characteristics that Dunbar has in common with the Gaelic *fili*. One of his poems, 51. " Inconstancy of Luve," is written in a form of stanza corresponding in practically all details to the *ochtfhoclach mór* or *beag*,[16] for example in the two-rhyme scheme.[17] The internal rhyme of 82. " Ane Ballat of our Lady " is certainly modelled after Latin hymns, but the firework display of internal rhymes in the last two stanzas of Dunbar's sections of 6. " The Flyting of Dunbar and Kennedie " seems rather to be derived from Gaelic models—as also in Kennedy's final stanza.[18] This would be even more true of 77. " A general Satyre," if we could be sure that it was Dunbar's. Dunbar frequently uses a special stanza for poems of a similar nature, for example, one running $a\ a\ B\ a\ B_4$, with a refrain, for petitions, etc., of a serious tone[19]; apt as this form may be for the content we should realise that both Scots poetry

[15] In the " Flyting," Dunbar seems to have understood " Kennedy " as *ceann eitigh*, " ugly head." One Roughead appears as a legal representative of the Kennedys in Edinburgh.

[16] Cp. W. P. Ker, " On a lyric stave called in Irish *ochtfhoclach bec*," in *Miscellany presented to Kuno Meyer*, ed. O. Bergin and C. Marstrander, Halle 1912. For a general survey of Gaelic prosody, see Douglas Hyde, *A Literary History of Ireland*, 1898; Kuno Meyer, *A Primer of Irish Metrics*; and *Tadhg Dall O' Ruiginn*, ed. Eleanor Knott, Irish Text Society, 22-3 (1922-6).

[17] In l. 16, Mackenzie misprints Bannatyne's " cure " as " care," thus obscuring the structure. " Cure, curiously " (for " care, carefully ") are much commoner in Middle Scots than in Southern English. It is, however, no more than a coincidence that *cùram* (itself derived from Lat. *cura*) also occurs frequently in Gaelic poetry.

[18] See below, pp. 109-13.

[19] *E.g.* 4, 8, 9, 12, 14-16, 20-1, 31, etc.; slightly varied in 3, 4, 10, 11, 60.

and Gaelic poetry has an extraordinary predilection for such traditional metres for special subjects.[20]

We find the same free movement from one traditional level to another in Dunbar's style. C. S. Lewis has pointed out that he uses his own everyday educated language in his moral poems (and, I should add, in most of the personal poems and petitions); the allegories and courtly poems require a higher style, the " aureate "; while comic and burlesque pieces seem best couched in a broad vernacular. For example :

(*a*) Schir, yit remembir as of befoir,
How that my youthe [a]is done forloir — *[a] is lost*
In your service, with pane and greiff....

(*b*) Ryght as the [a]stern of day [b]begouth to schyne, — *[a] star [b] began*
Quhen gone to bed war Vesper and Lucyne,
I raise and by a [a]rosere did me rest : — *[a] rose garden*
Up sprang the goldyn candill matutyne,
With clere [a]depurit bemes cristallyne, — *[a] purified*
Glading the mery foulis in thair nest....

(*c*) [a]Iersch brybour baird, vyle beggar with thy [b]brattis, — *[a] Irish robber bard [b] rags*
Cuntbittin [a]crawdoun Kennedy, coward of [b]kynd, — *[a] coward [b] disposition*
[a]Evill farit and [b]dryit, as [c]Denseman on the [d]rattis, — *[a] ill-favoured [b] shrunken [c] Dane [d] wheels*
Lyke as the [a]gleddis had on thy [b]gule snowt dynd....[21] — *[a] kites [b] yellow*

There is frequent misunderstanding of aureation, this rich decoration with polysyllabic words of French and Latin origin. In principle it is an enrichment of the vernacular such as Chaucer had achieved, or as the *grands rhétoriqueurs* had aimed at in fifteenth-century France. If the aureate style of the Scots Makars looks to us so much more rhetorical and " sugared " than Chaucer's, yet there are two facts that we must not overlook. From the inception of the Auld Alliance towards the end of the thirteenth century, the Scots tongue has had many close relations with French and Latin that have not passed

[20] After writing this, I find a mention of Dunbar's " verse patterns and forms resembling the Gaelic ' strict forms'," by Maurice Lindsay, " Poetry," in *Some Scottish Arts*, ed. J. M. Reid, 1951, p. 41.

[21] (*a*) 20. " To the King," ll. 1 ff. ; (*b*) 56. " The Goldyn Targe," ll. 1 ff. ; (*c*) 6. " Flyting," ll. 49 ff.

through the general medium of English, as any page in the *Scottish national Dictionary* will show. This holds true of most phases of Scottish culture (*e.g.* music), and in the age of James IV Scotland had a strongly Continental outlook, developing cultural and diplomatic relations with France, Italy, Spain, Denmark. Secondly, not even the milder forms of aureation survived the Reformation (1560) and the Union of the Crowns (1603), which together deprived Scotland of a court language.

In Henryson's " hamelier " output there are few traces of aureation : Dunbar, the court poet, provides many elaborate examples. Aureation serves a well-defined artistic purpose : decoration on a small surface. Dunbar's word pictures are highly coloured, but he does not employ a continuous spectrum : rather he aims at the harder and more brilliant colour-contrasts of a miniature or a piece of enamelling—" anamyllit " indeed is one of his favourite words.[22] Look at the sumptuous colours of 82. " Ane Ballat of our Lady " or the heraldic tracery of 55. " The Thrissil and the Rois." [23] The Gaelic poets go even further in the elaboration of the smallest detail and achieve a close parallel to their book-illustrations, or to their sculpture as seen in the Celtic crosses. We find Dunbar half-way towards such ornamentation, and Miss Taylor speaks of a " richly enamelled picture," and of " hard surfaces, enamelled or otherwise."

Surfaces ? Yes. On the one hand, Dunbar is a highly personal poet, in the sense that he is chiefly preoccupied with such matters as are immediately of interest to himself personally—his own headache, his own poverty and insecurity, his own transitory moods, his own jealousies, dislikes and grievances. In handling this subject-matter, he is solely concerned with bare surface appearances, and external details. His poems are not in any sense confessional documents : from them we learn little about the man himself—his abiding passions, his faith, his later priesthood ; one semi-autobiographical piece leaves us in some doubt whether he was a novice or a friar of the Franciscan order (4. " How Dumbar wes desyrd to be ane Freir "). His court life produced a number of official elegies and panegyrics, as well as the ceremonial allegory in which he celebrates the marriage of his

[22] It is also popular, though less so, with other writers of the time ; we find it in *The Kingis Quair* (st. 48), and in Gavin Douglas.

[23] For an ingenious use of the coat-of-arms in the stained-glass windows installed in Holyrood Abbey in honour of this union of the thistle and the rose, see Baxter, *op. cit.*, p. 113. Henryson had used heraldic emblems in " The Trial of the Fox."

King with Princess Margaret of England.[24] But even in his court poetry Dunbar is chiefly concerned with the minor incidents of court life—such as his own feud and subsequent reconciliation with the Keeper of the Queen's wardrobe, a dance in the Queen's chamber, a mock tournament for the favours of a negress, or one of the King's amorous escapades.[25] The King's greatness is passed over in silence, and we listen in vain for any echo of the great events of the time : even Flodden itself is not mentioned. Did Dunbar then have no sense of greatness? I cannot help thinking of a version of the death of Queen Maeve, the greatest figure in Irish sagas beside Cuchullin, where she gets her death from a hard cheese flung against her forehead. And her husband and king is henpecked. The Irish sagas are very chary of unqualified praise, and the Celtic poet revels in the all too human weaknesses of his " heroes." This seems part of the democratic sense of equality that is found in all Celtic peoples : the Scots are as capable of hero-worship as anybody, but they are suspicious of anybody posing on a pedestal, and of any merely inflated " greatness," which they will puncture by such caustic remarks as " I kent his grandfaither." This reduces things to their proper proportions and re-establishes equality within the clan. We shall have to return to this peculiarly Scottish form of democracy, especially in dealing with Robert Burns.

One consequence is that we cannot trace the development of Dunbar's personality or even arrange most of his poems (as Schipper tried to do) in a fixed chronological sequence ; there are some very few that can be dated by their allusion to an event of court life,[26] or by being among the first Scottish prints by Chepman and Myllar. Internal criteria fail, as Dunbar's different *genres* represent different moods, not different periods. A survey must rather be achieved by grouping according to content or tradition : (1) personal and occasional

[24] No satisfactory answer has yet been given to the question why Dunbar (l. 189) expressly mentions 9 May, 3 months before the wedding, as the date of composition ; and the suggestion that he wanted to be in time for remuneration is altogether too lame. But 9 May was a red-letter day in Scotland, being the anniversary of the " Translation of the Bones of St Andrew," the patron saint of Scotland : cp. Penrose Forbes, *Kalendars of Scottish Saints*, 1872. And Gavin Douglas writes his Prol. XII on 9 May—the only date he expressly mentions.

[25] In 27. " The Wowing of the King quhen he was in Dunfermline," the King is not mentioned by name, but may well be represented by the " tod." The Stewarts were red-haired, and at Court James V was nicknamed " the Red Tod."

[26] Dunbar's refs. to the " Lord Thesaurair " in 24. " Welcome to the Lord Treasurer " have caused difficulty (cp. Baxter, 183 f. ; Schipper, p. 229). It seems certain, however,

poems, among them the petitions ; (2) moral and religious subjects ; (3) courtly allegories ; (4) extravaganzas, as this group may provisionally be called. The dividing lines are not always clear-cut, and there are overlappings between, for example, groups (1) and (4). We must devote special attention to the courtly poems and the extravaganzas.

Allegory was, to the medieval man, a natural form of thinking : this was how he visualised virtues and vices ; and in order to see how much he relied on it, we need only look at the sculptures at the doors of the medieval cathedrals. Dunbar's allegorical poems have less kinship with this medieval allegory than with the court masques, dances, and allegorical pageants of his own day, in which deep allegorical significance was sacrificed to quasi-dramatic spectacular effect. As a case in point, let us consider that aureate, richly enamelled poem, 56. " The goldyn Targe." It begins—in the conventional dream garden—with a riot of sensuous images : sounds, shapes, textures, and above all (ll. 10 ff.) colours :

Full angellike [a]thir birdis sang thair [b]houris — [a] *these* [b] *Hours*
Within thair [a]courtyns grene, in to thair bouris — [a] *curtains*
  Apparalit quhite and red wyth blomes suete ;
Anamalit was the felde wyth all colouris,
The perly droppis schake in silvir schouris,
  Quhill all in balme did branch and [a]levis [b]flete. — [a] *leaves* [b] *float*

These images have no *allegorical* significance : but they have their own sensuous vitality, and for Dunbar, at any rate, all their value resides in the sheer delight experienced merely in contemplating them. Not that he has an eye for landscape : he is less interested in the larger and more permanent aspects of the external scene than in his own fleeting impressions of brilliant details, and in the pictures which

---

that at least in the last two stanzas " my awin Lord Thesaurair " is Dunbar's pension which will from now on be his treasurer, and is consequently welcomed ; and perhaps this may hold true of the poem as a whole. Dunbar's alarm, ere Lord Treasurer had passed " Fra toun of Stirling to the air," may also refer to Dunbar's own mockery at the flying experiments of Damian, Abbot of Tungland (esp. 39. " The Birth of Antichrist," 38. " The fenyeit Freir of Tungland "). Damian, a leech and also an alchemist, was in high favour with the King, and Dunbar's raillery might well have shattered his hopes of a benefice. " Air," in the sense of itinerant courts of justice, occurs only in this poem, and it is quite possible that Dunbar was indulging in a play on the different meanings of the word.

they evoke in his own mind. Here, for example, are his descriptions—first (ll. 16 ff.), of the dawn :

To part fra Phebus did Aurora [a]*grete,* — [a] *weep*
Hir cristall [a]*teris* I saw [b]hyng on the flouris, — [a] *tears* [b] *hang*
[a]Quhilk *he for* [b]*lufe all drank up* wyth his hete... — [a] *which* [b] *love*

—secondly (ll. 22 ff.), of roses sprinkled with dew :

The rosis yong, new spreding of thair [a]knopis, — [a] *buds*
War *powderit* brycht with *hevinly* [a]*beriall* droppis, — [a] *beryl*
Throu *bemes* [a]rede *birnyng as ruby sperkis...* — [a] *red*

—thirdly (ll. 26 f.) of light bathing the forest :

The *purpur* hevyn, [a]*our scailit in silvir* [b]*sloppis,* — [a] *over-scaled* [b] *(?) patches*
[a]*Ourgilt* the treis, branchis, lef, and barkis... — [a] *over-gilded*

—and fourthly (ll. 30 ff.), of water reflecting sunlight :

... the lake as *lamp* did [a]leme of licht, — [a] *gleam*
Quhilk schadowit all about wyth twynkling glemis ;
That [a]bewis bathit war in secund bemys — [a] *boughs*
Throu the [a]reflex of *Phebus visage* brycht. — [a] *reflexion*

The charm of Dunbar's ceremonial poetry chiefly arises out of such exquisite images of the passing moment as these. The frequent intrusion of extraneous elements (such as those italicised in the above quotations) helps not only to define the images themselves, but *also to connect them with other images*, and so to endow them with an additional vitality. When Dunbar speaks (l. 51) of " a saill, als quhite as blossum upon spray," we may be reminded of the Imagists : there is also a more significant parallel with Gaelic poetry.

The allegory proper begins with the disembarkation (ll. 55 ff.) of a band of gods and goddesses. Dunbar scarcely troubles to visualise them in any detail, and most of their numerous attendants—Nurture and Lawlynes, Gud Fame, Hie Degree, and all the rest of them—are mere abstractions, evidently of no interest to him. His poem exhibits none of the structural ramifications, the complex meanings, of a medieval allegory ; its whole allegorical theme can, indeed, be summed up in one bare sentence : Resoun with his golden targe valiantly defends the poet against the assault of Beautee and her supporters, but is blinded and overcome. This may seem scanty and inadequate for a poem of 279 lines ; but Dunbar is less interested in allegorical profundity than in the world of the senses, in rapid dramatic action, and in distinct, instantaneous sense images. Much depends on rapid and intimate observation, as when Presence (ll. 204 ff.) throws a powder in Resoun's eyes—

> And than as drunkyn man he all [a]forvayit : *[a] went astray*
> Quhen he was blynd, the fule wyth hym thay playit,
> And banyst hym amang the [a]bewis grene *[a] boughs*

—or when Beautee seems, after this, " lustiar of chere." This abundance of sense images enriches the end of the " allegorical " action with full-blooded life : Eolus blows, all the gods and goddesses go on board, a broadside is fired, making the rocks echo and the smoke rise to the sky, and (l. 241)

> For rede it semyt that the raynbow brak.

As in a masque, the artist has achieved an effective curtain. After this, he awakes, delights in the morning, and salutes Chaucer (" rose of rhetoris all "), Gower, and Lydgate, who with their " sugarit lippis and tongis aureate " would have been able to render what he had seen.

Dunbar's manipulation of the allegorical machinery is purely perfunctory, and " The goldyn Targe " is not in the fullest sense an allegory.[27] It illustrates two of Dunbar's most characteristic traits—namely his addiction to subjective impressionism, and his concision. As we have seen, Henryson's poetry is full of images derived from an exact observation of nature, and so is Barbour's ; but in both cases these images are firmly subordinated to a larger design. Dunbar's somewhat different *milieu* did not provide so many opportunities of observing nature ; but the eye that he brought to bear on it was quite as exact as Henryson's, and images of nature are the very stuff and substance of his poetic vision. There is no other poet of the Middle English period whose works contain such a wealth of dazzling colours and other pulsating sense images as, for example, 55. " The Thrissil and the Rois," 44. " To the Merchantis of Edinburgh," 47. " The Tretis of the twa mariit Wemen and the Wedo." We even meet with an occasional synæsthesia—as in " The Thrissil and the Rois," l. 6 :

> Amang the tendir odouris reid and quhyt.

And in such passages as the opening and closing sections of " The twa mariit Wemen," the concentrated immediacy of the imagery is such

[27] Similarly, of 63. " The Merle and the Nychtingaill," C. S. Lewis says (p. 92 f.) that " Dunbar's interest is not in the morality but, once more, in the world of ear and eye, in morning sunlight on running water. . . ."

that it foreshadows what, in another connexion, Bernhard Fehr called *gesteigerte Sinnlichkeit* (" heightened sensibility ").

This way of seeing things cannot properly be called objective; yet it derives all its impulses from exact observation of the objective external world. Dunbar's heightened sensibility also enabled him to enrich the traditional *Natureingang*—already in his time a somewhat hackneyed convention: in 10. " Meditatioun in Wyntir " even a rather pale picture of winter suffices to establish the intended mood. In 55. " The Thrissil and the Rois," in which he combines heraldic imagery with the conventional May morning and the conventional dream, he gives it a delightfully unconventional (and Scottish) twist. When May summons him to sing her praises, the poet (ll. 29 f., 33 ff.) is reluctant to forego his sleep :

> ' Quhairto,' quod I, ' sall I uprys at morrow,
> For in this May few birdis herd I sing ?...
>
> Lord Eolus dois in thy sessone [a]ring ; — [a] *reign*
> So [a]busteous ar the blastis of his horne, — [a] *rough, boisterous*
> Amang thy [a]bewis to walk I haif forborne.' — [a] *boughs*

After this, his obedience and subsequent account of the crowning of the Lyon, the Egle, the Thrissil and the Rois, is of course all the more effective.

In the extravaganzas, Dunbar's powers of observation are still more freely exercised—as for example in the final stanza of 38. " The fenyeit Freir of Tungland " :

> The air was [a]dirkit with the fowlis, — [a] *darkened*
> That come with [a]yawmeris and with yowlis, — [a] *loud cries*
> With [a]skryking, [b]skrymming, and with scowlis, — [a] *screeching* [b] *darting*
> To tak him in the tyde.

And even his religious poetry (as already remarked) gains depth when his theme is such that he can visualise it in terms of a concrete picture. This ability to visualise an experience—or, rather, to *reconstitute* it in terms of all five senses—is closely connected with the fact that abstract ideas play so little part in Dunbar's poetry, and that so much of it arises out of definite situations, actual occasions, and concrete events.

In *The Testament of the Papyngo*, Sir David Lyndsay says of Dunbar, he " language had at large." This has often been taken to imply that Dunbar was verbose and prolix : but Lyndsay was actually referring to Dunbar's command of words, and to his mastery of aureation.

Dunbar was an artist who did not lose himself in verbiage. His longest poem, 47. "The Tretis of the twa mariit Wemen and the Wedo," contains no more than 530 lines. None of Dunbar's allegories is infected with the longwindedness of the type; in the quick-footed 54. "Bewty and the Presoneir" there is no real moral intent, and Dunbar's presentation is so concise that the action throughout occupies the screen. The "Lament" derives its momentum largely from that characteristic economy of utterance which also intensifies the dramatic impact of 43. "Tydingis fra the Sessioun," 4. "How Dumbar wes desyrd to be ane Freir," and 9. "How sall I governe me?" True, there are no examples of laconic understatement in moments of intense pathos—but then no such moments of intense pathos occur in Dunbar's poetry.

In Dunbar's courtly and allegorical poems, the influence of Chaucer can always be felt; but, both in impulse and in execution, his comic and satirical pieces are purely Scottish. Scurrility, of course, is not by any means unknown in later medieval English and Continental literature, which abound in burlesques, satires, *poèmes à mal mariée*, *tensons*, *estrifs*, and *fabliaux*: but these are usually in a somewhat different key. As C. S. Lewis rightly asserts, any comparison of Dunbar's "twa mariit Wemen and the Wedo" with Chaucer's "Wife of Bath" is wide of the mark; for whereas Chaucer is portraying a character rich in humanity, Dunbar is confronting us with a "practical joke" set in an "idyllic frame." Nor does Chaucer's well-told lascivious anecdote "The Miller's Tale" have any close parallel in Dunbar's poetry. Generally speaking, Dunbar has a certain affinity with the Goliardic spirit. This appears most obviously in such a poem as 40. "The Testament of Mr Andro Kennedy"; but a closer resemblance might perhaps be detected in Dunbar's *fabliau* 27. "The Wowing of the King quhen he wes in Dumfermeling."

Many threads go to make the coarse and colourful web and woof of Dunbar's "comic" poetry. Allegory is turned inside out when the seven deadly sins dance their wild reel. And just as allegory and aureation reflect the gorgeous Court pageants and tournaments, so Dunbar's extravaganzas often represent the "antimasque" of contemporary chivalry, such as James IV's mock tournament in honour of a negress—in which [28] the victor

> Sall kis and withe hir go in grippis...

[28] 37. "Of ane Blak-moir," ll. 18, 23-5.

while the vanquished—the rhyme was too good to miss—

> Sall cum behind and kis hir hippis,...
> My ladye with the mekle lippis.

We may think, too, of the burlesque pageants of the Boy Bishop, the Abbot of Unreason, or the King and Queen of the Bean.[29] As so much stained glass and ecclesiastical sculpture testifies, such things were quite common in the later Middle Ages. Yet the question remains why they awoke such powerful echoes in Scotland, from Dunbar and those anonymous predecessors and contemporaries whose work is preserved in the Bannatyne Manuscript, down to Burns's *Tam o' Shanter*, "Holy Willie," and *The Jolly Beggars*. C. S. Lewis's explanation of the scurrility of Dunbar's comic poetry is that such piquant fare was still relished in the best society. But this was, as we shall see if we here turn aside to consider the history of Gaelic poetry, only half the story.

From the earliest times until well on in the seventeenth century, the Gaelic tradition in poetry was dominated by the *filidh* or learned hereditary bards, who, with their jealously guarded professional secrets, were second only to the King himself in influence, prestige and precedence. They excelled in invective and panegyric composed according to strict metrical and poetic rules. If a *fili* was slighted, if the hospitality extended to him fell short of his often exorbitant demands, he instantly retaliated with a savage invective. It was popularly believed that such invective could literally raise blisters, and since nobody willingly had contact with those cursed by the bards, it could actually ruin its victim, his kith and kin.[30] Gaelic, of course, is not the only literature in which invective occurs ; but nowhere else does it have so much demonic force, nor is it delivered with so much zest, so much abandon, so much reckless exaggeration, as, owing to the impulsive Celtic temperament, in Gaelic poetry.[31] Even when, in the seventeenth century, the old learned bards themselves "fell upon evil days," this tradition was carried over into the vernacular Scottish Gaelic poetry of the seventeenth and eighteenth

[29] Baxter, p. 153.

[30] W. B. Yeats uses the power of the old poet as the theme of *On the Threshold of the King*, but his bard is rather a languid descendant of his elders with their power of words. In Scotland the *filidh* and *bards* (of a lower order) grew so exacting that from 1449 on they had to be repressed by law, esp. in the Statutes of Iona (1609).

[31] For some fine renderings from Middle Irish into English, see James Stephens, *Reincarnations* (1918). Tradition stresses that Columba's curse was powerful.

centuries ; and the works of such popular (*i.e.* post-bardic) poets as John MacDonald of Keppoch (Ian Lôm), John MacCodrum, Alexander MacDonald (Alasdair macMhaighstir Alasdair), and Duncan McIntyre (Donnchadh Bàn) contain many satirical poems of unusual savagery. In eulogising the Gaelic language, Alexander MacDonald gives several reasons for its supremacy over all other languages—it is strong, fluent, copious, resonant, and so forth—but the first is that it is the one language in which, since the Tower of Babel, bard or satirist can scold best :

Is i an aon chànain
am beul nam bàrd 's nan éisg,
as fearr gu càineadh
bho linn Bhàbeil féin.[32]

[It is the one speech,
in mouth of the bards and satirists,
best for scolding
since the time of Babel itself.]

Modern Scottish speech, too, is often said to be unsurpassed for deflating an opponent.

From the earliest times, Celtic literature also displays a propensity for the grotesque—especially grotesque exaggeration : one example that comes readily to mind is the classical description of the madness of Cù Chulainn, the greatest of all Irish heroes. It is above all the gruesome that is represented as grotesque.[33] This is the outcome of a reckless irreverance, an eldritch imaginative propensity that may run away with the poet, and lead him to perform all sorts of intellectual antics ; often, too, it may involve him in violent rebellion against any merely conventional moral and religious orthodoxy. The Irish sagas are full of this spirit of rebellion, and reckless irreverence (side by side with fervent devotion) finds its climax in Middle Irish poems (*The Old Woman of Beare*, *Gormfleith*). Many renderings or reincarnations of old poems by Frederic Robert Higgings, Austin Clarke, James Stephens, Padraic Colum and others breathe the same characteristically Celtic spirit of rebellion, and the same passionate

[32] *Aiseirigh na seann Chanain Albannach* (see *The Poems of Alexander Macdonald*, edd. Revs. A. and A. Macdonald, Inverness, 1924, p. 6, and *Bardachd Ghaidhlig, 1550-1900*, ed. W. J. Watson, 2nd edn., 1932.

[33] Cp. Rudolf Thurneysen, *Irische Helden- und Königssage* (Halle 1921), p. 178 ; Kenneth H. Jackson, *A Celtic Miscellany* (London 1951) pp. 38-41, 55 ; Magnus Maclean, *Literature of the Celts*, 2nd edn., p. 166.

irreverence is frequently discernible in the works of such writers as James Joyce, Sean O'Casey, Liam O'Flaherty in Ireland, and Rhys Davies in Wales.

If we view Dunbar's temperament in the light of this tradition we shall at once detect a strong family likeness. His poems are not humorous, like Chaucer's ; nor are they in the strict sense satirical, for Dunbar uses no moral yardstick. In 47. " The Tretis of the twa mariit Wemen and the Wedo," Dunbar did not set out to compose a satire on women, or to censure feminine immorality ; he took far too much mischievous delight in his chosen subject for that. As C. S. Lewis reminds us, it is well to bear in mind the effect of its first recital at Court : after the idyllic introduction the ladies and nobles must have settled down to another courtly allegory, only to be roughly shaken out of their composure by the startling scurrility of the remainder of the poem. But among Dunbar's audience any who had protested would only have laid themselves open to the retort " If the cap fits . . ." ; and we can easily imagine the roar of laughter that must have greeted the sly insolence of the last line :

> Quhilk wald ye [a]waill to your wif, [b] gif ye suld wed one ? — [a] *choose for your wife* [b] *if*

It has sometimes been argued that the insolent scurrility of the bulk of the poem jars inartistically with the idyllic beauty of the opening and closing sections, or alternatively that this is merely an artifice by which Dunbar seeks to underline the total depravity of the two married women and the widow. Such criticism, however, falls wide of the mark. Dunbar is not concerned to classify things as good and evil : he wishes rather to present a picture of life as he sees it, life as a natural unity to be relished by the free and uninhibited use of all human senses and faculties, " lower " as well as " higher." Yet it is precisely this contrast between " higher " and " lower " which gives point to Dunbar's ribaldry. Hence the effective insolence of the last line ; hence, too, the wealth of affectionately recorded detail, as in the conclusion (ll. 512 ff.)—

> ... the day did up daw, and dew [a]donkit flouris ; — [a] *moistened*
> The morrow myld wes and meik, the mavis did sing,
> And all [a]remuffit the myst, and the meid smellit— — [a] *removed*

and in the unforgettable picture (l. 186 f.) of the debauched husband grown impotent before his time—

He dois as [a]dotit dog that [b]damys on all [c]bussis, — [a] *foolish* [b] *makes water* [c] *bushes*
And liftis his leg apone loft, [a]thoght he [b]nought list
pische. — [a] *though* [b] *does not wish to*

From the inclusion of so many piquant details the poem derives its scurrilous, dynamic vigour, as well as its homeliness; and such quietly spoken epithets as " this semely," " this amyable," make the underlying contrast all the more grotesque, and all the more ludicrous.[34]

It is precisely in these respects that " The twa mariit Wemen " differs so markedly from the *poèmes à mal mariée.* In its companion piece, 46. " The twa Cummeris "—who manage to get through Lent with a bottle of wine at their elbow while still sadly lamenting the lean times—we meet with the same wild eldritch delight in grotesque invention and the same irresponsible irreverence with no moral undertone. Dunbar is no hater of women. He can express all the purity of an almost Mariolatrous reverence (45. " In Prais of Wemen," 52. " Of Luve Erdly and Divine," 63. " The Merle and the Nychtingaill "). The beautiful and the grotesque dwell side by side in his breast. Both form part of the same undivided world: but within it there can be little doubt that Dunbar's own personal predilection was for the grotesque, and that his keenest delight was in the elfin cantrips of his extravaganzas—in which aureate representations of virtue would plainly be out of place, and the wild reel of the vices is brilliantly depicted in plain Braid Scots of unbounded vigour and vitality. It is easy, at first sight, to mistake 57. " The Dance of the sevin deidly Synnis " and 58. " The Sowtar and Tailyouris War " for two more examples of the conventional *danse macabre*, with its parody of those things that were most terrifying to the medieval mind; but in many respects—such as their wild and extravagant absurdity, their grotesque insolence, the gusto of their invective—these poems stand in reality much closer to Gaelic than to Continental tradition. In them, Dunbar is not concerned with abstract vices; the figures in which he personifies them are drawn from real life, and derive their own vitality from his power of concise visualisation[35]: in the " Dance," Pryd is like a swaggering young nobleman who wastes his substance (ll. 17, 22, 25 f.) with riotous living—

[34] For a study of " The twa mariit Wemen," see James Kinsley, *Medium Ævum*, XXIII (1954).

[35] Cp. the abstract figures in the petitions, *e.g.* 21. " None may assure in this Warld," ll. 36-9.

With hair wyld bak and bonet on syd...
Mony prowd [a]trumpour with him trippit... — *[a] deceiver*
[a]Heilie harlottis [b]on hawtane wyis — *[a] disdainful scoundrels* *[b] haughtily*
Come in with mony sindrie [a]gyis— — *[a] guise*

while Yre (ll. 32 ff.) is like a reiving Borderer with his moss-trooping retainers—

His hand wes ay upoun his knyfe,
He [a]brandeist lyk a [b]beir : — *[a] swaggered* *[b] bear*
Bostaris, braggaris, and [a]barganeris, — *[a] wranglers*
Efter him passit [a]in to pairis, — *[a] in pairs*
All [a]bodin in [b]feir of weir ; — *[a] arrayed* *[b] accoutrements of war*
In [a]jakkis, and [b]stryppis and bonettis of steill, — *[a] padded jerkins* *[b] strips*
Thair leggis wer [a]chenyeit to the heill.... — *[a] chain-mailed*

Dunbar's poems cannot properly be called " comic " ; they have a *demonic* quality which C. S. Lewis for one regards as specifically Scottish. This demonic quality (to mention only one example) is conspicuous in much of Burns's work ; it also crops up extensively in Gaelic poetry. It may also be discerned in François Villon—who has had a strong fascination for several modern Irish and Scottish writers (J. M. Synge, Michael Scott ; R. L. Stevenson, Tom Scott, Alexander Scott)—and partly for this reason both Burns and Dunbar have been compared with Villon. In its treatment of a daringly irreverent theme, Dunbar's " Testament of Mr Andro Kennedy " has, as already remarked, a certain obvious affinity with the Goliardic spirit ; but the mood is essentially light-hearted, and the rebellious note which Dunbar strikes is entirely his own—and at the same time (ll. 105 ff.) characteristically Celtic :

I will na preistis for me sing,
  Dies illa, dies ire ;
[a]Na yit na bellis for me ring, — *[a] nor yet*
  Sicut temper solet fieri ;
Bot a bag pipe to play a spryng,
  Et unum [a]ail wosp *ante me.* — *[a] wisp of straw signifying an ale house*

The poem as a whole is built on the clash of sacred associations and a very profane sentiment ; the final effect, however, is ludicrous, not coldly blasphemous, and there are no signs of any such inward conflict as raged incessantly in the depths of Villon's soul. Rather, we find the same ironic self-revelation as, much later, in Burns's "Holy Willie's Prayer."

Dunbar's wildest exuberance goes into his flytings. "The Flyting of Dunbar and Kennedie" is only an example of one side of this category, essentially a verbal contest between two equally matched opponents. "The fenyeit Freir of Tungland," "The Dance of the sevin deidly Synnis," and several of the petitions all really belong to the same species; and, on a more general level, invective is an essential ingredient of many of Dunbar's poems. Flytings, of course, are not confined to Scottish literature; Mackenzie points to Greek, Arabic, Italian, Provençal, Celtic. Dunbar's flytings have little in common with that purely formal exercise the *tenson*; and only 63. "The Merle and the Nychtingaill" and 52. "Of Luve erdly and divine" may reasonably be regarded as examples of the *estrif* or the *débat.* With their ebullient gusto Dunbar's flytings belong rather to Gaelic tradition—with which Dunbar's opponent Kennedie may well have been familiar. Dunbar seems to have more substance, more hard personal attack. Flyting, in Scottish literature, is usually, though not always, a kind of intellectual game in which two highly trained contestants engage in a battle of wits; but it is also a display of sheer imaginative versatility, and each strives to surpass the other in carrying certain extravagant details to the extreme limits of absurdity, as in the stanza with which Kennedie triumphantly brings "The Flyting of Dunbar and Kennedie" (ll. 545 ff.) to an end:

Deulbere, thy spere of [a]were, but feir, thou yelde, — [a] *war*
  Hangit, [a]mangit, [b]eddir-stangit, [c]strynde stultorum, — [a] *bewildered* [b] *with adder's sting* [c] *race, kind*
To me, maist hie Kenydie, and flee the felde,
  Pickit, wickit, convickit Lamp Lollardorum,
  Defamyt, blamyt, schamyt, Primas Paganorum.
Out! Out! I schout, apon that snowt that snevillis.
Tale tellare, rebellare, induellar wyth the devillis,
  Spynk, sink with stynk *ad Tertara Termagorum.*

George Bruce, himself a poet, has recently [36] compared the logically exhaustive pattern found in such poems with that of those Celtic sculptures in which the artist, not content with mere matters of fact, may pursue any particular detail—for example the tail of an animal

[36] In a talk on "The Scots Tongue in Poetry," given under the auspices of the British Council at Aberdeen on 2 Feb. 1955.

—further and further and further, until he has filled the extreme limits of the surface on which he is working.

In the " Lament," Kennedie gets (ll. 89 ff.) a whole stanza to himself—

> Gud Maister Walter Kennedy
> In poynt of [a]dede lyis veraly, — [a] *death*
> Gret reuth it wer that so suld be

—and, as these lines show, flyting does not necessarily imply personal hostility, but may actually express genuine regard and liking ; often flyting seems most satisfying between friends, not only because, in the words of a favourite Scots proverb, " nippin and scartin's Scotch fowk's wooin," but because it enables words to be used, and things to be said, that otherwise could not, without bloodshed. Considering that the Scots, as a nation, are passionately addicted to argument—eristic rather than dialectical argument, to use the Platonic terms—it is not surprising that they should have evolved this highly dramatic way of expressing themselves. Though often described as a by-product of Calvinism, this argumentative spirit existed in Scotland long before the Reformation, and there are traces of it in Henryson's poems " Aganis haisty Credence of Titlaris " and " Sum Practysis of Medecyne," and even in the disputes of the three hens (in " The Taill of Schir Chantecleir and the Foxe ") and of the Fox, the Wolf and the Cadger. It is also singularly persistent, and even if Dunbar's " Complaint to the King aganis Mure " (who " magellyt " Dunbar's poems) lacks the universality of Burns's appeal, it still has much in common with Holy Willie's plea—" and dinna spare ! "

3. Gavin Douglas

It would no doubt be very rewarding to study GAVIN DOUGLAS (*c.* 1474-1522), later Bishop of Dunkeld, against the wider European background of his time. Such a study would reveal how in his work the Middle Ages overlap with the New Learning, presenting a continuity, not a break. Douglas's *Eneados* is one of the great Renaissance translations. In it he makes it his purpose to bring one of the very greatest classical authors within reach of the common reader. He shows a respect for the letter of his original that is wholly new ; and such is his reverence for Virgil, both as a man and as a poet, that he reviles Caxton's so-called *Aeneis,* and even censures the liberties that Chaucer had taken with his author (Prol. I, II.14). In many ways the Prologues of the *Eneados* represent the beginnings of literary criticism (Prols. I, V, VI, IX), and Douglas ponders the problem of choosing between a literal translation and one that attempts to reproduce the style as well as the meaning of the original (Prol. I, II.14 f. ; " Dyrectioun of his Buik," IV.225). He quotes his authorities, and adopts the educated Renaissance man's slightly patronising attitude towards the unlearned ; yet he includes a translation of the " Thirteenth Book " of the *Aeneid,* by Mapheus Vegius (Maffeo Veggio). His style and his theory of the epic show a similar mixture of old and new. Douglas retains the Christian interpretation of Virgil and the Catholic system of thought, and he writes allegories—but he fills them with a new meaning, and he comes within striking distance of Sir Philip Sydney's theory of an epic as a sugar-coating for a moral pill (Prol. I, II.9.16-20). But Douglas has been unduly neglected ; none of these studies has been undertaken ; and (though it is in progress) not even the Scottish Text Society edition of his works has yet been published.[1]

Not less interesting is Douglas's place in the Scottish tradition.

[1] In effect, this leaves only *The poetical Works of Gavin Douglas, Bishop of Dunkeld,* ed. JOHN SMALL, 4 vols., Edinburgh 1874, from which all quotations are taken. Small begins his line-numbering afresh on each page, and refs. are here given as follows : *En.* V.iv = *Eneados,* Bk v, ch. iv ; Prol. IV = Prologue to *En.* IV ; *P.H.* = *Palice of Honour* ; II.21.8 = Small, VOL. II, p. 21, l. 8.

See also L. Maclean Watt, Douglas's *Aeneid,* 1920 (insubstantial) ; J. W. Bennet, " The early Fame of Douglas' *Eneados,*" in *Modern Language Notes,* LXI (1946) ; W. Beattie, " Gavin Douglas's *Palice of Honour,*" in *The Times Literary Supplement* for 23 Feb. 1946 ; B. Dearing, in *Proceedings of the Modern Languages Association,* LXVII (1952) ; Heather

His *Eneados* (1513) is the most sustained work in Scots poetry, and, considering the scale, the most consistent. In order to achieve this result, he had had to labour away at the problem of widening the Scots tongue's range of expression, forging it and reforging it until it was capable of expressing anything. He does not go in for Scottish concision or understatement ; dogmatically he will sometimes say a thing three times over in different words. Like Dunbar (and, to a lesser extent, Henryson [2]), Douglas moves freely from one level of poetry to another, with appropriate modulation of language, style, and metre. In this connexion, it is illuminating to compare the May idyll of the Prologue to the *Palice of Honour* (1501) with the grotesque eldritch episode in the same poem (1.7-8, especially " the fisch yelland as eluis schoutit "), with its harsh final consonants and heavy alliteration.[3] In the *Eneados*, there is a similar contrast between the aureate magnificence of Prol. I and the rhymed alliterative bob-and-wheel of Prol. VIII, a passionate flyting against the corruption of this false world. Here we have plain Braid Scots, containing words of Norse and Gaelic origin, with stressed metre and knotty alliteration up to six times in a line and often of two initial consonants. The rugged dynamic force of Prol. VIII contrasts no less sharply with the serenity of Prol. XII, (the " May Prologue "), or with the hymn-like severity of Douglas's invocation of the Creator in Prol. X, where there is a rich admixture of Latin words, in forms terminated by the stress : *etérn*, *glór*, *creát*, *generát*, *incommíxt*, etc. [4] There is also a wealth of long vowels, with consonants checking the movement here and there, and an occasional pause for an unstressed syllable. This creates a slow solemnity, like the heavy pealing of a cathedral bell.

There is nothing artless or inadvertent about Douglas's use of these different levels. At the beginning of Prol. IX, in three stanzas of rich internal rhyme suggestive of Latin hymns,[5] he

---

MacDermid, *Gavin Douglas, Translator of Virgil's Aeneis,* unpublished M.A. Thesis, Univ. of Liverpool, 1954. See, too, Mary Ringsleben's unpublished Ph.D. Thesis on Douglas, Aberdeen Univ., 1956.

[2] Cp. Cresseid's complaint, and " Sum Practysis of Medecyne." Henryson also shows signs of using an ornate style for comic purposes.

[3] Cp. *P. H.* (1.21.8, 65.28).

[4] These are commoner in Scots than English, and one of them at least (*glóir*) has also penetrated into Gaelic.

[5] It is rather, however, the Gaelic type of internal rhyme (see below, pp. 109-12). We have here several examples of the Gaelic *aiccill* (anticipation) : a preceding end rhyme is echoed somewhere in the next line—*e.g.*, in the above, " m*oyr*—acc*or*ding," " her*o*ycall—n*o*billnes," " w*ord*—sp*ort*is."

first appeals for sincerity and constancy, but then (III.205.19 ff.) breaks off—

> Eneuch of this, us nedis prech na moyr,
> Bot, accordyng the purpos said tofoyr,
> The [a]ryall style, [b]clepyt heroycall, — [a] *royal* [b] *called*
> Full of wirschip and nobillness [a]owr all, — [a] *over*
> Suld be compilit [a]but tenchis or voyd word, — [a] *without taunts*
> Kepand honest [a]wys sportis quhayr thai [b]bourd, — [a] *wise* [b] *jest*
> All [a]lous langage and lychtnes [b]lattand be, — [a] *loose* [b] *letting*
> Observand bewte, sentens, and gravite.

Further, he suggests (206.7 ff.)

> we [a]aucht tak tent — [a] *ought to heed*
> That baith accord, and [a]bene convenient, — [a] *be*
> The man, the sentens, and the knychtlike stile....

And, still more specifically, in writing (206.14 ff.) of dignified deeds :

> Full litill it wald delite
> To write of [a]scroggis, broym, haddir, or [b]rammale : — [a] *stunted shrubs, broom, heather* [b] *small branches*
> The [a]laurer, cedir, or the palm triumphale, — [a] *laurel*
> Ar mayr [a]ganand for nobillis of estait : — [a] *fit*
> The muse suld wyth the person [a]aggre algait. — [a] *agree always*

Douglas strictly observes this rule, not only in his choice of language, but also in his use of alliteration. In allegorical, courtly, or discursive passages like those quoted above there is, very occasionally, an almost unintentional alliteration. The more "hamely" the subject and language, the more dominant does alliteration become. It bursts forth whenever the flyting mood takes charge, as above, in the exceptional line "All lous langage and lychtnes lattand be," in Prol. VIII (*passim*), and in Prol. I (II.8.4) :

> I spittit for despyt to see [a]swa spilt... — [a] *so spoilt*

It is noticeable, too, that Douglas's nature scenes are heavily alliterated, as, for example, in his descriptions of May (Prol. XII), a June evening (Prol. XIII), and winter (Prol. VII) ; in the latter we are forcibly reminded of Henryson's verse-portrait of Saturn. This points rather to native seasonal songs, than to Chaucer and the May convention, as being here the ultimate source of Douglas's inspiration.[6]

The usual verdict is that with all its fidelity Douglas's translation of the *Aeneid* has more rugged vitality, more rustic vigour, more fire,

[6] See K. Hurlstone Jackson, *Studies in early Celtic Nature Poetry*, Cambridge 1935, pp. 149 ff.

more self-assertion than Virgil's *Aeneid.* Douglas, it is said, is more rugged, Virgil more supple. C. S. Lewis maintains, however, that we have too classically solemn a picture of the *Aeneid*, and that Douglas's *Eneados* has more of the essential Virgil ; while Ezra Pound is convinced (in *How to read*) that the translation is better than the original. Be that as it may, Douglas's characteristics are closely akin to those of the Scottish tradition, and there is no doubt that in some passages—notably the sea scenes [7]—Douglas's imagery is more vivid and more concrete than Virgil's and shows more delight in detail. Douglas's language, too, has more life in it : it teems with images of nature, and seems racier and closer to the soil.[8]

Gavin Douglas's poems reveal a man of distinctly virile, almost angular, character,[9] who has no sympathy with the softness for women that had led Chaucer (Prol. I, II.17.20 f.) to

> set on Virgile and Eneas this [a]wyte, *[a] blame*
> For he was ever, God [a]wait, wemenis friend. *[a] knows*

Douglas is disgusted at weak undignified indulgence in love and lust, and in Prol. IV he points (II.165.10 f.) to the medieval legend of Aristotle's debasement :

> Men sayis thow bridillit Aristotle as ane hors
> And [a]crelit up the [b]flour of poetry. *[a] basketed [b] flower*

Virgil can teach us, he adds (II.167.20), to be moderate in love and wine :

> Childir to [a]engener [b]ois Venus, and nocht in vane ; *[a] engender [b] use*
> Have na surphat, drink nocht bot quhen thow art
> dry.

This leaves no place for courtly love or amorous play, any more than in the *Kingis Quair* or *The Testament of Cresseid.* That is " unlefull luffe " (Prol. IV). Yet Douglas is remarkably concrete when thundering against the " schamefull play " in May, with its stealthy whisperings and meetings.[10]

[7] *E.g. En.*, BK. I, cap. iii (II.26.17 ff.).

[8] See, for example, the passage from *En.*, BK. V (II.234.17), quoted below, p. 84.

[9] He reveals little of his own career and background ; and though he came of one of the leading Scottish families, rose early to high office, and went abroad on various missions, his poetry betrays neither the subtlety of the diplomat, nor the decorum appropriate to the episcopate.

[10] Douglas himself probably had illegitimate children (Small, VOL. I, p. cxxv).

This brings us to the question of Douglas's religious and moral attitude. *The Palice of Honour* is more than a pageant of figures in allegorical trappings ; it tries to *solve* a genuine moral question : how, and on what basis, to achieve honour. In the Prologues of the *Eneados*, his most important original contribution to poetry, Douglas stresses the fact that he does not, like Virgil, intend to glorify false gods or to preach the transmigration of souls—a doctrine for which he seeks a Christian interpretation, concluding that his " philosopher naturall " must have had intuitions of Hell, Purgatory, and the Deadly Sins, of Mary in the shape of the Sibyl, of Satan in that of Pluto, and so forth (Prols. VI, X). This is truly medieval, and, as Douglas points out, Augustine himself had quoted the Sixth Book of the *Aeneid* (Prol. VI), There is, of course, in this bishop-to-be, much theological orthodoxy, as in his account of the Trinity : according to him, its three Persons correspond to the soul's three faculties, namely intelligence or understanding, which " considers the thing before " ; " raison," which " decernis " ; and " memor," which " kepis the consait " (Prol. X). Douglas also vividly compares the Trinity with fire, which combines flame, light, and heat. Most of this is highly conventional ; here and there, however, he strikes an original note.

In this same Prologue, Douglas invokes God as the Creator of all things, who also in His wisdom ordained the course of the world and the seasons. He is " incomprehensabill," and not even from His creation can man comprehend Him. God is in everything, with no diminution of Himself. These arguments are not exceptional in the medieval Church, and are to be found in Augustine ; but nowhere are they expressed so absolutely. Still more surprising is a passage (Prol. XI, IV.6.19 ff.) on grace and redemption :

I say, [a]be grace ; for quhen thou art in grace, — [a] *by*
Thou may [a]eik grace to grace, ay moyr and moyr. — [a] *add*
Bot quhen thou fallys be syn tharfra, allace !
Off thy meryte thou gettis hyr nevirmor :
Yit quhen thou dewly disponis [a]the tharfor, — [a] *thee*
Doing all that in [a]the thar may be done, — [a] *thee*
Of hys gudnes the etern Lord [a]alssone — [a] *as soon*
Restoryis [a]the meryt, wyth grace in [b]erlis of glore.[11] — [a] *thee* [b] *earnest of glory*

[11] Similarly, in *P.H.*, Pt. III : if you fall into sin, the ship of grace is wrecked and you will drown, " Except be faith ye find the plank agane/Be Christ, wirking gude warkis I understand " (I.53.23 f.)

Here there is no mention of confession and absolution, of the intercession of the Church, or of the mediation of the saints ; even more than in Barbour and Henryson, the individual has to settle his account with God Himself, and salvation is not the reward of good works, but the free gift of God to a soul that has striven hard to respond to God's offer. This passage is almost exactly attuned to the innermost principle of the Kirk of Scotland, as defined by a former Moderator, G. D. Henderson : " The Christian privilege and responsibility of each child of God, the freedom of the individual Christian to study and reflect, and to make his personal response to every divine offer and challenge." [12] The emphasis that Douglas lays on the prevenience of God's grace can be traced back to Augustine ; but Calvinism itself was based on this aspect of Augustinian teaching.[13] Those passages in which Barbour, Henryson, and Douglas lay so much stress on the *personal* response of the individual to the challenge of the Divine Will clearly foreshadow the predominant ideas of the Scottish Reformation. Indeed, it may be said that Protestantism and Presbyterianism would never have taken such firm root in Scotland if the soil had not long been ready for them.[14] Like Barbour and the Declaration of Arbroath, Douglas is very close to Calvin (and Augustine) in his insistence on law and justice as the divinely ordained foundations of freedom. In Prol. XI (IV.I.17 ff.) he discountenances war (and chivalry) except in so far as " the ground of batale " is " fundyt apoun rycht " :

> Nocht [a]for thou [b]lyst to mak discentioun, — [a] *just because* [b] *wish*
> To seik occasionis of contentioun,
> Bot [a]rype thy querrell, and discus it plane : — [a] *examine*
> Wrangys to redres suld [a]weyr be [b]undertane, — [a] *war* [b] *undertaken*
> For na conquest, [a]reif, [b]skat, nor [c]pensioun. — [a] *rapine* [b] *tax* [c] *tribute*

Without God's help, the power of man is indeed feeble. Citing Aristotle's *Ethics*, Douglas then goes on to distinguish " hardyment " from " fuyl hardyment " and from cowardice. (The parallel with

[12] G. D. Henderson, *The Claims of the Church of Scotland*, 1951, p. 6. It has been suggested that Douglas may later have inclined to the new teaching (see Æ. J. G. Mackay's preface to his edn. of John Major's *History of Greater Britain*, Scottish History Society, 1892).

[13] Cp. Henderson, *op. cit.*, pp. 39 f.

[14] Cp. the attitudes of Barbour, Henryson and Douglas with that of the Presbyterians as summed up by G. D. Henderson : " They looked to God with respect and fear. An inscrutable but admittedly all-wise and ultimately benevolent, though austere, Providence was recognised as constantly present in the individual's experience " (*op. cit.*, p. 41).

Barbour is, however, even more striking than that with Aristotle, in view of Douglas's insistence on the importance of being " auyse ".)

It is, however, in the tone of his religious and moral teaching that Douglas is closest to the spirit of Presbyterianism, for he seems to have been gripped by a haunting suspicion that we shall have to pay for all our happiness :

> All erdly glaidnes [a]fynysith with wo. *[a] finishes*
>
> Temporall joy endis with wo and pane.
>
> ... erdlie plesour endis oft with sorrow, we see.[15]

and there is even an occasional outburst of fire-and-brimstone sermonising (Prol. IV). Like so many other Scottish writers, Douglas displays a deep delight in rational argument. Barbour and Henryson had been able to indulge their love of argument in the bygoing : Douglas is no less impatiently assertive, but has to save up his comment until he has finished a book of the *Aeneid*—but then it bursts forth all the more impetuously. On contemplating Caxton's mutilations of Virgil's *Aeneid*, Douglas is filled with righteous indignation (Prol. I), and the mere thought that his own translation will have its critics causes him to flare up as in a flyting. At one moment he will observe the poetic convention of modesty and will apologise for his rough verse—but it is not so bad as to give anybody the right to criticise it, and damnation take all who despise it or mutilate it ![16] " After all," he exclaims (Prol. IX, III.207.26-7), " I myself

> Can nocht persaue a falt in all my wark,
> Affectioun sa far my raysson blyndis."

Quite as impatiently as Carlyle, he rails (Prol. III, II.116.17) at those who see nothing more than a fable in the story of the Minotaur :

> Tharfore wald God I had thair [a]eris to pull, *[a] ears*

and (Prol. VI, III.1.11) at those who think the Sixth Book of *Aeneid* was all " japis " or " auld idolatreis " :

> O hald your pece, ye verray goddis apis !

[15] Prols. II (II.67.23), IV (II.171.28), and V (II.222.12). And cp. Prol. IV (II.169.28) : " Bot all your solace sall returne in gram [sorrow]."

[16] Prol. I (II.19) ; " Dyrectioun of his Buik " (IV, 224 ff.) ; " Exclamatioun aganis Detractouris and oncurtas Redaris, that bene our studius, but occasioun, to note and spy owt faltis or offencis in this volum, or ony othir crafty warkis " (IV.229 f.) ; " Here followis the tyme, space and dait " (IV.231).

" Na, na," he stamps his foot (Prols. I, IV, V, etc.) ; he will not report any mere " gabbing " (II.9.25). His impatience breaks forth (Prol. VI, III.2.25, 3.1) in rhetorical questions :

> Schawis he nocht heir the synnis capitall?
>
> Ar all [a]sic sawis fantasy and in vane? — [a] *such sayings*

It is only natural, of course, to speak like this in the midst of an argumentative outburst. In Scotland, however, as Sir Walter Scott often points out, questions are commonly used instead of statements or answers ; and in Gaelic it is a perfectly normal way of telling a story.[17] This imparts a subjective colouring, and greatly intensifies the dramatic quality latent in all Scots speech ; in Douglas's poetry it has the same effect, though it occasionally tends to produce an inflated style.

But as a rule Douglas's language is pithy, richly and vividly descriptive and pungently realistic : on occasion, it is also scurrilous—even in passages of " knychtlike stile." The sharp clarity of Douglas's pictures is due chiefly to the precision with which he marks the details, as when in *En.* V.iv (II.234.17 ff.) he describes the laughter which arises when one of the Trojans falls into the sea during the Naval Games :

> The Troianis [a]*lauchis fast* [b]seand him fall, — [a] *laugh* [b] *seeing*
> And, hym behaldand swym, thei [a]*keklit* all ; — [a] *cackled*
> Bot [a]*maist*, thai maiking [b]*gem* and *gret riot*, — [a] *most* [b] *game*
> To see hym *spout salt wattir* of his *throt.*[18]

Often, too, he heightens the effect by means of comparisons and contrasts, through which, more even than the other Makars, he projects into the context an image of his own that is a great deal more vivid than the thought he is actually expressing ; often, indeed, this gives the subjective impression more emphasis than the objective fact. Where, he asks in Prol. I (II.15.10 ff.), is there a vernacular that

[17] For example, " Có a thachair orm air an rathad ach Iain ? " (" Who met me on the road but John ? " = " I met John on the road.") Any page of J. F. Campbell's *Tales of the West Highlands and Islands* will provide frequent examples. It has been argued that this trick of Scots speech was borrowed from Gaelic.

[18] Our italics. It is instructive to compare this with the original (*Aen.*, x.181-2) : " Illum et labentem Teucri et risere natantem, /et salsos rident revomentem pectore fluctus." Virgil's " *et . . . et . . . et* " is rendered by the ascending scale of laughter : but Virgil's rather tame " *risere . . . rident* " becomes " lauchis fast . . . keklit all . . . maiking gem and gret riot " ; while for " *salsos . . . fluctus* " and " *revomentem pectore* " Douglas substitutes the much more definite " spout salt wattir of his throt."

provides such clearly-defined terms as " *genus, sexus, species, obiectum, subiectum* " :

He [a]war expert culd fynd me termes [b]twa, — [a] *would be . . . who* [b] *two*
[a]Quhilkis ar [b]als rife amange clerkis in scule — [a] *which* (pl.) [b] *as*
As euir *fowlis plungit in laik or puile.*

Intensification of this subjective element leads on occasion to that extravagant, grimly humorous exaggeration which we have so frequently remarked elsewhere, as in Prol. I (II.19.7-8) :

[a]Beis nocht [b]our studious to spy a mote in my ee, — [a] *be* (imp.) [b] *over*
That in your [a]awin a *ferry* [b]*bote* can nocht see. — [a] *own* [b] *boat*

Douglas strove consciously to widen the scope of " Scots "—as he was the first to call it instead of " Inglis " [19]—by making it more flexible, more academically precise, more copiously rhetorical, more aureate. What higher standard could he have chosen than Virgil's " *di parlar sì largo fiume* " ? What better task than that of translating the *Aeneid*? Yet his own characteristic idiom, so pithy and so picturesque, is closely akin to folk-speech ; and the proverb, sometimes Biblical, sometimes vernacular, is one of its essential ingredients (Prols. I, II.19.9, and IX, III.205.13, 207.24) :

And do to me as ye wald be done to.

Do tyll ilk wyght as thou done to wald be.

The blak [a]craw thinkis hir [b]awin byrdis [c]quhite. — [a] *crow* [b] *own* [c] *white*

Douglas's imagery is largely derived from nature, as seen in Scotland, and also from Scottish folklore. Thus in introducing the Sixth Book of the *Eneados*, he says (Prol. VI, III.2.1 f.):

All is bot [a]gaistis and elriche fantasies, — [a] *ghosts*
Of browneis and of bogillis full this buke.[20]

This was what enabled him to write his great nature poems, the first in Scots or English in which landscape is depicted solely for its own sake.

Apart from a passing reference to Boreas and Eolus the whole of the winter poem (Prol. VII) is founded solely on Scottish experience, and it contains a wealth of sharply-defined sense images drawn from

[19] Prol. I (II.7.4), etc.

[20] Cp. *P.H.*, Pt. I (II.13.19). " Brownies " were a species of hobgoblin formerly believed to frequent farmhouses ; " bogle " is still the Scots name for a scarecrow.

a multiple awareness of nature that was to remain unrivalled until the eighteenth century. The sun hangs low down on the horizon, the days are short, and rivers run " reid on spait with watteir broune." For winter in Scotland is not so much a time of sharp ringing frost, with a thick blanket of snow, but rather of biting winds, sleet, hail, and blinding snowstorms, of low drumly clouds racing across white skies ; a time of miry roads, when the land lies bleak and barren, and long icicles bedeck the crags. All this is wonderfully depicted, with frequent alliteration, and a wealth of epithets coldly expressive of privation : " barrand, strypyt [stripped], nakyt, fadyt, widderit." Even the stars look hostile. We hear the wind whining, we see the husbandman drenched and exhausted ; the birds shiver on bare branches, the deer come down into the glens, the sheep bield themselves as best they can against the braeface, and in the byre the cattle huddle together for warmth. It is not a winter in which warmth is to be got by exercise, but one that cuts to the bone and dazes the blood. The cold gets inside you : there is no defence against it.

Douglas's picture of all this—and here he excels even the nature poets of the eighteenth century—is not static. Often—as in the expressive line (III.76.5) :

> The wynd maid [a]wayfe the [b]reid weyd on the [c]dyk   [a] *wave* [b] *red weed* [c] *wall*

—his sharp eye registers a movement, slight in itself, which yet serves to emphasise the stark fixity of the wintry landscape. Douglas's picture of winter, like Henryson's, is highly subjective : we are made aware of the cold by the poet's account of his own reactions to it, and see him at his fireside, trying to defeat it by means of a " mychty drink " and double wraps, or in bed, beneath three blankets, with his head wrapped up against the frost. Through the window-panes he sees the wintry constellations, hears the " wyld elriche screik " of the hideous owl, the whistle of the " gled [kite]," or the cry of the wild geese in their Y-formation high in the " lift." At daybreak, he opens the window " on char [ajar] " : the day is " bla," " wan," " har "—a powerfully evocative use of bleak vowel sounds and wintry Norse words.[21] The dew has frozen, the " branchis brattlys," hail hops on roof and road. Quickly he shuts the window, " chiverand for cauld," and tries (III.78.22) :

> ... wyth hait flambe to [a]fleme the fresyng [b]fell.   [a] *expel* [b] *cruel*

[21] *Bla* < Icel. *blar,* " livid, black-and-blue " ; *har* < Icel., " cold, nippy."

The Virgil on his desk, with so much still to be translated, makes his spirit sink lower still. With a sigh, however, he takes up his yoke—Book Seventh, and how well it matches this dreary environment !—and goes on with his translation. This is not really a description of winter : it is rather the evocation of a winter mood, and by his choice of metres, words, and sounds, he enables us to relive his own wintry impressions of intense cold, of eldritch uncanny noises, and of scenes the mere sight of which is enough to induce shivering.

Douglas's elaborate descriptions of a May day and a June evening (Prols. XII, XIII) contain more classical mythology, and the diction is more aureate. But the things to which he applies these aureate terms are native to Scotland—like (Prol. XII, IV.86.4 ff.) the " Nymphis and Naedes,"

> [a]Syk as we [b]clepe wenchis and damysellis, — [a] *such* [b] *call*
> In [a]gresy gravis wandrand by spring wellis. — [a] *grassy groves*

And elsewhere (IV.89.17), in speaking of Philomene, Esacus and Peristera, Douglas explains :

> I meyn our [a]awin native bird, gentill [b]dow... — [a] *own* [b] *dove*

and then paints in the sheen of its coloured plumage. The scene is decidedly Scottish : the midsummer sun setting far in the north, the cobwebs (IV.85.18 ff.), the insects—" midgeis, fleyis [flies], emmitis [ants], byssy beis " (Prols. XII, XIII) : what other poet had ever evoked vibrant summer heat so vividly by painting the incessant flitting to-and-fro of so many different insects, or used the sudden stillness, when all this movement ceases, half so skilfully to suggest the close of day ? These two prologues mark the climax of the heightened sensibility that we found in the older Scottish literature. Colours, forms, smells, sounds are seized with a precise and instantaneous awareness of shades and values such as no Scots or English poet had previously attained. Observing the pale flowers, Douglas remarks (Prol. XII, IV.83.22) :

> Sum [a]wattry hewit as the [b]haw wally see, — [a] *watery-hued* [b] *wan wavy*
> And sum [a]depart in freklys red and quhyte, — [a] *divided*
> Sum brycht as gold with aureat levys [b]lyte.[22] — [a] *little*

Elsewhere (Prol. XIII, IV.173.25-6), he comes very close to impressionism :

[22] And cp. *P.H.*, Pt. III (I.52.20), where a ship appears " With blanschit saill milkquhite as ony snaw."

The dewy grene, [a]pulderit with [b]daseis gay — *[a] powdered [b] daisies*
[c]Schew on the sward a cullour dapill gray. — *[a] showed*

And in this description (Prol. XII. IV.84.9 ff.) of a lily, the concentration of sensuous images—smell, touch, taste, and sight—is so intense and so varied as almost to constitute a synæsthesia :

The balmy vapour from thar sylkyn [a]croppis — *[a] tops*
Distylland hailsum sugurat hunny droppis,
And sylver [a]schakaris [b]gan fra levis [c]hyng, — *[a] thin metal plates [b] did [c] hang*
Wyth crystal [a]sprayngis on the verdour [b]yyng. — *[a] stripes [b] young*

" Crystal," " bedit," " perlis," " pulderyt "—by means of such words, Douglas tries always to transmit an *exact* image[23] ; we see the fire in a dewdrop or the pattern of the shadow of trees and towers contrasting with the light, and the " illuminate air " (Prol. XII). The local accuracy of such images, and the frequency with which they occur in the May Prologue and elsewhere, are both reminiscent of Gaelic poetry.[24] But Douglas also instils a sense of the *rhythms* of nature, and his May Prologue is no mere catalogue. It has little in common with the emblematic background tapestry of the conventional May prologue in medieval poetry. Far more than James I, Henryson or Dunbar, he conveys an impression of the changes, the *stirrings*, great and small, that are incessantly in progress. Sometimes the hint is so delicate that (IV.83.15, 25, 29) it may easily be missed :

Soft [a]gresy verdour *eftir balmy schowris* — *[a] grassy*
On curland stalkis *smyling* to thar flowris...

The dasy [a]*dyd on breid* hir [b]crownell smaill. — *[a] spread out [b] little crown*

The [a]flour delice *furth spred* his hevinly hew.... — *[a] fleur de lys*

But here is his description (Prol. XIII, IV.168.12) of the " gloaming " —Scotland's long, long summer evening :

All byrnand reid [a]*gan walxin* the evin sky, — *[a] did grow*
The son enfyrit haill....

[23] Cp. above, p. 84, n. 18.

[24] It should not be overlooked that Douglas was himself bishop of a Gaelic-speaking diocese, in which many of the clergy may still have been acquainted with traditional Gaelic poetry. Douglas's own all-too-human treatment of Venus may perhaps have been tinged by Celtic notions of heroes.

In this slow-fading light, with its soft shades, the tip of every blade of grass catches the dew, which falls (IV.169.2 ff.)

> as [a]lemand [b]beriall droppis... — [a] *gleaming* [b] *beryl*
> Lyke cristall [a]knoppis or small silver bedis. — [a] *knobs*
> The lycht [a]*begouth* to [b]*quynkill owt* and *faill*, — [a] *began* [b] *twinkle*
> The day to [a]*dyrkyn, decline*, and [b]*devaill.* — [a] *darken* [b] *descend*

Presently the shadows grow deeper, up goes the bat with " hir pelit ledderyn [naked (*lit.* peeled) leathern] flycht," the lark settles down to rest,

> Out owr the [a]swyre swymmis the [b]soppis of mist, — [a] *gorge* [b] *clouds*

and night at length casts her mantle. Darkness enfolds man, beast, " fyrth," and forest ; peace descends on cattle and deer ; even the restless activities of the insects cease. Metrically, too, this remarkable passage shows fine modulation and masterly control of pace. Line by line, a reader who cares to make the experiment of reading it aloud will find himself lowering his voice in expectation of the final cadence : but cadence succeeds cadence, and the long syllables go on soothing the reader's ear, till his voice sinks finally to its lowest pitch, and the last cadence of all leaves behind it a sense of absolute tranquillity.

Equally enchanting is Douglas's description (IV.173.7 ff.) of the short June night, during which, in Scotland, it never becomes completely dark. Waking after his dream of Mapheus Vegius, Douglas looks about him, and this is what he sees :

> Yonder doun [a]dwynis the evin sky away, — [a] *fades*
> And upspryngis the brycht dawing of day [25]
> Intill ane other place nocht far [a]in sundir, — [a] *apart*
> That to behald was plesans, and half wondir.

The stars fade one after another, and morning is here. Douglas paints it in with a wealth of adjectives richly expressive of joyous activity—" blyth," " bissy," " blyssful "—and (IV.173.17) full of lively vowels :

> Sone our the fe*i*ldis sch*i*nis the l*y*cht cl*ey*r.

What a contrast here with winter's " bla," " wan," " har " ! The

[25] Observe the different rhythm of these two lines.

scene is alive with Nature's creatures—birds, cattle, poultry—and (IV.173.27) as part of the slow awakening of the world we see

> The mysty vapouris springand up full sweit.

And in Prol. XII, Nature's underlying rhythms are interpreted (IV.82.18 ff.) as those of one vast living organism :

> The [a]sulye spred hyr braid bosum [b]on breid, *[a] soil [b] widely*
> Zephyrus' confortabill inspiratioun
> For till [a]ressaue [b]law in hyr [c]barm adoun. *[a] receive [b] low [c] womb*

As here portrayed, nature breathes, loves, cherishes. Many of the countless details which go to produce this impression are, in themselves, so trivial, that we ourselves may scarcely be conscious of them. But the final effect is that in these Prologues we see for always what we have sometimes felt (Lewis).

III

Ebbing: David Lyndsay

TILL THE DAYS of Walter Scott, SIR DAVID LYNDSAY OF THE MOUNT (1486/90-1555) was the most widely read and frequently printed of the Makars; among the Scots peasantry his name was almost proverbial. The reasons for this popularity are highly revealing.

David Lyndsay was of gentle birth. At an early age he obtained various positions at Court and was "usher" to Prince James, later King James V; and reminiscences of teaching and amusing the royal child occur in his "Dreme" and in his "Complaynt."[1] Later, as Lyon King of Arms and as one of his King's most important diplomats, he served on many official missions; as Lyon, he was also responsible for organising spectacular Court functions. But none has so eloquently championed the common people as this influential courtier. When he says that his verse and language are rough and rustic, and that they lack the aureate elegance of Dunbar or Douglas,[2] he is not showing conventional modesty. His works were meant for "rurall folk" (*Papyngo*, 66). When he uses a courtly style, it often is almost in order to parody it, as in the "First Epystyll" of the *Papyngo*; in *Ane Satyre of the Thrie Estaitis*,[3] Sensualitie speaks in aureate Chaucerian stanzas as long as she keeps up her pretence (ll. 499 ff.), but in Braid Scots tail-rhyme as soon as she drops her mask. Lyndsay's natural medium is colloquial Scots, with occasional drastic violence. Listen to John the Common Weill, who is half-incredulous, half-stammering with happiness, when he hears (*Thrie Estaitis*, ll. 2417-8) the good tidings of reform, and, pushing his way through the crowd to get closer, exclaims:

[1] Full titles: "The Dreme of Schir David Lyndesay" and "The Complaynt of Schir David Lindesay" (hereinafter cited as "Dreme" and "Complaynt"). All quotations are from *The Works of Sir David Lindsay of the Mount*, ed. Douglas Hamer, S.T.S., 4 vols., 1931-6. See also *Ane Satire of the Thrie Estaitis*, ed. James Kinsley, with essays by Agnes Mure Mackenzie and Ivor Brown, 1954; and H. Aschenberg, *Sir David Lyndsays Leben und Werke*, München Gladbach 1891.

[2] Cp. esp. *The Testament and Complaynt of our Soverane Lordis Papyngo* (hereinafter cited as *Papyngo*), ll. 15-30.

[3] Hereinafter cited as *Thrie Estaitis*. See below, nn. 19-21.

> Out of my [a]gait, for Gods saik let me ga : [a] *way*
> Tell me againe, gude maister, quhat ye say.

It is when, as in this passage, Lyndsay's ear is tuned in to the language of common folk that he finds his true inspiration and achieves his most genuinely dramatic effects. He reflects the sound common sense of the folk, including their proverbs,[4] their shrewdness, their desire for firm ground under their feet, and their realistic suspicion of gambling. " Wo to the realme that hes ouir young ane king " (" Dreme," l. 1011)—that is the keynote of Lyndsay's political complaint, and in *The Complaint and public Confessioun of the Kingis auld Hound, callit Bagsche,*[5] instead of the Wheel of Fortune, he gives us (l. 151) a picturesque Scots proverb : " Hiest in Court, nixt the weddie [gallows]." Lyndsay's humour consequently inclines to coarseness and obscenity, but it also has (*Thrie Estaitis,* l. 1527) the grim dramatic quality of folk speech :

> Na [a]cuir thow nocht, man, for my thrift. [a] *care*
> [a]Trows thou that I be daft ? [a] *believest*

Lyndsay's metres are commonly of the more popular variety. He does use the Chaucerian stanza and a few other courtly forms, and the framework of his poems is usually modelled on courtly originals. There are occasional instances of decorative alliteration, and one (*Papyngo,* ll. 647 ff., 1172 ff.) of ornate internal rhyme. In the *Thrie Estaitis,* however, Lyndsay shows that he is more at home with bob-and-wheel stanzas and tail-rhymes, which go to meet popular taste. Among the latter, there are many with curtailed second parts (for example, *a a b a b*), and one of these is the earliest occurrence of the Burns-stanza in Scotland ($a\ a\ a_4\ b_2\ a_4\ b_2$).

Not that Lyndsay had neglected the study of Chaucer and his contemporaries.[6] His earliest extant poem, the " Dreme " (1528), begins with the conventional sleepless night and the dream vision ; but, apart from this, its realistic and intimate specification of local and personal details is quite un-Chaucerian. Moreover, it is a January night—winter again !—with snow and hail, and the contrast

[4] J. Kissel, *Das Sprichwort bei dem mittelschottischen Dichter Sir David Lyndesay,* dissertation, Erlangen 1892, enumerates 173 proverbs or proverbial expressions.

[5] Hereinafter cited as *Bagsche.*

[6] Cp. A. Lange, *Lyndesays Monarche und die Chronica Carionis,* Giessen 1904, and E. Koeppel, " Sir David Lyndesays Anspielungen auf mittelenglische Dichtungen," in *Archiv für das Studium der Neueren Sprachen,* CVII (1902).

of the bleakness of nature with the poet's colourful memories of summer creates the desired atmosphere of " mutability " for his dream. In passages like this, where he conjures up a concretely visualised scene,[7] Lyndsay has the sensuous suggestiveness and intensity that we found characteristic of Douglas, Dunbar and Henryson ; but, unlike them, he has too much to say, and all too easily becomes prolix. Perhaps being a teacher to the prince had made him dogmatic and encyclopædic.

The dream proper, a vision of Hell, Paradise, the elements, and earth, seems to follow the European pattern. But the longest single part of the poem (ll. 799-1015) is a view of Scotland and her fate, seen with common sense and realism. This harnessing of allegory to a popular patriotic purpose is quite out of accord with the older convention, and it was one of the ways in which " Davie Lyndsay " endeared himself to the common folk of Scotland. The poet asks his guide, Remembrance, why Scotland is so poor. He sees fish, mountains with " bestiall," valleys of corn, rivers, lochs, hunting, " halkyng," deer, springs, rich finds of metals, even gold, silver and precious stones. The luxury of wine and spices she may lack, but food, drink, clothing are abundant, nor are there (ll. 834-5)

> More fairer peple, nor of gretar [a]ingyne, — [a] *intellect*
> Nor of more strenth gret dedis tyll indure.

The answer is that Scotland suffers (ll. 847 ff.) from lack of " governyng," of due enforcement of her laws, of far-seeing policies, and consequently of peace. If the shepherd sleeps, the flock will fall prey to the wolves. In his dream the poet sees a gaunt, rugged " berne [man] " coming across the fields, a " pyikstaff " in his hand as if he had gone from his home. It is " Jhone the Comoun Weill," whom we meet again in the *Thrie Estaitis* : the fact that Lyndsay twice personifies the Common Weill as a peasant or bonnet laird is highly significant. John is " disgysit," " disherissit," neglected. Polecye has fled to France, his sister Justice is all but blind (ll. 947 f.). In the lawless Border John had almost been slain,[8] the " sweir swyngeoris [lazy rogues] " of the Highlands drove him away, in the outer Islands and in Argyll he found " unthrift, sweirnes [sloth], falset, pouertie, stryfe " (l. 965). From the Lowlands he was expelled by profit ; the clergy practice simony ; " Covatice " is everywhere.

[7] *E.g. Bagsche, passim* ; *Papyngo*, ll. 90 ff., 154 ff., and several scenes in the *Thrie Estaitis*.

[8] These were the years just before James V tried to impose order in the Borders by expeditions that are reflected in the ballads (*e.g.* " The Song of the Outlaw Murray ").

John the Common Weill will not, he says, be able to return home (ll. 1004-5)

> ... tyll that I see the countre gydit
> Be wysedome of ane gude auld prudent kyng.

This is a new use of allegory ; the allegorical figures enable Lyndsay to express abstract political ideas in concrete pictures with sharp contemporary and local characteristics. Lyndsay is the most eloquent and convinced exponent of the " democratic attitude " that is such a marked feature in Scottish literature. Henryson had expressed the dignity of the peasant ; to Lyndsay, a cobbler or tailor has greater ethical worth than bishop or prelate, because they thoroughly *know* their trade (*Thrie Estaitis*, ll. 3127 ff., 3344 ff.).[9] Lyndsay's manly independence has its noblest ring in *Bagsche* (1533-36) and in the " Complaynt " (*c.* 1529). He has never been able to beg favours, he says, and even now (" Complaynt," l. 31) " I wyll nocht flyte ".[10] In the *Papyngo* (1530), the dying parrot appeals (l. 303) to his monarch, James V, to choose his council regardless of " blude, ryches or rent," and urges him to read history, the chronicles, and statecraft for half an hour a day. " Lerne to be ane kyng," he cries (l. 287) ; and in the *Thrie Estaitis* Lyndsay explains (l. 1605) what he means :

> Quhat is ane king ? nocht bot ane officiar,
> To caus his [a]leiges live in equitie. [a] *subjects*

This is the true state doctrine of the Reformation, but it is also the state doctrine of the Declaration of Arbroath and of Barbour's *Bruce* : it is the task of a king to defend the God-given " fredome " and " richt " of the people. The supreme effort must be for peace, which best serves the common weal.[11] Most of the reforms in the *Thrie Estaitis* are designed to promote the common weal, by strengthening the rule of law on which the security of the common man depends.[12]

[9] It is puzzling that the two passages are so far apart. Diligence in the meantime fetches three " Doctores " to demonstrate knowledge and preaching ; this would be more intelligible if the incompetence of the prelates had been established previously, after the testing of the tradesmen.

[10] Lyndsay was banished from Court when the Earl of Angus, Queen Margaret's second husband, had the young James V in his power (1524). The King escaped in 1528, and by 1530 Lyndsay was back in office.

[11] So, too, in the *Thrie Estaitis*, and in *Ane Dialog betuix Experience and ane Courteour, of the miserabyll Estait of the Warld* (often referred to as *The Monarche*, but here cited as *Dialog.*) Lyndsay had belonged to the peace party that had tried to restrain James IV back from the recklessness (as it seemed to them) of the course that led to Flodden ; see W. Murison, *Sir David Lyndsay, Poet, and Satirist of the Old Church*, Cambridge, 1938 ch. 1.

[12] See esp. §§ 2-5, 7, 11, 13 and 15 of the " First Act," in *Thrie Estaitis*, ll. 3793 ff.

The democratic element in Scots literature is one of its most striking characteristics. What other literatures have so many kings and peasants among its poets, or indeed any kings at all who wrote popular poetry ?[13] " Democratic " is really not the correct word ; it is rather a free manliness, a *saeva indignatio* against oppression, a violent freedom, sometimes an aggressive spirit of independence or egalitarianism. If often lacks the constructive impulse that we are accustomed to regard as part of democracy. It is sometimes explained as the result of the Celtic " polity " in which each, whatever his rank, is first and foremost a member of the clan, and also as a result of the pressure from England ; and freedom from Roman rule may also have meant absence of the Roman civic spirit.[14] As a small country, Scotland may also have had a less exclusive separation of classes than, for example, France and England ; that was certainly the impression formed by the French knights in Scotland in Barbour's time. The less rigid stratification of society in Scotland appears everywhere in Scottish literature, and it has also been suggested as one of the reasons why Scotland is so much richer in Gaelic vernacular poetry than Ireland.[15] One expression of the Scots " democratic spirit " is the Scottish love of arguing about fundamentals from purely individual points of view. There is truth in the saying that while the English discuss things in order to reach agreement, to find a compromise, the Scots argue in order to disagree, to make their point, to assert their rugged independence and individuality. It is an innate tendency to challenge blind acceptance. It was also carried over into Presbyterianism, with its reliance on intellectual conviction, and Presbyterian church-government helped to perpetuate and to intensify the old spirit. Religion is not, to the Scots, beyond argument, nor God an unapproachable power, but an authority with whom each individual can and must discuss his own plans. This is not a fruit of Calvinism, as we have seen in connexion with Barbour, Henryson, and Douglas ; the familiar approach to God is simply the religious aspect of the old Scots spirit of independence.[16] In its negative form, this spirit becomes prideful arrogance and an envious

[13] *Christis Kirk on the Grene* and *Peblis to the Play* (see below, pp. 114, 120) are often attributed to James I, sometimes to James V, who is also credited with some ballads, *e.g.* " The jolly Beggar " and " The Gaberlunzie Man." Another poem of his (which has not come down to us) occasioned Lyndsay's " Answer to the Kingis Flyting."

[14] Cp. Ian Finlay, *Scotland*, Oxford 1945, pp. 8-10.

[15] See below, pp. 186, 197.

[16] Cp. Finlay, p. 15.

dislike of anybody who is finer, more original, and more sensitive than others or seeks to rise above the common level. The saying " I kent his grandfaither " is meant to keep an upstart in his place.[17]

Democracy and social justice are Lyndsay's main themes. They induced him to champion the cause of the Reformation ; and his criticism of the Old Church was the greatest single cause of the immense popular vogue that he enjoyed.[18] Biting satire against abuses among the clergy occurs in " The Dreme " and *Papyngo*, and is the essence of the *Satyre of the Thrie Estaitis*. The latter was performed before the royal family on 6 January 1540, fully twenty years before the Scottish Reformation, in a version[19] of which no text survives. In 1552 followed an open-air performance in Lyndsay's native Cupar (Fife), from which Bannatyne gives us extracts,[20] and in 1554 yet another version[21] was performed before the burgesses of Edinburgh and probably also the Queen Regent. For the public performances at Cupar and Edinburgh the text was much enlarged. It is full of allusions to local and contemporary events, and conveys a sharp picture of the social conditions of the time : abuses in the Church ; the pest (ll. 2594 ff.) of beggars, pardoners, bards, pipers and other retainers ; the tricks (l. 4056) of the merchants who " mix Ry-meill amang the saip [soap] " and cheat the simple peasant women ; the Border cattle-thieves who flourish under the protection of the great lords. Perhaps because they had fewer opportunities for whole-sale corruption, the burgesses are let off more leniently than the two other Estates. Even so, all three come in for caustic satire.

The play opens with Rex Humanitas pampered and led by the nose by Flatterie, Falset, Sensualitie, Dissait (in disguise), while Veritie and Chastitie are shut in the stocks and lawlessness is rampant. In an interlude, the extortion of " corpse-present [death duty] " by the

[17] Cp. (the modern) Alexander Scott's verse " Letter to Robert Fergusson," in *Robert Fergusson 1750-1774*, essays, ed. S. G. Smith, Edinburgh 1952 : " And praise wi pounds a fremmit [foreign] bard far raither Nor fling a meck [ha'penny] tae ' Him ? I kent his faither ! ' "

[18] Cp. W. Murison (above, n. 11).

[19] Known as *Version I*. For a synopsis, see HAMER, VOLS. II, pp. 1-6, and IV, pp. 125-9.

[20] Known as *Version II*, for which see *The Bannatyne Manuscript*, ed. W. Tod Ritchie, S.T.S., VOL. III (1928), pp. 87-238 ; and HAMER, VOLS. II, *even*-numbered pp. 10-404, and IV, pp. 129-240. According to HAMER (VOL. IV, p. 139), " Bannatyne was clearly unaware . . . that his text was that of the Cupar performance only."

[21] Preserved in a quarto edn. printed by Robert Charteris, Edinburgh 1602, and known as *Version III*, for which see HAMER, VOLS. II, *odd*-numbered pp. 35-405, and IV, 125-9. According to HAMER (VOL. IV, p. 129), *Version III* is " a slightly revised form " of *Version II*. Our quotations are accordingly from *Version III*.

priest makes the peasant a Puir Man whom the Pardoner robs of his last groat. But Divyne Correction is on the way (l. 1594),

To [a]teill the ground that hes bene lang [b]vnsawin ; [a] *till* [b] *unsown*

and the Parliament of the Thrie Estaitis is summoned for reform measures. They come in walking backward, but John the Common Weill shows up their true leaders : Covetice and Sensualitie among the clergy ; Publick Oppressioun among the secular Lords ; Falset and Dissait among the burgesses. When these all have been put behind lock and key, the reform measures advocated by John the Common-Weill are carried—against the violent opposition of the clergy, where their own vested interests are threatened. The ignorant prelates are replaced by learned preachers ; Flatterie, under his mask as a Freir, expelled ; and the other vices hanged. And Pauper fervently implores the King not to let these good laws be a dead letter only. But what here looks like the dreichest of dreich fare is in fact an ample and spicy banquet.

Lyndsay does not break with the Old Church, but he wants to see it reformed. To him, the roots of the evil are ecclesiastical property,[22] which leads to covetice and worldliness (" First Act," [23] §§ 7, 10-13, 15), and compulsory celibacy, which produces immorality (§§ 6, 14). Learning and preaching should be the inalienable mark of the clergy (§§ 8-9, 12)—then the whole people will stand up to defend its Kirk (§ 1).

Most of Lyndsay's reforms are social. He does not touch dogma —let the Doctores explain the Trinity (" Dreme," l. 546). Still, he calls for the translation of the Bible as a source of truth. Characteristically, the Vices in the *Thrie Estaitis* quote the saints more frequently than the Virtues do. In the *Papyngo*, Lyndsay exposes the abuse of the confessional ; in *Kitteis Confessioun* (1540s)—if it is his—he advocates voluntary confession, not to a priest, but to God Himself. In the *Thrie Estaitis* John the Common Weill says his creed to his Lord directly, and adds the article concerning the Church (ll. 3024 ff.) only after renewed command :

I [a]trow *Sanctam Ecclesiam*, [a] *believe in*
Bot nocht in [a]thir Bischops nor thir Freirs, [a] *these*
Quhilk will, for purging of thir [a]neirs, [a] *kidneys*
[a]Sard up [b]the ta raw, and doun the uther. [a] *fornicate* [b] *the one row*
The mekill Devill [a]resave the [b]fidder. [a] *receive* [b] *cart-load*

[22] In 1552, the Church owned half of Scotland's total revenue. According to G. M. Thomson, Scotland's higher clergy must have been conspicuous, even in that age, for licentiousness.
[23] *Thrie Estaitis*, ll. 3793 ff.

To which Divyne Correction himself replies (ll. 3029 f.) :

> Say quhat ye will, Sirs, be [a]Sanct Tan, [a] (?) *St Anne*
> Me think Johne ane gude Christian man.

Elsewhere (ll. 1160-1) Veritie speaks to God in a tone we know from Henryson :

> Get up, thow sleipis all too lang, O Lord,
> And mak sum ressonabill reformatioun.[24]

It is remarkable that Lyndsay was already expounding some of the principal ideas of the Reformation in the " Dreme " (1528) and the *Papyngo* (1530). This raises the question whether Lollardry had, in Scotland, already joined forces with the Continental Reformation. Since the records of the Inquisitorial Court have disappeared, it is difficult to reconstruct the history of the Lollards in Scotland.[25] But most Scottish students at Oxford went to Balliol College, where Wycliffe was Master ; in 1365 alone, eighty-one Scottish students were permitted to study in Oxford, and we know, too, that Barbour had accompanied students to that university. Under Albany, Governor of Scotland during the captivity of James I, we hear of the first Lollard burned in Scotland (James Resby, 1407), and Andrew of Wyntoun praises Albany as a sworn enemy of the heretics. James I's Parliament of 1424-5 at Perth made the bishops responsible for stamping out Lollardry. A disciple of Johan Huss, Paul Craw (or Crawar) was burnt at St Andrews in 1433, and as late as 1494 thirty people from Kyle in Ayrshire were accused of Lollardry before James IV, but escaped the fire as some " great familiars " of the King were among them. According to John Knox,[26] they were accused of refusing tithes, demanding the abolition of sacerdotal celibacy, and proclaiming that only God could forgive sins, not the Pope or the clergy. In " The Flyting of Dunbar and Kennedy " both poets use " Lollard " as a term of abuse, and Kennedy also refers to Lollardry elsewhere.[27]

To Lyndsay his own poetry was less important than the message which it conveyed. Therefore he repeats himself in characters, ideas,

[24] Cp. *Dialog*, ll. 2701 ff.

[25] For the following details and also for some other historical information, I am indebted to Mr W. R. Humphries, Lecturer in Scottish History, University of Aberdeen.

[26] See *John Knox's History of the Reformation in Scotland*, ed. W. Croft Dickinson, 2 vols., Edinburgh 1949, VOL. I, pp. 7-11.

[27] *E.g.* in *The Bannatyne Manuscript* (above, n. 20), VOL. II, pp. 131 ff.

episodes, phrases, rhymes, and his 18,000 lines are wholly unrevised. Lyndsay is not a formal artist ; to him, poetry serves a purpose—as it was to do under the Presbyterians. At first sight, the *Thrie Estaitis* may be of the same type as the slightly older English *King Johan* by John Bale, who also employs the morality play as a weapon for the Reformation. In *King Johan*, abstract moral and political conceptions are transformed into symbolic figures, which then disguise themselves as historical personalities : thus, Privat Welth becomes Nobility, which then disguises itself as Cardinal Pandulphus ; Sedition becomes a Monk, who subsequently assumes the guise of Stephen Langton. This brings the drama within striking distance of the chronicle play. There is admittedly a certain resemblance to it in the first part of the *Thrie Estaitis*, when Flatterie and his consorts disguise themselves as a Freir, and so on ; but Lyndsay does not specifically identify these symbolic figures with particular historical personalities or events. On the other hand, his satire is saturated with local, social, political details that add up to a precise picture of the conditions of the age. Bale's figures are chessmen in an allegorico-historico-political game ; Lyndsay's are men of real life, of his own environment, in an allegorical cloak.

But Lyndsay does not think allegorically. Allegory is not, in his hands, a conventional way of expressing, in poetry, an intricate and subtle system of thought, or of representing abstract vices and virtues with their innumerable attributes : it is a means of presenting a real social and political problem in terms of a concrete picture that we can actually visualise, and it enables Lyndsay himself, in presenting it, to keep his feet on the ground. The abstract thought that the common weal is suffering poverty is translated (ll. 2438, 2456) into a picturesque, proverbial image that leaves a lasting impression in the mind—it " gars John the Common Weill want his warm clais [clothes]." Similarly, Flatterie (ll. 602 ff.) is " new landit out of France " ; Dissait (l. 656) is " counsallor to the Merchand-men " ; only John the Common Weill (ll. 2543 f.) shall stand at the bar of the tribunal, and so forth. This sharper realism favours a stronger dramatic quality : Falset (ll. 793, 849 ff.) follows the example of the other vices, disguises himself as a monk, and calls himself Sapience—but then forgets his new name. In the heat of the argument, Spiritualitie is provoked into saying (l. 2910) that he himself has never read the New Testament ; and on being told that this is the Apostle Paul's own commandment, hotly retorts (ll. 2915) :

Sum sayis be him that wore the croune of thorne,
It had been gude that Paull had [a]neir bene borne. [a] *never*

The *Satyre of the Thrie Estaitis* is a rather isolated example of early Scottish drama.[28] Among Lyndsay's tasks at Court was the arrangement of plays: he directed the pageant to welcome James V's second Queen, Marie de Lorraine, and "The Iusting betuix Watson and Barbour" was part of these festivities. Lyndsay shows considerable dramatic talent—more, certainly, than his English contemporaries. Though it could stand thorough pruning,[29] the *Thrie Estaitis* has, despite its length, a remarkable unity. Lyndsay at least sees things dramatically, in terms of action and tension, and he enters the minds of his figures so as to make them speak in character: Flatterie's report of the voyage from France (ll. 602 ff.) is a fine example. This makes the characters sufficiently individual—look at Spiritualitie thundering his "How dare you!" The chief source of Lyndsay's dramatic power is the tension of argument, that good Scots art. It is this that gives the second part its strength, and the dispute between the Thrie Estaitis themselves is one of the highlights of the play: how well observed is the intervention (ll. 2928 ff.) of the Third Estait. Compared with this, the more allegorical first part looks old-fashioned. The learned disputations, on the other hand, may be an essential part of Lyndsay's message, but are apt to become dogmatic and boring. But when he is visualising a realistic and definite scene, and comes closest to the sharp, precise Scots speech, Lyndsay is brilliant.

Lyndsay's racy dramatic idiom fits naturally into the conception of the Scots literary tradition that we have already formed. His subject-matter only occasionally affords scope for understatement (*Papyngo*, l. 171):

God [a]wat [b]gyff [c]than my hart wes wo begone. [a] *knows* [b] *if* [c] *then*

But we find examples of the tension that arises from contrast ("Complaynt," "Prolong" [*sic*] to the "Dreme"); of extravaganza ("The Iusting betuix Watsoun and Barbour"); and of the spirit of flyting, if not of its artistic formalism. When, in "The Answer quhilk Schir Dauid Lindesay maid to the Kingis Flyting" (*c.* 1535), he puts on his Sabbath braws and uses the Chaucerian stanza, he is speaking with his tongue in his cheek. In other places ("Dreme," ll. 211, 224,

[28] For the later development of Scottish drama, see below, pp. 311 ff.

[29] Such as it had from Robert Kemp in the acting version performed at the Edinburgh Festival (1948-50).

266) he wields the whip of alliteration with the best of them. And in the *Thrie Estaitis* (ll. 2444 ff.), listen to the rumbling anger of Johne the Common Weill :

> Thair [a]canker cullours I ken them be the heads... [a] *cankered*
>
> Loe quhair the [a]loun lyis lurkand at his back... [a] *worthless fellow*
>
> Thou feinyeit Flattrie, the feind fart in thy face !

Lyndsay's animal poems are, too, an essential link in the Scottish tradition. Though it clearly foreshadows the later Scottish species of animal testaments and mock elegies, his *Papyngo* echoes the true medieval style ; but *Bagsche* is distinctively Scottish. It is the first dog-poem in Scots or English ; it considers the sturdily independent dog as a kind of equal, a comrade ; and it has much in common with Henryson's *Fabillis*, or Dunbar's most manly " Petition of the Gray Horse, Auld Dunbar," the Gaelic poets, or Burns. Here I do not postulate a literary influence, but rather a popular traditional attitude towards animals.

The history of Scottish poetry from Barbour to Lyndsay is at the same time the history of the birth of a culturally distinct Scots language. Barbour stands on the threshold ; his language can still be called Northern English, though in its idiom it has a character of its own. But the literary Scots of Henryson and Dunbar, and still more so that of Douglas and Lyndsay, is a language in its own right. True, it has as many links with English as *Schwyzerdytsch* [30] with German, or Norwegian with Danish ; yet, phonetically and morphologically, in word usage, in the Celtic and Scandinavian derivation of much of its vocabulary, and in its submerged Celtic sentence-pattern, it has a character markedly its own. In a sense, the Makars themselves created this language, each in his own field widening its scope, opening up new depths, and enlarging its power of expression. A language that finally ranges from ecclesiastical and social satire to the pathos of Cresseid, from a remarkable translation of the *Aeneid* to the flytings, from Henryson's tenderness to Dunbar's ornate pageantry, cannot be called a restricted language. It was still growing, and had not yet developed the idiom of prose or of abstract reflexion and speculation.

[30] The German language as spoken in Switzerland.

Although it is Lyndsay whose Scots is closest to folk speech, the same characteristic frequently occurs in the works of the other Makars. Their Scots is forcibly expressive, it repeatedly achieves contrasts of a harsh Northern vitality, and has a tendency towards concreteness and realism that already appears in Barbour. In it we also recognise a highly dramatic quality derived no doubt from its close connexion with common speech, song, and dance. The concise, tender, compassionate intimacy of Henryson's Scots, in particular, is immensely expressive and admirably sustains his many fine strokes of psychology: here, in its own limited field, Scots has developed powers of expression and modes of utterance to which English can show nothing analogous ; and anybody who tries to translate into English " The Uponlandis Mous and the Burges Mous," the beginning of " The Taill of the Paddok and the Mous " or of *The Testament of Cresseid*, the passages I singled out in the *Thrie Estaitis* or in the *Eneados*, will recognise the loss of expression. Dunbar extended the range of Scots, both in the direction of courtly and ornamental aureation and in that of that wild eldritch extravaganza which forms a link with Gaelic tradition, and thus made it more sophisticated, and at the same time more vividly scurrilous. If the contrasts to which this gives rise are often of immense dramatic tension, they are only enhancing a quality fundamental to Scots, which, as we have seen repeatedly, is able to bind opposites in sharp juxtaposition. Douglas subjected the Scots tongue to the severe discipline of a huge, sustained task, and the Scots tongue's suggestive force was one of the essential instruments of his success. Lyndsay finally applied it to express questions of statecraft, and at the same time linked it still further with folk speech.

As yet there is no decline, even if Lyndsay has not the poetic qualities of the other Makars. After Flodden (1513), there is, however, a flattened summit ; the courtly element begins to fade into the background, and we see in front of us a dangerous sign-post : poetry is being used as a weapon in political or religious controversy. But before we can proceed to investigate later developments we must have a look at the teeming life that lies behind the radiant figures of the great Makars.

IV

The Pattern left in the Sand: The Background of the Minor Poets from the Fourteenth to the Seventeenth Century

This is not so much a history of Scottish literature as a survey of it in which we have made it our governing aim to spotlight those characteristics which crop up so regularly in the works of some outstanding Scottish writers that they together make up a tradition. If we would see these characteristics not merely as individual traits, but rather as personal formulations of certain traditional attitudes, we must at least glance at the background against which they stand out so vividly. In it we shall also discern the earliest manifestations of certain changes, at first almost imperceptible, but soon more violent, which mark the end of this first brilliant phase of the tradition ; these fainter lines of the background will, moreover, dominate the canvas which the eighteenth century is presently to fill with fresh light and colour.

Though time has dealt heavily with early Scottish literature, several large works that have not yet been mentioned in these pages have come down to us. There is the almost legendary beginning with Thomas Learmonth of Ercildoun (now Earlston) in Lauderdale, *alias* Thomas the Rhymer, who is credited with a *Tristrem.* There are the rhymed alliterative tales often connected with the equally dim figure of " Hucheone of the Awle Ryale," [1] to whom Andrew of Wyntoun attributes at least *The Pistill* [*Epistle*] *of Susan,*[2] *The Awntyrs of Arthure,*[3] and *The Quatrefoil of Love.* Some also consider him to have been the author of *Perle* and *Sir Gawain and the Grene Knight.* Here, indeed, much evidence speaks apparently in favour of English origin. In *Perle,* however, as compared with contemporary English poetry, the late Agnes Mure Mackenzie detects the same literary method, the

[1] *I.e.,* ? Sir Hugh of Eglinton, d. 1381.

[2] See *Scottish alliterative Poems,* ed. F. J. Amours, S.T.S., 1897, pp. 172 ff.

[3] See *op cit.,* pp. 117 ff., and Sir W. A. Craigie, " The Scottish alliterative Poems," in *Proceedings of the British Academy,* XXVIII (1942), pp. 217-36.

same aureation, the same delight in gorgeous decorative detail, the same frank homely realism, and the same eye for nature in its harsher aspects, as in the poetry of the Scots Makars ; and though much early Scottish poetry is metrically as intricate, English poetry has nothing similar to show until Swinburne. Two later examples of the alliterative poem that must also be mentioned are Holland's *Howlat* (*c.* 1450),[4] a bird allegory of pro-Douglas political tendencies, and *The Tale of Rauf Coilyear* (*c.* 1470),[5] a vigorous and amusing piece in which, characteristically, everything is turned upside down in favour of social equality and the common man.

In failing to deal with *Wallace*,[6] traditionally attributed to " BLIND HARRY," at considerable length, we are admittedly doing it an injustice. If Barbour's *Bruce*, with its essentially historical interest in the hero, foreshadows the great Scottish biographies of Boswell and Lockhart, this narrative account of Scotland's great popular hero Wallace, compiled a hundred years later, with its delight in semi-fictitious dramatic episodes, its sense of character and picturesque situation, taps the vein of Walter Scott. Though sometimes long-winded and tedious, Blind Harry, whoever he may have been, has nevertheless the same sharp eye for revealing sensuous detail, the same gift of clear-cut visualisation, and the same shrewd folk-speech (" deir eneuch ") as Henryson :

The ship master on to the top he went ;
Southwest he saw, that trublyt his entent,
Sexten salis arayit all [a]on raw, — [a] *in a row*
In colour reid, and towart him [a]couth draw. — [a] *did*
The gliterand [a]son apon thaim schawit brycht, — [a] *sun*
The se about enlumynyt with the lycht.[7]

Zepherus began his morrow cours,
The swete vapour thus fra the ground [a]resours. — [a] *rises*
The [a]humyll breyth doun fra the hevyn [b]awaill, — [a] *gentle* [b] *sank*
In every meide, bathe fyrth, forrest, and daill ;
The cler [a]rede among the [b]rochis rang — [a] *note* [b] *rocks*
Throuch greyn branchis quhar byrdis blythly sang.[8]

[4] See BANN. (below, n. 12), VOL. IV, pp. 128 ff., and *Scottish alliterative Poems*, pp. 47 ff.

[5] See *op cit.*, pp. 82 ff.

[6] *The Actis and Deidis of . . . Schir William Wallace*, ed. J. Moir, S.T.S., 3 vols., 1885-9. See also W. A. Craigie, " Barbour and Blind Harry," in *Scottish Review*, XXII (1893), and G. Neilson, " Blind Harry's ' Wallace '," in *Essays and Studies*, I (1910).

[7] *Wallace*, IX.61 ff.

[8] VIII.1186 ff.

‘ Slepand as swyn ar all [a]yone fals [b]menyhe ; — [a] *that* [b] *band of men*
Na Scottis man is in that cumpané.’
Than Wallace said ; ‘ Giff thai all [a]droukyn be, — [a] *drunken*
I call it best with fyr [a]sor thaim to se.’ [9] — [a] *sore*

[a]Traistis rycht weill all this was [b]suth in deide, — [a] *believe* [b] *true*
[a]Suppos that it no poynt be of the creide.[10] — [a] *even though*

[the enemy]
Als fersly fled as fyr dois off the flynt.[11]

★ ★ ★

Most of the Scottish poetry written between 1450 and 1580 that is still extant is contained in three sixteenth-century manuscript anthologies, namely the Bannatyne (1568),[12] the Maitland Folio (*c.* 1570-85),[13] and the Maitland Quarto (1586).[14] *Colkelbie's Sow* [15] contains allusions to about fifty songs ; while about fifty titles of tales, forty of songs, and thirty of dances are listed in the *Complaynt of Scotland*,[16] and more than two dozen popular songs were adapted to the purposes of a reformed Kirk in the *Gude and Godlie Ballatis*.[17] In his “ Lament,” too, Dunbar names many contemporary Scottish poets ; and others are mentioned by Lyndsay and Douglas. But even among those whose names have actually come down to us, most are shadowy figures of little or no substance ; and we only possess scraps of what must have been a flourishing tradition, with its own wide and variegated repertoire of songs and poems. (This must be borne in mind in dealing with such poems as “ Of the Malyce of Poyetis.”) [18]

Conscious and deliberate artistry such as we have already seen in Dunbar seems to have been the chief characteristic of this tradition ;

[9] vii.357 ff. [10] v.213. [11] vi.314.

[12] *The Bannatyne Manuscript*, ed. W. Tod Ritchie, S.T.S., 4 vols., 1928-34. Written “ in tyme of pest ” by George Bannatyne, the final draft contains just over 400 items. Here cited as Bann.

[13] *The Maitland Folio Manuscript*, ed. W. A. Craigie, S.T.S., 2 vols., 1919-27. It was compiled by Sir Richard Maitland of Lethington. Here cited as Mait. F.

[14] *The Maitland Quarto Manuscript*, ed. W. A. Craigie, S.T.S., 1920. Essentially an extract from the Folio for one of Lethington's daughters. Here cited as Mait. Q.

[15] See below, pp. 106 ff. and n. 20.

[16] Ed. J. A. H. Murray, E.E.T.S., 1872, pp. 66 and lxxxvii ff.

[17] Ed. A. F. Mitchell, S.T.S., 1897.

[18] Mait. F., vol. i, pp. 325 f.

high style or flyting, true lyric or extravaganza, devotion or irreverence, aureation or broad vernacular constantly merge and separate like the fleeting reflexion of branches on broken water.[19] A most remarkable example is *Colkelbie's Sow*.[20] To label it a parody (or set of parodies) is really to miss the point. Unlike *Sir Topas* or *Rauf Coilyear*, it does not follow a single line of development : indeed it can be much more accurately described as a theme and variations, and there is nothing like it for centuries to come.[21]

The " *Prohemium* " is in the heroic style of the four-beat couplet —and decorated in the MS. with a coat of arms. The " *Prima Pars*," in a furiously reeling dance of two-beat couplets, tells the story of Colkelbie, who sells his sow for three pennies. One of these he loses ; with it, a man who finds it buys one of the sow's pigs, which a harlot steals to crown a feast at which she entertains all her friends, but under the butcher's knife the little pig gives a terrified whine, and the sow breaks loose with all the other swine, rescues her offspring, and races away with it, pursued helter-skelter by the madhouse crowd of the party. Needless to say, the pig grows to be the strongest boar the world has ever seen and is victorious over all other animals. This part of the poem has the same eldritch extravagance as Dunbar's " Dance of the sevin deidly Synnis " or " The Sowtar and Tailyouris War," and the story is told with the same furious whirl and absurd capers—flying off at a tangent every few lines to trace a fantastic pattern, and carrying logic to the extremes of illogicality exactly as in the flytings.

But enough " off thir mokking meteris and mad matere " (II.1) : in the next part, the story of the second penny is told, in the true style of romances, the four-beat alliterative couplet. Colkelbie gives this penny to a blind old man led by a young girl of excellent beauty, who grows up in Colkelbie's house and marries his son. The King of France sees the young couple, and is so impressed by the young woman's beauty, and by her husband's valour, that he takes them

[19] Therefore we cannot profitably assign these poems to the poet's youth, maturity, etc., as in *The Poems of Alexander Montgomerie*, ed. J. Cranstoun, S.T.S., 1887, here cited as (Montgomerie's) *Poems*, ed. CRANSTOUN ; now largely superseded by Stevenson's supplementary edn. (for which see below, n. 37). Some of these supposedly " mature " poems are found in the Bannatyne MS, compiled when Montgomerie was just over 20 !

[20] BANN., VOL. IV, pp. 279 ff.

[21] It is worth noting that a pibroch or piece of *ceòl mór* (classical Highland bagpipe music) normally consists of a ground (*ùrlar*), followed by a standard sequence of variations —*siubhal*, *taorluath* and *cruinnluath* (often extremely complicated)—after which the ground is often repeated. The structure of *Colkelbie's Sow* is surprisingly similar.

to his court and finally honours them with an earldom (named Flandria, from their names Flannislie and Adria). The narrator is an old woman, who points out the five wisdoms which it exemplifies, and explains what each of the three pennies and each particular incident symbolises. She also repeats the story of the first penny, but in knightly style and with a *moralitas*.

Finally, the story of the third penny is told, in high style, in aureate heroic couplets, with next to no alliteration. Colkelbie hoards this penny for fifteen years, but then buys two dozen eggs as a present for his godson, whose parents, however, contemptuously reject the gift. Out of the eggs are hatched Chantecler, Pertelot, Sprutok and all their tribe. The birds multiply and go on multiplying, until, at his godson's coming-of-age, Colkelbie can hand him a net profit of more than £1000, making him the richest and mightiest man in the country. Here we have almost a legend of a saint, poetically interwoven with strands of moral and philosophical reflexion.

This fifteenth-century " theme and variations " is one remarkable example of conscious artistry—almost of virtuosity. Another is the anonymous poem, " Quhair-of to wryt,"[22] in the *a a b a b* stanza that Dunbar used to express moral reflexion. It is in their professional preoccupation with form, and especially in the skill with which they elaborate complex decorative patterns of rhyme and alliteration, that the conscious artistry with which the anonymous Scottish poets of the early period went about their work stands most conspicuously revealed.[23] More often than not, they accept the narrow limitations of a form which demands special sequences of terminal and internal rhymes and heavy alliteration ; and within this framework they are not satisfied until they have adorned the last square inch of surface with intricate beauty. In its extreme forms, this conscious artistry becomes sheer virtuosity,[24] and one cannot fail to see that it arises from precisely the same æsthetic attitude as Celtic art : Sir James Fergusson traces it [25] in the elaborately knotted carvings on Celtic tombstones, in the thematic development of pibroch, in the figures of the traditional Lowland country dances, and in the inlaid orna-

[22] Mait. F., vol. i, pp. 237 f.

[23] In Scottish painting, according to Stanley Cursiter (*Scotland*, ed. H. W. Meikle, p. 199), the most notable qualities have been " the rich full colour and sense of pattern."

[24] Cp. Bann., vol. ii, pp. 52 (" O nicht of nicht and licht of licht most cleir "), 182 (" Remember man on endless hellis vexatioun ") ; and vol. iii, p. 291 (" Flour of all fair-heid gif I sall found the[e] fra.").

[25] In *The Green Garden : A new Collection of Scottish Poetry*, Edinburgh 1946, p. xvi.

mentation of eighteenth-century pistols, etc.—to which might well be added the intricate metrical patterns of Gaelic poetry. Let us first examine some salient characteristics of sixteenth-century Scots prosody.

The first to catch the eye is alliteration, which had flourished in the West Midlands of England during the fourteenth century and is generally believed thence to have spread northwards.[26] In Scotland, however, the old rhymeless long line survives in one example only, Dunbar's " The twa mariit Wemen and the Wedo " ; alliteration is much more frequent with rhyme added (see beginning of this chapter). Purely decorative alliteration, moreover, was superimposed on the Chaucerian verse forms, and is quite common in all Scots poetry of the fifteenth and sixteenth centuries. True, we do not find it in Alexander Hume, but Alexander Scott and Alexander Montgomerie both frequently make use of it. The amount of alliteration varies considerably : it is most thickly laid on in numerous contemporary flytings, in which alliteration, especially of sibilants, often gives scorn a cutting edge ; in his *Reulis and Cautelis to be observit and eschewit in Scottis Poesie* (1585), James VI sanctions this " tumbling verse," and quotes Montgomerie.[27] Alliteration continued to be used in extravaganza. In the " high style," too, it was still regularly used in conjunction with aureation ; but here it went out of fashion somewhat earlier, under the influence of the *dolce stil nuovo* of the Italian sonneteers.

There has been much speculation as to why alliteration flourished so vigorously in Scotland long after it had been forgotten in the South. Sir William Craigie suggests that it was due to the fact that the Scots tongue, with its combined English and Scandinavian vocabulary, was very rich in words. The stronger accentuation of Scots which leans so heavily on the initial consonant, may also have had something to do with it.[28] But probably there was more in it than that.

Stanzas built on alliteration, terminal and internal rhyme had been the rule in Irish syllabic poetry.[29] The Middle Irish prose tale *Cath Finntraga* (Battle of Ventry) [30] carries alliteration to its extreme

[26] *E.g.* by Sir W. A. Craigie in " The Scottish alliterative Poems " (above, n. 3).

[27] See *The Poems of James VI of Scotland*, ed. J. Craigie, S.T.S., VOL. I (1955), p. 81. For a general survey of the work of Scott, Montgomerie, and other late sixteenth-century Scottish poets, see below, pp. 126 ff.

[28] Cp. George Blake in his novel *The Shipbuilders* (1935), where he attributes the passionate vehemence of Scots speech to its wealth of explosive consonants ; see below p. 324.

[29] See above, p. 61 and n. 16

[30] Ed. and tr. Kuno Meyer (in Anecdota Oxoniensia : medieval and modern Ser. I), PT. IV (1885), p. 27.

limits by arranging twenty-seven adjectives in alliterative groups of three. From before 1400 till well on into the sixteenth century alliteration was a dominant element chiefly in the Irish and Scottish Gaelic " inflated " prose style,[31] but also in poems like the " Incitement of Harlaw " and in some Scottish Gaelic poems in the Book of the Dean of Lismore.[32]

Thus heavy alliteration combined with rhyme is contemporary in both Scots and Gaelic, and even if there was no direct influence there must have been a common taste in a public that was partly bilingual. The Irish origin of Gaelic alliteration rules out a purely one-way influence from English.

Similarly with the richness in rhymes. The complicated rules which govern the use, in Gaelic poetry, of rhyme and alliteration are most strictly applied in the old syllabic metres. Here, for instance, is a specimen of *séadna*, one of the favourite syllabic metres, as used in a fourteenth-century Scottish Gaelic poem :[33]

> Dál chabhlaigh ar Chaistéal Suibhne,
> suairc an eachtra i nInis Fáil ;
> marcaigh ag tráchtadh na dtonna,
> glantair bárca donna dháibh.
>
> [Tryst of a fleet against Castle Sween,
> welcome is the adventure in Inis Fáil ;
> horsemen travelling the billows,
> brown barks being cleansed for them.]

In this metre the number of syllables in each line, and in the last word of each line, is given by the formula $2(8^2+7^1)$. The stanza consists of two couplets linked together by terminal vowel rhyme (F*á*il—dh*á*ibh). In the first couplet, there is alliteration between the last stressed syllable of l. 1 and the first stressed syllable of l. 2 (Suibhne—suairc) ; in the second, there is internal vowel rhyme between the last word of l. 3 and the second-last word of l. 4 (dt*o*nn*a*—d*o*nn*a*), and alliteration between the second-last and the last stressed syllables

[31] According to C. W. Dunn, " Highland Song and Lowland Ballad," in *University of Toronto Quarterly*, XVIII (1948), p. 8, this " florid use of alliteration " is " particularly Celtic."

[32] See *Scottish Verse from the Book of the Dean of Lismore*, ed. W. J. Watson, Scottish Gaelic Text Society (hereinafter cited as S.G.T.S.), 1937, no. XXIX ; and cp. " Oisin's Eulogy of Finn," in Magnus Maclean, *The Literature of the Celts*, p. 125.

[33] Attributed to Artur Dall mac Gurcaigh, and apparently written in 1314 ; see *Scottish Verse from the Book of the Dean of Lismore*, pp. 6 ff., 257 ff.

of l. 4 (donna—dháibh). All these associations are obligatory. Some of the other rhymes, alliterations and assonances that the stanza contains are also required, but free as to their *position* : one pair of alliteration in each of the first three lines (chabhlaigh—Chaistéal ; eachtra—nInis ; tráchtadh—dtonna), and two pairs of internal rhymes between ll. 3 and 4 (m*a*rcaigh—gl*a*ntair ; tr*á*chtadh—b*á*rca). Others again are incidental : (ch*a*bhlaigh—Ch*a*istéal ; S*u*ibhne—s*u*airc ; m*a*rcaigh—tr*á*chtadh ; dt*o*nna—d*o*nna ; gl*a*ntair—b*á*rca). Thus there are, in this stanza of thirty syllables, eight paired rhymes (two obligatory, two optional as to their position, and four adventitious), and six paired alliterations (two obligatory, three optional, and one incidental)—a total of fourteen such relationships ; and only six out of the total of twenty words do not show obligatory rhyme or alliteration, or both combined. And as if this were not enough, a further requirement is that (like many Scots poems of the period considered in this chapter) the poem should begin and end with the same word ; in this case the last line (unfortunately defective) is :

[ ] triath deacair an dál. [ ] hard the meeting.

None of the Continental literatures—not even medieval Latin poetry with its wealth of rhyme—contains anything nearly so intricate. Internal rhyme occurs not infrequently in Old French and Middle English poetry, and there are one or two examples of it in Chaucer. In Scots poetry, however, there are over a hundred poems—not always the best—in which all forms of internal rhyme are used, either throughout, or at any rate in the concluding stanzas. One line may contain as many as four sectional rhymes :

Prudent/maist gent/[a]tak tent/and prent/the wordis [a] *take care*
Intill/the bill/with will/thame still/to face.[34]

And inverse rhyme may echo the end of one line (or half-line) at the beginning of the next, similar to Gaelic *aiccill*, as in these examples :

O [a]leving Lord, that maid baythe hevin and hell [a] *living*
Fra us expell/this creuell civile [a]weir [a] *war*
That all this yeir/[a]hes done this cuntre quell, [a] *has . . . quelled*
[a]That nane can tell/how thai sall keip thair [a]geir [a] *so that* [b] *property*
Nor without [a]feir/quhair thai sall rest and dwell.[35] [a] *fear*

[34] Envoi to Alexander Scott's " New Yeir Gift to the Quene Mary, 1568," in BANN., VOL. IV, pp. 235 ff.

[35] Sir Richard Maitland, " Aganis the Divisioun of the Lordis," ll. 1 ff., in MAIT. F., VOL. I, pp. 303 f.

I wald [a]se mare nor ony thing I sie ; *[a] see more than*
I sie/not yit the thing that I desyre :
Desyre/it is that does content the [a]ee ; *[a] eye*
The ee/it is [a]whilk settis the hairt in fyre.[36] *[a] which*

All the cæsuras may have rhyme patterns of their own, independent of, or connected with, the end-rhyme scheme, a common couplet-arrangement being :

a *a*
a *B*.

In a handful of poems we even find a constant reshuffling of the same elements, as in

Polwart, ye peip like a mouse amongest thornes ;
Na cuning ye keip ; Polwart, yee peip ;
Ye luik lyk a sheipe [a]and ye had two hornes ; *[a] if only*
Polwart, ye peip like a mous amongest thornes.[37]

Various types of internal rhyme are found in Barbour,[38] Henryson,[39] Douglas,[40] and Lyndsay [41] : but it occurs much more frequently in Dunbar, Kennedy and Robert Sempill, and in many popular and satirical poems of the sixteenth century ; and, most frequently of all, in Alexander Scott and Alexander Montgomerie during the second half of the same century. In reading Alexander Scott's song " Favour is fair," [42] nobody can fail to be aware of its intricate metrical and alliterative pattern :

Favour is fair in luvis [a]lair, *[a] lore*
Yit freindschip [a]mair bene to commend ; *[a] more is*
But quhair despair bene adversare,
Nothing is thair bot wofull end.[43]

[36] Alexander Montgomerie, Sonn. XLII, in *Poems*, ed. CRANSTOUN, pp. 109 f.

[37] *Polwart and Montgomerie Flyting* : " Montgomerie to Polwart," ll. 1 ff., in *Poems of Alexander Montgomerie*, ed. J. Stevenson, supplementary vol., S.T.S., 1910 (here cited as (Montgomerie's) *Poems*, ed. STEVENSON), pp. 129 ff.

[38] *E.g.* IX.39-40.

[39] *E.g.* " Prayer for the Pest " (HARVEY WOOD, pp. 163 ff.), ll. 65-88.

[40] Esp. Prol. III, *passim.*

[41] Esp. in the *Papyngo.*

[42] In *The Poems of Alexander Scott*, ed. J. Cranstoun, S.T.S., 1896, (here cited as (Scott's) *Poems*, ed. CRANSTOUN), pp. 64 f., and BANN., VOL. IV, pp. 5 f. See, too, *Poems by Alexander Scott*, ed. Alexander Scott, Saltire Classics, 1952, in which, however, the texts are " modernised."

[43] Giving the rhyme-scheme (*aa*)(*ab*)(*aa*)(*ab*), where (*ab*) signifies a line having two halves, of which the first rhymes *a*, the second *b*. Note the alliteration.

As used in Scots poetry, internal rhyme often has rather a jarring effect and is usually much harsher than it is in Gaelic poetry. This is partly because the positions of internal rhymes are not fixed so rigidly in the Gaelic metres ; and partly because only vowels are rhymed in Gaelic, while all that is required of the consonants following the rhyming vowels is that they must belong to one of six groups of roughly similar consonants. Thus Gaelic rhymes are midway between the rigidity of true rhyme and the freedom of mere " assonance," and the resultant vowel harmony is less insistent than what an Irish writer has referred to as " the drums and fifes of rhyme." [44] There are traces, in Scots poetry, of this flexibility : rhymes are occasionally shifted, and rhyme sometimes gives place to assonance, as in Alexander Scott's love-song " Ye blindit *lu*varis, *lu*ke." [45]

It can scarcely be doubted that internal rhyme came into Scots poetry from medieval Latin, French, and English poetry ; but doubtless it was because it satisfied the needs of a public that had in some measure inherited the æsthetic values of Gaelic poetry that it enjoyed, in Scotland, such a special vogue. Gaelic poetry was, for the most part, transmitted orally. Though some Scots poets *may* never have read or heard a single line of Gaelic poetry, many of those for whom they wrote may well have inherited a predilection for the intricate metrical patterns of Gaelic poetry. Theirs was evidently the taste that most Scots poets of the fifteenth and sixteenth centuries were trying to satisfy when they lavished so much care on such ornamental features as alliteration and internal rhyme. We are not able to say whether Gavin Douglas deliberately adopted a Gaelic metre, or whether his ear was unconsciously following Gaelic modes, when he constructed such a very Gaelic rhyme pattern as :

[44] J. Patrick Byrne, " Assonance and modern Irish Poetry," in *Dublin Magazine* July-Sept. 1938, pp. 52-62. There are said to be about 300 rhyme-systems in Gaelic poetry. For a useful account, see *Bardachd Ghaidhlig*, ed. W. J. Watson, 2nd edn., Stirling 1932, pp. xxxvi-lxiii. In a typical *rann* of one *cumha* (lament) printed by Watson, the stressed vowels form the following pattern :

— a — — a —   — a — — ia — o
— i — — a —   — a — — ia — o
— i — — ó   — i — — ò — — o
— a — — à   — a — — à — o

All the correspondences are intentional, esp. those of the second and fourth stressed vowels in each line (Watson, *op. cit.*, pp. lvii-viii). I have known students, themselves native Gaelic-speakers, to fail or hesitate when asked to point out the rhymes in a stanza.

[45] In Scott's *Poems*, ed. CRANSTOUN, pp. 85 ff., and BANN., VOL. IV, pp. 102 ff.

The balmy vapour from thar sylkyn croppis
Distylland hailsum sugurat hunny droppis,
And sylver schakaris gan fra levis hyng
Wyth crystal sprayngis on the verdour yyng.[46]

As time went on, some of the resultant forms—such as the anonymous Chaucerian stanza "Quho wald do weill," [47] and that astonishing *tour de force* the "Ballat of Hairtis" [48]—became increasingly artificial, and increasingly full of mannerisms. Often—especially in its later developments, this late-sixteenth-century Scots poetic style is almost indistinguishable from Euphuism. Yet it had begun to take shape long before the conceits of Antonio de Guevara and his school appeared in Britain. Its characteristic modes of utterance truly expressed the spirit that underlies all Celtic art, and some of them have recently re-emerged in the work of James Joyce and other Anglo-Irish writers.

It is also important to realise that the rhythms of Scots poetry were largely determined by music, and especially dance music. In Gaelic, every poem is primarily a song, and it and its tune are virtually inseparable. In Scots—though many have come down to us without the tunes that originally belonged to them—most poems were songs, too, until well on in the eighteenth century, as witness the *Gude and Godlie Ballatis* or the lists in the *Complaynt of Scotland*.[49] The metre used by Montgomerie in *The Cherrie and the Slae* is that of "The Banks of Helicon," a tune said to have been composed in 1556 by the music master of the Chapel Royal; and in the seventeenth century, the Sempills of Beltrees, who form an essential link with the eighteenth, wrote songs in forms that were to become traditional poetic metres.

[46] Prol. xii (iv.89, ll. 9 ff.), giving the following scheme:

—	—	—	ai	—	—	—	yl	—	o	—
—	yl	—	ai	—	u	—	u	—	o	—
—	yl	—	ai	—	—	—	—	—	y	
—	y	—	ai	—	—	—	—	—	y	

—with complex additional alliterations (*s*, *cr*, *h*, *v*).

[47] Bann., vol. ii, p. 184.

[48] See Scott's *Poems*, ed. Cranstoun (above, n. 42), p. 30, and Bann., vol. iii, pp. 293 f.; in which the constant harping on the word "hairt" (nineteen times in one stanza!) provoked even Alexander Scott to exclaim (*Poems*, ed. Cranstoun, pp. 31 f., and Bann., vol. iii, p. 315) "For quhy it is so full of hairtis That myne within my bosum stairtis."

[49] *Complaynt* (above, n. 16), pp. 64, lxxxii ff. Recent discoveries (esp. the Dalhousie MS) have rescued the tunes of several of Scott's and Montgomerie's poems; the second of Thurston Dart's broadcasts on "Early Scottish Music" (B.B.C. Third Programme, 14 June 1955) contained one of Scott's, and four of Montgomerie's. In the first few years of its existence, the Edinburgh University School of Scottish Studies has collected 5000 folk songs and tunes, Scots and Gaelic.

The lilt of music and the steps of the Scottish country dances are at the bottom of much in Scottish poetry : the use of traditional metres, often very complicated ; of internal rhymes that might just be musical phrases ; and of frequent refrain on a thematic word, as in that well-known poem, in double common metre, in which Francis Sempill of Beltrees—his subjects being a dancer, Maggie Lauder, and a piper, Rab the Ranter—strikes, as it were, a recurrent tonic or dominant by ending the successive stanzas with the rhyme-words " L*au*der," " ch*an*ter," " ch*an*ter," " d*an*cer," " L*au*der." [50] The underlying musical pattern sustained the lively rhythm and dance of Scots verse forms even when they were no longer meant to be danced or sung.

The origin of some traditional Scots stanzas can be traced back to English models, but, once transplanted, they underwent a subtle change of mood and meaning. Dunbar's meditative pattern *a a b a b* continues to be frequent throughout our period, sometimes with a mock moral purpose. The most popular metre, however, sometimes simplyc alled " Scottis meter," is the eight-line *a b a b : b c b c* with four, five, or three feet ; it is often handled very deftly, the turn after the fourth line starting the counter-argument as if with a slightly raised voice. The interposition of short lines (of only one or two beats) between longer ones and the sharp scansion of the verse by means of internal rhyme are both nicely adjusted to the argumentative cast and shrewd humour of the Scottish mind ; while the short " bob " before the refrain of *Peblis to the Play* or *Christis Kirk on the Grene* is like a gasp or a sudden proud toss of the head :

To danse thir damysellis thame [a]dicht, — [a] *made ready*
  [a]Thir lassis licht of [b]laitis, — [a] *these* [b] *manners*
Thair gluvis wes of the [a]raffell rycht, — [a] *doeskin*
  Thair [a]schone wes of the [b]straitis, — [a] *shoes* [b] *kersey*
Thair kirtillis wer of [a]lyncome licht, — [a] (?) *Lincoln cloth*
  Weill prest with mony plaitis :
Thay wer so [a]nyss quhen men thame [b]nicht — [a] *fastidious* [b] *approached*
  Thay squeilit lyk ony [a]gaitis, — [a] *goats*
                So lowd,
At Chrystis-kirk on the grene that day.[51]

[50] According to the rules of Gaelic prosody, these are all strict rhymes.

[51] Giving the formula $a_4b_3abab\ ab : c_1D_4$ (*that day*)—in which b_3 means a line of three feet, rhyming *b*, and D_4 (*that day*) means a line of four feet invariably ending " that day." See BANN., VOL. II, p. 262, ll. 10 ff., and cp. Scott's " Justing and Debait," in Scott's *Poems*, ed. CRANSTOUN (above, n. 42), pp. 9 ff., and BANN., VOL. II, 343 ff., in which the stanzas 1-19 end " that day," stanza 20 " that nycht."

Three forms of this period need special consideration : the bob-and-wheel stanzas, the " Standard Habbie " or " Burns stanza," and the sonnet.

Stanzas in which, as in a reel, a careful build-up is followed by a sudden whisking movement always had a strong attraction for Scottish poets. The alliterative tales already mentioned usually have a bob and wheel.[52] In the long lines of the rather similar form adopted, with modifications, in parts of the *Polwart and Montgomerie Flyting*,[53] the speaker is only sparring with his opponent ; in the short ones following, he delivers a flurry of quick jabs. After the face-round of the bob, the wheel may also express intense personal feeling,[54] or fervent devotion,[55] sharply contrasted with the restrained, almost meditative, mood of the long opening phrases. The stave of *Christis Kirk on the Grene* is similar, but somewhat simpler. Its lively end is reminiscent of the steps of certain old traditional dances ; later, it came to be traditionally regarded as the proper metre in which to depict popular amusements.[56] The musical origin of the stanza used by Montgomerie in *The Cherrie and the Slae* [Sloe] has already been mentioned. Here is a typical stanza (ll. 29 ff.) :

The dew as dyamontis did [a]hing — *[a] hang*
Upon the tender [a]twiskis ying, — *[a] twigs*
  Owertwinkling all the treis
And [a]ay quhair flouris did [b]flureis fair, — *[a] wherever [b] flourish*
Thair suddenlie I saw repair
  Ane swarme of sounding [a]beis. — *[a] bees*
Sum swetlie hes the hony socht,
  [a]Quhill thay war [b]claggit [c]soir ; — *[a] till [b] clogged [c] sore*
Sum willinglie the wax hes wrocht
  To keip it up in store ;

[52] See for example the *Pistill of Susan*, in *Scottish alliterative Poems* (above, n. 2), which exemplifies the common formula $abab\ abab_4 : c_1 : ddd_2\ c_2$—where c_1 is the " bob," and $ddd_2\ c_2$ the " wheel."

[53] See, for example, " The second Pairt of Polwarts third Flyting," in Montgomerie's *Poems*, ed. STEVENSON (above, n. 37), pp. 173 ff., which exemplifies the formula $abab\ abab_4 : c_4ddd_3\ c_2$.

[54] As in the love-poem " In May in a morning " (BANN., VOL. III, pp. 285 ff.), the formula being $(ab)(ab)(ab)(ab)_4\ c_1 : ddd_3c\ _2$—in which $(ab)_4$ means a line containing four feet, and divided into two halves, the first of which rhymes *a*, the second *b*.

[55] As in Maitland's " Prayer " (MAIT. Q. LXXIII) with its formula $abba\ accd_5 : ee_2\ d_5$.

[56] Cp. Scott's " Justing " (above, n. 51).

So heipping, for keiping,
  Into thair hyves thay hyd it ;
Preciselie and wiselie
  For winter thay provyd it.[57]

Before Montgomerie adopted it, it had already been used by (among others) Sir William Kirkaldy of Grange in his *Ballat of the Captain of the Castle* (1571),[58] in which the first section usually contains an exposition, followed by a defiance in the second part (often introduced by " but "), while the quick rhymes of the wheel are used for flyting. Montgomerie finds a more congenial use : the lyric part with its tail-rhymes paints a picturesque and idyllic background ; the common metre of the middle brings action, chiefly in the first person ; and the wheel contains either a dancing lilt (" Sum singing, sum springing "), or a more meditative strain ; in the second half of the poem, with its insistence on argument, the wheel is like a last argumentative thumping on the table, as when Hope exclaims (ll. 538 ff.) :

Allace, man, thy cais, man,
  In [a]langerring I lament : — [a] *lingering*
Go to now, and do now,
  That Courage be content !

The Burns stanza [59] occurs, with no special characteristics, in troubadour lyrics of the twelfth century and soon appears in English poems and miracle plays.[60] In Scots, Lyndsay's *Satyre of the Thrie Estaitis* contains one rather nondescript example ; and the rest of the sixteenth century yields some two dozen instances all told, with some closely similar forms.[61] The sharply accentuated end is used by Alexander Scott for argumentative purposes, almost for flyting, but it may also be used humorously to express intentional naïveté,[62] mock love,[63] or satire. The stanza is usually couched in homely

[57] Giving the exceptionally complex formula $aa_4b_3\ cc_4b_3 : d_4e_3d_4e_3 : (ff)_2g_3\ (hh)_2g_3$, in which *f* and *h* normally have feminine endings : note that in Scots " wiselie " is pron. " wicelie," thus rhyming strictly with " preciselie," and that there is frequent alliteration. For text, see Montgomerie's *Poems*, ed. STEVENSON, pp. 2 ff., and *The Cherrie and the Slae*, ed. H. Harvey Wood, London 1937.

[58] In *Satirical Poems of the Time of the Reformation*, ed. J. Cranstoun, S.T.S., 2 vols., 1891-3, VOL. I, pp. 174 ff.

[59] $aaa_4b_2\ a_4b_2$. For specimens, see below, pp. 172, 177 ff., 208 f., 213.

[60] Cp. *The Poetry of Robert Burns*, Centenary Edn., edd. W. E. Henley and T. F. Henderson, 4 vols., 1896, VOL. I, pp. 335 ff.

[61] With, for example, b_1, b_3 or b_4 instead of b_2.

[62] As in " I met my lady weil arrayit," BANN., VOL. III, pp. 32 f.

[63] As in " In somer quhen floris will smell," *op. cit.*, pp. 26 f.

and expressive language.[64] The practice of ending it with a reiterated thematic word [65] can be traced back to a comparatively early date, and when, in the seventeenth century, the Burns stanza re-emerges after a period of neglect, it is in the guise of full-blown mock-elegy, such as " The Life and Death of the Piper of Kilbarchan, or The Epitaph of Habbie Simson," [66] by Robert Sempill of Beltrees—a poetic *genre* that has been a great favourite ever since. Sempill uses the first three lines to build up a picture that he suddenly pulls down in the short turn, and after a shrewd comment in the penultimate line (a_4) he falls back in gruff resignation : " but now he's *dead.*"

Is there, perhaps, a connexion between this special use of the Burns stanza and *ochtfhoclach mór*,[67] the metre of Gaelic *cumha* (lament, elegy), which first emerged in the sixteenth century? *Ochtfhoclach mór* is a stressed metre ; it has a refrain word, and in rhythm and structure closely resembles the first half of the Burns stanza. The rather similar *ochtfhoclach beag* [68] was used for the dance tunes allied with many Gaelic and Scots poems of tail-rhyme structure, such as Montgomerie's " Hay, nou the day dauis [dawns] " [69], and *ochtfhoclach mór* might also have reached non-Gaelic audiences on the wings of a common music.[70]

The sonnet belongs, in Scotland, to the court of James VI. There are several hundred Scottish sonnets, chiefly by Montgomerie, John Stewart of Baldynneis, and William Fowler. These are mostly in the " Spenserian " form—which Scottish poets used years before Spenser.[71] The Scottish sonnet seems partly to have grown out of

[64] As in " The Cruikit Liedis [lead] the Blinde," in *Satirical Poems . . . of the Reformation* (above, n. 58), VOL. I, pp. 128 ff.

[65] *E.g.* " away " in Maitland's " Satire on the Age," in MAIT. F., VOL. I, pp. 37 ff., and " vane " in Scott's " Pansing of lufe quhat lyf it leidis," in BANN., VOL. IV, pp. 96 f.

[66] Cp. below n. 119 ; reprinted in many anthologies, *e.g.* G. Eyre-Todd, *Scottish Poetry of the 17th Century*, 1895.

[67] Lit. " great octosyllabic."

[68] Lit. " Little octosyllabic."

[69] See Montgomerie's *Poems*, ed. CRANSTOUN, pp. 193 f. Dunbar and Douglas both mention the tune (" Hey tuttie, taittie," said to have been sung by the Scottish troops at Bannockburn), and the *Gude and Godlie Ballatis* give it sacred words.

[70] Cp. above, p. 61, n. 16. Lowland tunes were similarly introduced into Gaelic poetry in the eighteenth and nineteenth centuries : *e.g.* Duncan McIntyre's " Cumha Coire a' cheathaich, air fonn *Flowers of Edinburgh*," and William Livingston's " Fios thun a' Bhaird, air fonn *When the Kye come Hame*."

[71] This does not necessarily mean that Spenser copied it from the Scottish sonneteers. Though James VI's *Essayes of a Prentice* (1584), for which see *Poems of King James VI* (above, n. 27), pp. 1 ff., might have reached him in Ireland, Spenser's own æsthetic tendencies were similar to those of his Scottish contemporaries, and in the sonnet concatenation was in either case the natural result.

existing Scottish metres. Occasionally, an additional quatrain *c d c d* was added to the conventional Scottish metre *a b a b b c b c*, giving *a b a b b c b c c d c d*. More frequently, an additional couplet *d d* was tacked on, giving *a b a b b c b c d d*. And in order to convert this further development into a sonnet, it only remained to make use of both modifications at the same time, giving *a b a b b c b c c d c d e e*. This concatenation destroys the internal structure and graceful curve of the Italian sonnet ; instead, we have again the intricately knotted ornamentation of the Celtic crosses. This line of development leads finally to sonnets [72] in which the end-rhyme immediately preceding is repeated at the beginning of the next line and many words are even alliterated. This makes for a more intellectual pattern ; indeed, the Scottish sonneteers seem to widen the scope of the sonnet and apply it to wider purposes than their English and Continental brethren. On the other hand, Montgomerie and Mark Alexander Boyd were writing a more Italian form of the sonnet a generation before anything comparable appeared in England.

* * *

On surveying the contents of the poems lumped together in this chapter we find, of course, much conventional matter : love and despair, praise and complaint, petitions and eulogies, devotional and moral meditation. In this period, which contains Alexander Hume's rhymed sermons and many translations of psalms and hymns, religious poetry plays a more prominent part than ever before or later. Deep-felt devotion is the keynote of some of the poems in Bannatyne's religious section [73] ; some of Montgomerie's psalms have the jubilant sound of church music ; and the *Gude and Godlie Ballatis*, besides translations and adaptations of secular songs, contain some fine poetical accounts of the reckoning between a soul and its Maker. Nowhere, however, do we find anything mystical or metaphysical.

The Scots poetic genius is at its best when instead of following general or alien conventions it asserts its own rugged individuality, its own angular independence. The most truly lyrical poems are not concerned with youth but, much less conventionally, with old age.

[72] Such as Montgomerie's sonnets XLII-III, XLV, LXIV, in his *Poems*, ed. CRANSTOUN, pp. 109-11, 120 f.

[73] *E.g.* " Cum haly spreit," " We that ar bocht," and Clerk's " My wofull hairt," in BANN., XXIV, XXXIII, XXXVI, VOL. II, pp. 54 f., 71 ff., and 77 ff.

The anonymous "Welcume, Eild"[74] belongs, with its suggestive reticence, to the finest Scots poetry; and its two pair of socks, mittens, and afternoon nap engage our sympathies just as effectively as the opening of *The Testament of Cresseid.* The love poetry, too, is less memorable for any purely conventional effusion of tender feeling—for though the sixteenth century yields several charming love lyrics, the Scot remains as chary as ever of expressing too much tenderness—than for the vaunting tone that rings through Alexander Scott's lines

> Als gud luve cumis as gais,
> Or rathir bettir,[75]

or in the clarion refrain

> I am as I am and so will I be.[76]

It is a note that is often struck in Scots folk poetry, and it is heard again and again in the love-poems of the Bannatyne collection.[77] Not all of them, however, express the same defiant attitude, and there is a deep Henrysonian pathos in Fethe's poem "Pansing [pondering] in hairt,"[78] with its compulsive refrain

> Cauld, cauld culis the lufe that kendillis owr het.

In the finer love poems, there seems to be an intellectual fibre giving body to the emotion, as in the anonymous "My hairt is heich aboif [above],"[79] or Scott's "Rondel of Luve"[80]:

> Lufe is ane fervent fyre,
> Kendillit without desyre:
> Schort plesour, lang displesour;
> Repentance is the hyre;
> Ane pure tressour without measure:
> Lufe is ane fervent fyre.

As in Dunbar, the most notable in the poems in these collections are the extravaganzas and "ballats of vnpossibiliteis."[81] True Scots

[74] MAIT. F. LIX, VOL. I, pp. 205 ff.; with which cp. Kennedy's "Honour with Age," Maitland's "Solace in Age," and Alexander Hume's "To his sorrowfull Saull, Consolation," *op. cit.*, pp. 234 f., 329 f., and *Poems of Alexander Hume*, ed. A. LAWSON, S.T.S., 1902, pp. 34 ff.

[75] "In June the Jem" (ll. 29 f.), in Scott's *Poems*, ed. CRANSTOUN (above, n. 42), pp. 71 f., and BANN., VOL. IV, pp. 15 f.

[76] Anon., BANN., VOL. IV, pp. 2 f.

[77] Often, too, as in Helen B. Cruickshank's poem "The auld Wife speaks" (*Up the Noran Water*, 1934), it is expressed in the proverb: "There's better fish still in the sea."

[78] BANN., VOL. III, pp. 343 f.

[79] BANN., VOL. III, pp. 307. f.

[80] Scott's *Poems*, ed. CRANSTOUN, pp. 81 f., and BANN., VOL. IV, pp. 95 f.

[81] *E.g.* "I yeid [went] the gait [road] wes nevir gane," "Quhen Phebus fair," "Quhen that the mone [moon]," and "Quhen Phebus into the west" (BANN., VOL. III, pp. 66 f., 356 ff., and VOL. IV, pp. 42 ff.).

extravaganza is much less fully exemplified in the obstreperous horse-play of *Christis Kirk* and *Peblis to the Play*—which have both commonly been over-estimated—than in the sheer grotesque absurdity of *Colkelbie's Sow*, and of many another poem which gives intellectual delight by tracing a fantastic but logical pattern that forms a comic counterpart to the complex traceries of Celtic carved stones,[82] or, in fiddle music, the intricate rhythms and wicked tunes of many strathspeys and reels.[83] Whereas "the Englishman," as the late Agnes Mure Mackenzie put it, "is swept off his feet by the grotesque, the Scot smacks his bonnet on his head and plunges overboard." As we have already had occasion to point out, the grotesque is also given a free reign in Irish literature. *MacConglinne's Vision* [84] is not of another "Schlaraffenland" or Land of Cockaigne, but has the intellectual sharpness of grotesquerie, down to the bed-tick of butter. Similarly, in Clerk's "Robeyn's Jock come [came] to wow [woo] our Jynny,"[85] the "tocher [dowry]" is given down to the very fleas. Such extravagance is a permanent characteristic of Scottish literature: "Lord Fergus Gaist" [86] has the same eldritch fantasy (though not the same artistry) as *Tam o' Shanter*; and in "The Blythsome Bridal" Francis Sempill of Beltrees reveals the same knack of seizing on idiosyncracies as Leslie Mitchell ("Lewis Grassic Gibbon"), who looks at the world described in *Sunset Song* (1932) through the eyes of the small crofters, which fasten on the abnormalities, moral and physical, of their neighbours, and magnify them to proportions of grotesque absurdity. With this goes much irreverence, and much Scots scurrility [87] sufficiently vigorous to vie with that of Dunbar and Burns.

The grotesque element in Scots is not strictly identical, however,

[82] There is perhaps an indication that this spirit was of Celtic origin in "The Droichis [dwarf's] Part of the Play" (see BANN., VOL. II., pp. 315 ff., and Dunbar's *Poems*, ed. MACKAY MACKENZIE, pp. 170 ff.), in which most of the grotesque figures are Gaelic.

[83] *E.g.* "Quhy sowld nocht Allane honorit be?", "Lord Fergus Gaist [ghost,]" "In Tiberus Tyme," "Sym of Lyntoun," "The dumb Wife," and Lichtoun's "Dreme" (BANN., VOLS. II, pp. 285 f., 303 f., and III, pp. 13 f., 31 f.; and MAIT. F., VOL. I, pp. 69 f., 173 ff.) Among modern Scottish composers F. G. Scott is outstanding in his mastery of this wicked grotesqueness.

[84] See *Aislinge Meic Conglinne*, ed. and tr. Kuno Meyer, 1892.

[85] BANN., VOL. III, pp. 15 ff.

[86] BANN., VOL. II, pp. 303 f.

[87] *E.g.* Robert Sempill's "Ballat upoun Margret Fleming," "Defence of Crissell Sandelandis," and "Ballat of Janet Reid"; the anonymous "Use of Court"; and Clappertoun's "Wa worth Maryage" (for which see BANN., VOL. II, pp. 327 ff., and MAIT. F., pp. 193, 243 f.)

with that seen in Gaelic literature : it belongs more definitely to this world, and often is tinged with a certain grimness. A characteristic example is the piece entitled "How the first Helandman of God was maid of ane horss turd in Argylle," with its hard, dry laugh, and its canny shrewdness :

God turned owre the horss turd with his pykit staff,
And up start a Helandman blak as ony [a]draff... — [a] *spent malt*
God than he [a]lewch and [b]owre the dyk lap.[88] — [a] *laughed* [b] *jumped over the wall*

This Lowland variety of grim humour is perhaps most characteristically presented in Moffat's "Wyf of Auchtirmwchty," which rehearses the age-old tale of a husband who rashly "swaps jobs" with his wife—to his own utter discomfiture.[89] There is no loud laugh, the poet presents nothing but the facts, but you see a mischievous twinkle of the eyes. This humour promotes some quite serious political satire. It also gives rise to a kindlier satire of manners ; and from *Peblis to the Play* to Fergusson's *Leith Races*, Burns's *Holy Fair*, and, in our own day, R. G. Sutherland's *Embro to the Play*, satirical accounts of popular behaviour at fairs and festivals have been a regular feature of Scottish poetry.

The subtlety which underlies the broad humour of these poems also begets mock-heroic poems full of hidden wickedness that may easily be overlooked. Here is one more example of the Lowland Scot's inherited mistrust of fine sentiment ; for when confronted by a parade of feeling that an Englishman might be tempted to handle somewhat cavalierly, it gives the Scot a malicious satisfaction to take it down by apparently taking it seriously. This appears clearly enough in the various "Justings" by Dunbar, Lyndsay and Alexander Scott : but most critics have overlooked the mockery in Montgomerie's best-known poem, *The Cherrie and the Slae* [90]—one of the most popular Scots poems for centuries. Cast in the complex lyric stave already

[88] BANN., VOL. III, p. 84 ; cp. above, p. 7.

[89] BANN., VOL. II, pp. 320 ff. There is a rather scurrilous Latin version in *Silva sermonum jucundissimorum* (Basle 1568), which Laing reprints in the appendix of his *Select Remains*. The Scots poem however has more in common with the Irish folk-tale retold by Pádraig Ó Siochradha ("An Seabhac") in *An Baile seo 'gainne* under the title "Seán Croidhechráidhte," and modernised by Sean O'Casey in his one-act play *The End of the Beginning*. No English version is known, and the Scots version followed by Moffat may have been derived originally from Gaelic tradition.

[90] Above, n. 57.

mentioned, the poem begins with a series of exquisite images of nature.[91] But when, wantonly, the poet wounds himself with Cupid's arrow and lies sick with mingled longing for the inaccessible cherry and disdain of the sour slae in easy reach, Hope, Courage and other allegorical figures step in and strive for his good as they see it. Though slightly dull, this long didactic sequel is never entirely serious. In a true allegory, Montgomerie would have had to adopt a high style; as it is, he often uses a broad and pithy Scots, with a fair sprinkling of proverbs and humorous thrusts. There is mischief in the poet's eye when Cupid behaves

So [a]moylie so coylie, — [a] *demurely*
He luikit lyk ane [a]sant, — [a] *saint*

or when the poet himself is " in sik a ferie-farye [confusion] " or " moir lyk ane attomie nor man "; when Courage exclaims, " He is bot daft that hes ado "; and when Will, on being told that the poet must first be made a man, ironically replies " He lookes like one at least "—and later is " angrie as an ape." [92] Ramsay and Burns recognised this when they used the stanza for comic verse. Montgomerie also stops short of full seriousness when the allegorical figures indulge in the national hobby of arguing, each obstinately trying to make his point; I wonder whether the poet had his eye on the divines of the day, when his figures argue about principles, completely losing sight of the issue for 400 verses (Despair, Danger, Dreid are called " prechours "). The arguments are sound, however, and the poem affords a wonderfully Scottish interpretation of the virtues of peasant prudence, shrewd calculation, foresight, realism, and tenacity (not to say obstinacy). Together with the forcible and picturesque language, this may well account for the fact that *The Cherrie and the Slae* went through twenty-two editions before the time of Burns.

No account of the salient features of Scots poetry of this period would be complete without another look at the flytings, of which some follow the formal pattern, while others are genuinely impassioned. Of the formal sort, the most important are " The Flytting betwix the Sowtar [shoemaker] and the Tailyor " [93] and *Polwart and Montgomerie*

[91] Cp. the stanza quoted above, pp. 115 f.

[92] For these quotations, see Montgomerie's *Poems*, ed. Stevenson, pp. 8, ll. 111 f.; 18, l. 237; 20, l. 253; 26, l. 350; 101, l. 829; and 103, l. 883.

[93] Bann., vol. iii, pp. 22 f.

Flyting.[94] Both are poured forth with, if possible, even less restraint than " The Flyting of Dunbar and Kennedy," and both make full use of traditional vocabulary and traditional methods. In the preface to the *Polwart and Montgomerie Flyting,*[95] we are told that though the contestants bark, they do not bite, and that their flyting is only a game, or at most an exercise in generous professional emulation; and be that as it may, there are dozens of vituperative poems, often called flytings,[96] in which—whatever the occasion—merely to let fly at somebody appears to be valued for its own sake. Holland's *Howlat* [*Owl*] suggests that he was conscious of the Celtic origin of flyting, for the rook, as a bard speaking a mixture of Scots and Erse and quoting Irish kings, produces a fine bit of flyting and threatens to " rhyme " them if he does not get his food and drink.[97] Similarly, in one of his sonnets, Montgomerie reminds his listeners that unless his demands are met, he is able to " eternize " their names ; and when, in another, he gives warning that once he puts his tongue to serious scolding " it brings the flesh, lyk bryrie [?], fra the banes [bones]," we instantly recall the Gaelic belief that a poet's curse could literally raise blisters.[98] The verse usually is heavily alliterated : sometimes, however, the opening is aureate—till the poet takes off his coat and rolls up his sleeves ; this recalls the similar device of contrast in Dunbar's " The twa mariit Wemen and the Wedo." Though rarely, if ever, absent in those flytings that are genuinely invective, the delight afforded by the creation of extravagant patterns is most pronounced in the more conventional ones.

The Scots poetry of the time also shows an undiminished feeling for nature, together with an assured mastery of detailed poetic landscape. This legacy from Henryson and Dunbar is particularly

[94] Above, n. 37.

[95] This preface (printed in Montgomerie's *Poems,* ed. CRANSTOUN, p. 57) is probably by Drummond of Hawthornden.

[96] Dunbar, Kennedy, Scott, Montgomerie, and Sempill are by no means the only authors whose flytings occur in BANN., MAIT., *Satirical Poems . . . of the Reformation* (above, n. 58), or even in the *Gude and Godlie Ballatis.* In Scots, " flyte " still means " scold."

[97] *Howlat* (above, n. 4), ll. 791 ff..

[98] See Montgomerie's Sonnets XX, LXII (" Apologie to the Kirk of Edinburgh "), in *Poems,* ed. CRANSTOUN, pp. 98 f., 119 f. ; and with the latter cp. E. G. Cox, " The Case of Scotland *vs.* Dr Samuel Johnson," in *Transactions of the Gaelic Society of Inverness,* XXXIII (1932), pp. 49 ff. Cranstoun's suggestion that " lyk bryrie " means " like mad " is most unconvincing, and (as Sir W. A. Craigie has suggested) the true reading is probably " brynie [breast plate]."—In *MacConglinne's Vision,* the scholar threatens to " satirise " those who refuse his demands.

conspicuous in "Quhen Tayis bank was blumyt brycht,"[99] in the first 350 lines of *The Cherrie and the Slae*, and in Alexander Hume's *Day estivall*.[100] The last is the most remarkable, for though the midday heat, the wine and the peaches perhaps are reminiscences of the poet's sojourn in France, the poem as a whole is devoted to nature, both for its own sake and as an integral part of human experience. Beginning with the light effects that he sees at sunrise, and following the day throughout its course, the poet observes the country folk and their activities, registers a richly evocative impression of vibrating midday heat—its stillness a-quiver with the humming of bees, while

> The stabill ships upon the [a]sey, — [a] *sea*
> [a]Tends up their sails to drie, — [a] *stretch*

and "ilk plaister wall" and pavement reflects the heat—and watches finally as the shadows lengthen and the west is "painted . . . pourpour." All these poems contain sharp observation and many precise perceptions of eye and ear.[101] All who know Scotland are well acquainted with the fascination of its transparent, evasive light : and in its ever-changing play on running water Scottish poets have found endless delight.[102] As we have seen, Montgomerie notes the dew "owertwinkling all the treis" ; and in his description of the cherries that hung above his head, like "twinkling rubeis round and reid," he tells how their "schaddow" showed in the river, and

> Reflex of Phebus in the firth
> [a]Now cullorit all thair [b]knoppis — [a] *(?) new* [b] *knobs*
> With dancing and glansing
> In [a]tirlis lik [b]dornik champ. — [a] *twirls* [b] *Tournay cloth*

Hume's eye is even more alert to such effects—not only to the stars and the sunrise, to resplendent sunlight,[102] to the dew, or to plumage

[99] BANN., VOL. III, pp. 296 ff.

[100] *Poems*, ed. LAWSON (above, n. 74), pp. 25 ff.

[101] Cp. Montgomerie, *The Cherrie and the Slae*, in which "Echo answerit ay," and a waterfall plays "the ci-sol-fa-uth cleif" (*Poems*, ed. STEVENSON, pp. 4, l. 48 and 8, l. 91) ; and Hume, *The Day estivall*, in which the "cessile air" of the afternoon is so silent that "hils and dails and forrest fair" re-echo "every cry and call" (*Poems*, ed. LAWSON, p. 28, ll. 85 ff.).

[102] Quite independently of Turner and Monet, William McTaggart (1835-1910) and many other Scottish landscape-painters have been fascinated by the problem of rendering light. See D. P. Bliss, "Painting," in *Some Scottish Arts* (above, p. 62, n. 20).

[103] To another anonymous Scottish poet his lady's hair seemed in his dream (BANN., VOL. III, p. 308, l. 16) "lyk the oppynnit silk." Unfortunately, two pages of the MS are missing, and this fine poem is incomplete.

shimmering in the sun, but also to the appearance of light as seen through mist and rain. Like so many Scots and Scottish Gaelic poets, he is fascinated by the crystal clarity of the burn—and by the trout and the salmon he sees in it, and in *The Day estivall* he describes (ll. 205 ff.) the special clarity of a reflexion seen in the light of evening :

What pleasour were to walke and see,
[a]Endlang a river cleare, *[a] along*
The perfite forme of everie tree,
Within the deepe appeare ?

Some of Hume's observations show a greater precision than ever before, occasionally even a scientific spirit. Sometimes he tries to isolate and analyse an impression, and so creates static moments of very sharp outline, as in this image (ll. 79 ff.) of trees and sea as they appear in the silent heat of noon :

[a]Nor thay were painted on a wall, *[a] than if*
[a]Na mair they move or [b]steir. . . . *[a] no more [b] stir*
The [a]wals, that [b]woltring wont to be, *[a] waves [b] heaving*
Are stable like the land.

The attitude that lies behind the fixity of these images is more intensely subjective than ever : as if to prove that all things, even perceptions, are relative, the poet takes the impressions that he receives from the outside world, and by refashioning them creates his own reality. (As we saw, there already were some hints of a similar tendency in Dunbar, and even in Henryson.) Often—as when, in " Tayis Bank," the brilliant flowers are " blacht [bleached] and blew "[104] beside the beauty of the poet's love—this refashioning of nature is somewhat conventional : but there is no reason to doubt that Montgomerie is describing an actual experience when he tells how he stared at the stars,

Sum reid, sum yallow, sum blew, sum grene

till everything appeared two to his " barbulyeit [bewildered] braine." The perfect expression of this subjectivising tendency occurs in " What is beauty ? "—a gem-like little poem, possibly by William Fowler :

I make thee faire in thinking thou art so.[105]

[104] BANN., VOL. III, p. 298, l. 65.

[105] See *The Works of William Fowler*, edd. H. W. Meikle, J. Craigie and J. Purves, S.T.S. 3 vols., 1914-40, VOL. I, p. 389.

With respect to style, too, the background of the fifteenth and sixteenth centuries repeats much that we have recognised in the foreground figures.[106]

★ ★ ★

But already we have overstepped the historical limit laid down at the beginning of this chapter. In making a brief retrospective survey of the development from the second half of the sixteenth century we must try to indicate how and why this tradition came to an end. It has often been suggested that the diaster of Flodden (1513) was the beginning of the end. Flodden was certainly a severe shock: but during the next half-century we have David Lyndsay and ALEXANDER SCOTT (*fl.*1545-68)—lesser poets, admittedly, but true exponents of the Scots tradition in literature. Scott's poems, which have been preserved only in the Bannatyne MS, are purely lyrical. In their usually intricate verse patterns, the rhythms of song and dance are elaborately embroidered with aureation and alliteration; but Scott also enriches the tradition with injections of the *dolce stil nuovo* of the Italianate school in European literature. Even so, Scott is no slavish imitator of foreign fashions. In his poetry, Petrarcan love keeps its feet on the ground, and there is something unusually hard about it; it speaks with a Scots accent, and native intellectual shrewdness. Scott's poems are not mere pegs on which to hang melodies; they are poems in their own right, and such is his mastery of the refrain that in it is concentrated—even more than in Dunbar—his quintessential meaning. His poetry shows, at any rate, that the Scots tradition was still capable of development.

In the meantime, Scotland was swung over to the Reformation (1560). Whether it is true or not, as sometimes alleged,[107] that Calvinism blighted the arts, it was bound to have deep effects on Scotland's national culture. It cut the old cultural ties with France; and although the Wedderburnes who compiled the *Gude and Godlie*

[106] *E.g.*, the keen sense of dramatic situation; the vivid comparisons; the tender intimacy; the reticence or understatement in expressing genuine emotion, cp. Hume, "To his sorrowfull Saull, Consolatioun" (above, n. 74); the spirit of democracy and independence, cp. Hume's "Epistle to Maister Gilbert Mont-creif" (in his *Poems*, ed. LAWSON, pp. 68 ff.), and Scott's "New Yeir Gift" (above, n. 34), with its echoes of John the Common-weill.

[107] *E.g.*, by Agnes Mure Mackenzie, Maurice Lindsay, and others. On the other side of the question, see M. P. Ramsay, *Calvin and Art* (1938: a most stimulating book), and Ian Finlay, *Scotland*, 1945, etc.

Ballatis sought to establish new connexions with Germany, Scotland as a whole now turned her face towards England, all the more so since the Bible itself, and most of the relevant controversial literature, were in English ; people became so accustomed to hearing and reading the Word of God in English that, perhaps unconsciously, they began to regard English as the proper language for all serious, dignified subjects. Many minds were absorbed by fervent controversies, while others tried to escape from contemporary life : there is an escapist attitude in some of the finest poems of the time. Some of the controversialists did not indeed throw in the whole of their forces : though, for example, the Bannatyne MS contains some delightfully indelicate poems by Robert Sempill, a precursor of journalism, he appears in *Satirical Poems of the Time of the Reformation*[108] as one of the most fanatically Knoxian writers. The poetry of ALEXANDER HUME (?1557-1609) is a good example of how some of the finest minds forsook poetry to serve a higher cause. In the dedication, "To the Scottish Youth," of his *Hymns* (1599, but dated 1594) he confesses that he too had followed the paths of secular poetry, which sings of fleshly, illicit love ; but now he sets out to show the right use of a Christian talent. His poems prove, as he acknowledges, that his "rule" precludes the writing of great poetry, inasmuch as it is the cause that matters, not the art, and he must not aggrandise himself. (Perhaps he had temporarily lost sight of the "cause" when he wrote *The Day estivall*, his finest poem.)

Was Scottish Calvinism the cause or the effect of so much that is characteristically Scottish ? The answer lies outside our scope. But we have seen that many of the characteristics often attributed to it —such as the austerity, the readiness to argue even with God, the shrewdness, the mistrust even of happiness[109]—were there from the beginning. Even before the Reformation, education had been, moreover, of prime importance in Scotland ; but, partly as a result of those characteristics, Scottish humanism flowed in narrower channels than elsewhere, and education was harnessed to severely practical purposes—certainly not to the cultivation of personality or to idle dalliance with mere beauty. In Scotland there were no University Wits.

The Renaissance indeed gained a foothold at the court of James VI : but here we come to another important factor in the decline of the

[108] Above, n. 58.

[109] Cp. Henryson and Gavin Douglas (above, pp. 50-1, and 83.

Scots literary tradition. James VI himself had literary ambitions. At court, he gathered together, and promoted, a number of writers, among them his friend [110] and distant kinsman ALEXANDER MONTGOMERIE (?1545-?1615), the last poet of the Scots tradition who mastered all its different modes: flyting, high style, popular pieces full of proverbial folk speech, and lyrical songs full of exquisite beauty [111]—in fact he seems almost a latter-day Dunbar. As a sonneteer he owed much to Ronsard. He it was who created the vogue of the Scottish sonnet; he helped, too, to introduce the Italian form, though here he had a predecessor in MARK ALEXANDER BOYD (1563-1601), by whom it was first taken up. But Montgomerie gradually lost contact with the essentials of the Scots tradition; his later poetry falls apart into various unconnected groups, and his work sometimes displays more form than substance. Yet he deserves a place of honour.

Mark Alexander Boyd's "Sonet," his only surviving poem, is contained in a single contemporary printed version now in the National Library of Scotland:

Fra banc to banc, fra [a]wod to wod, I rin — *[a] wood*
[a]Owrhailit with my feble fantasie, — *[a] overwhelmed*
Lyc [a]til a leif that fallis from a trie — *[a] to*
Or til a [a]reid owrblawin with the wind. — *[a] reed*
Twa gods [a]gyds me: the ane of tham is blind, — *[a] guide*
Ye, and a [a]bairn brocht up in vanitie; — *[a] child*
The nixt a wyf ingenrit of the [a]se, — *[a] sea*
And lichter [a]nor a [b]dauphin with hir fin. — *[a] than [b] dolphin*

Unhappie is the man for evirmaire
That [a]teils the sand and [b]sawis in the aire, — *[a] tills [b] sows*
Bot twyse unhappier is he, I lairn,
That [a]feidis in his hairt a mad desyre, — *[a] feeds*
And follows on a woman throu the fyre,
Led [a]be a blind and [b]teichit [a]be a bairn. — *[a] by [b] taught*

This sonnet sums up much that is best in the tradition of the Makars. In the simplicity and directness of the language, as well as in the use of metre for the sake of intensity of expression, we seem to have

[110] At least until he was banished from Court.

[111] *E.g.*, in addition to those already mentioned, "Quhat mightie Motione," "Evin dead behold I breath," "In throu the Windoes of myn Ees," "Adeu, O Desie [daisy] of Delyt" (*Poems*, ed. CRANSTOUN, pp. 135 f., 158 f., 161 ff., 189 f.).

swung back full circle to Henryson. But Boyd shows himself a man of the Renaissance, not only by dealing in classical mythology, but also by the intensely personal note of his poem ; his sonnet illustrates how well Scots poetry was able to keep contact with the European development[112]—and be none the less Scottish for that : what other poetry could be shrewd enough to speak of Venus as a " wife " ? Mark Alexander Boyd has shed the artificiality that had become so conspicuous in the Scottish tradition of the sixteenth century, and like Henryson he achieves his greatness by clothing a serious subject of general cultural importance in the colloquial speech of his country : the form is that of a courtly lyric, the language simple and of the folk —art and folk poetry combine to create such an intensity of passion, such a fire of emotion as only the greatest poetry has. We see the Scots intense economy of expression, the translation of thought into a sharp and realistic picture, and the harshness that stifles a sob. This is the last example for centuries where popular and literary poetry touch.

The Anglicising tendency that had set in even before the Union of the Crowns (1603) was accelerated by the removal of the Court from Edinburgh to London. The courtly poets who followed the King south soon strove to write English. Their work, neither better nor worse than that of most of their English brethren, was soon merged in the broad stream of English poetry. Few books, moreover, were yet printed outside London ; and for all these reasons, Scots seemed doomed as a language fit for serious literary purposes. Sir Robert Aytoun (1570-1638),[113] who had studied in Paris and lived at court, wrote English even before the Union of the Crowns. He was followed by William Drummond of Hawthornden (1585-1649),[114] whose largely imitative poetry hardly contains anything Scottish, except an " Entertainment " given by the City of Edinburgh for King Charles, and some short humorous pieces that the author did not care to publish.

[112] In this connexion, Mr R. L. C. Lorimer has pointed out to me that the last line of Boyd's " Sonet " is, in effect, a compressed translation into Scots of the last two lines of Ronsard's sonnet " Qui voudra voir . . . " (*Oeuvres choisies de P. de Ronsard*, ed. C. A. Sainte-Beuve, Paris 1879, pp. 1f.): ". . . que l'homme se deçoit / quand plein d'erreur *un aveugle* il reçoit / *pour sa conduite*, un enfant pour *son maistre*." It would be interesting to know how many more echoes of sixteenth-century French poetry Boyd's sonnet contains.

[113] His English poems were edited by C. Roger 1844 (revised 1871) : see also *Transactions of the Royal Historical Society*, 1 (1875).

[114] See *The poetical Works of William Drummond of Hawthornden*, ed. L. E. Kastner, S.T.S., 2 vols., 1913.

At Court we also find Drummond's uncle, William Fowler,[115] the Queen's secretary ; Sir William Alexander, Earl of Stirling (1580-1640),[116] with his Senecan tragedies ; Sir David Murray of Gorthy (1567-1629)[117] ; Sir William Mure of Rowallan (1594-1657)[118] ; and others. Their poetry reflects the life of the Stuart Court, though still with a certain shrewdness, and an occasional earthiness. They do not seem like provincials come up to the capital, but have something of the European outlook of Scottish culture : both Fowler (who translated *Il Principe*) and John Stewart of Baldynneis went back to Petrarch, Tasso, and Ariosto, and Montgomerie to Ronsard ; while Drummond borrowed from the Pléiade, from Italian and even Spanish poets, and his library was a fine picture of European culture.[119]

Now that the vital connexion between courtly and popular was severed, the sap went out of Scots literary poetry. The Kirk appropriated some of what was left. But below the surface there remained popular poetry, never printed, in " guid hamelie Scots " that seemed unfit for higher and more intellectual purposes. Untouched by the Renaissance and the new humanism, it survived with the dance tunes to which its metres were adapted, and when sometimes we catch a glimpse of it it retains many traditional characteristics, as in the poems of the Lairds of Beltrees, Robert Sempill (or Semple), the father (1595) and Francis, the son (1616-82).[120] Their work is one of the few surviving links between the Scots poetry of the late sixteenth century and that of the revival that took place during the eighteenth ; but only its more popular elements were destined to provide materials for Burns : Sempill's mock elegy of Habbie Simson, the song of the dancer Maggie Lauder and the piper, the folk amusement of " The Blythsome Bridal " or " Hallow Fair ", the folk-song " Old Longsyne ", or the humorous allegory " The Banishment of Poverty." But there was another powerful stream of oral popular poetry, the ballads.

115 Above, n. 105.

116 See *The poetical Works of Sir William Alexander, Earl of Stirling*, edd. L. E. Kastner and H. B. Charlton, S.T.S., 2 vols., 1921-9.

117 See his *Works*, ed. T. Kinnear, Bannatyne Club, 1823.

118 See *The Works of Mure of Rowallan*, ed. W. Tough, S.T.S., 2 vols., 1898.

119 See his *Works*, ed. Kastner, introd.

120 There is some doubt as to the attribution of " The Blythsome Bridal " and " Maggie Lauder " ; they may be by other hands, or, more probably, re-workings of older popular poems, as " Old Longsyne " almost certainly is. See *The Poems of the Sempills of Beltrees*, first collected edn., with notes and biographical notices, Edinburgh 1849.

V

A Treasure-trove: The Scottish Ballads

"A BALLAD," says Gordon Hall Gerould, "is a folk-song that tells a story with stress on the crucial situation, tells it [dramatically] by letting the action unfold itself in event and speech, and tells it objectively with little comment or intrusion of personal bias."[1] We are not concerned here with theories of ballad origin, but it is essential to understand that the present form of the ballads with which we are concerned is largely determined by two factors: singing and tradition. Whether ultimately derived from a form of dance or not—and there is no evidence in Scotland of danced ballads[2]—the ballads were sung to a recurrent tune[3] which helped to shape the metrical form, often including a refrain which gives a touch of lyricism[4]; strophic singing also strengthened the emphasis on what was essential, focussed the action sharply, and created a suitable medium for the "leaping and lingering" pace (Gummere) of the ballads. No matter by whom it was originally composed, every ballad

[1] See G. H. Gerould, *The Ballad of Tradition*, 1932, (hereinafter cited as GEROULD), p. 11.—Unless otherwise stated, all quotations in this chapter are from the standard collection, *The English and Scottish popular Ballads*, ed. F. J. CHILD, 5 vols., 1882-98 (reprinted New York 1956). In accordance with custom each is cited by means of the number that Child assigns to it, and after a CHILD number, "A.2.1" means "version A, stanza 2, line 1." See also *English and Scottish popular Ballads*, edd. H. C. Sargent and G. L. Kittredge, based on CHILD, 1 vol., 1904; and *Border Ballads*, ed. W. Beattie, Penguin Books, 1952, which contains a good Scottish selection.

Recent studies include G. H. GEROULD (above); Edwin Muir, "A Note on the Scottish Ballads," in *Latitudes*, 1924; W. J. Entwistle, *European Balladry*, 1939 (corrected 1950), here cited as ENTWISTLE; E. K. WELLS, *The Ballad Tree*: *A Study of British and American Ballads* (with 60 traditional ballads and their tunes), 1950, here cited as WELLS; M. J. C. HODGART, *The Ballads*, 1950, here cited as HODGART, and W. Macneile Dixon, "English and Scottish Ballads," in *An Apology for the Arts*, 1944. Cp. also E. K. Chambers, *English Literature at the Close of the Middle Ages*, Oxford Histories of English Literature, 1945.

[2] The "dances" of "Robene Hude," "Thom of Lyn," and "Jhonne Ermistrang" are mentioned in *The Complaynt of Scotland* (above, p. 105, n. 16), pp. 66, lxxxvii: but these are not likely to have been, in the accepted sense, danced ballads.

[3] On the music, see esp. HODGART and GEROULD. Usually it is modal, monodic, and homophonic. Scottish ballad tunes have close affinities with Gaelic folk music (cp. HODGART, and M. Lindsay in *Some Scottish Arts*).

[4] Refrains occur more frequently in oral tradition than in MS or printed versions, in which they are often dropped for convenience' sake. Ballads which Child printed without refrains have since been found with them (WELLS, ch. 4).

was created anew, *re-made*, every time it was sung, and its final form was thus in effect a product of communal " editing "[5] as it was handed down in oral tradition. Thus ballads throve in, and expressed the attitude of, small homogeneous communities which remained untouched by the " art " or " literary " poetry of the time, and thus were free to develop a set of poetic conventions totally their own. These led to the use of a standard vocabulary and certain stock phrases, and similar incidents were narrated in the same or similar words (so that whole stanzas were sometimes borrowed from other ballads), with incremental repetition, conventional colours, and so forth. Out of these " primitive " conventions (or simplifications) there arose a stylised but apparently artless poetic form which allowed all the more intensity and set free the individual imagination. Being (in the sense already defined) of communal origin, the ballads are rich in old folklore harking back to pre-Christian times ; they contain a whole network of primitive taboos,[6] magic numbers, old superstitions, and a powerfully expressive pagan mythology, all fundamentally symbolic of the essential realities of human experience. For reasons given below, this element of folk-belief and paganism is especially prominent in the Scottish ballads.

Balladry is international, and ballad themes have wandered freely to and fro.[7] It may seem that in setting out to study the Scots ballads as a branch of the national literature, or even in calling them Scots, we are begging a very big question. As already emphasised, all ballads are, however, a communal product, and have, therefore, a communal spirit. It is only to be expected that the communal spirit expressed in the Scots ballads will, in many respects, resemble the spirit of the common folk in other countries : but if it is truly communal it must also display its own specifically Scottish, national characteristics. In this chapter we are faced, therefore, with a twofold question : How do the Scottish ballads, or the Scottish versions of international ballad themes, compare with those of other countries, and what place do they have in the total pattern of Scottish poetry ?

Ballads have an unusually important place in Scottish literature : perhaps only Denmark has such a large, compact body of ballads of

[5] See Sir Alexander Gray, *Arrows, a Book of German Ballads and Folksongs attempted in Scots*, 1932, preface.

[6] For an excellent summary, see Wells, ch. 5.

[7] Cp. Entwistle. According to Gerould, 80 or 90 of the 305 ballads in Child have been shown to be " international," though partly of British, partly of European origin ; and 25 ballad stories are common to Britain and Scandinavia, but to no other country.

such artistry, poetic intensity, and dramatic power. Some of Barbour's lines read as if they had been taken over from ballads, and the songs sung by "young wemen" about Sir John de Soulis (*Bruce*, XVI.519) may actually have been ballads; if so, Barbour's mention of them is the earliest reference to ballads in Scottish literature. Pitscottie's account of Johnny Armstrong in his *Chronicle* corresponds *verbatim*, in all the more striking incidents, with "Johnie Armstrong"[8]; and several known ballads are referred to by name in *The Complaynt of Scotland* (*c.* 1550), which mentions the ballads of "the battle of the Hayrlau (Harlaw)" of 1411 and on "the huntis of Chevet" and "the Perssee and the Montgumrye met,"[9] as well as the "dances" of "Thom of Lyn," "Robene Hude" and "Johnne Ermistrang." The heyday of Scottish ballads was in the sixteenth, seventeenth, and eighteenth centuries[10]; their transmitted form belongs, as a rule, to the eighteenth century, when they were first collected and printed. All the evidence suggests that in Scotland ballads were handed down (and continuously re-created) in a living, unbroken oral tradition from before the Reformation (1560) until the time of Allan Ramsay and even of Walter Scott. A late gleaning early in the present century produced a rich harvest in the North-East,[11] and the School of Scottish Studies in Edinburgh is still finding living ballads.[12] In England, on the other hand, broadsheets, and the minstrels before them, had had their effect on the ballad,[13] and the eighteenth century brought a revival, not a continuation (WELLS). The later date of the extant form of Scottish ballads—few go back to before the sixteenth century—has usually been taken to imply that they flourished later in Scotland.

[8] CHILD, 169.C. Pitscottie's account (for which see Lindesay of Pitscottie's *Historie and Chronicles of Scotland*, ed. Æ. J. G. Mackay, S.T.S., 3 vols., 1899-1911, VOL. I, p. 335), includes all the most striking incidents, and some actual phrases, *e.g*, "He weened he was king as well as he," "What wants that knave that a king suld have?" and "I have asked grace at a graceless face." This shows how closely the language of the ballads was related to common Scots speech. Cp. below, pp. 144-50 (n. 68).

[9] Probably earlier versions of "The Battle of Otterburn" and its variant "The Hunting of the Cheviot" (CHILD, 161-2). The battle was fought in 1388.

[10] Cp. CHILD, 169-206, 208-10.

[11] The late GAVIN GREIG's *Last Leaves of traditional Ballads and ballad Airs collected in Aberdeenshire*, ed. A. Keith, Aberdeen 1925 (here cited as GREIG), contains between 1 and 14 new versions of each of 108 of the ballads in CHILD.

[12] Some years ago, Mr H. Henderson, one of the School's research fellows, obtained in living oral tradition near Turriff (Aberdeenshire) versions of a number of ballads, among them "The Earl of Aboyne" (CHILD, 235), which were known from an 18th-cent. MS, but had never been heard sung before.

[13] Owing to the Kirk's early control of the press, Scotland can boast practically no early broadsides of ballads.

But on the other hand we have the well-known close relationship of the Scots and the Danish ballads, and in England, too, the area of the Danelaw is the most fertile in balladry. Strong though they were, trade connexions alone can hardly be responsible ; the reason for the relationship must be sought at an earlier date, when Danes were constant " guests " on the shores of the country. The existing evidence, in my opinion, tends rather to prove that the tradition of creating and re-creating ballads has never died out in Scotland—though of course, its later stages are much better known to us than its earlier ones.

★ ★ ★

What are the reasons for the greater vitality and importance of the ballads in Scotland ? The answer lies partly in the fact that ballads thrive best in the harsh social climate of a border community, and this first category of BORDER BALLADS is the most important. England and Scotland of course had a common border : both geographically and politically, however, it was much more important to Scotland, the smaller country. And Scotland had other borderlands. Significantly, the Battle of Harlaw (1411), which was only in fact an ordinary feudal conflict,[14] is interpreted in the ballad of the same name (CHILD, 163) as a decisive encounter between Highland and Lowland, Gael and Saxon ; and it is in Aberdeenshire, where Highland and Lowland meet (and where Harlaw was fought), that the richest living tradition of balladry exists.

Oddly enough, the struggle of Gael with Norseman in the West Highlands and Islands seems to have left very little trace in Scotland's balladry. The usual verdict is that the Gaels with their strict and artistic bardic poetry never developed ballads.[15] This may be true of Ireland, but in Gaelic Scotland we find a vigorous strain of folk

[14] Alexander, Earl of Ross (whose daughter had become a nun), d. 1406. Alexander's sister m. Donald, Lord of the Isles, who in her name laid claim to the vacant earldom. Alexander's father-in-law, Albany, the Governor of Scotland, also laid claim on behalf of his son, John, Earl of Buchan. Donald (who had a Lowland mother and had offered his allegiance to Henry IV of England) was opposed by the Mackays and the Frasers before finally encountering the Earl of Mar and the Provost of Aberdeen with a force of Lowlanders at Harlaw in 1411.

[15] See D. Corkery, *The hidden Ireland*, 1925, p. 63, followed by ENTWISTLE and others.

poetry which at least has much in common with ballads.[16] There are a number of songs on battles and executions that have many of the characteristics of the true ballad—its symbolism, selectively dramatic presentation, localism, conventional colours, intensity and " primitive " style—and also like all ballads presuppose some knowledge of the events which they narrate : these characteristics are obvious in the lament for Gregor Roy McGregor of Glenstrae, beheaded at Kenmore in 1570, or in that for Donald MacDonald, killed in the Battle of Cairinnis in 1601, a poem written by his foster-nurse, Nic Coisean.[17] But the development of Scottish Gaelic popular poetry with ballad characteristics is much too recent to take advantage of the typical ballad situation as it had existed at the time of the clash between Gael and Norseman. Nor are these Scottish Gaelic poems truly ballads : most of them are in the first person, and are both more lyrical and more specific than most true ballads. Both as regards motifs and outlook, the ballad tradition finds a closer parallel in Scottish Gaelic folk tales, such as " An dà Chraoibh Ghaoil (The two Love Trees) " or " An Nighean a reiceadh (The Lass who was sold)." [18] These are remarkably different from Irish folk tales : in the Scottish tales, according to John G. McKay,[19] the acquisition of anything coveted is usually fatal, and there is accordingly a flavour of tragic fatalism which I for one find strongly reminiscent of the ballads.

The Border was a melting-pot into which were thrown Gaelic and Cymric Celt, Dane and Angle, Scot and Englishman. Here we find traditions of King Arthur and William Wallace interwoven with survivals of paganism, Norwegian saga, and Border history. The nonsense refrain of some ballads, as well as some counting-out games of the nursery, are sometimes believed to be remnants of Gaelic or Cymric.[20] The unusual predominance of the mother in the Scots ballads is perhaps a faint echo of the matrilineal social system of the

[16] See D. S. Thomson, " Scottish Gaelic Folk-poetry *ante* 1650," in *Scottish Gaelic Studies*, VIII (1955), pp. 1 ff. Cp. also *Heroic Verse from the Book of the Dean of Lismore*, ed. and tr. N. Ross, S.G.T.S., 1939, pp. xvi ff., and D. S. Thomson, *Macpherson and his Sources*, 1951, pp. 3 ff.

[17] For the first, see *Comhchruinneacha do dh' Orain taghta, Ghaidealach*, ed. Paruig Mac-an-Tuairneir (Patrick Turner), Edinburgh 1813, p. 286, and *Bardachd Ghaidhlig*, ed. W. J. Watson, 2nd edn., Stirling 1932, pp. 244 ff., for the second, *The Macdonald Collection of Gaelic Poetry*, edd. A. and A. Macdonald, Inverness 1911, pp. ix f., 31.

[18] See *More West Highland Tales*, ed. J. G. Mackay, VOL. I (1940), pp. 278 ff., 292 ff.

[19] *Op. cit.*, p. 277.

[20] WELLS, pp. 95, 158.

Picts (and the Gaels ?),[21] and in " Bewick and Graham " [22] we are reminded of the Celtic custom of fosterage.

Topographically, the Border was cut off from the rest of Scotland by a belt of hill and muir, and from the South by the Roman Wall ; historically, it was a country of almost incessant warfare ; politically and culturally, it was more or less autonomous—a " debatable land " possessed by a sturdy race of freedom-loving outlaws who honoured valour above victory, and were incapable, even when defeated, of admitting they were beaten. Though often at feud with one another, the Borderers stood together against any outsider, especially the " King of Lothian," who is usually represented as an arch-traitor who stabs the patriotic Border heroes in the back because he covets the gear and goods that they have won from the hated Southron.[23] In this connexion we remember, too, the bitter words of David Lyndsay, the Lowlander, against the reivers and the lawlessness of the Border.

Yet " lawlessness " is not quite the right word, for the Borderers have their own strict code :

> ' And whae will dare this deed avow ?
> Or answer by the Border law ? '

In times of peace (" truce " is the word the ballads use !) it might still be legitimate to redress private wrongs by cattle-raiding or by rescuing a friend from prison : but to take prisoners or to destroy a castle on the other side of the Border was regarded as an act of treachery.[24] The Borderers seem constantly on the alert, watching for the fire on their laird's " peel " summoning them to repel a raid by the Southron. In this area of changing frontiers and frequent forfeiture, the grouping, however, is not strictly national. A disinherited

[21] See J. Weisweiler, " Die Stellung der Frau bei den Kelten und das Problem des ' Keltischen Mutterrechtes '," in *Zeitschrift für Celtische Philologie*, XXI (1940), pp. 205-79 ; N. K. Chadwick, " Pictish and Celtic Marriage in early Literary Tradition," in *Scottish Gaelic Studies*, VIII (1955), pp. 56-115 ; and *The Problem of the Picts*, ed. F. T. Wainwright, 1955, pp. 25-8, *et. pass. m.*

[22] CHILD, 211.

[23] Cp. " The Lament of the Border Widow," " Johnie Armstrong," " The Laird o Logie," and " The Outlaw Murray " (CHILD, 106 (pp. 429-30), 169, 182, 305). The career of John Armstrong of Gilnockie (hanged 1530, by James V, with 50 of his followers) provides historic proof of the independence of the Border reivers : his raids extended on either side of the Border, and were the subject of a conference between commissioners of both Kingdoms.

[24] Cp. " Kinmont Willie " (CHILD, 186), 5.2-3, 11.1-2. For the text of this and some other ballads, *e.g.* " Jamie Telfer of the Fair Dodhead " (CHILD, 190), we are dependent on Scott, who appears to have tampered with them.

or exiled chief may raid from the South, as did Douglas in the time of James III ; Hobie Noble, the exiled Englishman who in several ballads fights for the Scots, is also a case in point, and the traditional objectivity of presentation even allows an English Border peasant to become the hero of a Scots ballad—but then he tricked the English lords even better.[25]

In the ballads, the Borderer's supreme loyalty is to his laird, who is more than a feudal lord and in many ways resembled the Highland chief who can command a true clan spirit. The laird's approval is required for any raid ; he protects the rights of his followers as he does his own, and his summons to " ride " is absolute :

> ' They that [a]winna ride for Telfer's [b]kye, *[a] will not [b] cows*
> Let them never look in the face o me ! '[26]

The ballads tell of the vigour and valour of men who act as members of their family, and are constantly on the alert to avenge its wrongs. This clannishness creates a sombre pattern of treachery and loyalty, cruelty and heroism; and (as evidenced by, for example, the ballads of Spain and Jugoslavia) there is no other soil in which the ballad grows so well.

The rude economy of the Border was based on cattle and sheep, and (apart from land itself) there was very little wealth that was not easily removable. When stocks ran short, and when, in autumn, " muir men had won their hay," the Borderer got ready to ride—in other words, to go cattle-raiding. Cattle-raiding indeed provides the ground-theme of the Scottish Border ballads, with such incidental variations as fights to rescue those captured in previous raids. Cattle-raiding is a common feature of any country possessing a similar economic and social structure, but only the Scots ballads, oddly enough, have taken it as a fundamental theme ; not even the ballads of the American South-West, otherwise so similar in attitude, have done so.[27] Here it may possibly be significant that the old Irish heroic tales are largely concerned with cattle-raids : *Táin Bó* . . . (cattle-raid) is the title of many an epic ; and in modern Gaelic, *tàin*, originally a raid, has the predominant meaning " cattle, flocks ; wealth in flocks." [28]

[25] See " Dick o the Cow " (CHILD, 185).

[26] See " Jamie Telfer of the Fair Dodhead " (CHILD, 190), 26.3-4.

[27] WELLS, p. 297.

[28] See M. Maclellan, *A pronouncing and etymological Dictionary of the Gaelic Language*, Edinburgh 1925, s.v. " tàin." In Gaelic that well-known seventeenth-century pibroch *The MacFarlane's Gathering* is called *Togail nam Bò* [*Cattle-lifting*], and the MacFarlanes lived on Loch Lomondside—another of the borderlands between Highland and Lowland.

It may also be significant that the unashamed and businesslike attitude towards cattle-lifting adopted in the Scottish Border ballads is closely paralleled by Barbour's attitude towards booty. According to the English account of the events leading up to the Battle of Otterburn, Percy boasts romantically that he will kill " the fattiste *hartes* in all Cheviat " ; but according to the Scottish account

> The doughty Douglas bound him to ride
> Into England, to drive a *prey*.[29]

A strong business-instinct pervades the Scottish ballads :

> ' Wi her I will get [a]gowd and gear ; *[a] gold*
> Wi you I neer got nane.' [30]

When, in two other ballads, those pursuing an escaped prisoner come up with him just as he and his rescuers get safely to the far bank of a flooded river, they ask that his fetters at least should be given back to them, for they were expensive enough ; but what true Scot would give them ? [31] Trickery, ruses, disguises are frequent in ballads of other countries, too,[32] but those in the Scottish ballads are in general less playful, they take on a sharper cutting edge in outwitting the Southron or outbargaining an overbearing lord, and there is more grimly dramatic enjoyment of each successive trick.[33]

Child's collection contains no less than sixty Border ballads, which thus form a considerable proportion of Scottish balladry in general, and themselves are part of a larger class usually described as " historical " ballads. Like them, the Border ballads present history plain, and as it appears to the common folk :

> ' 'Tis scarcely ten, now,' said the King ;
> ' I heard the clock mysell ! ' [34]

[29] Cp. " The Hunting of the Cheviot " (Child, 162), A.2.1, and " The Battle of Otterburn " (Child, 161), C.1.3-4.—Stealing also figures prominently in the Jugoslav ballads, but in the much more romantic form of bride-stealing.

[30] " Fair Annie " (Child, 62), A.1.5-6.

[31] See " Jock o the Side " (Child, 187), B.33 ; " Archie o Cawfield " (Child, 188), A.43. Jock keeps *his* fetters (B.34.1-2) to shoe his mare ! There are, however, exceptions to the general rule. In " Lang Johnny More " (Child, 251 ; almost a parody of 99, 100), the Scots refuse a " tocher [dowry] " from the English King after freeing Johnny from the prison into which the King had thrown him for falling in love with the Princess.

[32] *E.g.* the Robin Hood cycle.

[33] *E.g.* " The Lochmaben Harper," " Dick o the Cow," " Jock o the Side," and " Archie o Cawfield " (Child, 192, 185, 187-8). In the two last, the horses are shod backwards.

[34] " Sir Hugh le Blond " (Child, 59), B.25.3-4.

What they report as fact is not historically reliable ; events that had no connexion with one another are freely intermixed, and though hours and seasons are often mentioned, no historical dates are specified, and the action takes place within the framework of a timeless chronology based on the incessant rhythms of the farmer's year :

The sun was na up, but the moon was down,
  It was the [a]gryming of a new-fa'n snaw.[35] — [a] *sprinkling*

It fell about the Lammas tide,
  When the muir-men [a]win their hay.[36] — [a] *get*

Unlike other ballads, the Border ballads have all the authenticity of a local (as opposed to a shadowy, universal) setting. It was no doubt because they were of clannish interest that so many place-names were included in these ballads ; in some cases the route followed in a raid can be re-established in all its details [37] ; in others, tales in which such details were not originally specified have been localised and so made more colourful. " The Battle of Harlaw ", [38] from the North-East, is unique among all other ballads in that it uses " dialect " as an index of nationality :

' Yes, me cam frae ta Hielans, man,
  An me cam a' ta wey.' [39]

As this occurs in all twelve versions [40] it must be an old, indeed probably an original, feature. The fact that they contain so much local detail has prevented the Border ballads from becoming traditional elsewhere : relatively few of them have migrated to America.

★ ★ ★

Secondly, there is an important group of Scottish ballads containing narratives of supernatural events many of them connected—at least

[35] " Jamie Telfer of the Fair Dodhead " (CHILD, 190), 7.1-2.

[36] " The Battle of Otterburn " (CHILD, 161), C.1.1-2.

[37] But sometimes, *e.g.* in " Lang Johnny More " (above, n. 31), London seems only a day's ride beyond the Border !

[38] CHILD, 163.

[39] A.4.1-2, showing that the speaker is a Highlander. Gaelic has no [đ]. Nominative and accusative are identical, even in pronouns : *chunnaic mi*, " I saw " ; *chunnaic e mi*, " he saw me." Some versions have " she " here for " me," but this is a fictitious though conventional rendering of Highland English ; cp. Robert Fergusson's " Leith Races " (below, p. 176), which has " she " and " her nanesel," for " I " and " my own self." In the present context, " she " could however be a rendering of Gael. *mise* [*miʃə*], the first person singular emphatic.

[40] 3 in CHILD, 163 ; 9 in GREIG, 50.

in origin—with Thomas the Rhymer. The supernatural plays a far more important role in Scottish ballads than in their English and Continental counterparts (Norwegian and Danish excepted).[41] The BALLADS OF THE SUPERNATURAL, especially the cycle about Thomas the Rhymer, are rich in echoes from the copious Celtic fairy lore, with the fairies coming out of their hills on Mayday and Halloween, the Gaelic Bealltainn and Samhuinn. We find many beliefs familiar from other Scots poems: the numerous taboo-names for the devil or for "the good folk," [42] magic numbers,[43] the way to the "other world" through a hill (Irish) or across the water, witches unable to cross running water, witch knots, and so forth. The frequent mention of "witches" must be considered as an outcome of the widespread witch-cult, itself partly a child of old pagan, Celtic mythology and social customs: the main festive days of the witch covens were Roodmas (the eve of Mayday) and Halloween, and if we read the report of the trial of Andro Man at Aberdeen in 1597 we are curiously reminded of the old Gaelic *compert* stories [44] and of the strange marriage customs of the Picts and Celts [45]:

> Thow confessis...thow begud [began] to have carnall deall with that devilische spreit, the Quene of Elphen, on quhom thow begat dyveris bairnis...Siclyk, thow affermis that the Quene of Elfen hes a grip of all the craft, bot Christsonday is the gudeman, and hes all power under God [= the "Devil"]...Thow affermis that the Quene is verray plesand, and will be auld and young quhen scho pleissis; scho mackis any Kyng quhom scho pleissis, and lyis with any scho lykis....

This is supported by the evidence of Marion Grant, whose trial took place at the same time:

> ...the Devill, thy Maister, quhome thow termes Christsonday, causit thee dans sindrie tymes with him and with Our Ladye, quha, as thow sayis, was a fyne woman, cled in a quhyt walicot [petticoat].[46]

[41] ENTWISTLE, pp. 230, 238.

[42] The *Scottish National Dictionary* contains all sorts of taboo-names used by fishermen, especially at sea.

[43] Is there perhaps any connexion between "Thomas Rymer" (CHILD, 37), A.2.3-4—"At ilka tett of her horse's mane/Hung fifty silver bells and nine"—and W. B. Yeats, "The wild Swans at Coole"—"Upon the brimming water among the stones/Are nine-and-fifty swans"? Though I have been unable to discover any trace of a belief that 59 is a magic number, it is well known that Yeats cultivated a "Celtic" mysticism.

[44] *I.e.* stories about the conception of certain heroes.

[45] See N. K. Chadwick (above, n. 21).

[46] Both passages are as quoted by M. A. Murray, *The Witch-cult in Western Europe* 1921, pp. 44-5.

But at the same time these very features that link the witch cult with old Pictish and Celtic customs establish a connexion with the ballads of "Thomas Rymer" or "Tam Lin" and their class: like the Pictish queen of old, the Queen of Elfland chose her own mates, and when their loves had been consummated

Hir hare it hange all ouer hir hede
Hir [a]eghne semede [b]owte, that [c]are were graye.[47] [a] *eyes* [b] *out* [c] *before*

We must remember that the witch cult seems to have been stronger in Scotland than in any other European country,[48] and that here the clash between this remnant of paganism and Christianity was often violent: after the Reformation only one Catholic was put to death, but between 1560 and 1700 hundreds, perhaps thousands of "witches." The special importance of the witch cult in Scotland partly explains the role played by the supernatural narratives in Scottish balladry, and at the same time the curious part which, as we shall see, the "De'il" has in Scots literature. Yet these strong influences, direct and indirect, of Gaelic and Pictish lore must not make us blind to the traces left in Scots ballads by the legends and myths of the ancient Britons, Angles, or Danes; if the Scottish fairies are of a harsher nature than their Irish cousins, that is largely due to this admixture from the various races that went to form the Scottish people.

* * *

There is, finally, a third type, usually called the "ROMANTIC" or "TRADITIONAL" BALLAD. It might be difficult to name any special characteristics of these which set them apart from ballads of other types. Yet they contain the pure essence of balladry, and provide many of the best examples of its technique. Their appeal is both universal and permanent. Many of them originated in (or were later adapted to) specific historical events or situations. In the course of time, however, all trace of the specific was washed away, and there remained only the elemental situations and passions of life, the bare bones of poetry, the stuff of life in any age.[49] They speak to us, not

[47] From "Thomas off Ersseldoune," one of the earliest known versions of "Thomas Rymer": see CHILD, VOL. I, p. 318, and 57 (Appendix), 23.3-4.

[48] Cp. M. A. Murray (above, n. 46); G. M. Thomson, *A short History of Scotland*, 1930; and R. Graves, *The White Goddess*, 1947, which, though tendentious, is stimulating.

[49] In such ballads as "Sir Patrick Spens," "The Death of Queen Jane," "The Bonny Earl of Moray," and "The Bonnie House o Airlie" (CHILD, 58.A, 170, 181, 199), the historical and political associations have almost completely been lost, and only the general human theme remains.

of a distant past, but of things always present—birth, death, love, the stark fact of human conflict in all its forms, the fiery cleansing of the human spirit in the furnace of passion. The presentation is bare and impersonal, and everything is reduced to the simplest possible terms: there is commonly a tragic theme, two (or at most three) characters, and no room for anything local or individual, or for much realistic detail. The first line or two of a romantic ballad may have retained just a touch of specific local colour to arouse interest—for example, in " Sir Patrick Spens,"

> The King sits in Dunfermling toune,
> Drinking the blude-reid wine [50]

—but this note is not sustained, and in most the opening situation is elemental enough and fits any generation: in a few lines we have setting, theme, characters—mother, son, lover, husband, symbols of life in any age—and the action is already in full swing.

In the Scots ballads, there is an intense preoccupation with the subject at the moment of passion, which, according to the contemporary Scots poet Sydney Goodsir Smith, *is* poetry itself, naked and burning. They speak to the heart, the imagination, not the mind; and abstract thought does not enter into them. In " Jock o the Side," [51] a Border ballad, the splintering of a prison door symbolises escape and freedom: in " Sir Patrick Spens " the golden combs with which the ladies adorn their hair symbolise the vanity of human wishes, and ironically contrast it with the tragic fate of Sir Patrick and his companions. Only in such details does realism obtrude itself—but as they are purely suggestive and symbolic they give the ballad its intensity, and its power lies in what is left untold:

> ' Gar warn the bows of Hartlie-burn,
> See them sharp their arrows on the [a]wa.' [52]   [a] *wall*

This symbolism covers the whole range of folk mythology, from a broken ring to the heel lost in walking up the steps.

The third group, with its truly human appeal, is the most truly international. Though they are unmistakably Scottish, the differences which stamp them as Scottish are differences rather of degree than of

[50] Child, 58, A.1.1-2.

[51] Child, 187.

[52] " Hobie Noble " (Child, 189), 16.1-2: " sharp " is Scott's emendation for the unintelligible " shaft " of the two original mss.

kind. Thus the dominant mood is deeply tragic and fatalistic, with less of the picaresque, and few moments of serenity : Robin Hood and his " merry men all " are typical enough of English balladry in general, but again and again in the Scottish ballads we hear the fatal footfall of monosyllables :

> But still the sea came in.[53]

Here it is particularly illuminating to compare " The twa Corbies [ravens] " with its English analogue, " The three Ravens." [54] In the English ballad, whose lyrical character is underlined by a refrain, the three ravens cannot come near the body of the newly slain knight, as his hounds and hawks keep a faithful watch, and his leman comes and kisses his wounds, and buries him. In " The twa Corbies," however,

> ' His hound is to the hunting gane,
> His hawk to fetch the wild-fowl hame,
> His lady's ta'en another mate,
> So we may mak our dinner sweet.'

and the tragic effect is heightened by the ironic contrast between the " twa corbies " and the knight—as he was and as he is :

> ' Ye'll sit on his white [a]hause-bane, — [a] *collar-bone*
> And I'll pike out his bonny blue een ;
> Wi ae lock o his [a]gowden hair, — [a] *golden*
> We'll [a]theeke our nest when it grows bare.' — [a] *thatch*

[53] " Sir Patrick Spens " (CHILD, 58), H.20.4. It is scarcely a coincidence that these monosyllables abound in the last lines of each stanza.

[54] Both in CHILD, 26. Child remarks that the Scottish verses " sound something like a cynical variation of the tender little English ballad." There is an excellent setting of them by F. G. Scott, who intensifies their grim irony by giving sts. 1 and 4 to the female voice : this avoidance of theatrical pathos is fully in accord with the spirit of the Scottish ballads. It is only fair to add that " The twa Corbies " may have been touched up by Scott or Hogg.—Often it is very difficult to determine which " readings " are original and which emendations. In " The Braes of Yarrow " (CHILD, 214), A.14.3, Percy's MS apparently read :

> She ' wiped ' the blood that trickled down . . .

In a note Child writes : " *The words in ' ' are so distinguished in the MS and are of course emendations* . . . ' wiped,' 14^3 *is probably substituted for* drank . . . " But in E (printed in Scott's *Minstrelsy* ; MS in Hogg's handwriting), the line reads

> She drank the red blood frae him ran . . .

and F (MS in Laidlaw's handwriting) has

> She drank the red bluid frae him ran.

The doom of all the vanity suggested by " bonny blue een " and " gowden hair " is sealed by the last word, " bare." No kissing of wounds here, nor a faithful lady dying of a broken heart " ere euensong," but a tragic fate :

> ' Oer his white banes, when they are bare,
> The wind sall blaw for evermair.'

" Ever " and " never " are characteristic expressions of the tragic fatalism of the Scottish ballads, and we remember the same note in the Scottish Gaelic folk tales. It is not, however, the fatalism of resignation, but of courage, almost defiance, in the face of this knowledge of fate. Like the heroes of old, the men of the ballads are ready for death, to " dree their weird " :

> A faint heart neer wan a fair ladie...
> There'll nae man die but him that's [a]fie.[55] [a] *doomed to die*

The flavour of the humour is distinctly Scottish. There are not so many humorous ballads as in other literatures, and their humour is sharper and has (especially at the moment of greatest dramatic tension) a laconic, tightlipped grimness that is characteristically Scottish. It is a humour that arises, often in face of danger and death itself, out of sharp contrast. A prisoner carried down a ladder in his irons will jest at the rough beast he is riding and at his cumbrous spurs, and when he is hastily hoisted sideways on to a horse, his rescuers will mock grimly,

> ' In troth ye sit like ony bride.' [56]

[55] " Jock o the Side " (CHILD, 187), B.20.2, 30.2.

[56] " Jock o the Side," B.25.4. Here may I record the impressions that my wife and I formed of the Border hills ? Our dominant impression was not so much of the loneliness, and the starkness of the outlines, as of the eerie, not quite transparent quality of the light, alike in dull weather and in sunshine. Here, strong sunlight may be bringing out the colours—for instance, above St Mary's Loch—hard and direct : but only a few hundred yards away the outlines become somewhat unreal—not indistinct, but rather *withdrawn*, as if behind a veil. (It must be due to the humidity.) And when, coming down from the moor, you see a herd of black cows half-a-mile away, where the sharpness of the landscape mellows, they look as if they came from another world ; I actually succeeded in catching this effect in colour photographs. In the moors round the Three Brethren, between Tweed and Yarrow, we were not so conscious of the loneliness as of a certain uncanny feeling apparently provoked by this unearthly light. Though we knew there was nobody for miles around, we felt we *must* look over our shoulders just in case there was somebody after all. And the crying of the whaups (curlews) went right through us ; in the mist it has a most uncanny sound. We have not experienced such feelings in any other place, and they have greatly enriched my understanding of the ballads. Altogether, we formed the

Here the grotesque humour may serve to relieve emotional tension ; at other times there is a sly shrewdness, almost a business-spirit in this humour : " I wot they cost me dear enough." [57] Fleeing with two stolen horses, the fool Dick o the Cow happens to stun his pursuer:

> ' Gramercie,' then can Dickie say,
> ' I had twa horse, thou hast made me three.' [58]

Elsewhere, in a skirmish, the English captain has a lance thrust through his thigh :

> If he had lived this hundred years,
> He had never been loved by woman again. [59]

The cattle he had stolen are retrieved, but with so many killed that

> ' Dear kye, I trow, to some they be.' [60]

Underneath all this grim humour and irony we feel, however, the same tenderness as in Henryson :

> O our Scots nobles wer richt [a]laith — *[a] loath*
> To [a]weet their cork-heild [b]schoone ; — *[a] wet [b] shoes*
> Bot [a]lang owre a' the play wer playd, — *[a] long before*
> Thair hats they swam [a]aboone. [61] — *[a] above*

---

impression that anybody who had to live in these stark, lonely hills, with their eerie light, could only prevent himself from turning melancholy, or superstitious, by developing a certain stern grimness of outlook. The superstition is enshrined in the Thomas Rymer cycle, the grimness in the Border Ballad : but of sentimental melancholy there is not a trace in the true Scottish Borderer !

[57] " Archie of Cawfield " (CHILD, 188), B.29.2.

[58] " Dick o the Cow " (CHILD, 185), 41.3-4 ; cp. " The Lochmaben Harper " (CHILD, 192), AC. 14-5, where the mare arrives at the harper's door together with the Lord Warden of Carlisle's " wanton brown " tied to her tail ; the servant-maid, " keeking " through the lock-hole

> 'O ! by my sooth,' then cried the lass,
> ' Our mare has gotten a braw brown foal !'
>
> ' Come, haud thy tongue, thou silly wench!
> The morn 's but glancing in your ee.'
> ' Ill wad my hail fee against a groat,
> He's bigger than e'er our foal will be ! '

[59] " Jamie Telfer o the Fair Dodhead " (CHILD, 190), 40.3-4.

[60] 41.2. Cp. Barbour's *Bruce*, XVIII.282 ff., where Earl Warenne is sent on a foraging expedition, but the Scots have removed all the cattle, and he only finds one cow : " ' Than, certis,' said he, ' I dar say/This is the derrest beiff that I/Saw euir yeit ; for sekirly [surely]/ It cost me ane thousand pund and mar ! ' "

[61] " Sir Patrick Spens " (CHILD, 58), A.8. (Really, however, I prefer the first line of this stanza as given in H [printed by Scott], 21.1 : " O laith, laith were our gude Scots lords . . . ").

This is one of the finest stanzas in Scots ballads. It illustrates the ballad technique of suggesting the beginning and the end, nothing more. Attention seems to be sharply focussed on realistic details, but in fact, the resultant images are inherently symbolic. The first two lines contain a grim, typically " democratic " comment of the vanity of the Scots lords : but the image of their hats swimming on the sea fully brings home to us the tragic pathos of the event.

The Scots tongue is an essential part of the means used in obtaining precisely this kind of effect. With its strong consonants and dynamic accentuation, Scots has a directness, tight-lipped brevity and concentration that enables it to give a single emotionally coloured word its full effect :

> The ankers brak, and the topmasts lap,
> It was sic a deadly storm ;
> And the waves cam oer the broken ship,
> Till a' her sides were torn.[62]

Read this stanza with English vowels and consonants (especially the English *r* !), with the mellower English accent and laxer English articulation (diphthongs !), and it becomes much less powerfully evocative of doom than it is in Scots. Scots lends itself easily to the ballad style, and Sir Alexander Gray translated German and Danish ballads and folk-songs into Scots,[63] because he found it impossible to translate them into standard English without sacrificing their essential flavour. A comparison with the originals brings out the characteristic qualities of Scots : " a wee bit room " is both more angular and more tender than " *ein Zimmerlein*." Scots is usually more forcibly realistic, more direct, more personal, and less solemn : often in listening to it one seems to catch an amused or even a mischievous twinkle in the speaker's eye.

The ballads contain many popular semi-proverbial phrases—such as " do or dee," " wield the brand," etc.—and have a pithily sententious outlook that emphasises a few essential values and has little room for subtlety of feeling.[64] In the Scots ballads, little stands for much : the listener has largely to construct his own picture of the event, and understatement of tragic facts is customary. " Gude

[62] " Sir Patrick Spens " (CHILD, 58), H.15.

[63] In *Arrows* (above, n. 5), and *Four-and-fourty*, Edinburgh 1954.

[64] Cp. " Lang Johnny More " (CHILD, 251), 4.1-2 : " But if a' be true they tell me now,/And a' be true I hear. . . . " Reading this, we may be reminded of Henryson's folk characters, or of *T. Cr.*, l. 64 : " Quha wait gif all that Chauceir wrait was trew ? "

eneuch " ; " dear eneuch " ; " And lang, lang may the maidens sit," [65] ; " And wow but they cam speedilie " [66] ; " But thinkna ye my heart was sair [sore] " [67]—these and a hundred other such phrases evoke echoes of the Makars, but there cannot be any doubt that this way of speaking itself comes straight from the mouth of the people.[68]

★ ★ ★

Ballads are highly dramatic. Instead of an account of the breaking of a sword there is a curse on the smith who forged it. As a rule, the dialogue is unassigned, and an occasional " he said " has no descriptive adverb. The dramatic effect is heightened by their intense pre-occupation with the core of a situation—usually a life-or-death conflict involving two or three characters. The fact that ballads were songs, and the use of incremental repetition, made it possible to jettison much strictly unnecessary connective material, and most ballads lead abruptly from one scene to the next, never to linger there for more than a stanza or two before making another equally bold leap forward. In the Scots ballads, as Muir suggests, the power of dramatisation that is characteristic of all ballads is at its strongest : " Lord Randal," " Edward," " The twa Corbies," " Sir Patrick Spens," " The Wife of Usher's Well," and, in a comic sense, " Get up and bar the Door," [69] are all essentially dramatic—and have, it may be observed, precisely the same dramatic spirit as most Scots poetry from Barbour's time

[65] *I.e.*, for ever : " Sir Patrick Spens " (CHILD, 57), A.25.1.

[66] In fact, they were fleeing for their lives : " Archie o Cawfield " (CHILD, 188), Bb (*i.e.*, as printed in later edns. of Scott's *Minstrelsy*), 17.2.

[67] " The Lament of the Border Widow " (for which see CHILD, VOL. II, p. 429), 6.1.

[68] The language of the ballads shows relatively strong traces of a Gaelic substratum. Thus " the-nicht, the-day," for " to-night, to-day," and " nor," for " than," are common enough in contemporary Scots speech : but cp. Gael. *an nochd, an diugh, am feasgar* ; and *na* (" than "), *no* (" no, nor "), both pron. [nə]. Again, in " Mary Hamilton " (CHILD, 173), A.14.3, we have " Let them never let on to my father and mother," and in G.13.3 " Oh never let on to my father and mother " ; cp. Gael. *nach leig ort,* lit. " don't leave on you." (Though these are perhaps the earliest instances of " don't let on," they are not mentioned in *N.E.D.*, s.v. " let," 33, which is wrong or at least sketchy in its etymology, and does not give due weight to the fact that practically all its examples are from Scotland). And in " The Trumpeter of Fyvie " (*alias* " Andrew Lammie " : CHILD, 233), A.7.3, we have " And ay his face to the nor-east," with which cp. Gael. *chuir mi m'aghaidh air . . .*, lit. " I put my face on . . .," *i.e.* " I went towards . . . " For further discussion, see W. J. Watson, " Some Interactions between Gaelic and English," in *Transactions of the Gaelic Society of Inverness*, XXXIII (1925-7), Inverness 1932, pp. 310-26.

[69] CHILD, 12, 13, 26, 58, 79 and 275.

down to the present day. Here we are plunged straight into the very heart of the fifth act, in the first two or three lines. From the outset, interest is concentrated on the central issue—usually the clash of two opposed wills—and the " montage " (by which I mean the technique of linking together significantly a series of quick " shots ") [70] is masterly. Such Scots ballads as " Edward," " Lord Randal," and " The twa Corbies," certainly display a much keener sense of drama than their English and Continental counterparts. The English ballads are in general a good deal mellower and more *domestic* than most of the Scottish ballads, and very few of them have the same tremendous concision.

The dramatic potency of the Scottish ballads is due partly to the strong sense of contrast that is so characteristic of Scots poetry, and of the Scots tongue. They do not contain much descriptive or decorative detail, and the details given—such as the fetters that weigh fifteen pounds, the exact length of a tree cut down to scale a prison wall, and the precise number of " naggs [notches] " on either side of it—often seem trivial enough.[71] Most of the colours mentioned are highly conventional, and the ballads do not contain much original imagery ; such as they do is usually of doubtful authenticity, and the romantic " impressionism " which appears in " The Douglas Tragedy "—

> They lighted down to tak a drink
> Of the spring that ran sae clear
> And down the stream ran his gude heart's blood,
> And [a]sair she gan to fear. — [a] *sore*
>
> ' Hold up, hold up, Lord William,' she says,
> ' For I fear that you are slain.'
> ' 'Tis naething but the *shadow of my scarlet cloak*,
> ' That shines in the water sae plain.'

—may possibly have been written into it by Sir Walter Scott.[72] Yet within the limits of their own conventions, the ballads evince a strong feeling for nature, a spontaneous delight in sensuous experience as such, that is recognisably akin to the spirit of the Makars. Often—

[70] Cp. S. Eisenstein, *The Film Scene*, 1943.

[71] Cp. " Jock o the Side " (CHILD, 187), A.17.4, B.11.3 ; " Archie o Cawfield " (CHILD, 188), A.22.3.

[72] Our italics. See " Earl Brand " (CHILD, 7), B.12, 13. The same may be true of " Jamie Telfer " (CHILD, 190), 36.3-4 : " The Dinlay *snaw* was neer mair white/Nor the *lyart* [grizzled] *locks* of Harden's hair."

as when, in " Tam Lin," [73] we are told that Janet waited at Miles Cross, and that there, about midnight, " she heard the bridles ring " —the detail that seems so trivial creates so irresistible an impression of authenticity as almost to persuade us that we, too, are present. There are signs, here and there,[74] of a rich sense of colour, and Hodgart asserts that the Scottish ballads are more extravagantly hyperbolical than others in their description of finery. There is also a strong sense of scenic and pictorial effect, and, though conventional, the pictures that it produces are often extremely vivid :

> ' O see ye not yon narrow road,
> So thick beset wi thorns and briers ? ' [75]

or especially :

> ' To seik het water beneth cauld ice,
> Surely it is a great folie—
> I haif asked grace at a graceless face,
> But there is nane for my men and me.' [76]

Here, too, winter provides some of the most striking pictures—Hell, characteristically, is " all so dreary wi' frost and snow " [77]—and the dominant mood of the ballads is indeed a frosty one.

Finally, it must again be emphasised that the chief peculiarity of the Scottish ballads is not so much that they are fundamentally different from other ballads, but that they tend to emphasise very sharply a number of general ballad characteristics. Yet many of these characteristics thus emphasised occur again and again throughout the whole corpus of Scottish poetry, and there is an obvious affinity between the Scottish ballads and the poetry of Barbour, Henryson, Douglas, Burns, and the modern makars. In Scotland, " the interactions of learned and folk poetry are never long quiescent, and in Lowland Scotland the native and scholarly streams constantly replenished one another." [78] James V was regarded as the author of two ballads, " The jolly Beggar " and " The gaberlunzie Man," [79]

[73] CHILD, 39, A.37.2.

[74] *E.g.*, " The gay Goshawk " (CHILD, 96).

[75] " Thomas Rymer " (CHILD, 37), A.12.1-2.

[76] " Johnie Armstrong " (CHILD, 169), C.22.

[77] " The Daemon Lover " (*alias* " James Harris " : CHILD, 243), F.14.2. It will be recalled that Gavin Douglas prefixed his winter prologue to the account of the Nether World in *En.* VII.

[78] WELLS, p. 75.

[79] CHILD, 279.

his forefather James I of two popular poems. Before English collectors took up the ballads and created a literary vogue for them, ballads had already produced " forgeries " in Scotland: Lady Wardlaw had passed off " Hardyknute " as a genuine ballad by 1719; David Mallet faked " William and Margaret " (1725); William Hamilton of Bangour wrote " The Braes of Yarrow " (1725), a sequel to the ballad of the same name,[80] and John Home's play *Douglas* (1755) was also based on a ballad. Here, too, we find in Scotland a constant interweaving of diverse traditions. This helped to fertilise Scots literary poetry. It helps also to explain the greater vitality of the Scottish ballads.

[80] CHILD, 214.

Part II

Autumn Tide

VI

Surging Up: The Eighteenth Century

THE SAVAGE STRIFE that went on in Scotland throughout the seventeenth century paralysed cultural life in many fields. Though its spiritual foundations had been stabilised by the end of the century, Scottish minds were bound to be deeply affected by the Parliamentary Union of 1707. It is no part of our present task to show why this should have produced a resurgence of the national spirit in the field of letters, or how Jacobitism, strictly a minority movement, became part of the national mythology. It is enough to say that the eighteenth century ushers in the second climax of Scottish literature.

However, there is one difference. Formerly—though this excluded Latin writers and Gaelic poetry—we could focus all our attention on one scene: now we must watch several. The orientation towards England foreshadowed by the Reformation and strengthened by the flitting of the Court to London, was made absolute by the Union. Not a few Scottish courtiers and noblemen (and some large landowners) increasingly made London their headquarters, and began sending their sons to school in England—especially to Eton. The native Scots tongue, already superseded in the Church by English, fell back even further as English seemed to be the politer (and also the more promising) language. These social developments had a deep effect on literature. Those who had gone south were the potential patrons, the leisured class who could have enjoyed poetry as an enrichment of life. As a result, literature became increasingly a product of an occasional spare hour in the day of a farmer or worker, with all the ensuing lack of finish and care—or else the writer obeyed the call of the South.

1. The Anglo-Scots

Of those who went south some merged into the general English (or British) [1] tradition and are of no consequence to our subject. Others,

[1] Though the Scots usually insisted on "British," the English did not bother themselves much with these niceties, and continued to say "English."

while trying to conform to the pattern of English letters, unconsciously carried with them part of the Scottish heritage, which broke out in their writing and enriched the general stream of English literature. If we want to have our perspective correct we must at least throw a passing glance at the elements thus, often unwittingly, introduced into English letters.

James Thomson (1700-48) affords the best example of the Scotsman seeking his fortune as a man of letters in London. Though he did not set out to revolutionise English poetry, that is precisely what his introduction of a new theme, nature, achieved in the long run. He was not steeped deeply enough in the Augustan tradition, and his topic came to him from his background. Nature, especially in its rougher aspects, is to him a reality. When, initially, he takes winter as his original subject, it is quite unnecessary for us to postulate an echo of Middle Scots poetry in Thomson or in his teacher Ricaltoun [2]; the prominence of this season in Scotland, the realism with which the Scots take account of the harshness of life, or even the insistence with which they dwell on it, are in themselves a sufficient explanation. The success of Thomson's *Seasons* is chiefly attributable to the fact that it chimed in so well with the rising belief of the time—and in particular with Deism. Still, Thomson's *Seasons* challenge comparison with corresponding poems or passages in older Scots poetry.

Their common ground is nature and country life as the topic of a whole poem, including nature's wilder aspects, with personal observations and impressions of life and movement. Thomson's poem, however, is longer, more comprehensive and systematic; it is decidedly didactic, and it pursues nature to a higher meaning, a philosophy. Though it may strike us as abstract and artificial, this moralising, with the "poetic diction" in which it is expressed, reveals the poet as a man of his century, and was much admired. It has few parallels in traditional Scottish literature. Long passages in Thomson have nothing of the direct and personal expression so characteristic of most of Scots poetry, or of the hard facts so sharply visualised in the poetry of Henryson, Montgomerie, and Alexander Hume; in place of suggestive compression we find solemn comprehensiveness. In the student societies of Edinburgh the young Thomson had conscientiously attempted to get rid of his Scotticisms and studied "correct" English almost as if it had been a foreign language. Scots,

[2] Ricaltoun's poem on winter was written shortly before Thomson's.

his mother tongue, was for informal, English for formal purposes ; this did not make for direct personal utterance. But whenever memories of his native country assert themselves, then (almost against his will, as his successive revisions show) Thomson is apt simply to picture a scene distinct in all its details, and highly dramatic : in *Winter*, the contrast between the cold outside and the warm inside environment, the sheep under the snowdrift, the shepherd lost in the snow, the robin ; in *Autumn*, the leaves that " slowly circle through the waving air " ; and, in *Spring*, the most intently and dramatically alive of all these scenes, the trout and salmon fishing. Apart from the Deistic " Hymn," posterity has most esteemed in Thomson's *Seasons* those vivid impressions which are most closely connected with the Scottish tradition. Atmosphere-painting and vivid impressions such as we see in *The Castle of Indolence* had been frequent in Scots poetry, and so had the predilection for formal intricacy which finds expression in the same poem's Spenserian stanzas.[3]

Other Scottish writers who belong to the common stream of British literature are William Falconer (1730-69), whose *Shipwreck*, the first long sea-poem in English, is neo-classical and long-winded, but shows an intense insistence on detail ; Tobias Smollett with his full-blooded and grotesque robustness ; and James Boswell, whose *Life of Dr Samuel Johnson* may be regarded as the first mature fruit of that preoccupation with character which we have already observed in Barbour, Henryson, and the ballads—not to mention the many " dramatic monologues " in Scottish poetry. Scottish painting, too, is strongest in portrait painters with their insistence on character, and Scotland gave birth to some of the best biographers : Barbour himself, Boswell, Lockhart, Carlyle. Writing at home, but for the wider British public, there is Robert Blair (1699-1746), apostle in *The Grave* of eighteenth-century melancholy ; again we find non-conformity with the dominant school and another unconscious step towards the Romantic revolt to which Scotland also contributed by her ballads and by Macpherson's *Ossian*. While the eighteenth century gave England much of her security and self-satisfaction, it was in Scotland an age of unbalanced tension, which accentuated that interior mistrust which not merely prevents the Scottish mind from accepting things at their face-value, but forces it to go on worrying away at them until it gets below the surface.

[3] Cp. Douglas, Prols. XII, XIII ; Alex. Hume, *The Day estivall*, and the Scots form of sonnet (above, pp. 87-9, 124-5, 117-8, respectively).

2. The North Britons and Scottish Prose

The nation's main cultural activity continued to be centred in Scotland—especially in Edinburgh. At the first lull in the fierce political strife which followed the Union and came to a head in 1715, the *ingenium praefervidum Scotorum* began to reassert itself. Its creative energies were discharged, however, into two quite different channels, between which, for a century to come, there was to be little direct contact. Some, who frequented such clubs as the Easy and the Cape, and contributed to or read *Ruddiman's Magazine*, wrote Scots and strove to resurrect the old national tradition: others, who belonged to the Select Society and supported the *Scots Magazine* and the original *Edinburgh Review*, wrote English and sought (not unsuccessfully) to make Edinburgh Europe's intellectual capital. Both these trends—national and European—had been inherent in the old unitary tradition of the country, but the new political regime drove them apart, and so denied them mutual stimulation.[1]

The *Literati*—as these literary North Britons liked to be called—rallied around David Hume (1711-76),[2] the philosopher. The theory of morals, æsthetics and criticism on which the movement as a whole was based first made its appearance in Francis Hutcheson's *Inquiry into the Originals of our Ideas of Beauty and Virtue* published in 1725—the year in which Thomson went off to England and Ramsay published *The Gentle Shepherd*. By the middle of the century, the voice of Scottish philosophy had gained the ear of Europe, and among the books which have permanently enriched its mind are: David Hume's *Treatise of Human Nature* (published unsuccessfully in 1739-40), *Enquiries* (*concerning Human Understanding*, 1748, and *concerning the Principles of Morals*, 1751), *Histories of Britain* (1754-62), and *Dialogues concerning Natural Religion* (1779); William Robertson's *History of Scotland* (1759) and of *Charles V* (1769); Hugh Blair's *Lectures on Rhetoric and Belles Lettres* [3]; and Adam Smith's *Theory of Moral Senti-*

[1] For a fuller account of the eighteenth-century background, see D. Daiches, *Robert Burns* (New York 1950, London 1952), which contains an excellent chapter on "The Scottish Literary Tradition," and his chapter on "Eighteenth-century vernacular Poetry" in *Scottish Poetry*, ed. J. Kinsley, 1955.

[2] See E. C. Mossner, *The Life of David Hume*, Edinburgh 1955, which contains much useful biographical and bibliographical information.

[3] Contains lectures delivered in 1760 (as Professor of Rhetoric) and in 1762 (as Professor of Belles-lettres); published 1783.

ments (1759) and *The Wealth of Nations* (1776). It was a world of thinkers and critics who inherited their intellectual subtlety and trenchant argumentative skill from generations of controversialists. By basing their philosophical system on principles derived from " common sense, individual introspection, or arguments from history or psychology " (Daiches), they conquered the intellectual sterility induced by an exclusive preoccupation with purely theological controversy ; by breaking up the hardened soil they also made it able to receive other seeds. All this foreshadowed the achievements in philosophy, mathematics, natural science, and medicine which were presently to make the Scottish universities admired throughout Europe, and helped to produce, in Scotland, a more tolerant religious and intellectual climate. Blair and Robertson both were ministers of the Kirk of Scotland ; Robertson was also the leader of the Moderates and Moderator of the General Assembly in 1763 ; and many of the clergy belonged to this social and intellectual circle—of which the sceptic David Hume was perhaps the most prominent representative. This thaw in the intellectual climate was presently to favour the growth of the other arts, too.

The *Literati* strengthened Scotland's ties with the Continent—especially with France and Holland.[4] They also gave Scotland a new self-confidence, and succeeded in making Edinburgh a real intellectual centre : only a generation or so after it had been necessary for Smollett and Allan Ramsay, the painter, to go south in search of a public, Scott and Raeburn found one ready-made in their own newly-awakened Edinburgh.

Hume and his friends were sincere patriots, but they scorned Scots and laboriously cultivated an English style.[5] It is sometimes suggested that this was because English was now the language of the upper classes, and had greater prestige. But that is only a partial explanation. English was now the dominant language in a United Britain, and since they made it their object to capture, in London and on the Continent, a market for Scottish books, it was obligatory

[4] According to G. M. Thomson, eighteenth-century Scotland still had closer cultural relations with Holland and France than with England. The Scottish universities were modelled on Continental systems ; in their libraries, Dutch books were especially common, if only because of the common interest in Roman law during a century in which law was all-important. In the 1760s, Hume was more at home in Paris than in London. Fashions in clothing, eating and drinking were Dutch or French.

[5] Hume in particular was very self-conscious about this, and asked Wilkes and others to point out any Scotticisms that he had unwittingly perpetrated.

for them to write English, as best they could. But by this date Scots would hardly have served their purpose even if they had wished to use it. In order to understand why, it is necessary to glance back at the brief and casual history of Scots prose.

★ ★ ★

The late fifteenth century produced a few Scots prose translations; but (perhaps chiefly because Scotland had so many European connexions), Latin was long preferred to the vernacular for all serious intellectual purposes. John Fordun, Hector Boece, John Major and Buchanan, all, as a matter of course, wrote their histories in Latin; in the Scottish universities lectures in all faculties continued to be given in Latin until well on in the eighteenth century; and only under Cromwell did the vernacular replace Latin in the courts. The first substantial Scots prose texts appeared in the second quarter of the sixteenth century: Nisbet's Scots translation of Wycliffe's New Testament (1530: first printed 1901) [6]; John Bellenden's translation of Hector Boece's *Chronicles of Scotland* (1533) [7]; and the anonymous *Complaynt of Scotland* (*c.* 1550),[8] itself partly a translation. Scots prose reached its high-water mark in ROBERT LINDESAY OF PITSCOTTIE'S *Historie and Chronicle of Scotland* (1575),[9] a sequel to Boece's Latin history. Lindesay has much in common with Barbour, Dunbar, and Henryson: his prose reveals the same dramatic sense of character, the same quick eye for graphic sensuous detail, and the same direct realism. His *Chronicle* is full of the spirit of the ballads—here, too, Johnny Armstrong asks "grace at a graceless face"—and his art is rather that of an accomplished story-teller than of a learned expositor and commentator.

Scots prose died out within the next few decades. The Reformation brought with it a flood of controversial literature in the vernacular, but for political reasons the bulk of it was in English. England was Scotland's chief Protestant ally against Romanism; the Geneva Bible and the Authorised Version were in English, and English became the language of the pulpit. There is only a handful of post-Reformation pamphlets in Scots, to these we may add the tracts of James VI,

[6] See *The New Testament in Scots*, ed. T. G. Law, S.T.S., 3 vols., 1901-5.
[7] Edd. W. Seton, R. W. Chambers, and E. C. Batho, S.T.S., 2 vols., 1938-41.
[8] Ed. J. A. H. Murray, E.E.T.S., 1872.
[9] Ed. Æ. J. G. Mackay, S.T.S., 1899-1911.

which, however, are of more biographical than literary significance. The most important Scots prose, for further development, might have been the hundred-and-fifty " Prayers Upon the Psalms " in the 1595 edition of the Scottish Psalter, which show the highest degree of development for speculative purposes.[10] There is some mixture of Scots and English, as in John Knox's *History of the Reformation in Scotland* or in James Melville's *Autobiography and Diary* ; the style here is similar to Lindesay's, with more of the grim Scots humour, more comparisons and contrasts, and perhaps more forcible directness ; the language is fundamentally Scottish in its underlying rhythm and pattern. John Knox's allusions make it evident that he knew the work of the Makars. Among Scottish writers of " English " prose one must mention Sir Thomas Urquhart of Cromarty (1605-60), whose translation of Rabelais is in English but has a fantastic wealth of vocabulary and an eldritch humour that rather recall the grotesque side of the Makars and have no parallel in English prose before the verbal artistry of James Joyce[11] ; it is Scots speech rendered into English.

Gavin Douglas, as we have seen, had deliberately attempted to widen the compass of Scots as a medium of poetry, but no similar attempt was ever made to enlarge the scope of Scots prose. What there was of it was vigorous and admirably picturesque ; but it had not been harnessed to any severely intellectual purposes, and, though well able to express both violent and tender passion, it did not lend itself to dispassionate speculation, reasoning, or learned discourse. During the seventeenth century, moreover, Scots prose ceased to be used either for spiritual or for courtly, sophisticated purposes. Eighteenth-century Scots was chiefly a spoken language, lacking in intellectual fibre and learned vocabulary. As such, it was ill suited to the needs of philosophers and historians like Hume, Robertson, and Adam Smith, who accordingly wrote English, much as the learned men of the Middle Ages had written Latin.

The North Britons scored all their greatest successes in philosophy and history. In poetry they failed miserably, and despite the great reputation that some of them achieved as writers on the philosophy of criticism, they were ludicrously mistaken in their own critical assessment of such works as Dr William Wilkie's *Epigoniad* and John Home's *Douglas*. They hailed Wilkie as the Scottish Homer (Hume),

[10] Reprinted in full in Adam Philip, *The devotional Literature of Scotland*, London n.y.

[11] In one place, Urquhart gives 71 characteristic animal noises where Rabelais has only 9.

ranked blind Dr Thomas Blacklock with Pope, and John Home with Shakespeare, glorified James Beattie's *Minstrel*, let their taste be regulated by Henry Mackenzie, the Man of Feeling, and all allowed themselves to be taken in by Macpherson's *Ossian*—all, that is to say, except David Hume, to whose preconceptions of the natural man Macpherson's shadowy heroes did not correspond.

There were various reasons why the North Britons went so far astray in these appraisals of contemporary Scottish poetry. For one thing, having staked the cultural future of their country on English, they were inclined to be over-enthusiastic about any manifestation of imaginative Scottish writing in English. For another, they started from certain critical and philosophical preconceptions, and when they found these applied in the works of their poet-disciples the *quod erat demonstrandum* of their theories seemed to have come full circle. Poetry, however, is not a thing of the speculative mind, but of the heart. English was the natural choice for their philosophical speculation ; but only Scots, their mother tongue, would have been capable of expressing their deepest and most intimate feelings. Though the best speculative prose of the Middle Ages is in Latin, the best medieval poetry is in the vernacular. And, finally, whereas poetry is part of a living tradition, made up of symbols, allusions, values felt and recognised by the community out of which it grows, the Anglo-Scottish neo-classicism of the North Britons was primarily a deliberate intellectual attitude ; and it is small wonder that Ramsay, Fergusson, and Burns wrote good poems in Scots, but invariably bad ones in English.

3. The Scots Tradition

This brings us to the trunk of the tradition, Scots poetry. Literary historians speak of a " revival " of Scots poetry in the eighteenth century. If this is meant to imply a recovery after a period of poor health it is perfectly correct, for though the stream of Scots poetry had dwindled away to a mere trickle—of which here a song, and there a longer poem, or perhaps elsewhere a dance, are all that have come to the surface—yet it had never entirely ceased to flow. The Kirk had appropriated some folk songs (*Gude and Godlie Ballatis*), and had tried to suppress dancing, but these oral and irrepressible forms of poetry and music had evaded a strict censorship of the press.

There must have been a substantial body of poems and songs, originals or rehandlings of old pieces. Some were printed in James Watson's *Choice Collection of comic and serious Scots Poems both ancient and modern* (I, 1706; II, 1709; III, 1711); some, by "other ingenious young gentlemen," went into Ramsay's *Tea-Table Miscellany* (from 1724). Many of these occasional poets were "bonnet lairds" indulging in a kind of quaint homeliness, like William Hamilton of Gilbertfield, who not only contributed "The Last Dying Words of Bonnie Heck," but began an exchange of verse epistles with Allan Ramsay and paraphrased *Wallace* (1722). Between Ramsay and Fergusson this stream of poets and songsters increases, each usually contributing a few items only. They carried on a living tradition that had come down on the wings of song and with the steps of the dance. George Eyre-Todd's two volumes of *Scottish Poetry of the Eighteenth Century* (1896) is overwhelmingly made up of songs and ballads,[1] often to old tunes. There are, for instance, two independent versions of "The Flowers o' the Forest," by Jean Elliot (1756) and Alison Rutherford (Mrs Cockburn), both going back to some ancient song on the seventy Selkirkers who did not return from Flodden Field. Jean Elliot's song has caught the rhythm, economy, and suggestive force of a truly traditional song:

I've heard them lilting at the ewe-milking,
  Lasses a-lilting before the dawn of day;
But now there is moaning in [a]ilka green [b]loaning; *[a] every [b] lane*
  The flowers o' the forest are a' [a]wede away... *[a] (?) withered*

In [a]hairst at the [b]shearing nae youths now are jeering; *[a] harvest [b] reaping*
  [a]Bandsters are [b]runkled and [c]lyart and grey; *[a] sheaf-binders [b] wrinkled*
At fair or at preaching nae wooing, nae [d]fleeching; *[c] grizzled [d] coaxing, wheedling*
  The flowers o' the forest are a' wede away.

Many an eighteenth-century Scots song jigs to the liveliest traditional dance rhythms—such as the Rev. John Skinner's "Tullochgorum," a modern song set to an old tune, in which the repeats at the middle of each stanza resemble nothing so much as the rhythm of the dancers' feet as they "set" to their partners—and make the listeners' feet, too, itch to join in. Throughout the seventeenth and eighteenth centuries this practice was common enough, and Robert Burns carried this on, adding to it his own consummate art.

[1] Cp. the imitations mentioned above, pp. 149 f.

Much of eighteenth-century Scots poetry embodies the tunes, verse forms, and rhythms of popular song and dance—a consequence of the fact that it was not so much literary as communal poetry : it grew out of the interactions between the individual and the community in the village pub or in the club at Edinburgh. These poets were not writing in an ivory tower, but recited or sang their verses, as it were, on the sounding board of the community, and a special stimulus came from the clubs of Edinburgh ; we need only look into the closes and wynds of the Old Town to see why this should be so. Rooted as it was in communal experience, their work is full of popular and patriotic sentiment, and serves social purposes. During the eighteenth century, folk festivals continued to provide Scots rhymers with subject matter, as in John Mayne's *Hallowe'en* (1780) ; conviviality and a congenial society proved a strong stimulus ; and the verse epistles and similar addresses which had hitherto occurred sporadically now became a regular species of Scots poetry.

There cannot be any mutual response between a poet and his audience unless there is an antecedent community of feeling. The chief reason why the vernacular Scots poetry of the eighteenth century has so much more vitality than contemporary literary poetry is that it was much more deeply rooted in the national character and in the national culture. Many of its most obvious characteristics are purely traditional, and are not drawn from literature, but rather from the life of the living community : for example, the proud note of independence in George Halket's " Logie o' Buchan " ; the shrewd " realism " and scornful scoffing at pretence of " Wooed and married and a' " and " The Rock and the wee Pickle Tow," both by Alexander Ross ;[2] the hint of a mischievous smile in Ross's second version of " Wooed and married and a' " ; the grim humour (" Deill break his legs ") of Adam Skirving's " Hey, Johnnie Cope "[3] ; the ubiquitous use of understatement ; the frequent and characteristic use of a series of symbolic pictures to express indirectly an overwhelming emotion, as in William Julius Mickle's " The Sailor's Wife " (1771) :

> ' And are ye sure the news is true ? '...
> ' His very [a]fit has music in't — [a] *foot*
> When he comes up the stair.'

[2] In Ross's pastoral *Helenore* (1768), the girl says of her parents " They ken [know] ye like me, and they ken ye've gear [possessions.]" Similarly Robert Crawford.

[3] A Jacobite song on the English commander at Prestonpans (1745).

There is the same tense contrast of hard facts with moods of intimate tenderness (for example, Skinner's " The Ewe wi' the crookit Horn "), the same directness of statement, the same power of sharp visualisation, and the same habit of presenting a subject in pictures, or by means of a vivid comparison (for example Ross's *Helenore*) as in older Scots speech and poetry. These traits are most pronounced in the poets of the North-East, Alexander Ross, George Halket, John Skinner.

Though it thus derived its vitality from the living community, the development of eighteenth-century Scots poetry was also conditioned by influences that were purely literary. Much older Scots poetry was printed (and so rescued from imminent oblivion) in James Watson's *Choice Collection*, Allan Ramsay's *Ever Green* (1724), David Herd's *Ancient and Modern Scots Songs* (1769),[4] and others. These anthologies had a powerful effect which we can best examine in the poetry of Burns's two predecessors, Allan Ramsay and Robert Fergusson.

* * *

ALLAN RAMSAY (1684/5-1758) [5] was the moving spirit in the " revival ". It was thanks to him that social life, poetry, conviviality, and conversation found their happy union in such small, intimate groups as the Easy Club (his favourite), and others. Ramsay was much more important as (in this sense) a leader than as a poet in his own right. He was not only an ardent patriot on the defensive after the " treason " of 1707 ; but a touchy and self-conscious nationalist, highly suspicious of all intrusive foreign influences. In him, for the first time, we find outraged nationalism taking the form of sentimental Jacobitism. These feelings inspired his editorial work, but his highflying ambitions for Scottish culture ranged far beyond these reactions of the moment. By 1718, the lad who had come to Edinburgh from Lanarkshire in 1700 to be a wigmaker, had become a bookseller who sought to cater for the intellectual needs of the

[4] Herd's was the only anthology that did not modernise the texts.

[5] See *The Works of Allan Ramsay*, edd. BURNS MARTIN and J. W. OLIVER (hereinafter cited as *Poems*), S.T.S., 4 vols., of which only 2 have so far been published (1945-53). See also *Selected Poems by Allan Ramsay*, ed. H. HARVEY WOOD, Saltire Society, 1940 ; and reprints (*a*) of *Ever Green*, 2 vols., 1876, and (*b*) of *The Tea-table Miscellany*, 1871. The best study is Burns Martin, *Allan Ramsay*, Harvard 1931 ; see also D. Daiches, in *Scottish Poetry*, ed. J. Kinsley, 1955, pp. 155 ff., and Andrew Gibson, *New Light on Allan Ramsay*, 1927, in which some controversial points are raised.

capital. By 1728 he had opened the first circulating library in Great Britain, and his bookshop was the chief Edinburgh meeting-place for all men of letters. In 1736, he published a collection of Scots proverbs ; in 1729, forty years before the foundation, in London, of the Royal Academy, he (and his son Allan Ramsay, the painter) helped to found the Academy of St Luke for encouraging arts, painting, architecture, sculpture in Scotland. He gave much support to the theatre, not only by providing it with scripts, by writing pleas and prologues, by writing and adapting plays, and by himself acting as a manager, but also by founding in Carrubber's Close in 1736 Edinburgh's first regular theatre. Here, however, his ambitions aroused violent opposition among those of the clergy who still regarded plays and worldly literature as " Deil's wark." Despite his gallant fight, Ramsay's theatre was doomed in any case by Walpole's Special Licensing Act of 1737.

Ramsay's most important cultural achievement was as an editor. In the Preface to his own *Poems* (1721) he had defended the Scots tongue for its originality and wealth—thus, it can express the same idea by " empty, toom, boss, hollow "—and when presenting his anthology of *Ever Green, a Collection of Scots Poems wrote by the Ingenious before 1600* (2 vols., 1724), he opened on a note of freedom and stressed that " when these good old *Bards* wrote, we had not yet made Use of imported Trimmings upon our Cloaths." Maintaining that Scottish poets should once more, as before 1600, look north and describe Scottish landscapes, he chastises those ignorant of their own language. The overwhelming majority of the poems in the *Ever Green* are drawn from the Bannatyne MS, which he was able to borrow, and Ramsay enlarges the known field of Scots poetry by including many of the Makars' works that had not appeared in Watson's *Choice Collection* : thus he reprints Henryson's " Robene and Makyne " and some of the *Fables* ; makes a representative selection of Dunbar's poetry, including the " Flyting," " The Thrissil and the Rois," " The goldyn Targe," " The fenyeit Freir of Tungland," " The Dance of the sevyn deidly Synnis," " Dunbar's Dregy," " Lament : Quhen he was sek," and various other pieces ; gives several of Alexander Scott's poems, among them the " Justing " ; and adds, for good measure, the frivolous compositions of Robert Sempill, several flytings, " Christis Kirk on the Grene," " The Wife of Auchtermuchty," " The Battle of Harlaw," and others. From various other sources he also raked together another thirteen pieces—among them Montgomerie's *The Cherrie and the Slae* and " Solsequium," two of the *Gude and Godlie*

Ballatis, "Johnie Armstrang," Lady Wardlaw's pseudo-ballad "Hardyknute," and two of his own poems, presented here to avoid political trouble. As it was his aim to arouse public interest in Scotland's heritage he took considerable liberties in presenting his texts. He did not quite meet with the expected success; no second edition was called for in his life-time, and only four followed between 1761 and 1876.

The success achieved by its modern companion, the *Tea-table Miscellany, a Collection of choice Songs, Scots and English* (starting in 1724) thus was all the more striking. It contains "old songs," "old songs with additions," songs by unknown authors, and songs with "new words by different hands." We find old acquaintances like "The blythsome Bridal," and versions of such well-known ballads as "The Bonny Earl of Murray," "Barbara Allen," "Sweet William's Ghost," "Johnny Faa." Though fourteen editions appeared during Ramsay's life-time, many of his revised versions are depressingly sentimental and make one long for the lost originals. Ramsay had neither an ear for music nor a sure feeling for folk poetry. He could indulge in the vilest obscenity. Usually, however, he tries to "genteelify" a song, and many of his love-lyrics are highly conventional. When he forgets his fine feelings, he can sometimes turn out honest work; and with its evocation of the mirk, uncanny night and the cosy ingle, and its joyous, bouncing rhythm, "Up in the Air" [6] (which Madge Wildfire sings in Scott's *Heart of Midlothian*) is undeniably a splendid drinking song. Ramsay did arouse the desired interest and so preserved many tunes from total oblivion. Within a year there appeared the *Orpheus Caledonius* (London 1725), containing some fifty Scots songs with their music, and the ensuing string of song-collections finally culminated in Johnson's *Scots Musical Museum* (1787 ff.).

Ramsay's original poetry is likewise an amalgam of English Augustan neo-classicism and Scottish popular tradition. (This was itself an effect of the dualism which the Union had produced in Scotland). Whenever he is dealing with an elevated subject or addressing a polite audience, Ramsay affects a genteel, Anglo-Augustan tone, almost as if he wished to travesty the mastery of several different stylistic levels achieved by the old Scots Makars. In these poems, he violates his own precepts by introducing Cupids and Sylvans into a

[6] *Poems*, VOL. I, pp. 174 f.

Scottish setting; some of the most pompous (such as "Content"[7]) read like taskwork, others (such as "Bessy Bell and Mary Gray"[8]) are marred by an occasional false note. On the whole, Ramsay does not succeed in reconciling traditional Scots values with his own eighteenth-century notions of enlightenment, good taste and social propriety; in particular, his professions of being "content with small wealth" do not ring true. A number of his poems are newspaper stuff (for example, "The Rise and Fall of Stocks"[9]) with no real poetic feeling, and owing to the background of the club Ramsay tends to speak at the top of his voice all the time. His humour occasionally has the Scots quality of shrewdness (answer to William Hamilton's "First Epistle"[10]), but all too often, as in "An Epistle to Mr James Arbuckle,"[11] it resembles the commercialised and unspontaneous humour of the professional *compère*.

Yet we must judge Ramsay by his achievements, not by his failures. His temperament was, as he himself said, "mair to mirth than grief inclin'd"; and in dealing with simple subjects where he is more at home, the note that he strikes is quite genuine. Though coarser and less polished than their models La Motte and Lafontaine, his fables are warmer and more vivid. The simpler and "hamelier" subject-matter of such pieces brings out the best in Ramsay, who shows genuine social sympathy, with just a touch of rebellion in it, and portrays his characters with sober realism. There is nothing genteel or affectedly idyllic about such poems as "The Lass with a Lump of Land" and "The Widow,"[12] or about "Lucky Spence's Last Advice"[13] (ll. 33 ff.):

> Be sure to [a]truff his pocket-book, — [a] *rifle*
> Saxty pounds Scots
> Is nae [a]deaf nits... — [a] *empty nuts*

Ramsay has a good ear for the speech of the common people, and his dialogue reveals a keenly dramatic sense of character. "Richy and Sandy,"[14] his pastoral dialogue on the death of Addison,

[7] *Poems*, VOL. I, pp. 90 ff.
[8] *Poems*, VOL. I, pp. 49 f.
[9] *Poems*, VOL. I, pp. 176 ff.
[10] *Poems*, VOL. I, pp. 118 ff.
[11] *Poems*, VOL. I, pp. 212 ff.
[12] *Poems*, VOL. II, pp. 282 f., 287 f.
[13] *Poems*, VOL. I, pp. 22 ff. According to Ramsay, Lucky Spence was "a famous bawd who flourished . . . about the beginning of the eighteenth century."
[14] *Poems*, VOL. I, pp. 106 ff.

is cannily mock-heroic, and the way in which he makes its two characters, Steele and Pope, take down each other, and Addison himself, is characteristically Scottish. On the other hand, Ramsay's predilections must be largely held responsible for the increasing tendency to consider Scots as best suited for low, " hamelie " subjects and domestic verse.

Ramsay's debt to the older Scots poetry is obvious, but his imitations of older poems, such as " Christis Kirk II, III," [15] and " The Monk and the Miller's Wife " (after *The Freiris of Berwick*),[16] are of simpler and tougher texture than their models. Still, Ramsay has learnt the art of setting the scene in a few sharp phrases which light up the background as briefly and sharply as a flash of lightning. With two or three quick brush-strokes, he can suggest a Scottish landscape ; very occasionally he even shows almost the same heightened sensibility as Dunbar :

> ...the sun was wading thro' the mist.

> ...let's fa' to wark upon this green,
> The shining day will bleech our linen clean ;
> The water's clear, the [a]lift unclouded blew, *[a] sky*
> Will make them like a lilly wet with dew.[17]

Ramsay also has some intuitions of Henryson's art of suggesting the tenderness that underlies the hard outer surface, and his apostrophe to his book—" Daft giddy Thing ! to dare thy fate " [18]—foreshadows Fergusson's " Ode to a Butterfly," or Burns's address " To a Mouse." On occasion, Ramsay's Scots is precise and admirably direct ; it has not yet degenerated into a pastiche as with later imitators.[19]

These gifts which Ramsay derived from older Scots poetry—of characterisation, of pithiness of language, and of suggestiveness—are most conspicuous in his various pastorals. In these, as in the fables, he re-established the link with the European tradition ; and both pastorals and fables are at once more imaginative, more serious, and of wider scope, than the rest of his Scots poetry ; on a smaller scale, they represent a similar widening of compass as Douglas had achieved with his *Eneados*. Ramsay's pastorals have their roots in the soil, and lack

[15] *Poems*, VOL. I, pp. 66 ff. [16] *Poems*, VOL. II, pp. 146 ff.
[17] *The Gentle Shepherd* (*Poems*, VOL. II, pp. 205 ff.), ACT I, sc. i, l. 111 ; sc. ii, ll. 9 ff.
[18] " The Conclusion," (*Poems*, VOL. I, pp. 245 f.), l. 5.
[19] *E.g.* " Ann [if] thou wert my ain Thing," in *Poems*, VOL. II, pp. 79 f.

the artificially idyllic quality that occurs so frequently in English pastorals. At first sight, *The Gentle Shepherd* is of purely conventional structure, with the usual love chain, and a rather strained *dénouement* which reflects contemporary notions of the genteel.[20] Yet it has the charm of novelty, largely because the *mise-en-scène*, especially in the earlier parts, is genuinely Scottish : romantic ideas of love are dramatically contrasted with the realities of life (wait till the arrival of " them brats " !), and the dialogue echoes the canny talk of a community which is familiar with the risks of farming, and refuses to take things at their face value. No wonder that *The Gentle Shepherd* was long a favourite in Scottish villages, or that one or two of the songs helped to maintain its popularity :

My Peggie is a young thing,
  Just enter'd in her teens,
Fair as the day, and sweet as May,
Fair as the day, and always gay :
My Peggie is a young thing,
  And I'm not very auld,
Yet well I like to meet her at
  The [a]wauking of the [b]fauld... [21] — [a] *watching* [b] *fold*

Allan Ramsay is not a poet of the first, or perhaps even the second rank, but his courageous initiative determined the path of poetry in Scotland for a century to come. Even in 1721, there were 464 subscribers for Ramsay's *Poems*. Such was his personal prestige that he succeeded in reinvigorating a tradition that many had thought moribund : but concerned as he was chiefly with low life, he made most use of the coarser strands of this tradition, and though he consolidated it and gave it, so to speak, more body, he was not notably an innovator. Yet he succeeded in stabilising (and in popularising) certain forms that had not strictly been traditional. By casting it in Standard Habbie, Robert Sempill of Beltrees had given the mock elegy, as we have seen, a special twist, and Watson's *Choice Collection* contained two more mock elegies cast in the same metre. Ramsay followed up this example with a whole series of mock elegies in Standard

[20] This was partly a result of the advice of Ramsay's friends, who had persuaded him to expand a single scene into five acts. Similarly, the ballad opera version which he was prevailed upon to write (1728) is very inferior.

[21] Still more recently, *The Gentle Shepherd* was performed at the Edinburgh Festival in 1949.

Habbie: on Maggie Johnston, an innkepeer; on Patie Birnie, a fiddler; on Johnny Cowper, a Kirk Treasurer's man, whose job it was to spy out vice; and on Lucky Wood, an ale-house keeper.[22] Ramsay's treatment is much less flexible than Sempill's, and usually he is not craftsman enough to end every stanza with the rhyme-word "dead." Yet (especially in the two elegies on Lucky Wood and on Johnny Cowper) he does sometimes catch the true spirit of the mock elegy, and it was thanks to him that the *genre* became traditional.

The mock elegy, and the "dying words," seem deeply rooted in Scottish life, and are intimately connected with certain other aspects of Scottish tradition. The sharp dramatisation in form of monologue or dialogue satisfies the desire for concreteness of character so often shown in Scots poetry, and the frequent choice of an absurd or somewhat grotesque subject gives ample scope for a clash of appearance and reality, of pretentious solemnity and shrewd realism; some of the "last dying words" have the same touch of caprice as the older tocher-poems. This finds an excellent expression in Standard Habbie ($aaa_4b_2\ a_4b_2$): the house of cards so cunningly built up in the three long lines of the first part of the stanza is triumphantly completed in the short line following—only to be demolished with a snap of the fingers in the compressed second half.[23]

The Goliardic tradition of the "testament" took on, as we have seen, a special twist in Dunbar's "Testament of Mr Andro Kennedy." In Lyndsay's *Testament and Complaynt of Papyngo*, we have the "last dying words" of an animal; and in its honest pathos his *Complaint of Bagsche* still more strikingly foreshadows the later development of the type, which reaches completion in William Hamilton of Gilbertfield's "Last Dying Words of Bonnie Heck, a famous greyhound in Fife" (Watson's *Choice Collection*).[24] Ramsay followed Hamilton's example in "The Last Speech of a Wretched Miser," and in "Lucky Spence's Last Advice," which contains the shrewd and scurrilous last words of a dying bawd; but here, too, there is a certain coarseness of texture in Ramsay's work, and little of the contrast between illusion and reality is left.

Another *genre* that Ramsay was quick to take up from William

[22] *Poems*, VOL. I, pp. 10 ff., 14 ff., 18 ff., 186 ff.

[23] This sudden reversal is highly characteristic, and seems to arise out of a trick frequent in common Scots speech. For notice of further developments of Standard Habbie, see below, pp. 176 f., 216.

[24] The collection also contains another poem of the same type entitled "The Mare of Collingtoun newly revived," and signed "P.D."

Hamilton of Gilbertfield was the humorous verse epistle, often in Standard Habbie. There had been verse epistles before, but Hamilton gave his a characteristic turn, and his exchange of epistles with Ramsay set the pattern for subsequent examples. These Scots epistles are not really self-revelations. It is as if the poet steps outside himself and watches himself speaking—eyeing himself shrewdly, with an occasional dry laugh or scathing comment on life in the accent of conversation. There is plenty of caustic humour, but no pathos; and even in bestowing praise where it is due the poet does not give himself away or allow his searching eye to overlook human weaknesses: Hamilton may voice his admiration for Ramsay's power of expression in Scots—but his shrewdness also imagines him looking up quaint old words in a dictionary. Ramsay composed a round dozen of various epistles, some in rather a Horatian style.

Ramsay's prosody also shows how successfully he consolidated the Scots poetic tradition. In an age that mainly relied on a few classic verse forms, he used an astonishing variety of metres: some have internal rhyme, there is frequent alliteration, and occasionally a whole poem is built on one set of rhymes or assonances. These more intricate patterns came to him, however, with the tunes. Examples are "Katy's Answer," "Genty Tibby and sonsy Nelly," "Up in the Air," "The Widow,"[25] the *Cherrie-and-the-Slae* stanza and his numerous variations of the common measure. His favourite metres were the octosyllabic couplet, the heroic couplet, the stanzas of *The Cherrie and the Slae* and of *Christis Kirk*, and especially Standard Habbie, which he made increasingly popular. Ramsay is not lucky with Montgomerie's elaborate stanza, but must be given credit for having recognised its humorous possibilities. He retained the original Christis-Kirk stanza in *Ever Green*, but adopted the modified form of Bishop Gibson's edition of 1691 (and of Watson's *Choice Collection*) in his own rehandling and additions, as well as in Scott's "Justing." Here, in Ramsay's spelling, is the third stanza of *Christis Kirk* in its original form:

Of all thir maidens myld as [a]meid, — [a] *mead*
  Was nane sae [a]jimp as Gillie: — [a] *neat*
As ony rose her [a]rude was reid, — [a] *ruddy complexion*
  Her [a]lyre was lyke the lillie. — [a] *flesh*

[25] *Poems,* VOLS. I, pp. 52, 173 f., 174 f.; II, p. 287 f.

ᵃFow zellow, zellow was her ᵇheid ; — *ᵃ full yellow ᵇ head*
But scho of lufe sae silly,
Thocht all hir kin had sworn hir ᵃdeid, — *ᵃ death*
Scho wald haif but sweit Willie,
Alane,
At Chryst-Kirk of the Grene that day.

For the bob and wheel (c_1 D_4) Ramsay substitutes [26] a simple refrain (C_2) ending in " day " :

Tho' a' her kin had sworn her dead,
She wa'd have but sweet Willy
Alane that day.

This may seem but a slight alteration, but it jettisons the short line c_1, with its diabolically proud back-toss of the head. The stanza thus lost its old capacity for capering extravaganza, and became rather a medium for humorous story-telling—an effect which mirrored Ramsay's own temperament.

★ ★ ★

If Ramsay's efforts may be said to have banked up the main stream of Scots poetic tradition at a time when it was in danger of oozing out and disappearing in a swamp, the genius of ROBERT FERGUSSON (1750-74) can be fitly described as a new spring that imparted to it an additional volume, depth, clarity, and bubbling vitality that were all its own. Fergusson has often been represented as merely a forerunner of Burns, but this youth who after the death of his father had to leave St Andrews to support his mother, and who, at night, relieved the drudgery of the law office in the congenial and stimulating society of his beloved Cape Club, was truly a poet in his own right. Considering that he was only just over twenty-four when he died, Fergusson may well be regarded as one of Britain's most remarkable poets.[27]

Fergusson was truly a poet, in the sense that he expressed his whole experience in a form that makes it significant for us. Fergusson

[26] *Poems*, VOL. I, p. 58.

[27] The standard edition is *The Poems of Robert Fergusson*, ed. M. P. MCDIARMID (cited below as *Poems*), S.T.S., 2 vols., 1954-6. See also *The Scots Poems of Robert Fergusson*, ed. Bruce Dickins, 1925 ; and (same title) ed. J. Telfer, 1948, which has helpful notes ; and *Selections from the Scottish Poems of Robert Fergusson*, ed. A. Law, Saltire Society, 1947. There is much useful biographical and critical material in *Robert Fergusson 1750-74, Essays by various Hands*, ed. S. G. Smith (hereinafter cited as *R. F.*, ed. SMITH), 1952.

realised, not only that Scots was now only a language of restricted use, but also that it consequently was no longer subservient to the needs of court poetry or of polite letters ; and he was the first Scottish poet who deliberately exploited the fact that " plain Braid Scots " was not encumbered with too many purely literary associations, and had none of the artificiality of a court language. The words and images in such of his poems as " Caller Oysters " are simple and direct, but their simplicity is not the kind that makes us wince. Scots poetry is often " unadorned, but passionate and penetrative as Hebrew eloquence," [28] and this directness and simplicity are precisely the characteristics which enable it to reach the heart of the matter, and, in a few terse phrases, to state the naked facts. When combined with Fergusson's power of imaginative visualisation, these purely linguistic qualities may enable his apparently impersonal satire to express, directly and without moralising, emotions that are both personal and universal :

> But Law is a draw-well [a]unco deep, — [a] *remarkably*
> Withouten rim [a]fock out to keep ; — [a] *folk*
> A [a]donnart chiel, whan drunk, may [b]dreep — [a] *stupid fellow* [b] *drop*
> Fu' [a]sleely in, — [a] *easily*
> But finds the [a]gate baith [b]stay and steep — [a] *way* [b] *hard to climb*
> Ere out he win.[29]

The Scots that Fergusson wrote derives its essential potency from sheer intensity of vision, and whether it was or was not " pure " vernacular Scots is therefore, from our point of view, an irrelevant question. There is no need to suppose that Fergusson is reporting anything that he has actually heard said when he appeals to " Aqua vitae " :

> Be thou prepar'd
> To hedge us frae the black banditti,
> The City Guard ; [30]

or even when he writes of Adam :

> Nor did he [a]thole his wife's upbraidin' — [a] *endure*
> For being [a]fou.[31] — [a] *drunk*

[28] See C. M. Grieve (" Hugh MacDiarmid ") in *R. F.*, ed. Smith, p. 67.
[29] " The Sitting of the Session," ll. 61 ff. (in *Poems*, VOL. II, pp. 208 ff.).
[30] " The Daft-days," ll. 64 ff. (in *Poems*, VOL. II, pp. 32 ff.).
[31] " Caller Water," ll. 5 f. (in *Poems*, VOL. II, pp. 106 ff.)

Yet in these and many similar passages he undoubtedly expressed what many shrewd Scots might inwardly have felt. Fergusson was not a song-writer, and his poetry seldom expresses his personal emotions. Yet, however grimly expressed, his humour is tender, and beneath his outward emotional restraint there is immense depth. "Daft gowk," he exclaims on seeing a butterfly in the street, "daft gowk, in macaroni dress."[32] In themselves, the words are sober enough, but who can fail to perceive the wealth of imaginative sympathy that they express for a gay, ephemeral fellow-creature?

Fergusson wrote no plays, and his poetry contains less dialogue than Ramsay's. Yet is is perhaps even fuller of sharp dramatic contrasts. Like so many Scottish poets, he had a keen sense of character and a shrewd appreciation of moral realities. His refusal to take people or things at their face value is reminiscent of Henryson's "How lang will this lest?"[33] and it makes his "Eclogue"[34] much more than merely an imitation of Ramsay's pastorals. Nor is it any wonder that the Scottish winter, contrasted with a cosy fireside, provides his finest settings, as in the "Eclogue" itself, where, now that his gentle bride has turned into a "flyting fury" of a wife, Sandie complains (ll. 92 ff.):

> I'll see a braw [a]reek rising frae my [b]lum, — [a] *smoke* [b] *chimney*
> An' [a]ablins think to get a rantin blaze — [a] *perhaps*
> To [a]fley the frost awa' an' toast my [b]taes— — [a] *frighten* [b] *toes*

—but she with her "gimmers [gossips]" will be sitting round the ingle and "crammin their gabbies wi' her nicest bits," and he "out-by maun [outside must] fill his crap/Frae the milk coggie, or the parritch cap."

Fergusson stands much closer than Ramsay does to the central core of the Scottish tradition. His senses are keenly alive to all kinds of impressions—colour, smell, taste, sound. In him there again flares up the real flyting spirit with all its virtuosity, as when he addresses the Tron-Kirk bell:[35]

> [a]Wanwordy, crazy, dinsome thing, — [a] *unworthy*
> As e'er was fram'd to [a]jow or ring! — [a] *toll*

[32] "On Seeing a Butterfly in the Street," l. 1 (in *Poems*, VOL. II, pp. 154 ff.).

[33] There are many correspondences between Fergusson's poetry and Henryson's, *e.g.* "The grace is said—it's nae o'er lang" ("The Election," l. 59; *Poems*, VOL. II, p. 188); cp. Henryson, *F.*, l. 278.

[34] *Poems*, VOL. II, pp. 85 ff.

[35] "To the Tron-Kirk Bell," ll. 1-2 (in *Poems*, VOL. II, pp. 97 ff.)

Often, as on this occasion, he allows his imagination to go rushing off to grotesque extremes of logic, or seizes on some slightly unusual characteristic, and by exaggerating it produces what seems to be a new being, as in this glimpse of Old Edinburgh :

Now morn, with bonny [a]purpie-smiles, — [a] *purple*
Kisses the air-cock o' St Giles ;
[a]Rakin' their [b]ein, the servant lasses — [a] *rubbing* [b] *eyes*
Early begin their lies and [a]clashes ; — [a] *gossiping*
[a]Ilk tells her friend of saddest distress, — [a] *each*
That still she [a]brooks frae scouling mistress ; — [a] *puts up with*
And wi' her [a]joe in turnpike stair — [a] *sweetheart*
She'd rather snuff the stinking air,
[a]As be subjected to her tongue, — [a] *than*
When justly censur'd in the wrong.[36]

The underlying principle is the same as that which the Makars observed in their extravaganzas ; but Fergusson's most extravagant flights of fancy are sober in comparison with theirs. Less impetuous, less wayward, and less irresponsible, they are always guided by reason, and often end in renewed contact with reality, as in his address " To the Principal and Professors of the University of St Andrews, on their superb Treat to Dr Samuel Johnson," [37] when, having imagined the striking effect that might have been produced by a meal of haggis " weel tottled in a seything pat," sheep's head, " white and bloody puddins routh," and " sma' ale," he drily concludes (ll. 57 ff.) :

Then let his wisdom [a]girn an' snarl — [a] *show teeth in rage*
O'er a weel-tostit [a]girdle farl, — [a] *oatcake baked on griddle*
An' learn, that [a]maugre o' his [b]wame, — [a] *despite* [b] *belly*
Ill bairns are ay best [a]heard at hame. — [a] i.e. *spoken of*

Because they are thus controlled by reason, Fergusson's flytings (for example, " The Rising of the Session," " The Sitting of the Session," " A Drink Eclogue ") [38] can convey much serious social criticism, but something of the old diabolical grotesquerie remains, and they have none of the chill of purely intellectual satire. Even in his choice of subjects—" Plainstanes and Causey [causeway]," Whisky and Brandy, his " auld breeks," a butterfly in the street [39]—he is at once

[36] " Auld Reikie," ll. 23 ff. (in *Poems*, VOL. II, pp. 109 ff.).
[37] In *Poems*, VOL. II, pp. 182 ff.
[38] In *Poems*, VOL. II, pp. 127 ff., 208 ff., 210 ff.
[39] *Poems*, VOL. II, pp. 122 ff., 210 ff., 215 f., 154 ff.

boldly inventive and daringly grotesque. Nor is there anything conventional in his treatment of them. Instead he enters whole-heartedly into his creations, and so gives them abundant life.

Unlike Ramsay, Fergusson had a strong sense of style, and was more of a deliberate artist than any other Scottish poet (not excepting Burns) between the last of the Makars and R. L. Stevenson. He had studied with profit the works of such English eighteenth-century poets as Pope, Gay, Gray, and Shenstone, and the high standard that he set himself in his own sophisticated verse may partly have been derived from them. But he thoroughly assimilated all that he borrowed furth of Scotland : in particular, he steered clear of the poetic diction of the time, and in his work such a cliché as " hireling damsels " is quite exceptional.[40] With few exceptions, he used only the simplest metres (especially Standard Habbie, and octosyllabic rhymed couplets), and he never uses the old intricate song-metres. The last trace of the old predilection for formal elaboration, heavily-incrusted surface ornament and complex concatenations of rhyme has disappeared. By introducing a new set of rhymes into the second half of the revised " Christis Kirk " stanza, Fergusson turns it into double common measure with a refrain. In this final form, it becomes an admirably flexible medium for narrative, but can no longer provide the same purely intellectual delight as in its original pattern. Fergusson's instinctive feeling for metres enables him to achieve, nevertheless, a harmony of form and content which makes his own verse sound entirely natural. Though he left no songs, Fergusson's rhythms sometimes develop the furious pace of a reel (" The Daft-Days "),[41] and he had a nice touch with a refrain—as in the " Elegy on the Death of Mr David Gregory," [42] when the refrain " But now he's dead " is suddenly ousted (ll. 39 ff.) by an entirely different end-rhyme, with its own significant associations :

For Gregory death will fairly keep
 To take his nap ;
He'll till the resurrection sleep
 As sound's a [a]tap. [a] *spinning-top*

The slow rhythm and long lines in alternate rhyme of " The Farmer's

[40] See *The Farmer's Ingle* (in *Poems*, VOL. II, pp. 136 ff.), l. 95. This statement does not, however, preclude deliberate use of poetic diction for such special effects as those discussed below, pp. 177-9.

[41] In *Poems*, VOL. II, pp. 35 ff.

[42] In *Poems*, VOL. II, pp. 1 f.

Ingle" convey something of the same evening calm as Gray's "Elegy" in its similar metre. Fergusson's stanza here is modified Spenserian *abab cdcd d*. All lines have five stresses, but the last usually has an additional pause, which makes it seem longer; and sometimes it has, in fact, six accents (as in Spenser's stanza):

Till death slip sleely on, and gi'e the hindmost wound.[43]

This shows the degree to which Fergusson assimilates foreign influences. The slow, full movement of the verse endows this poem with a natural dignity such as Scots poetry had not known since the time of the Makars:

Whan gloming grey out o'er the welkin [a]keeks,	[a] *peeps*
Whan Batie [a]ca's his [b]owsen to the byre,	[a] *drives* [b] *oxen*
Whan Thrasher John, [a]sair dung, his barn-door [b]steeks,	[a] *sore wearied* [b] *shuts*
And lusty lasses at the [a]dighting tire:	[a] *winnowing*
What [a]bangs fu' leal the e'ening's coming [b]cauld,	[a] *overcomes full thoroughly* [b] *cold*
And [a]gars [b]snaw-tapit winter freeze in vain;	[a] *causes* [b] *snow-crested*
Gars [a]dowie mortals look baith blyth and [b]bauld,	[a] *gloomy* [b] *bold*
Nor [a]fley'd wi' a' the [b]poortith o' the plain;	[a] *frightened by* [b] *poverty*
Begin, my Muse, and chant in hamely strain.[44]	

Here there is no quaint rustic humour, no false humility, no abject self-consciousness: for Fergusson sees life whole and describes it as he sees it.

Fergusson's favourite stanza was Standard Habbie. The poems in which he uses it range from the flytings to the mock elegies; several of the latter, with their refrain "But now he's dead," are perfect masterpieces. Some of the poems in this stanza express honest sentiment; others are humorous, sententious, or, on occasion, caustically satirical. In each of these applications, Fergusson manages by skilful manipulation of the two short lines to achieve a different effect. In "Leith Races" [45] and in "Hallow-Fair," [46] he uses his own modification of the "Christis Kirk" stanza to depict the holiday crowds, and his tight-lipped comment makes the short refrain ending in "day" (or "night") a success; that he also wrote "The Election" [47] in the same metre had given it in his hands, from the

[43] "The Farmer's Ingle" (above, n. 40), l. 36.
[44] ll. 1 ff.
[45] In *Poems*, VOL. II, pp. 160 ff.
[46] In *Poems*, VOL. II, pp. 89 ff.
[47] In *Poems*, VOL. II, pp. 185 ff.

beginning, a sarcastic twist. He usually casts his dialogues in heroic couplets, or sometimes in octosyllabic couplets, which he also uses for his more serious satires, for his odes and addresses, and for " Auld Reikie," [48] his most ambitious poem.

In trying to assess the magnitude of Fergusson's contribution to the development of the Scottish tradition in poetry, we must not overlook the fact that his purpose was consciously patriotic. Most of his Scots poems appeared in *Ruddiman's weekly Magazine, or Edinburgh Amusement* (1772-74), a periodical devoted to the discussion of various aspects of Scottish culture, and some of them were directly inspired by articles which it had published.[49] Fergusson's was, however, a disappointed nationalism, and (as often in Scotland ever since the Stuart cause ceased to be an actual political danger) it took the form of romantic Jacobitism. Though scarcely a defeatist, Fergusson was culturally and politically on the defensive, and (if only because the dividing line between national and foreign could no longer be taken completely for granted) highly suspicious of foreign influences.[50]

Fergusson's main gift to Scots poetry was—or at least might have been—the contemporary and metropolitan character of his work. He was a man of the city, acutely aware of what went on around him and spontaneously writing down his experience with a new freedom from limitations. All his predecessors had been content, since Scots had become a vernacular, only to express in it the " hamely," humorous, mocking side of their nature. In his verse, Fergusson sought to express the *wholeness* of experience, and used Scots to emphasise its actuality. In the " Elegy on the Death of Scots Music," [51] there is first a deliberate contrast between classicism and " hameliness." The classicism is most pronounced in the second and third stanzas :

Round her [Music] the *feather'd choir* would *wing*,
Sae bonnily she wont to sing,
And [a]sleely *wake the sleeping string*, — [a] *slily, skilfully*
Their sang to lead,
Sweet as the zephyrs of the spring ;
But now she's dead.

[48] Above, n. 19.

[49] See J. W. Oliver, "Fergusson and *Ruddiman's Magazine*," in *R. F.*, ed. Smith, pp. 84-98.

[50] Cp. " The Daft-Days," " Elegy on the Death of Scots Music," " Hame Content," " To the Principal and Professors of the University of St Andrews," and "A Drink Eclogue " (in *Poems*, vol. ii, pp. 32 ff., 37 ff., 157 ff., 182 ff., and 210 ff.).

[51] In *Poems*, vol. ii, pp. 37 ff. All italics and quotation marks in the following extract from this particular poem are mine.

Mourn [a]ilka *nymph* and ilka *swain*, — [a] *every*
Ilk sunny hill and [a]dowie glen ; — [a] *gloomy*
Let *weeping streams* and *Naiads drain*
Their fountain head ;
Let *Echo swell the dolefu' strain*,
Sin' Music's dead.

In the fifth [52] and sixth stanzas the change of key already foreshadowed by " dowie glen " takes place :

Nae lasses now, on [a]simmer days, — [a] *summer*
Will [a]*lilt at bleaching of their* [b]*claes* ; — [a] *sing cheerfully* [b] *clothes*
Nae [a]herds on Yarrow's bonny [b]braes — [a] *herdsmen* [b] *hillsides*
Or banks of Tweed
Delight to chaunt their [a]*hameil* lays, — [a] *home-bred*
Sin' Music's dead.

At [a]glomin now, *the bagpipe's* dumb, — [a] *gloaming*
Whan *weary* [a]*owsen hameward come* ; — [a] *oxen*
Sae sweetly as it wont to [a]*bum*, — [a] *drone*
And *pibrachs* [a]*skreed* ; — [a] *were played briskly*
We never hear its *warlike hum*,
For Music's dead.

In the ninth stanza, having thus shown that he can beat the classicists at their own game, and what can be done with Scots, Fergusson makes explicit the point of the comparison :

Now foreign sonnets [a]bear the gree — [a] *hold first place*
And [a]*crabbit queer variety* — [a] *perverse*
Of sounds fresh sprung frae Italy,
A bastard breed !
Unlike that saft-tongued melody
Which now lies dead.

And though here, too, there are still some playful touches, there can be no mistaking the scornful underlying seriousness of the two remaining stanzas :

Cou'd " [a]Laverock at the dawning day," — [a] *lark*
Cou'd " [a]Linties chirming frae the spray," — [a] *linnets warbling*
Or " Todling burns that smoothly play,
O'er [a]gouden bed," — [a] *golden*
Compare wi' [a]*Birks of Indermay* ? — [a] *favourite Sc. tune*
But now they're dead.

[52] Though here, too, there are still (*e.g.* " chaunt their . . . lays ") a few further touches of classicism.

O Scotland ! that cou'd [a]yence afford *[a] once suffice*
To [a]bang the pith of Roman sword, *[a] overcome the strength*
[a]Winna your sons, wi' joint accord, *[a] will not*
To battle speed,
And fight till MUSIC be restor'd,
Which now lies dead ?

With all its beguiling sweetness and stateliness, this poem is quite as much a criticism of Anglo-Scottish poetic diction as it is a lament for Scots music, and it reveals the subtlety and skill with which Fergusson himself used Scots.

In the " Elegy on John Hogg, late Porter in the University of St Andrews," [53] Fergusson probes the moral and intellectual cast of a mind formed by popular Presbyterianism. Here, too, there is (ll. 55 ff.) an implied contrast between plain Braid Scots and the language, remote though dignified, of the Authorised Version :

' It's i' the psalms o' David writ
That this wide warld ne'er shou'd [a]flit, *[a] remove* (*intrans.*)
But on the waters [a]coshly sit, *[a] snugly*
Fu' [a]steeve and lasting.' *[a] firm*

All this betokens a more serious attitude towards the vernacular, and Fergusson raised it once more almost to the status of a language. In " The Ghaists : A Kirkyard Eclogue," [54] self-conscious " hameliness " gives way (ll. 55 ff.) to an assured gravity :

Think na I vent my well-a-day in vain ;
[a]Kent ye the cause, ye sure wad join my [b]mane. *[a] knew [b] complaint*
Black be the day that e'er to England's ground
Scotland was [a]eikit by the UNION's bond ; *[a] added*
For mony a [a]menzie of destructive ills *[a] host*
The country now [a]maun brook frae mortmain bills *[a] must endure*
That void our testaments...

Elsewhere,[55] we find the same deliberate gravity in scenes of nature :

Tho' simmer's [a]gane, an' we nae [b]langer view *[a] gone [b] longer*
The blades o' [a]claver [b]wat wi' pearls o' dew. *[a] clover [b] wet*
Cauld winter's bleakest blasts we'll [a]eithly [b]cowr, *[a] easily [b] recover from*
Our [a]eldin's driven, an' our [b]har'st is [c]owr ; *[a] fuel [b] harvest [c] over*

[53] In *Poems*, VOL. II, pp. 191 ff. [54] In *Poems*, VOL. II, pp. 141 ff.

[55] In " An Eclogue " (between " Geordie " and " Davie " ; *Poems*, VOL. II, pp. 82 ff.), ll. 9 ff.

Our [a]rucks fu' thick are stackit i' the yard, — [a] *stacks*
For the Yule-feast a [a]sautit mart's prepar'd ; — [a] *salted bull or cow*
The [a]ingle-nook supplies the simmer fields, — [a] *chimney corner*
An' [a]aft as mony gleefu' [b]maments yields. — [a] *often* [b] *moments*

The language used by Fergusson in the opening stanza of " The Daft-Days," [56] his first poem in Scots, seeks, for the first time since the Renaissance, to widen its scope :

Now [a]mirk December's [b]dowie face — [a] *dark* [b] *doleful*
Glowrs [a]owr the [b]rigs wi' sour grimace, — [a] *over* [b] *ridges*
While, thro' his *minimum* of space,
    The bleer-ey'd sun,
Wi' blinkin light and stealing pace,
    His race doth run.

From naked groves nae birdie sings,
To shepherd's pipe nae hillock rings,
The breeze nae od'rous flavour brings
    From *Borean* cave,
And [a]dwyning nature droops her wings, — [a] *dwindling*
    Wi' visage grave.

But above all, Fergusson is the poet of Edinburgh. He does give some glimpses of nature, and with its richly evocative pictures of farm life " The Farmer's Ingle " is not only a better poem than Burns' well-known piece " The Cotter's Saturday Night," but is perhaps the best of its kind in Scots or English literature. But, probably because they arise directly out of his own experience, Fergusson's pictures of life in Edinburgh are still more vivid. He sketches many fine portraits of the city itself in all its moods—especially the wintry ones :

Cauld blaws the nippin north wi' angry [a]sough, — [a] *moaning sound*
And showers his hailstanes frae the Castle [a]Cleugh — [a] *cliff*
O'er the Greyfriars.... [57]

In this harsh environment, cosy interiors seem all the warmer and more alluring, and in such a poem as " Caller Oysters," [58] with its glimpse of an oyster cellar where a congenial company unbuttons in

[56] In *Poems*, VOL. II, pp. 32 ff.

[57] *The Ghaists* (above, n. 54), ll. 7 ff.

[58] In *Poems*, VOL. II, pp. 66 ff.

friendly talk, the spirit of contrast inherent in all Scots speech and poetry thus receives (ll. 37 ff.) the fullest scope :

When big as [a]burns the gutters [b]rin, — *[a] mountain streams [b] run*
[a]Gin ye hae catcht a [b]droukit skin, — *[a] if [b] soaked*
To Lucky Middlemist's [a]lowp in, — *[a] jump*
And sit fu' snug
O'er oysters and a dram o' gin,
Or haddock [a]lug. — *[a] ear*

Fergusson can catch better than anybody the moods and movements of a crowd of holiday-making fair-goers. Often, it is true, the strength of the picture lies chiefly in its sharp observation of details and individual impressions : but this enables Fergusson to express the spirit of the crowd, and, as we have seen, Scots poetry is usually more interested in the details of a mosaic than in the total conception or structure.

It is in " Auld Reikie " [59] that Fergusson best evokes the metropolitan atmosphere. Here, too, the contrasts that he paints in with such an extraordinarily rich vocabulary, and with such fine control of tempo, are the main foundation of his success. The " bonny purpie-smiles of morn " may " kiss the air-cock o' St Giles," but they also hear the " lies and clashes " of " servant lasses," mingled with their tales of the " sad distress " they have to brook, and protestations that they would rather " snuff the stinkin' . . . air in turnpike stair " than stand the whims of " scoulin' mistress." There is even more inherent contrast in Fergusson's pictures (ll. 117 ff.) of the " macaroni," and (ll. 87 ff.) of the whore :

Near some lamp-post, wi' [a]dowy face, — *[a] gloomy*
Wi' heavy [a]ein, and sour grimace, — *[a] eyes*
Stands she that beauty [a]lang had [b]kend, — *[a] long [b] known*
Whoredom her trade, and vice her end....
And sings sad music to the [a]lugs, — *[a] ears*
'Mang [a]burachs o' damn'd whores and rogues.... — *[a] crowds*

Here contrast is made to express the diversity—both of lives and events—that goes to make up a city's day. Fergusson's realism is unshrinking, he also sees the seamy side of Edinburgh, but he is not morbid and does not moralise, nor does he exhibit Edinburgh life as a curiosity. He accepts it as it is, in all its complexity and all its

[59] Lit. " Old Reeky," i.e. Edinburgh (in *Poems*, VOL. II, pp. 109 ff.).

humanity, savouring it with all his senses—and Fergusson certainly does not forget smell! His greatest sympathy is with (ll. 247 ff.) the ordinary folk of his town:

> In afternoon, a' [a]brawly buskit, — [a] *dressed in their best*
> The [a]joes and lasses [b]loe to frisk it: — [a] *sweethearts* [b] *love*
> Some tak a great delight to place
> The modest [a]*bon-grace* o'er the face; — [a] *bonnet*
> Tho' you may see, if so inclin'd,
> The turning o' the leg behind.
> Now Comely-Garden, and the Park,
> Refresh them, after [a]forenoon's wark.... — [a] *morning's*

It is not merely that Fergusson has found a new milieu or subject. He brings into Scottish poetry a metropolitan spirit that he may have learnt from Pope and Swift. It is the antithesis of kailyard parochialism, it is a poetry that looks ahead. It has a bite, a sense of actuality, and even a touch of sophistication, such as had not been seen in Scots poetry since the Court had migrated to London. "Between Fergusson and MacDiarmid, Scotland remained a parish as far as her writers were concerned." [60]

* * *

The verse forms used by the Scots vernacular poets of the eighteenth century were, in general, much simpler than those so often adopted by the Makars: and there is in their work little of that conscious artistry which had prided itself on its mastery of several distinct levels of style, of that purely æsthetic enjoyment of form which had produced so much metrical intricacy and artificiality. Though something of the old spirit survived in the tunes to which many of their poems were set, internal rhyme and alliteration have lost their old prominence, and the metres themselves have hardened into a few fixed forms. Once it set in this was a continuing process. Was this simply a consequence of the fact that the migration of the Court had deprived Scotland of anything resembling a leisured class? Or of the fact that English (as we have seen) had ousted Scots as the language of intellectual discourse? Or are its causes rather to be sought more strictly within the limits of the eighteenth century?

The want of a leisured class must certainly have helped to restrict

[60] S. G. Smith, in *R. F.*, ed. SMITH, p. 30.

the scope and subject matter of eighteenth-century Scots poetry. There is little religious or contemplative poetry ; no attempt at anything analogous to aureation ; and only an occasional glimpse of " high life." But there is also less nature poetry ; and though there is certainly some underlying extravagance in the last wills and mock elegies, and in some of the folk songs, such flyting as still occurs is more earthbound, less apt to fly off at a tangent, than in former days ; for example, the lovers' oaths in *The Gentle Shepherd*, which are merely, by sixteenth-century standards of " unpossibilities," rather a mild brew. This cannot have been due to lack of models, of which Watson's *Choice Collection* and the *Ever Green* both contain plenty in many different metres.

But if some traditional characteristics of Scots poetry are apparently on the wane, other traits are becoming increasingly prominent. Serious poems seem to have lost contact with contemporary European trends, and are increasingly stiffer and more austere ; while comic verse (which is much more plentiful) is becoming " hamelier " than ever —and more provincial. Though there is less sensuous impressionism, there is more grim humour and more realism, and the old shrewdness often displays a frankly more businesslike bent. And, above all, the mocking spirit, which sees through pretence and excels in taking it down, now has pride of place, and satire takes on its keenest edge. Was this merely an expression of the spirit of the eighteenth century ? Or of the personal idiosyncrasies of those concerned ? Or, now that Scotland is no longer an independent nation, have the Scots themselves become cynically mistrustful of all that is grand or high-sounding ?

Though there may be something in each of these explanations, undoubtedly there is more to it than that : for whereas all the most obviously Celtic characteristics of Scots poetry are on the decline, those which express a more Lowland outlook [61] are now predominant. This tallies with the picture historians give us.[62] Scotland has always had two cultures—Lowland Scots and Gaelic. In the time of the Makars, there may have been friction between the two ; but at least there had been contact. Gaelic and Lowland Scots met and mingled at the Court of James IV, and strong pressures which made for amalgamation seem to have continued into the reign of James V. All that is amply attested by the Celtic qualities that can be seen in the Lowland Scots poetry of the fifteenth and sixteenth centuries.

[61] As defined, *e.g.*, by Ian Finlay, *Scotland*, 1945.

[62] Cp. G. M. Thomson, *A Short History of Scotland.*

Yet (as many allusions in Dunbar's poetry show) there had always been a mutual antagonism between Gaelic and Lowland Scots. Though some of the largest Highland clans embraced the Protestant cause, the Reformation drove a wedge between Highland and Lowland. After the removal of the Court, there was less chance of mutual fertilisation, and all the wars that followed helped to deepen the gap. Both before and after the Union, the policy pursued by Scotland's rulers was often intended to sharpen and exploit existing differences between Highlanders and Lowlanders,[63] and during the eighteenth century these differences were still further accentuated by the ever-increasing contrast between Lowland prosperity and Highland poverty. Altogether, it is hardly surprising that Scots poetry should have become less Celtic and more Lowland during this period.

One further reason should not be overlooked : the direct impact of the Reformation. Presbyterianism was itself partly an outcome of the dominant traditional characteristics of the Scottish nation, but was bound in turn to modify them in certain ways. Though the Kirk (or at any rate its Presbyteries) has often attempted to circumscribe the freedom of creative writers,[64] it is a wild exaggeration to maintain that its influence on literature has been purely negative. In Calvinism, which he describes as " rigorously logical, indeed materialistic and mechanical in character," John Speirs [65] sees the root of many characteristics of Scottish eighteenth-century society which were really asking for social satire of the type of the " Elegy on John Hogg " ; [66] but this is only skimming the surface, and it can hardly be doubted that the influence of the Reformation went a good deal deeper. Who would deny that the tradition of the Covenanters, whose sayings read like bleak austere poetry, has left its mark deep on the national character? As Miss M. P. Ramsay has pointed out,[67] the Calvinist ideal in art is defined by Calvin's sentence : " But forasmuch as carving and painting are the gifts of

[63] One of the things that caused deepest resentment was quartering of the Highland troops among the Covenanters of South-west Scotland to prevent any repetition of the Pentland Rising.

[64] Cases in point are those of John Home, himself a minister, who had to resign his charge because of *Douglas* ; Burns, who was ordered to stop writing secular poetry ; John Wilson, who had to sign, before being appointed a teacher, a kirk document to effect that he would write no more secular verse ; and, in our own day, Robert Kemp, one of whose Scots plays was censured by the Presbytery of Ayr when performed on TV in 1956.

[65] " Tradition and Robert Fergusson," in *R. F.*, ed. Smith, pp. 106 ff.

[66] In Fergusson's *Poems*, vol. ii, pp. 191 ff.

[67] *Calvin and Art, considered in Relation to Scotland*, Edinburgh 1938.

God, I require that they be both pure and lawfully used " ; and by his further requirement that art should only present what the eye was capable of grasping. Hence arises the realistic, moral, and distinctly Protestant conception of art that we find in Holland, another Calvinist country. This is certainly the conception which dominates the work of the Scottish portrait-painters of the seventeenth and eighteenth centuries, from Jamieson to Robert Aikman and Allan Ramsay ; and even though some of the poets were at loggerheads with the Kirk, its influence is also apparent in eighteenth-century Scots poetry. The Protestant realism at least is there, with its insistence on fact and character, while much of the gusto, wild fancy, and irresponsibility of the older period have disappeared.

4. The Scottish Gaelic Tradition

Finally, no history of Scots literature in the eighteenth century would be complete without some account of Scottish Gaelic literature. I am not qualified to write authoritatively about Celtic poetry, nor is it essential to my present purpose that I should. But if we wish fully to understand the Lowland Scots tradition, we must at least take a glance in the bygoing at the traditional poetry of the Highlanders.[1]

Though Gaelic-speaking Scotland had originally been part of a common Gaelic sphere of culture with its heart in Ireland, the Norse invasions severed many bonds, and *The Book of Deer* contains some twelfth-century marginal notes in a Scottish variety of Gaelic. As shown by *The Book of the Dean of Lismore* (1512-26) [2]—the earliest

[1] It seems incredible that nothing has yet been done to compare the Gaelic, Scots and English branches of Scotland's national literature. A useful though uncritical and unsatisfying survey of Sc. G. literature is contained in Magnus Maclean, *The Literature of the Celts*, 2nd edn. 1926, and *The Literature of the Highlands*, 2nd edn. 1925. See also *Bardachd Ghaidhlig 1550-1900*, a verse anthology, ed. W. J. Watson, 2nd edn. (cited below as B. G.) 1932, which contains a helpful introduction ; D. S. Thomson, " Scottish Gaelic Folk-poetry *ante* 1650." in *Scottish Gaelic Studies*, VIII (1955) ; *Reliquiae Celticae*, edd. A. Cameron and J. Kennedy, 2 vols., 1892-4 ; *Carmina Gadelica* (*Ortha nan Gaidheal*), a collection of hymns, incantations, etc. ed. A. Carmichael, 1900 (2nd edn., ed. A. Matheson, 5 vols., 1928-56) ; *Deirdire*, traditional prose tales, ed. A. Carmichael, 1914 ; and *Rosg Gaidhlig*, a prose anthology, ed W. J. Watson, 1929.

[2] See (1) *Scottish Verse from the Book of the Dean of Lismore*, ed. and tr. W. J. Watson, S.G.T.S., 1937, cited below as *S.V.L.* ; and (2) *Heroic Verse from the Book of the Dean of Lismore*, ed. and tr. N. Ross, S.G.T.S., 1939, cited below as *H.V.L.*

Highland manuscript anthology, compiled a generation or so before those of Maitland and Bannatyne—the influence of the Irish bardic schools still remained dominant, even in Scotland, for several centuries. Forty of the sixty poets named in this collection were Scottish, and were either professional or hereditary bards, or titled amateurs (Thomson). The book contains several " Ossianic " ballads,[3] together with many elegies, satires, incitements to battle, and some moral and didactic verse. Among other striking features of these poems one might mention frequent outbursts of flyting often combined with extravaganza [4]; the occurrence of a mock elegy and at least one animal poem [5]; occasional heavy alliteration,[6] and a gradually increasing preponderance of end-rhyme.

But the downfall of the Lord of the Isles in 1494 cut the ground from under the feet of the classic bard dependent on his chief; and with the Flight of the Earls in Ireland in 1603 the stage is set for the modern school of poets, unprofessional and untrained. The old rigid categories of eulogy, elegy, satire, lose their supremacy, and slowly make way for wider themes; the esoteric poetic language of the learned bards is superseded by a colloquial Gaelic which still, however, contains many echoes of bardic heritage; and the old strict forms and syllabic metres are soon replaced by more varied verse and stressed metres, which, though less strict, are not less intricate.[7] Stressed poetry is more obvious in Scottish Gaelic than in Irish,[8] because there are so many labour songs (especially waulking songs), with their strong rhythms. There arises a new class of poets drawn from all social levels, of which the principal figures are, in seventeenth-century Scotland, Máiri Nighean Alasdair Ruaidh (Mary

[3] Printed in *H.V.L.* See also J. F. Campbell, *Leabhar na Féinne*, 1872, which contains some 54,000 lines of heroic Ossianic verse; there is even a theory that the Ossianic epic cycle is of Scottish origin with Irish offshoots.

[4] Some of the poems in *S.V.L.* resemble the later Scots tocher [dowry] poems, *e.g.* Nos. III (pp. 14 ff.) and XXIX (pp. 218 ff.), and " poems of impossibilities," *e.g.* No. XXX (pp. 224 ff.), with which cp. also the Irish *MacConglinne's Vision.*

[5] Cp. *S.V.L.*, Nos. III (pp. 14 ff.) and XVII (pp. 140 ff.).

[6] Cp. *S.V.L.*, Nos. II (pp. 6 ff.; quoted above, p. 109) and XXIX (pp. 218 ff.).

[7] According to D. S. Thomson (above, n. 1), and O. Bergin, " The Origin of modern Irish rhythmical Verse," in *Mélanges linguistiques offerts à Holger Pederson*, p. 280, stressed metres had already appeared sporadically in the 11th and 15th cents., so that they may have existed side by side with syllabic poetry as the ordinary form of folk poetry or popular verse, later to become dominant with the decay of bardic authority. Mr R. L. C. Lorimer informs me that *ceòl mór* (" pibroch," *i.e.* the classical Highland bagpipe music of the 17th and 18th cents.) *may* similarly have developed out of an earlier popular vocal music.

[8] Cp. W. J. Watson, *B.G.*, pp. xviii ff., xxxii ff.

MacLeod, *c.* 1615-1707),[9] Iain Lóm (John MacDonald of Keppoch, *c.* 1620-*c.* 1710), and Eachann Bacach (Hector Maclean, *fl.* 1648). Their poetry is transitional, and still has many strong links with the past in style, diction, and choice of subject; Mary MacLeod's poems are elegies and panegyrics on her chief, MacLeod of MacLeod, and his immediate kinsmen. But poetry also began to be composed about such new (or at any rate non-bardic) subjects as love, political questions transcending the interests of single clans, and so forth; and the style of the new poets is fresh, spontaneous, and sincere. Poetry is no longer, in their eyes, a mystery, an esoteric craft. It is an art, a means of self-expression, a "sensuous attempt to convey music in words"[10]; and the feeling for vowel harmony is at its strongest in their verse. From 1640 or so until the end of the eighteenth century, many of the new poets, if not most, were strongly attached to the Stuart cause. Scottish Gaelic poetry received its strongest impetus from the last Jacobite rebellion,[11] and reached the peak of its achievement during the fifty years which followed the final downfall of the Stuart cause at Culloden in 1746. Alasdair macMhaighstir Alasdair (Alexander MacDonald, *c.* 1700-*c.* 1770),[12] whose poems were the first Scottish Gaelic verse printed (1751), and, at his best, Donnchadh Bàn nan Oran ("fair-haired Duncan [McIntyre] of the Songs," 1724-1812)[13] are perhaps the two finest poets Scottish Gaelic has had; while Iain Ruadh Stiùbhart (John Roy Stewart, 1700-52), Rob Donn [Mackay] (1714-78)[14] with his love songs, elegies, and satires, Dugald Buchanan (born 1716) with his spiritual songs, Iain MacCodrum (1710-1796),[15] Uilleam Ros (William Ross, 1762-90),[16] are themselves no mean poets.

Here a brief account of the work of ALEXANDER MACDONALD,

[9] See *Gaelic Songs of Mary MacLeod*, ed. and tr. J. C. WATSON, 1934, which contains a useful introduction. See also the unpublished thesis (Aberdeen 1956) on Mary MacLeod by Dr Anne Mackenzie.

[10] M. Maclean, *The Literature of the Highlands*.

[11] Cp. *Highland Songs of the 'Forty-five* (*Duain Ghàidhealach mu Bhliadhna Theàrlaich*), ed. and tr. J. L. Campbell, 1933.

[12] See *The Poems of Alexander MacDonald*, edd. (with verse "translation") A. and A. MACDONALD, Inverness 1924 (of little real scholarly value; cited below as *Poems*).

[13] See *The Songs of Duncan Ban McIntyre*, ed. and tr. A. MACLEOD, S.G.T.S., 1952; here cited as *Songs*.

[14] See *Orain agus Dain le Rob Donn macAoidh*, ed. A. Gunn and C. MacFarlane, Glasgow 1899.

[15] See *The Songs of John MacCodrum*, ed. and tr. W. MATHESON, S.G.T.S., 1938; here cited as *Songs*.

[16] See *Gaelic Songs by William Ross*, ed. G. CALDER, 1937.

DUNCAN MCINTYRE, and IAIN MACCODRUM may help to illustrate some of the essential qualities of the new Scottish Gaelic poetry, at any rate as these appear to me. Even today, Scottish Gaelic-speakers have a special affection for the songs of Duncan McIntyre, which almost sing themselves ; but by common consent Alexander MacDonald was the greatest poet of the three.

Perhaps the first impression that the work of these three poets produces is that few languages are so richly poetical as Gaelic, with its immense vocabulary, sensuous precision, and subtle modes of expression ; but if the reader's own conceptions of poetry are based chiefly on a study of West European literature, his dominant impression may well be that their poems have no organic structure —no plot, no exposition, no climax, and no moral content.[17] There is no epic—even the longest of them are not much more than 500 lines in length—and no drama : nothing, indeed, that would have needed a sustained effort and an underlying intellectual system. But Gaelic poetry has its own principles of composition —that is why it is in some respects so different from European, or from classical, poetry—and its lack of structure is often only apparent.

Take Duncan McIntyre's " Praise of Ben Dorain," [18] which with its 554 lines is his longest poem. It is in form an imitation of pibroch or classical bagpipe music. A stately " ground " (*ùrlar*) is followed by a lively first variation (*siubhal*). When these have alternated three times, the ground is resumed for the last time, and leads finally to the *cruinnluath*, a fast and extremely lively concluding variation. McIntyre's sole theme is the praise of Ben Doran, a mountain in Glen Orchy, south of Rannoch Moor, on which he had once been employed as a stalker or forester. This is, of course, a limited subject ; but in each successive ground and variation, he turns it round and round—naming many different parts of the mountain and the memories they evoke in him, cataloguing its plants, and describing the life of the deer that he has so often stalked there—until he has exhausted its possibilities, and has thus brought his poem to an end. Here, and in most Gaelic poetry, the aim is completeness combined with

[17] Cp. Stanley Cursiter, formerly Director of the National Galleries of Scotland, in *Scotland*, ed. H. W. Meikle, p. 201 : " Sculpture has never held an important place in Scottish art. From whatever cause, the urge to give shape to thought in terms of volume and planes has offered less attraction than the possibility of using colour and pattern. It is indeed in ' pattern ' that [Scottish] sculpture has had some distinction."

[18] *Moladh Beinn Dobhrain*, in *Songs*, pp. 196 ff.

sharp clarity of detail. That is why the canvas is so small. The subject must be one that the poet knows intimately,[19] and he must confine himself entirely to his immediate surroundings, but must also be a sufficiently accomplished technician to be able, not only to fill the whole of this limited surface, but also to unify his design by integrating it, in all its elaborate details, with an intricately concatenated metrical pattern. The parallel with Celtic sculpture is obvious.

The requirement that the subject must be turned round and round till all its possibilities are exhausted gives rise to a series of exact pictures, each adding some fresh detail—with never a repetition.[20] This in turn gives rise to a profusion of descriptive epithets [21]—itself a natural outcome of the highly substantival and adjectival character of the Gaelic language. As many as three or four adjectives (some compound) are often placed side by side in one line, without a conjunction or even a comma, as in Duncan McIntyre's "Song to Summer":

> Gu tarrgheal ballbhreac bòtainneach
> sgiathach druimfhionn sròinfhionn guailleach.[22]

> [(Calves) bright-bellied, spot-speckled, stout-legged,
> whiteflanked, white-backed, white-nosed, high-shouldered.]

Vivid though such static descriptions often are, the charm of the best Gaelic poetry lies rather in what is left half-said, and therefore in the subtlety of Gaelic syntax, which has a strongly modal and con-

[19] It is said that many fine pibrochs have been lost because the pipers who knew them would not play them unless they were "note-perfect." Cp. *S.V.L.*, No. XXXVI (pp. 248 f.): "Woe to the man who has lost his voice, and has a flood of song, and cannot sing with them, and knows not how to hold his peace. . . . Woe to him that clutches often at the fruit his hand cannot reach. . . ."

[20] Cp. the wealth of technical detail in Alexander MacDonald's elaborate sea-poem *Clanranald's Galley* (*Birlinn Chlann Raghnaill*, in *Poems*, pp. 370 ff.); in the 16th-cent. "An Duanag ullamh" (*B.G.*, p. 259); and in Duncan McIntyre's *Praise of Ben Dorain*, which contains, *e.g.*, a precise description of a gun-lock, lists of the plants eaten by red deer, and much minute topographical detail, chiefly of interest to stalkers (*Songs*, ll. 2792 ff., 2950 ff., and *passim*). Cp. too, McIntyre's precise description ("Oran do Chaiptein Donnchadh Caimbeul," in *Songs*, ll. 941 ff.) of Capt. Campbell's sword: "Lann ùr nan trì chlaisean . . . 'S i sparrt' an ceann aisneach (New blade of triple fluting. . . . Firmly fixed in a ribbed hilt)."

[21] Which sometimes, in inferior work, degenerates into mere wordy frothiness: cp. Watson, *B.G.*, introduction.

[22] "Oran an t-Samhraidh" (*Songs*, ll. 2728 ff.).

ditional approach [23] which enables a poet to catch the most transient images in a swift series of phrases powerfully suggestive of light and movement : a shaft of sunlight bright " as a dash of lime," the " foam-white rowing," a glittering pool, and even the quick shimmer of trout jumping, when for a split second we see flashing scales and spots. This impressionism, amounting almost to *pointillisme*, runs all through it, and is indeed its chief charm. I do not know any other poetry (though Scots poetry perhaps comes second) in which colours and other sensuous impressions play such an essential role. These numerous minute images suggest to the mind a totality, a special mood. There is little or no philosophical reflexion, the pictures are quick flashes or miniatures complete in themselves, never vague, often dynamic. Gaelic poetry demands a picture rounded off within the couplet, or at least the quatrain. With its substantival approach (" he put sharpness on it " instead of " he sharpened it "), and its paratactic sentence structure, which prefers a sequence of clauses linked merely by *agus* (" and ") to one of clauses subordinated by means of other conjunctions, the Gaelic language inevitably gives rise to this kind of impressionism. In poetry, the effect is heightened, for in trying to render his own impressions the poet gives us a precise description not only of the thing perceived, but also of the image which it creates in his own mind. To call this comparison or metaphor does not fully do justice to it : it is better described as a flashing-together of two pictures, the more concrete one giving substance to the less tangible. Thus Gaelic is pictorial even when most abstract : the notes from MacCrimmon's pipe chanter are as numerous as the midges around a roe-buck in summer-time ; his fingering on the chanter suggests wicker-work ; somebody may be as full of loyalty and valour as a sea-piet's egg of food (Alexander MacDonald). In Duncan McIntyre's " Song to his Bride " [24] it may at first seem odd to find her compared to a sapling, a sea-trout, etc. But all the qualities that he enumerates —suppleness, sweetness, whiteness, etc.—together make up his total impression of the woman he loves, and each also suggests to him the image of something else that he loves dearly : trees and saplings,

[23] Thus the potential mood is often used to make a positive statement polite : " B'e mo chomhairle dhuit sin a dheanamh," *i.e.* " It were my advice to you to do it." On the other hand a statement may for emphasis be put in the form of a conditional sentence : " Chunnaic e tigh beag fada uaidhe, agus'ma b'fhada uaidhe, cha b'fhada esan g'a ruigheachd," *i.e.* " He saw a little house a long way off, but if it would be a long way off, he would not be long reaching it " (from J. F. Campbell's *West Highland Tales*).

[24] " Oran d'a Cheile nuadh-phosda," in *Songs*, pp. 114 ff. See esp. ll. 1668-83, 1732-9.

blossom, a sea-trout, a swan, the morning star, apples, quartz, bog-cotton. And to anybody who does not know that the tree, with its sap, is traditionally a symbol of the chief and of his blood, the following stanza from the older bardic poem by Cathal macMuiredhuigh (MacVurich) would be totally unintelligble :

Mo bile bugha fa mheas
  mo chridhisi an cuanna cas
  mc flatha air nàr foilghedh fes
  mo chrios catha an boinn gheal bras.[25]

[My tree of virtue in fruit,
  my heart the handsome curly one,
  the son of a prince from whom knowledge was not concealed,
  my belt in battle the intrepid fair drop.]

This is almost the technique of the Imagists as practised in Ezra Pound's " In a Station of the Metro."

This technique tends to obliterate the line between animate beings and inanimate objects. Any familiar object, such as man's pipes, fiddle, musket, halbert, may be addressed by name as a person, usually indeed as his sweetheart ; in the case of the *pìob mhòr* this is not at all astonishing, because to the piper the bag seems to be breathing, as if he had his arm round a girl's waist. It is not only in Gaelic poetry that an animal may be treated as a person, or at any rate as an embodiment of valour and honesty ; but the extent to which this is done in Gaelic poetry is remarkable. And that preoccupation with the immediate object of attention which is so characteristic of Gaelic poetry gives added intensity and makes these personifications all the more vivid. In one of his songs, Duncan McIntyre praises a gun " whose striker never refused to spark for him " ; [26] in another he addresses his own gun in terms that have the same feeling of comradeship as Burns's " Auld Farmer's New-year Morning Salutation to his auld Mare Maggie " :

Hóro mo chuid chuideachd thu,	[Ho-ro, my own comrade,
Gur muladach leam uam thu....[27]	Sad am I without thee...]

[25] *Reliquiae Celticae* (above, n. 1), VOL. II p. 240. The last line of the previous stanza is " Mo re lán is mabhall úr," *i.e.* " My full star and my new apple," and the passage as a whole is addressed to Donald, the poet's chief, though this is only implied, and there is no address in the second person.

[26] " Cumha Ghill-easbuig Ach-Chaladair [Lament for Archibald Campbell of Achallader] " : *Songs*, ll. 1175 f.

[27] " Oran do'n Ghunna dh'an Ainm nicCòiseim [Song to the Gun called Coiseam's Daughter] " : *Songs*, ll. 3320 f.

Still more remarkable, however, is the Scottish Gaelic poet's attitude to nature. He describes it with so much absorption that his own personality is dropped entirely out of view. He almost identifies himself with his object. In Alexander MacDonald's " Song to the 'Sugar Burn'," [28] the honey-covered leaves " creep backwards " out of sight of the children ; and Duncan McIntyre knows the deer so well that he smells what they smell, feels what they feel, sees the world with their eyes. (In the " hermit poetry " of the eighth to the tenth centuries, as Professor Kenneth H. Jackson points out, there is such intimate sympathy with the wild creatures among whom the hermits lived that the poet almost becomes one with them, or own brother to them, as if hardly conscious of any distinction between man and animal.[29]) It is an attitude that makes all nature a living being, and in Alexander MacDonald's " Curse on the Hillock " [30] the hillock itself is no longer a part of the landscape, but a living person, a fellow-creature, an agent in the life of men : this is a subject to which we shall recur in speaking of the " pandemonism " or " animism " of such writers as Hardy, Stevenson, G. D. Brown and Neil Gunn.

These new nature poems are perhaps the most remarkable achievements of eighteenth-century Gaelic poetry. Much has been made of James Thomson's (and Allan Ramsay's) influence on the seasonal poems of Alexander MacDonald, Duncan McIntyre, Rob Donn, Ewen MacLachlan, William Ross, and Dugald Buchanan, but Thomson and Ramsay only influenced them in the choice of subject : the keen delight in sensuous detail that they show in execution is purely Gaelic. It is a measure of the Gaelic poet's characteristic clannishness that nature always means his own glen, his own mountain, his own burn.[31] There is nothing vaguely sentimental about the nostalgia that Duncan McIntyre feels in Edinburgh : it is thoroughly realistic and is sharply focussed on precise pictures.

Perhaps the first thing that strikes one is the lack of a horizon

[28] " Oran do Allt an t-Siùcair " : *Poems*, pp. 44 ff.

[29] K. H. Jackson, *Studies in early Celtic Nature Poetry*, 1935. A fine example is *Pangur Bàn*, a hermit's poem on his white cat (K. Meyer, *Selections from ancient Irish Poetry*, 1911).

[30] " Aoir a' Chnocain " : *Poems*, pp. 276 ff.

[31] Cp. Duncan McIntyre, " Oran do Ghleann Urchaidh [song to Glen Orchy]," " Oran Coire a' Cheathaich [Song to Coire a' Cheathaich, lit. Corrie of Mist]," *Moladh Beinn Dobhrain* [Praise of Ben Dorain], " Cead deireannach nam Beann [Final Farewell to the Hills]," in *Songs*, pp. 160 ff., 164 ff., 196 ff., 386 ff. ; and Alexander MacDonald, " Oran do Allt an t-Siùcair [Song to the 'Sugar Burn']," in *Poems*, pp. 44 ff.

and of distant views even in Alexander MacDonald's sea-poems "Iorram Cuain [Rowing Song]" and *Birlinn Chlann Raghnaill* [*Clanranald's Galley*].[32] Instead, attention is concentrated on the immediate environment, precise details of which are listed with meticulous care. In his *Praise of Ben Dorain*, Duncan McIntyre gives a topographical account of the vegetation that is almost scientifically exact; he knows what kinds of grass will grow at such-and-such a spring, when the deer will feed in such-and-such a corrie, what they will eat, and so forth.[33] There is no general survey; the poet concentrates exclusively on the things with which he is immediately concerned, and his description of them is highly specific. His beloved deer are not conventional figures, like those in Landseer's paintings; they are living individuals, and he notes, for example, that the brows and eyelids of one particular hind show that she is healthy. As there is no ground-plan, the details are such as might apply to any mountain, but the order in which the images actually present themselves, and the impressions they evoke, are peculiar to this one particular locality as only the poet knows it. In total effect, the details are so vividly portrayed that they come fully to life. The detailed portrayal of nature in such a poem as Alexander MacDonald's "Oran do Allt an t-Siùcair [Song of the 'Sugar Burn']" has the same purely æsthetic fascination:

'S do bhoirchean daite, sgùm-gheal,
Tiugh, flùireineach, dlùth, tlàth....

[Thy banks coloured, foam-white,
thick, flowered, close, gay...];

the horse quenching its thirst in the cold brook and hearing its murmuring voice; the jumping trout; the foam rising in the milking-pail; the azure jewel flashing on each blade of grass.[34] The hallmark of eighteenth-century Gaelic nature poetry is indeed that almost everything that is said is purely factual, and that nothing is said that

[32] *Poems*, pp. 364 ff., 370 ff. The *iorram*, a specific form, has a strong rhythm based on that of an oarsman's pull and forward swing. As kings and chiefs were often buried in the island of Iona, the rhythm of the *iorram* became that of the *cumha* or lament.

[33] Cp. *Songs*, ll. 2934 ff., 3102 ff., etc. According to H. R. Fletcher, in *Scotland*, ed. H. W. Meikle, pp. 20 f., several plants found in the Highlands "are remarkable for their rarity, being confined in their few known localities to a very small area. For instance, on the wet rocky ledges of the Cuillin, and nowhere else, grows the Alpine rock cress."

[34] *Poems*, pp. 44 ff. (see esp. pp. 46, 47, 50).

does not express the object itself. Nature is valued solely because of the æsthetic delight which it affords ; there is no philosophical reflexion on it, no pantheism.

Of other species, there are eulogies and elegies (*marbhrann*, " death-song " ; *cumha*, " lament ") as of old, partly with traditional phraseology ; clan poems, incitements to battle, political songs, labour songs,[35] boat-songs, etc. New patterns are created in love-songs,[36] which—even where, as in William Ross's, Burns's influence is felt—are equally exhaustive in their enumeration of precise descriptive detail. Though, as in Scots, there had hitherto been little religious poetry, the state of mind induced by the final defeat of Jacobitism, and by the subsequent social and economic changes, was more receptive to it. Ever since the middle of the eighteenth century, hymns have been an essential feature of Gaelic poetry ; and even mysticism has made its appearance (especially in Dugald Buchanan, David Mackellar, and Donald Macrae).

Another highly remarkable feature is the so-called humorous or satirical poetry. Both terms are inadequate ; for it is really a mixture of humour and satire, with a strong dash of mocking diablerie thrown in for good measure. Alexander MacDonald, Duncan McIntyre, John MacCodrum, and Rob Donn all helped to develop the mock elegy which had already appeared in Gaelic poetry, and is so conspicuous in Scots eighteenth-century vernacular poetry ; and the eighteenth century produced mock elegies on a pet dove, a dog that broke through the ice, a cock that a hunter mistook for a kite, a ewe that had given the poet all his livelihood, a man whom Satan laments as unequalled in roguery. Though they are not so well-defined a species in Gaelic as in Scots, there is in these elegies an exuberant mockery which tends to run away with the poet and certainly has little in common with contemporary English mock elegies—for example, Gray's " Ode on the Death of a favourite Cat." Taken together, the essence of all these poems is that they express the spirit

[35] In " Morag " (*Poems*, pp. 148 ff.), Alexander MacDonald very skilfully disguises a political poem as a " waulking song " in which he addresses his Prince as " Morag of the wavy hair," and begs him to come and help to waulk the red cloth. Either he was using a conceit already popular in the Highlands, or his song gave rise to the traditional " Coisrigheadh an Aodaich [The Conservation of the Cloth]," in *Carmina Gadelica* (above, n. 1), VOL. I, p. 306.

[36] At a slightly later date, these are sometimes concerned with the parting of two lovers on the shore where those evicted in the Clearances are embarking for America—a setting that naturally tends to produce melancholy.

of—all in one—flyting, extravaganza, defiance of social convention, diablerie. Love, pride, hatred, obscenity and sensuality, are all richly and compassionately intermixed in the poet's soul. The spirit flares up at any touch of harness, and the same full-blooded vehemence goes into incitements to battle, political invectives, bawdy songs and drinking choruses ; these bards are no prudes, and on occasion their language is extremely scurrilous.

The drinking-songs make use of such motifs as that the son of malt makes the coward a hero and enables the dumb to speak ; such motifs no doubt were common currency throughout Scotland, and some of them also appear in the drinking-songs that Burns fashioned or refashioned out of the traditional materials available to him.[37] The Gaelic drinking-songs, however, are more precise and show more sensuous subtlety than contemporary Scots specimens—for example, Alexander MacDonald's " Royal Bottle Song " : [38]

'N uair bheirear a botul an staipeal
'S a chromar ri cab a chluas,
'S éibhinn a' ghogail là earraich,
Cagar searraig ris a' chuaich....

'S binne d' easraich dol 's a' chupan,
Copadh usgraichean gu d' bheul,
Na co-sheirm organ is chruitean
An talla druidte le 'n cuid theud.

'S binne na ceòl coilich-choille
Bhiodh ri coilleig air an tom,
Dùrdail a' bhotuil ri gloine,
Crònan loinneil thoilleadh bonn.[39]

[37] Cp. John MacCodrum, " Caraid agus Namhaid an Uisge-bheatha [Friend and Foe of Whisky]," *Songs*, ll. 551-2 : " Fear gun cheiltinn air cùinneadh/'N am bhith dlùthachadh ris," *i.e.* " A man who does not hide his money when one draws near to him "—almost an anticipation of Burns's " Surely you'll be your pint-stowp [stand me a pint], And surely I'll be mine." Is there a similar insistence on *treating* in any non-Scottish drinking-songs ?

[38] " Oran rioghail a' Bhotuil," in Poems, pp. 200 ff.

[39] *Poems*, pp. 206-7. " When the stopper is removed from the bottle, and the ear is bent to its mouth, it is delightful, on a spring day, to hear the clucking, the whispering, the flask makes to the bowl. . . . Sweeter the cascade thou makest going into the cup, the jewels foaming to thy lip, than the harmony of organ and harps of many strings played together in a closed hall. Sweeter than the music of the woodcock, as he sings on the hillock, is the murmuring of the bottle to the glass—a cheerful croon well worth a coin." Cp. John MacCodrum (" Caraid agus Namhaid an Uisge-bheatha "), *Songs*, ll. 490-2 : " My bottle, held by the neck, makes froth on my stoups—what delectable music to me their gurgle and clink [*an crònan 's an gliog*] ! " It is characteristic of Gaelic that it can find a word precisely denoting each of the sounds made by whisky when poured into a glass.

Flyting is evident in dozens of poems, against a rival or a neighbour, a bad tailor or a rascally shoemaker, the Unclothing Act or political opponents. Perhaps the finest example is John MacCodrum's "Dispraise of Donald's Pipes." [40] After a deceptively restrained opening, the poet's soaring imagination hurries him off on the wildest flights of fancy, but even when he is intent on pushing exaggeration to its extreme limits, his descriptions are still as perfectly concise, and as exhaustive as ever :

> Ceòl tha cho sgreataidh
> Ri sgreadail nan ròcas,
> No iseanan òga
> Bhiodh leointe chion bhidh...
> Mar rongan bà caoile
> 'S i faotainn a 'bhàis.[41]
>
> [Music as scunnersome
> as screeching of rooks,
> or young birds
> pained by lack of food....
> Like the rattle of a lean cow,
> and she nearing her death.]

Many of the flytings are dramatic verse dialogues, in which two bards flyte one another, sometimes with violent obscenity ;[42] and besides these there are some other dramatic verse dialogues—between the emblems of two chiefs, between a friend and an enemy of whisky, between Prince Charles and the Gael, and so forth.

Thus there is, on the one hand, plenty of grotesque exaggeration : but, as in Scots, there is also plenty of understatement. As a rule, Gaelic uses more words than are strictly necessary, and is often expressively emphatic. In voicing painful emotions or tender feeling, it however prefers understatement, and sorrow and pathos are usually expressed in language of unaffected simplicity. Inward emotion is often indicated by contrasting outward appearances : "after the battle each man draws his half-pay, while he [the hero of the elegy]

[40] "Diomoladh Pìoba Dhomhnaill Bhàin" : *Songs*, pp. 62 ff.

[41] *Songs*, ll. 959-62, 1036-7. Note the onomatopoeia.

[42] Cp. Alexander MacDonald, "Rannan eadar am Bàrd agus an t-Aireach Muilleach [Verses between the Bard and the Mull Herdsman]," in *Poems*, pp. 280 ff. ; and Duncan McIntyre's songs "Do Charaid Tailleir air son Cuairt shuirghe [To a Tailor's Friend anent a courting Visit]" and "Do'n Taillear [To the Tailor]," in *Songs*, pp. 86 ff., 90 ff.

has been left behind, stockstill upon the battlefield." [43] As in Scots, understatement is often effected by negation (" to be outstripped was not this breed's experience " ; " I mislike not your style "), or by not specifying the full amount (*gu leoir*, lit. " enough," instead of " very "). This unsentimental style is specially effective in two well-known eighteenth-century Gaelic songs on old age—Duncan McIntyre's " Cead Deireannach nam Beann [Final Farewell to the Hills] " [44] and John MacCodrum's " Oran na h-Aoise [Song of Old Age]."[45] Certainly there is no false pathos in the latter's final " I dislike thy approach." Indeed, with its metrical austerity, its factual approach, and even its keen sense of the absurdity of old age (which leaves the top of the head rather ugly), it effectively refutes the whole conception of " Celtic Twilight."

One further aspect of eighteenth-century Gaelic literature remains to be mentioned : the emergence of folk-poetry [46] in the mid-century MS collections, and its influence on the recognised poets. Scottish Gaelic folk-poetry is immensely richer than Irish. The reason may be, in part, the stronger bardic tradition in Ireland, but Derick Thomson suggests that the chief reasons to which it was due were (1) that class differences were less marked in Scottish clans, so that even the humblest clansman enjoyed a higher social status than the Irish peasant, and (2) that the educational system perhaps was more egalitarian.[47] This popular poetry was usually simpler, with more end-rhyme and end-assonance, and less ornamentation and internal rhyme ; but when with the new popular poets it achieves a higher social status, some of the older adornment comes back. Thomson finds a certain affinity with balladry in heroic folk poems,[48] but these Gaelic poems and songs are usually more specific and personal, and are often in the first person. Of relevance for us are the bold images, vivid visualisations, the " impossibilities " that are a feature in Gaelic love-songs to the present day, and the waulking-songs in dialogue that begin with a praise of one's own birthplace and end in vituperation of one's partner's.

After all this it scarcely seems necessary to sum up all the points of contact between Scots and Gaelic literature. The chief respects in

[43] Duncan McIntyre, " Cumha Ghill-easbuig Ach-Chaladair [Lament for Archibald Campbell of Achallader] " : *Songs*, ll. 1145 ff.

[44] *Songs*, pp. 386 ff.

[45] *Songs*, pp. 14 ff.

[46] See D. S. Thomson (above, n. 1).

[47] Cp. above, p. 127.

[48] See above, pp. 134 ff.

which Scots differs from English poetry are that it shows a stronger feeling for colour (and for other sense-impressions) ; its imagery is sharper and more detailed ; it is capable of much greater metrical complexity ; is apter to personify inanimate objects ; takes a keener interest in nature, especially in its wilder aspects ; is full of the spirit of clannishness ; and makes a speciality of flyting and extravaganza. All these features are still more strikingly characteristic of Scottish Gaelic poetry, which also differs from Irish poetry in showing a stronger folk element, a more " democratic " spirit, a harder core and firmer substance, " more simplicity and straightforward diction," [49] and (in its understatements) greater restraint—if not grimness—in expressing tender feeling. Once again, these are the very points of contact with Scots. It does not matter whether the resemblance between Scots and Scottish Gaelic poetry are attributable to literary influence (and in fact *literary* influences cannot have had much effect on a learned but illiterate islander from North Uist like John MacCodrum), or to an originally Celtic common taste, or to a common national tradition and a common national character. What the resemblances establish is that though the great majority of the poets on either side did not even understand the other side's language, there was in fact a good deal of common ground.

[49] One Irish scholar, Douglas Hyde, stresses these features of Sc. G. poetry, " while Irish has more melody and word-play, but also nebulousness and unmeaning sound." Another, Daniel Corkery, finds Sc. G. simpler and more direct than Irish poems (*The hidden Ireland*, 1925, p. 130). See also M. Maclean, *The Literature of the Celts*, p. 251.

VII

High Water Mark

1. Robert Burns (1759-96)

SCOTLAND's national bard has been the subject of so much study, criticism, and eulogy that it hardly seems possible to shed new light on any single facet of his achievement.[1] Yet some new aspects do emerge in the fresh perspective which results if we consider his work in relation to the development of the Scots literary tradition as a whole.

Though Henry Mackenzie's legend of the " heaven-taught ploughman " has long been discredited, Burns himself helped to create it, and as long as the " Immortal Memory " is honoured, it will never entirely die out. Yet we know how diligently Burns studied the literary heritage of his own country, and what were considered the classics of eighteenth-century English poetry. Burns was nothing if not an artist ; he took his stand on Scots popular tradition, and within the compass of the Scots tongue he played on several different registers. His faults were not those of a man who had read little, but of one whose reading had not been sufficiently discriminating. Any literary history of today enumerates all that Burns inherited from past Scots literary tradition : the mock elegies, often on animals or living people ; the violent satires ; the poems on country fairs, folk life, and amusement, including drinking-songs ; verse epistles, often of a humorous type containing mutual admiration and winding up with the hope of a convivial evening together ; and of course the folk-songs. It

[1] For a full critical evaluation of Burns's achievement, the reader may be referred to D. Daiches, *Robert Burns*, New York 1950, London 1952.

Quotations in this chapter are from *The Poetry of Robert Burns*, edd. W. E. HENLEY and T. F. HENDERSON (" Centenary " edn., cited below as H. & H.), 4 vols., 1896-7. See also *Works*, ed. W. Scott-Douglas, 6 vols., 1877-9 (new edn. 1895) ; *Life and Works*, ed. R. CHAMBERS, revised by W. WALLACE, 4 vols. 1896 ; *The Songs of Robert Burns, now first printed with the melodies*, ed. JAMES C. DICK, London 1903. Selections : *Poems*, edd. H. W. Meikle and W. Beattie, Penguin 1946 ; ed. L. Brander, World's Classics 1950. For correspondence, see *Letters of Robert Burns*, ed. J. DE LANCEY FERGUSON, 2 vols., Oxford 1931. The best biographies are Hans Hecht, *Robert Burns, the Man and his Work*, tr. J. Lymsburn, London, 1936, and F. B. Snyder, *The Life of Robert Burns*, 1932.

is also a commonplace that Burns adopted, and artistically perfected, the metres traditionally associated with each of these familiar types: Standard Habbie—which he makes so popular that it is now called the Burns stanza—for elegies, epistles, and many occasional poems; the Christis-Kirk stave in its revised form, sometimes with Fergusson's greater freedom of rhymes, for fairs, crowd scenes, popular festivities; the complicated Cherrie-and-Slae stanza with its musical background. Usually, too, it is pointed out that in his refrains Burns faithfully observes certain established conventions: in an elegy each stanza usually ends on "dead," in the Christis-Kirk stave on "day" or "night." Finally, Burns's debt to Allan Ramsay and Robert Fergusson is invariably recognised. To the latter it was great indeed. Burns had almost given up poetry when Fergusson's works fell into his hands and showed him what could be done with the vernacular, and many of Burns's poems are undisguisedly developments of Fergusson's. Burns expresses his admiration in the lines:

> O thou, my elder brother in misfortune,
> By far my elder brother in the Muse! [2]

In this Indian summer of the Scots literary tradition, Burns was the commanding figure who by sheer force of personality raised Scots vernacular poetry to the level of high art; and in this Fergusson may well be regarded as having been his fore-runner.

If we wish really to understand Burns's place in the tradition, we must, however, go deeper than this, and in this chapter I shall try to answer these four questions: (1) What conclusions does Burns's work enable us to draw about the use of Scots or English in Scottish poetry? (2) How did the eighteenth-century reduction of Scots to the status of a socially restricted vernacular affect his verse? (3) What less obvious features of the Scottish tradition are found in Burns? (4) Is it true that Burns accepted the convention as it left the hands of his predecessors and contributed nothing except his own personality (Henley)?

In answer to the first question, it is not enough to quote Burns's own statement that he never composed successfully in English, for even in his Scots poems he often slips into English—or something closely resembling it. In "Tam o' Shanter," [3] most of the comments

[2] "Apostrophe to Fergusson" (H. & H., VOL. II, p. 211).
[3] H. & H., VOL. I, pp. 278 ff.

expressing communal attitudes or the imagined words of the different characters are in plain Braid Scots :

> Ah, Tam ! Ah, Tam ! thou'll get thy [a]fairin ! *[a] present from a fair*
> In hell they'll roast thee like a herrin ! [4]

But in one, at least, the tonality is somewhat different :

> Care, mad to see a man sae happy,
> E'en drown'd himsel amang the [a]nappy . . . *[a] ale*
> Kings may be blest, but Tam was glorious,
> O'er a' the ills o' life victorious ! [5]

Though all this is still unmistakably Scots, only a small change of spelling (" *Tom* was glorious," etc.) is required to make the second of these couplets *visually* indistinguishable from English. This foreshadows a distinct change of key :

> But pleasures are like poppies spread,
> You seize the flow'r, its bloom is shed ;
> Or like the snow falls in the river,
> A moment white—then melts for ever ;
> Or like the borealis race,
> That flit ere you can point their place ;
> Or like the rainbow's lovely form
> Evanishing amid the storm.[6]

On the printed page, these lines *are* almost indistinguishable from English.[7] Immediately after them, Burns returns, as it were, to the home key—

> Nae man can tether time or tide ;
> The hour approaches Tam [a]maun ride ; [8] *[a] must*

—and in order to maintain the poem's linguistic unity, they have to be *pronounced* with a Scottish accent. Thus they fall within the compass of Scottish speech, and the language employed in them cannot strictly be called " English " ; perhaps it should rather be termed " near-English," " Anglo-Scots," or " Scots-English." Here it is used—like a lifted forefinger—" to point a moral and adorn the

[4] Ll. 201-2. [5] Ll. 53 ff. [6] Ll. 59 ff.

[7] Almost, but not quite : cp. " Or like the snow falls [= that falls] in the river," and the rhyme " river—ever."

[8] Ll. 68 f.

tale," and there is about it a certain slight hint of Augustan poetic diction. Characteristically, however, the abstract is presented in a series of concrete images from nature. This is no language " alien " to Burns, nor of " thought " as against " emotion " (Muir). It is the voice of the pulpit tradition, and consequently the school tradition, which ever since John Knox had found expression in English (but English close enough to the Scots way of speech, with its emphasis on the concrete). However, the language here is not Biblical, which would have implied an affinity with Holy Willie. (But it is remarkable that both the " Address to the unco Guid " and " Holy Willie's Prayer " [9] end on an approximation to standard English, too.)

Near-English of this type gives " Tam o' Shanter " a touch of perfection. In " The Cotter's Saturday Night," [10] English has, however, a very different effect. The description of supper and family worship in the second and third stanzas (the real beginning of the poem) are grand, and hold out the promise of a still nobler achievement. The slow movement of the verse suggests gravity as well as weariness, and English—Biblical English—is used to describe family worship. All this is as it should be. So far Burns moves within native traditions.

Yet even here there are signs of danger. The sentence-structure is loose and un-Scottish. In " the miry beasts retreating frae the pleugh," the word " retreating " seems wrong,[11] and when one comes to the " lisping infant," [12] one can only suppose that Burns is now writing a language which he did not speak, had never heard spoken, and had only known in books. Elsewhere (especially at the beginning and again at the end) the language is glaringly artificial, and in place of the poet's own personality there is only a sham elegance, a drooping, affected posturing :

> I've pacèd much this weary mortal round,
> And sage experience bids me this declare . . . [13]

This is not Burns at all, but a schoolboy who has been given an essay to write. Indeed, most of Burns's poems in the eighteenth-century

[9] H. & H., VOLS. I, pp. 217 ff. ; II, pp. 25 ff.

[10] H. & H., VOL. I, pp. 106 ff.

[11] St. ii, l. 3 : contrast with Burns's song " The Lea Rig " (H. & H., VOL. III, pp. 284 f.), st. i, ll. 3-4 : " And owsen [oxen] frae the furrowed field *Return* sae dowf [dull] and weary, O."

[12] St. iii, l. 7.

[13] St. ix, ll. 3-4 ; cp. st. v, ll. 5-6 : " The parents partial eye their hopeful years, Anticipation forward points the view," in which the poet's combination of concrete and abstract is singularly inept.

Augustan or sentimental diction read like a task in Latin versification set at school, complete with lofty sentiments and all.[14] When he is at his best, as in " The twa Dogs," " The Holy Fair," and " Tam o' Shanter,"[15] Burns flashes abstract ideas together and presents them in terms of a convincing picture taken from real life, and often including local allusions :

> The fear o' Hell's a hangman's whip
> To [a]haud the wretch in order.[16] — [a] *hold*

> While Common-sense has [a]taen the road, — [a] *taken*
> An' [a]aff, an' up the Cowgate — [a] *off*
> Fast, fast that day.[17]

Without in any way impairing the validity of the abstract ideas expressed, this intensifies their impact ; sometimes, as in " The Ordination,"[18] abstract conceptions of vices and virtues are made to resemble real actors wearing masks—very much as they were in Dunbar.

So there are really *three* strata of language in Burns : the Scots of the folk and of native poetry ; the near-English (or Scots-English) of the pulpit ; and Burns's own variety of literary neo-classical Augustan English. Only the last of these was diametrically opposed to his own genius, and it alone rings false. Burns lacked the power of assimilating the English literary fashion and making it his own ; he had less of it, for instance, than Fergusson. But were his contacts with Thomson and Shenstone, Pope and Young, *The Man of Feeling* and *Tristram Shandy*, entirely fruitless ? They certainly exercised a chastening influence on the riotous feelings in his breast, as he himself will tell us[19] ; they heightened and widened his sympathy with all beings, as is best seen in " To a Mouse,"[20] which is artistically unified, whereas (as underlined by the use of " daisy " instead of " gowan ")

[14] *E.g.* " To Ruin " (H. & H., VOL. I, pp. 139 f.), " at whose destruction-breathing word," etc. ; and the " Address to Edinburgh " (H. & H., VOL. I, pp. 239 ff.), " Edina ! Scotia's darling seat ! " (This line was aptly displayed on the Floral Clock in Princes St. Gardens, Edinburgh, at a time when Sir Will Y. Darling was M.P. for South Edinburgh).

[15] H. & H., VOL. I, pp. 9 ff., 36 ff., and 278 ff.

[16] " Epistle to a young Friend " (H. & H., VOL. I, pp. 140 ff.), st. viii, ll. 1-2.

[17] " The Holy Fair " (H. & H., VOL. I, pp. 36 ff.), st. xvi, ll. 7 ff.

[18] H. & H., VOL. I, pp. 210 ff.

[19] Cp. Burns's autobiographical letter to Dr John Moore, *Letters* (above, n. 1) VOL. I, No. 125.

[20] H. & H., VOL. I, pp. 115 ff.

its companion piece " To a Mountain Daisy "[21] remains a conceit. It delivered him from the danger of parochialism and helped him to find the uninhibited attitude towards popular superstition that makes the success of " Tam o' Shanter."

This linguistic stratification is curiously reminiscent of the different levels of style so characteristic of the poetry of the Makars, with its power of effortless transition from one to another. But this very comparison emphasises the restricted scope of eighteenth-century Scots poetry, and in this respect it seems almost a travesty of the work of the early masters : the courtly and ceremonial side is crippled ; morality either moves on borrowed stilts or mocks barefoot ; and the satiric and folk element has an unhealthy preponderance—rather as if Dunbar had written " The twa mariit Wemen " and " The Dance of the sevin deidly Synnis," but not " The Thrissil and the Rois " or any of his other allegorical and religious poems. Whereas Dunbar's bells often peal joyfully enough, Burns's have nearly always a sombre reverberation, with overtones of harsh and bitter mockery :

> Orthodox ! Orthodox !—Wha believe in John Knox . . .[22]

It was a stunted tradition that Burns inherited. His genius raised it to the highest artistic level. But could his achievement stem the tide ? In propounding his hypothesis that Scotland has developed a split mind which feels in Scots and thinks in English, Edwin Muir lays much stress on those technical and artistic deficiencies of eighteenth-century Scots vernacular poetry which arose out of the fact that Scots was no longer a language for all purposes.[23] It would not, however, be strictly accurate to say that Burns in his Scots poems only expresses emotion of a level that is not heightened by thought—see, for example, " To a Mouse "—or that thought could only have been expressed in English. Burns, it is true, was not a highly educated poet, nor always a very critical one, but, given his temperament and its background, that was only to be expected. In his Scots poems, Fergusson, the townsman and ex-student, shows more intellectual substance, more invention, sometimes more relevancy, more critical ability, and, in adapting foreign models, a surer touch. Burns's achievement lies in other fields, in which he is unrivalled. He has

[21] H. & H., vol. i, pp. 136 ff.

[22] " The Kirk's Alarm " (H. & H., vol. ii, pp. 30 ff.), l. 1.

[23] Cp. chapters entitled " Language " and " Comparative " in E. Muir, *Scott and Scotland*, 1936.

his finger tighter on the pulse of the common people, and, transcending time and place, his unique personality achieved art-poetry of a universal appeal. It was, in some measure, his lack of formal education which made it possible for him to salvage and preserve the Scottish folk songs, an achievement of immense cultural importance : collecting, sifting, preserving what was valuable, retouching, joining, recreating, till the spirit of folk song is clothed in consummate art. Dr Daiches's study of " Auld lang syne " reveals his mastery of this refining and restoring process.[24]

Such a study shows at the same time that Burns stands in the very heart of the Scottish tradition and of the Scots way of speech. The nostalgic feeling of change and passing time is evoked, not by abstractions, but by pictures of concrete experience of a wider symbolic significance. The strength of Scots has always been centred in its power of giving direct, concrete expression to emotions which specifically arise out of a given situation. We find this directness everywhere in Burns [25] ; the abstract and the universal is always closely bound up with a definite situation (as in a proverb) and assumes general symbolic value by a step so quick and direct that we are not even aware of it, as in

> The best-laid schemes o' mice *an' men*
> Gang aft [a]agley ; [26] — [a] *askew*

in

> Twa dogs, that were na [a]thrang at hame . . ., [27] — [a] *busy*

where there is a similar interlinking of the animal with the human plane ; and in

> We twa hae paidl'd in the burn,
> Frae morning sun till dine . . ., [28]

with its matter-of-fact plural (or dual), which admits *any* man or woman to a half-share in this reminiscence of lost childhood.

If concreteness is one salient feature of Scots speech, another is

[24] D. Daiches, *Robert Burns*, pp. 356 ff.

[25] Cp. " The Holy Fair," " Death and Dr Hornbook " (H. & H., vol. i, pp. 36 ff., 191 ff.), and many of the songs.

[26] " To a Mouse, on turning her up in her Nest with the Plough " (H. & H., vol. i, pp. 115 ff.), st. vii, ll. 3-4 (our italics).

[27] " The twa Dogs " (H. & H., vol. i, pp. 9 ff.), ll. 5-6.

[28] " Auld lang syne [Old long ago]" (H. & H., vol. iii, pp. 147 ff., st. iv, ll. 1-2

a shrewd sense of reality. It finds its favourite expression in a bob or a short line :

> He gied me thee o' [a]tocher clear, — [a] *dowry*
> An' fifty mark.[29]

There is none of the sentimentalism which mars "The Cotter's Saturday Night," but only a level-headed realism, when, in "The twa Dogs," [30] Luath describes (ll. 112 ff.) the joys of a cotter's life :

> Their [a]grushie weans an' faithfu' wives . . . — [a] *thriving children*
> An' [a]whyles twalpennie worth o' [b]nappy — [a] *sometimes* [b] *ale*
> Can mak the bodies [a]unco happy. — [a] *remarkably*

These lines are wholly devoid of irony—which is reserved for the next couplet :

> They lay aside their private cares
> To mind the Kirk and State affairs . . . ;

in them, as in the pledge in "Auld lang syne" [31]—

> And surely ye'll [a]be your pint-stowp, — [a] *stand me a pint*
> And surely I'll be mine—

Burns shows the same unashamed acceptance of reality as Barbour and Henryson.

The same underlying realism also gives rise to many unconventional songs : not of youth or spring or romantic love, but of approaching old age—and married happiness [32] ; of winter [33] ; of courtship in its worldlier aspects [34] ; of connubial strife [35] ; and of economic stress.[36] They repeat the pattern of the great past, the wonderful poems on age in Bannatyne and Maitland Mss., the great tradition of winter scenes, and the defiant note of love-songs.

[29] "The auld Farmer's New-year Morning Salutation to his auld Mare, Maggie" (H. & H., VOL. I, pp. 100 ff.), st. iv, ll. 3-4.

[30] H. & H., VOL. I, pp. 9 ff.

[31] St. ii, ll. 1-2.

[32] *E.g.* "John Anderson, my Jo, John" (H. & H., VOL. III, p. 63).

[33] *E.g.* "Winter," "A Winter Night," "Up in the Morning early," and "Thou gloomy December" (H. & H., VOLS. I, pp. 134 f., 225 ff. ; III, pp. 15 f., 185 f.).

[34] *E.g.* "Whistle owre the Lave [rest] o't," "My Tocher [dowry] 's the Jewel," "What can a young Lassie do wi' an auld Man," and "A Lass wi' a Tocher" (H. & H., VOL. III, pp. 58, 90, 93 f., 229 f.).

[35] *E.g.* "O, merry hae I been teethin a Heckle" and "Husband, husband, cease your Strife" (H. & H., VOL. III, pp. 66 f., 239 f.).

[36] *E.g.* "O, that I had ne'er been married" (H. & H., VOL. III, p. 206) : "Now I've gotten wife and bairns, An' they cry 'Crowdie [meal and water]' evermair."

Often the harsh wintry setting and the inhospitable world outside are painted for the sake of contrast with a warm cosy interior.[37] This contrast has always been a favourite one since Henryson's *Testament of Cresseid*, and it has always suggested danger outside. The harsh contrast between the inclement outside and a cosy inglenook may be an all-too-common experience in Scotland ; but it must also be remembered that contrast—especially emotional contrast with its consequent tension—figures so much more prominently in Scottish than in English poetry. Burns makes full use of contrasts : between the " cauld blast " and the " shelter " to heighten the dramatic note;[38] between the scenes of youth and maturity to create the impression of change in " Auld lang syne." Burns is a master of antithetical juxtaposition, as in these examples from " The Holy Fair " :

Here some are thinkin on their sins,
  An' some upo' their [a]claes. . . . *[a] clothes*

How monie hearts this day converts
  O' sinners and o' lasses ! . . .

There's some are [a]fou o' love divine ; *[a] full, drunk*
  There's some are fou o' brandy.[39]

We find this especially in Burns's crowd scenes with their heterogeneous motion. The humour of " The Holy Fair " lies essentially in the flatness of the contradictions—which suggests how questionable the attitude behind these " grace-proud faces " really is. The quick thrust of a bob is a splendid way of flinging a contrast at a listener, and of course is specially effective in showing up hypocrisy, as is amply shown by " The Ordination " or " Holy Willie's Prayer." [40] The whole of the latter is one single play on contrast in all its variations : between the rigidly orthodox words and the vile profanity behind them ; the apparent humility and the incredible selfishness that does not even know it is selfish ; the lechery of " Thy servant true " ; and so on to the " mercies temporal and divine," and the " grace and gear " of the end of the prayer. This reverses the practice of adapting secular poems to spiritual purposes as the *Gude and Godlie Ballatis* had done, and recalls Dunbar's irreverent travesties of the Office of the Dead, etc.

[37] Cp. " The twa Dogs," " The Cotter's Saturday Night," " Tam o' Shanter," and " The jolly Beggars " (H. & H., VOLS. I, pp. 9 ff., 106 ff., 278 ff. ; II, I ff.).

[38] " O wert thou in the cauld Blast," H. & H., VOL. IV, p. 43, st., i, ll. 1, 4.

[39] " The Holy Fair " (H. & H., VOL. I, pp. 36 ff.), sts. x, ll. 1-2 ; xxvii, ll. 1-2, 5-6.

[40] H. & H., VOLS. I, pp. 210 ff. ; II, pp. 25 ff.

The preponderance of contrast, however, cannot fully explain the dancing irresponsibility and the lashing whip of Burns's language; his poems often go far beyond the limits of conventional satire. Like Dunbar, he is well aware of the latent vituperative potentialities of Scots, with its wealth of consonants and consequent easy alliteration. In the harsh alliterations of the opening of "A Winter Night" [41]—

> When biting Boreas, fell and [a]doure, — [a] *hard*
> Sharp shivers thro' the leafless bow'r—

Burns is using essentially the same technique as Henryson in his description of Saturn: and in "The Holy Fair" how much force there is in the violently ejected consonants of Black Russel's sermon:

> A vast, unbottom'd, boundless pit,
> Fill'd [a]fou o' [b]lowin brunstane. . . . [42] — [a] *full* [b] *flaming*

This has too much of the exuberant gusto of flyting to be truly satirical. Of all Scots poets of recent centuries Burns has most of the true flyting spirit [43]; and there is more than a trace of its fantastic pattern in certain passages of "The Holy Fair," "The Brigs of Ayr" or "The jolly Beggars." [44] Like the Makars of old, Burns has, too, a specially rich and succulent vocabulary to go with it [45]—the glossary for these passages always swells disproportionately: and like that Middle Irish poet who took offence on being refused the "loan" of a glass of beer, he flares up at an inhospitable innkeeper at Inverness who keeps him waiting while he serves a duke's party.

This passionate spirit expresses itself in various ways. In the ode "To a Louse, on seeing one on a Lady's Bonnet at Church," where, however distorted, the pattern of everyday life is still clearly discernible in a wonderfully new perspective, it merely gives ridicule a special tang:

> O Jenny, [a]dinna toss your head, — [a] *do not*
> An' set your beauties a' [a]abread! — [a] *abroad*
> Ye little [a]ken what cursèd speed — [a] *know*
> The [a]blastie's makin! — [a] *blasted creature*
> [a]Thae winks an' finger-ends, I dread, — [a] *those*
> Are notice takin!

[41] H. & H., VOL. I, pp. 225 ff.
[42] "The Holy Fair" (above, n. 39), st. xxii, ll. 1-2.
[43] See also Burns's fine flyting in *Letters*, VOL. II, No. 77.
[44] H. & H., VOLS. I, pp. 36 ff., 200 ff.; II, pp. 1 ff.
[45] See, *e.g.* his "Address to the Deil" (H. & H., VOL. I, pp. 47 ff.).

O wad some Pow'r the giftie gie us
To see oursels as ithers see us !
It wad frae monie a blunder free us
An' foolish notion :
What airs in dress an' gait wad lea'e us,
An' ev'n devotion ! [46]

Elsewhere, however, it finds outlet in such grotesque, irresponsible extravaganza as in these lines, with their mock-solemn polysyllabic words and rhymes :

Now a' the congregation o'er
Is silent expectation :
For Moodie [a]speels the holy door, — [a] *climbs*
Wi' tidings o' damnation ;
Should Hornie, as in ancient days
'Mang sons o' God present him,
The vera sicht o' Moodie's face
[a]To 's ain het hame had sent him, — [a] *to his own hot home*
Wi' fright that day. [47]

Horse-play of the " Christis-Kirk " type also lives on in Burns's election poems, and the beginning of " The Election "—

Fy, let us a' to Kirkcudbright . . .

—is a direct echo of " The blythsome Bridal "[48] : while the reeling dance of grotesque fun of the tocher-poems is repeated in " Duncan Gray," [49] a song set to " that kind of light-horse gallop of an air, which precludes sentiment." [50]

Except in some of the songs, Burns usually relies on understatement as a means of expressing the deeper emotions ; in such poems as " The auld Farmer's New-year Morning Salutation to his auld Mare, Maggie," [51] and even in such of the songs as " Auld lang syne " and " John Anderson, my Jo, John," [52] the real emotion remains implicit and is not specifically mentioned. And, like most of his predecessors, Burns resorts to wild irresponsible extravaganza only in representing human absurdities and eccentricities.

[46] " To a Louse " (H. & H., VOL. I, pp. 152 ff.), sts. vii-viii.
[47] " The Holy Fair " (above, n. 39), st. xii.
[48] See H. & H., VOL. II, pp. 193 ff., and (for notes) 402 ff ; cp. above pp. 120, 130.
[49] H. & H., VOL. III, pp. 23 f., 215 f.
[50] Burns to Thomson, quoted in H. & H., VOL. III, p. 454.
[51] Above, n. 30. [52] Above, nn. 29, 33.

Flyting and extravaganza run like a red thread through the literature of Britain's whole Celtic fringe. True flyting, as we saw it in Dunbar, has little in common with satire and social criticism. It is essentially an act of revolt, primitive and unashamed, against all socially-imposed restraint ; it revels in the sensuous as such ; and in seeking to assert its own stubborn individualism it is quite prepared to let everything else " gang tapsalteerie," or to the Devil if need be. There is much more of this hilarious *abandon* in Burns's poems than there is in Fergusson's ; that is perhaps the chief reason why Fergusson's seem more rational, and Burns's have more zest. Burns stands closer, in some respects, to Dunbar. " O my Luve is like a red, red Rose " [53] is one of the tenderest love-songs ever written ; yet he also addressed his Muse as a " hizzie " and revelled in the obscenities of many of the poems in *The merry Muses of Caledonia*—some of which were his own compositions.[54] There is in all this an obvious parallel with the sensuous amorality, the all-inclusive tolerance, of Dunbar's " Twa mariit Wemen," and Burns seems often to have felt the same irresistible desire to deflate conventional poetic sentiment.

The Merry Muses perhaps seem less attractive to us than they did to Burns. But in " The jolly Beggars," [55] he composed a pæan of amorality which can scarcely fail to touch a hidden chord in every human heart. This " irresistible presentation of humanity caught in the act and summarised for ever in the terms of art " [56] is in the form of a cantata : each of its various component songs has its own contribution to make, and the result is summed up in the chorus of the concluding air : [57]

> A fig for those by law protected !
> Liberty's a glorious feast,
> Courts for cowards were erected,
> Churches built to please the priest !

Thus the " bard of no regard," [58] whose reckless defiance of social convention is essentially an expression of his own uncompromising artistic integrity, succeeds in transforming the beery swagger of the

[53] H. & H., VOL. III, pp. 143 f.

[54] Daiches, *Robert Burns*, pp. 310 ff. An edition of *The merry Muses* by S. G. Smith is in preparation.

[55] H. & H., VOL. II, pp. 1 ff. ; first published posthumously, as a chapbook, 1799.

[56] H. & H., VOL. II, p. 291.

[57] " See the smoking Bowl before us " (H. & H., VOL. II, pp. 17 ff.).

[58] " I am a Bard " (H. & H., VOL. II, pp. 15 f.), l. 1.

jolly beggars into a vision of humanity at its most natural which is remarkable for its breadth and depth of meaning.[59]

Two points must be realised in connexion with " The jolly Beggars." First, it is the fullest symposium of the Scottish tradition. There is no other compilation in which we find such a wealth of old motifs, songs, tunes, Scottish metres,[60] and echoes of the Makars, brought freshly to life in a congenial form. Secondly, the beggar as a symbol of anarchic freedom can be traced back to Goliardic tradition ; he figures in " Merry Beggars " and " The happy Beggars," two poems in the *Tea-Table Miscellany* which served Burns as models for his cantata ; and it is characteristic of Scots tradition that " The jolly Beggar " and " The Gaberlunzie Man " should both—rightly or wrongly—have been attributed to James V, and " Christis Kirk on the Grene " and " Peblis to the Play " to his royal ancestor James I. The beggar also figures prominently in modern Irish literature—for example in John Millington Synge's play *The Shadow of the Glen*, in which he represents freedom and fulness of life.

Each of the three Celtic countries of Britain has developed its own unusually fervent variety of religion and its own unusually oppressive ecclesiastical organisation ; and in all three of them—priest-ridden Ireland, chapel-ridden Wales, and presbytery-ridden Scotland—we find, from the Woman of Beare and Gormfleith to James Joyce, Liam O'Flaherty, Sean O'Casey, or Rhys Davies, from the Makars to Burns and C. M. Grieve, the same violent rebellion against conventional morality.

In Scotland, the brunt of Burns's ferocious attack on Calvinist orthodoxy fell on the reactionary party popularly referred to as the Auld Lichts [61] ; Burns rarely attacked the Kirk or Christianity as such. Dunbar's " anticlerical " poems had been travesties of Holy Offices or sacraments ; as we have seen, they were full of gusto, but contained little thought. Burns, too, could strike a hymn-like note [62]

[59] As often with Burns, he pitches a similar theme in a different key in the " Epistle to Davie " (H. & H., VOL. I, pp. 117 ff.). We find many such counterpieces : *e.g.* the love-songs and the bawdy poems ; " The Cotter's Saturday Night " and " The twa Dogs," etc.

[60] *E.g.* the *Cherry-and-the-Slae* stanza ; common measure ; tail-rhyme ; *Christis-Kirk* stave ; short couplet ; Standard Habbie ; 8-line stanza ; the popular *aa, ab* : *cc, cb* with its internal rhyme ; and many song metres.

[61] We need not here go into the development of Scottish church polity, or of religious and philosophical thinking, during the eighteenth century, nor into Burns's own personal reasons for taking up an anti-orthodox position. We are concerned with literary form and expression, and with the recrudescence of this symptom in Scottish literature.

[62] *E.g.* the " Address to the unco Guid " (H. & H., VOL. I, pp. 217 ff.).

or parody a prayer,[63] but he had to reckon with a Kirk in which ritual had been suppressed, and its place taken by rationalistic dogma, predestination, Sabbatarian zeal,[64] rigid severity, and stern disapproval of worldly joy. With quasi-Satanic passion Burns traces out the consequences of accepted orthodoxy until it stands fully revealed in all its inherent logical and moral absurdity. Holy Willie's abstract theological premises are entirely orthodox, but as they are set against the realities of life, we behold his cunningly worming mind wresting them to his own purposes—and orthodoxy is blasted to pieces.

The Kirk of Scotland had nourished, even among the common people, generations of fervent controversialists; and in his attack on the intellectual arrogance, complacent ignorance and bigoted self-righteousness of the Auld Lichts, Burns turned the Kirk's own weapons against them. Burns's attack, however, does not take the form of mere rational satire; it is in itself a liberating outburst of zest and vitality. Confronted by the doctrine of original sin "sax thousand years ere my creation," [65] the natural man laughs it out of existence. As he appears in such poems as "Tam o' Shanter" and the "Address," the Deil [Devil] is not the formidable Adversary so often denounced from the pulpit, but the Deil of popular belief, who has been aptly described as himself a "tricky rascal" who likes to enjoy himself, courts the lasses, whistles, dances, drinks, cannot get rid of his cloven hoof, and frequently disguises himself as a fisher or a workman, or in a dark suit like a kirk-elder.[66] The names by which he is addressed —in Gaelic, Dòmhnull Dubh (Black Donald); and in Scots, Auld Clootie, Hornie, Nick, or even Nickie Ben, with its twofold diminutive —are expressive of an affectionate familiarity which goes back to pre-Calvinist times, and is oddly reminiscent of the familiarity of attitude towards God so often found in earlier Scots poetry. But when the Auld Lichts proscribed, as Devil's work, such harmless amusements as singing and country dancing, there must have been many who felt, with Burns, that perhaps after all the Devil was not so bad as

[63] *E.g.* the "Address to the Deil" and "Holy Willie's Prayer" (H. & H., VOLS. I, pp. 47 ff.; II, pp. 25 ff.).

[64] The Scottish Sabbath is found in its most extreme form in the W. Highlands, where there are no local buses, ferries, etc., on Sundays. Here, however, it is perhaps not entirely due to Presbyterianism, for a Gaelic poem of not later than the early sixteenth century begins "Ni math siubhal san Domhnach [It is not good to travel on Sunday]" (*S.V.L.*, pp. 240 ff.).

[65] "Holy Willie's Prayer" (above, n. 63), st. iii, l. 5.

[66] R. M. Douglas, *The Scots Book*, 1935, pp. 104 ff. See also ch. vii ("Gaelic Proverbs") of M. Maclean, *The Literature of the Highlands* (above p. 185, n. 1), pp. 149 ff.

he was called. In his own "Address to the Deil," Burns ends on a delightfully paradoxical note :

An' now, auld Cloots, I [a]ken ye're thinkin, — [a] *know*
A certain Bardie's rantin, drinkin,
Some luckless hour will send him [a]linkin, — [a] *hurrying*
To your black Pit ;
But, faith ! he'll turn a corner [a]jinkin, — [a] *dodging*
An' cheat you yet.

But fare-you-weel, Auld Nickie-Ben !
O, wad ye tak a thought an' [a]men' ! — [a] *mend*
Ye [a]aiblins might—I dinna ken— — [a] *perhaps*
Still hae a stake—
I'm [a]wae to think upo' yon den, — [a] *woeful*
Ev'n for your sake ! [67]

Satan mending and even redeemed—what glorious laughter in the teeth of brimstone sermons on predestination !

It was largely an outcome of the same sturdy individualism that Burns maintained such an outspokenly egalitarian attitude in politics. The egalitarian spirit which we discerned in earlier Scots poetry [68] had found fuller expression in Presbyterian church-government. This had given it a democratic twist, and had also imparted a new strength, a spiritual conviction, that we see in those stubborn independents the Covenanters, whose stronghold was, it should be remembered, in the South-West. Burns's egalitarianism was fully in harmony with the spirit of the age, and he often voices or echoes the French revolutionary ideal of *Liberté, Egalité, Fraternité.*[69] Two types of poem which Burns often used to express such ideas were the verse epistle in the Scottish style (*i.e.* between equals protesting their independence), and the animal poem.

Animal poems have always been a distinctive feature in Scotland's poetry, and honesty had often been represented by a horse (Dunbar) or a dog (Lyndsay). Poems in which animals represent such qualities as courage had played an important part in Gaelic poetry. In Lowland Scots poetry, as we have seen, Henryson had given the fable a novel twist ; by envisaging the mouse, the swallow, the lion, and all the rest, both as animals and as symbolic figures, and by

67 "Address to the Deil" (above, n. 63), sts. xx-xxi.

68 Above, pp. 31, 51, esp. 94-6, etc.

69 *E.g.* "The Author's earnest Cry and Prayer," "A Dream," "The jolly Beggars" (esp. "See the smoking Bowl," st. ii, ll. 1-2 : "What is title, what is treasure, What is reputation's care ?"), "Is there for honest Poverty ?" (H. & H., vols. i, pp. 26 ff., 68 ff. ; ii, pp. 17 ff. ; iii, pp. 271 ff.).

projecting human values into an accurately observed world of animals, he had reduced the human world to its essentials and had brought out its deepest meaning. But Burns was not acquainted with Gaelic poetry, and of Henryson's *Fabillis*, only " The Lion and the Mouse " and a garbled version of " The two Mice " were accessible to him in the *Ever Green*. Burns thus inherited the tradition in a degenerate form, namely the mock elegy, in which the animals are made to speak with quaint humour, and act like men, without sharing in human values, as they do in Henryson. " The Death and dying Words of Poor Mailie " [70] belongs to this latter category, and it is remarkable that Poor Mailie's words are overheard by a half-wit. In " The twa Dogs," however, Luath and Caesar are first presented as animals, and the passage immediately preceding their dialogue contains a finely-observed account of dogs at play.[71] Long before that, however, at the words " that were na thrang at hame," the human analogy is very skilfully introduced, and it is kept up until we accept the dogs not only as animals, but also as symbolic figures ; the sly connexion of Luath, the " ploughman's collie," with the heroes of Ossianic legend even widens the scope beyond the present, and the way in which Burns thus brings animal and human into a common focus is very reminiscent of Henryson.

" The auld Farmer's New-year Morning Salutation to his auld Mare, Maggie," [72] is of a different type, also represented by John Skinner's song " The Ewe wi' the crookit Horn." The animal is envisaged purely as an individual animal which is, however, a man's trusted companion. This calls forth more tenderness than the peasant would otherwise express or even experience, for this particular animal is, *to him*, a symbol of his own past life, of mutual dependability, of affection. " To a Mouse " and " To a Louse," [73] on the other hand, are rather in the style of the conventional European animal allegory, with its more general moral ; the accurate observation of the animals as creatures, however, and the method by which the poet establishes a connexion between the poor mouse and himself, are devices more prominent in Scottish literature.

But it is not only animals that appear as actors in Burns's poems : the Brigs of Ayr, a haggis, a daisy—anything can come to life. This

[70] H. & H., VOL. I, pp. 53 ff.

[71] " The twa Dogs " (above, n. 28), ll. 36 ff.

[72] Above, n. 30.

[73] H. & H., VOL. I, pp. 115 ff., 152 ff.

of course is a common poetic device, but, as far as I am aware, it is only in Gaelic poetry that personification occurs nearly so often, or achieves such intensity, as in Scots. Unlike their nearest analogues in such medieval English poems as *The Owl and the Nightingale* or *The Body and the Soul*, these Scots personifications are not meant to serve a didactic purpose. Rather, they arise out of an essentially dramatic attitude, which finds expression whenever a human mental process is projected into an object and the object itself thus comes to life. Sometimes the object or objects personified are, so to speak, the proponents of the poem as a whole. More often, however, their role is incidental, like that of the nuts roasted to see how the couples which they represent will get on :

> Some kindle [a]couthie, side by side, *[a] friendly*
> An' burn thegither trimly ;
> Some start awa wi' saucy pride
> An' jump out-owre the [a]chimlie *[a] chimney*
> Fu' high that night.[74]

Usually, dramatic monologue is better adapted to this type of personification than dialogue, which often is dramatic only in form. " O, wert thou in the cauld Blast " is more inherently dramatic than " Husband, Husband, cease your Strife," " Holy Willie's Prayer " than " The twa Herds." [75] The presentation of Holy Willie is intensely dramatic, and the psychological insight which Burns brings to bear on him is so penetrating as almost to make our flesh creep—in the same way as in James Hogg's *Confessions of a justified Sinner*, where this worming one's way into a bigoted mind, however, lacks the saving grace of humour. In Scots literature it is often the feelings of others that are expressed, from inside their minds. Most of Burns's lyrics really are not outpourings of his own self. The strength of " Tam o' Shanter " is largely due to the way in which the poet, as it were, flits in and out of Tam's mind, sometimes (as when the landmarks between Ayr and Alloway assume such an air of sinister foreboding) seeing the world through Tam's eyes, sometimes seeing Tam through his own. The comments which interrupt the narrative really arise out of this dramatic tension in which Tam and the narrator are both involved ; and this is reminiscent of the way in which (as we have seen) Barbour and Henryson often obtrude their own personalities into the tales they have to tell.

[74] " Halloween [All Hallows Eve] " (H. & H., VOL. I, pp. 88 ff.), st. vii, ll. 5-9.

[75] H. & H., VOLS. IV, p. 43 ; III, pp. 239 f. ; II, pp. 25 ff. ; and II, pp. 20 ff. F. G. Scott's new setting of " O, wert thou in the cauld Blast " beautifully brings out its dramatic quality.

I cannot quite agree with the verdict that Burns accepted the tradition as it had come from the hands of Ramsay and Fergusson, and added nothing besides his own personality. Some of the points made in the last few pages show that he at least widened it and recovered ground unknown to the seventeenth and eighteenth centuries. For generations no Scots poet had had such close affinities with the Makars. (It does not matter to us whether this recovery of ground was due to literary influences or spontaneously arose out of the life of the people.)

This view tends to be confirmed if we take account of certain features of Burns's use of metre. It is obvious, of course, that he refined some of the commonest traditional metres—for example, he increased the flexibility of Standard Habbie, by exploiting (especially in the short lines) its latent capacity for modulation from understatement to reminiscence, from reticence—almost reluctance to express one's feelings [76]—to a sly sarcasm that depends on form and association :

Is just as true 's the Deil's in hell
Or Dublin city.[77]

More significantly, however, he also used more varied metres than any of his immediate predecessors. In " The jolly Beggars " and in " Mary Morison " [78] we recognise the old eight-lined " Scottis metre " —*abab* : *bcbc*—with the same characteristic " turn " as of old. He uses the elaborate Cherrie-and-Slae stave in seven different places, and it seems to go specially well with his hilarious *abandon* : the calm of the exposition and the ballad-like movement of the middle part finally explode in the violent agitation of the end. Significantly enough, Burns sometimes modifies this stanza : thus in the eighth " Recitativo " of " The jolly Beggars," the first line of each phrase (*i.e.* ll. 1, 4, 7, 9) has a strong cæsura, and the two halves may be joined by assonance :

Then owre again//the jovial [a]*thrang* — [a] *throng*
The Poet did request
To [a]lowse his *pack*,// an' [b]wale a [c]*sang*, — [a] *untie* [b] *choose* [c] *song*
A ballad o' the best.[79]

In " Halloween," there is often a similar internal rhyme in ll. 1, 3, 5, 7, of its Christis-Kirk stanza [80] ; or, alternatively, the last stressed syllables in both halves of these lines alliterate :

[76] Cp. above, pp. 206, 209.
[77] " Death and Dr Hornbook " (H. & H., VOL. I, pp. 191 ff.), st. ii, ll. 3-4.
[78] H. & H., VOL. III, pp. 286 f.
[79] " The jolly Beggars," Rec. VIII (" So sung the Bard " : H. & H., VOL. II, p. 17), ll. 7-10.
[80] Cp. also " The Holy Fair " (above, n. 17), st. xxviii, ll. 1, 3.

Amang the bonie winding banks,
  Where Doon rins, [a]wimplin, clear ; [a] *meandering*
Where Bruce ance ruled the martial ranks,
  An' shook his Carrick spear. . . . [81]

A close investigation will reveal many internal rhymes—not as chance occurrences, but as a pattern, and occasionally they show a softer effect like an echo :

> But Homer-like the [a]glowrin byke. . . .[82] [a] *scowling swarm*

Perhaps these internal rhymes are no more deliberate than a thump on the table to heighten the dramatic effect, or a proud snapping of the fingers expressive of the heightened hilarity associated with the Cherrie-and-Slae stave. But what about Burns's use of alliteration? We have already seen how Burns uses alliteration in combination with a mass of other consonants in depicting winter, and Hell as it figured in an Auld Licht sermon.[83] In " The Whistle," [84] the heavy alliteration and the anapaests evoke the spirit of an heroic epic—here of drinking. In the " Address to the unco Guid " the incidental alliteration is more like a resounding echo from the roof of the church, heightened by other word echoes of a less easily definable nature, all underlining the hymn-like effect :

Ye see your state wi' th*eirs*[1] comp*ar'd*[1, 2]
  And shudder at the [a]n*iffer*[3] ; [a] *exchange*
But cast a moment's f*air*[1] reg*ard*,[1, 2]
  What maks the m[4]ighty [a]d*iffer*[3, 4] ? [a] *difference*
Discount what scant occ*a*[5]sion g*ave*[5, 6] ;
  That purity ye pr*ide in*[7] ;
And (what's aft m*ai*[5]r than a' the [a]l*ave*[5, 6]) [a] *rest*
  Your better *a*[5]rt o' h*idin*[7].[85]

[81] " Halloween " (above, n. 74), st. ii, ll. 1-4.
[82] " I am a Bard " (above, n. 58), st. i, l. 3.
[83] Above, p. 208. Cp. " The jolly Beggars," Rec. II (H. & H., VOL. II, p. 4).
[84] H. & H., VOL. I, pp. 304 ff.
[85] " Address to the unco Guid " (H. & H., VOL. I, pp. 217 ff.), st. iii. Note that, though so spelt, " regard, mighty, art " are in Sc. pronounced " regaird, michty, airt." The second line alone seems to lack an additional internal relationship, but, at least in my ear, " shudder "—" niffer " evokes a definite echo-effect.

Here is a sound pattern of such intricacy as Scottish poetry had not known since Alexander Scott, and it greatly intensifies the sarcasm of the last two lines in naked colloquial language. In "The Kirk's Alarm,"[86] rhythmic means produce the effect of the pealing of church bells, and the internal vowel rhymes, echoes, and alliterations of "Wandering Willie" may have been suggested by the traditional tune:

> Winter winds blew loud and cauld at our parting.
> Fears for my Willie brought tears to my ee;
> Welcome now, [a]Simmer, and welcome, my Willie, — [a] *summer*
> The Simmer to nature, my Willie to me![87]

In "Tam o' Shanter," alliteration and sound patterns are used to trace the figures of a whirling Scottish country dance:

> The piper loud and louder blew,
> The dancers quick and quicker flew,
> They reel'd, they set, they cross'd, they [a]cleekit, — [a] *linked arms*
> Till [a]ilka carlin swat and reekit.[88] — [a] *every old woman*

Mackenzie and Calder maintain that Burns's verse sometimes has regular Gaelic *aiccill* (anticipation), as in

> But still keep something to yours*el*
> Ye scarcely t*ell* to [a]onie.[89] — [a] *any*

Other examples, well worth quoting, are:

> She tauld thee weel thou was a [a]sk*e*llum, (1) — [a] *good-for-nothing*
> A bl*e*(1)thering, bl*u*(2)stering, [a]dr*u*(2)cken bl*e*(1)llum.[90] — [a] *drunken babbler*

> There sat a b*o*(1)ttle in a [a]b*o*(1)le — [a] *recess*
> Bey*o*(1)nt the [a]ingle l*ow*(2); — [a] *flame of the fire*
> And ay she t*oo*(3)k the tither [a]s*ou*(3)k — [a] *suck*
> To [a]dr*ou*(3)k the [b]st*ou*(3)rie t*ow*(2).[91] — [a] *drench* [b] *dusty flax*

86 H. & H., VOL. II, pp. 30 ff.

87 "Wandering Willie" (H. & H., VOL. III, p. 208), st. ii, as amended by Erskine with Burns's approval.

88 "Tam o' Shanter" (H. & H., VOL. I, pp. 278 ff.), ll. 145 ff.

89 "Epistle to a young Friend" (H. & H., VOL. I, pp. 140), st. v, ll. 3-4 (quoted in *Gaelic Songs by William Ross*, edd. J. Mackenzie and G. Calder, 1937, "Note on Burns' Influence on Ross."

90 "Tam o' Shanter" (above, n. 88), ll. 19-20.

91 "The weary Pund o' Tow" (H. & H., VOL. III, pp. 108 f.), st. ii. In both these examples, there is of course also much alliteration. In the second, rhyme 1 receives much less emphasis than rhyme 3, which is much as it so often is in Gaelic.

In the first stanza of " Thou ling'ring Star " [92] they find *aiccill* throughout (at least as assonance) and additional alliteration ; and they believe that his might have been inspired by his Highland tours. Not all of their examples, however, seem entirely convincing.

Taken together, these features of Burns's use of metre reveal a love of pattern, of decoration on a small surface, which is not so exuberant as in some of the Makars, but serves the same artistic purpose ; and when Henderson says that Burns makes no special attempt at rhymed or rhythmical effect, one cannot possibly agree with him.

It is a curious thing that most of the respects in which Burns adds to the eighteenth-century tradition, and in which he comes nearest to the Makars, are those which lean towards the Celtic conception of poetry. While we had seen a hardening of Lowland characteristics in the eighteenth century, Burns displays a certain balance. Though Burns may never have heard the Gaelic that at his time may still have been spoken in remote parts of Ayrshire [93]—John Galt shows more marked traces—its spirit was still in the air, colouring the speech and thought of the people, and Burns can frame a genuinely Gaelic phrase like " and I sae weary fu' o' care." [94] The whole ethos of south-west Scotland is still perceptibly quite different from that of the Borders ; and any receptive visitor who goes to Ayr from Selkirk will probably agree with me that the ways in which Burns differs from Scott are still reflected in the Ayrshire way of speaking, with its lilting sentences, and in the easy sociability, reckless love of independence, and political radicalism of the people of the South-West. Galloway in particular was long regarded as a hotbed of rebellion and was always a problem to the Scottish kings.

Our view of Burns gains further confirmation if we consider what he does *not* give us in his poetry. Like the great majority of Scots

[92] H. & H., VOL. III, pp. 71 ff. (It should be appreciated that in ll. 2, 8, of this stanza, " early " and " groans," though so spelt, might well, in Sc., be pronounced " airly " and " grains," thus giving the required vowel-rhymes).

[93] Down to the seventeenth century, Galloway and the S.W. had some Gaelic-speaking ministers ; and in his chapter on " Celtic Literary Revivals " in *The Literature of the Celts* Magnus Maclean quotes the 1891 census figures according to which there were in Ayrshire, nearly 100 years after Burns's own death, 1654 native Gaelic-speakers, and 1827 others who were bilingual. Of course it does not follow that these or their parents were natives of the county. See W. L. Lorimer, " The Persistence of Gaelic in Galloway and Carrick," in *Scottish Gaelic Studies*, VOLS. VI, pp. 113 ff., VII, pp. 26 ff. (1949, 1951), where all the evidence seems to imply an earlier extinction of Gaelic in the South-West.

[94] " The Banks o' Doon " (H. & H., VOL. III, p. 124), st. i, l. 4. Cp. W. J. Watson, 'Some Interactions between Gaelic and English," in *Transactions of the Gaelic Society of Inverness*, XXXIII (1925-7), Inverness 1932, pp. 310 ff.

and Scottish Gaelic poets, he left no long, sustained efforts, no meditative or philosophical poetry, and was exceptional only in showing no historical or antiquarian interest in the past. Little suspecting that he himself was destined to become one of the curio-hunter's chief victims, he laughed at an antiquarian's treasured finds as " a fouth [plenty] o' auld nick-nackets."[95] His Highland tours prompted only a number of conventionally sentimental Jacobite songs in which he shows no real sense of history, and even of the ballads themselves his works contain only a few faint echoes. What links Burns most strongly to the older poetic tradition is his attitude to nature. To anything in the immediate natural environment—the gowans, the banks, the braes—he gives an instant response. But there is no horizon. Of the sun setting behind the crags of Arran (which today thousands of trippers and holiday-makers flock to see) he has not a word to say. Though he spent most of his life within smelling-distance of it, the sea is only, in his poetry, an element which sunders friends and lovers. And towards the mountains and the starry sky he shows a similar attitude.[96] The Falls of Foyers, near Loch Ness, only inspire some trite generalities. His attitude to nature therefore is not in any sense a romantic attitude : he does not try to " interpret " it ; he does not discern in it a kindred spirit which speaks to man ; he does not abandon himself to it, or even proclaim its grandeur. Doubtless it arose out of a working farmer's humdrum, everyday experience of nature ; doubtless it also owed something to neo-classical conceptions. Yet it undoubtedly coincided with the whole general trend of Scots and Scottish Gaelic poetry, in which, as we have seen, nature plays such an important part, and so many poems are entirely devoted to a precise and remarkably direct observation—not, however, of the scenery as such, but of the immediate natural environment.

I have not attempted to do justice to Burns the artist, or Burns the national bard: but this has been excellently done elsewhere. My task was rather to assess his place in the Scots tradition. Perhaps the chief result of our enquiry has been to show that, unlike his imitators, who mistook his directness for " hameliness," Burns, at his best, was always immediately and intimately in contact with the environment, social as well as natural.

[95] " On the late Capt. Grose's Peregrinations " (H. & H., vol. 1, pp. 289 ff.), st. vi, l. 1.

[96] The stars are not often mentioned in Scottish poetry. Strange though it may seem, the stars are much less conspicuous in Scotland than on the Continent. Several of my friends confirmed my impression that even on a dark winter night one can hardly see the Milky Way. Doubtless it is due to the humidity, which so often also blots out the horizon. Is that why both stars and horizon are so seldom noticed in Scottish poetry ?

2. Walter Scott

There is no need to attempt, in this connexion, a full evaluation of WALTER SCOTT (1771-1832) : that has been done elsewhere, successfully and in greater detail,[1] and many writers have censured his shortcomings, admired the magnitude of his achievements, and analysed the secrets of his success. At first sight, Scott apparently has little to do with the old Scots literary tradition. In fact it is safe to say that he was by far the most *original* literary genius that Scotland has yet produced ; for whereas no other Scottish writer explored and conquered so much virgin territory, and had so little real following in Scotland, he opened up new vistas in fiction-writing all over Europe, and his historical novels, at any rate, are an integral part of world literature. Where, then, does the Scots literary tradition come into it ?

In trying to understand Scott's achievement, let us first eliminate what we will not find in him. He is not primarily concerned with individuals in the context of daily life and business ; he does not pry into the private inner life of the soul, or into the dark abysses of its deepest passions—love, pride, hatred,[2] ambition, the desire for revenge. Sex, feminine psychology, and the analysis of morbid mental states—these all lie outside the field of his novels, which deal chiefly with man in his public aspects. Nor is Scott interested in speculation, theories of history, or metaphysics, and his nearest approach to the expression of religious feeling is an occasional disquisition on questions of church history, politics, or dogma. His own religious outlook prevented him from doing justice to the deep principles of the Covenanters, whose sometimes fanatical religious convictions were allied with an inherent belief in civil rights which Scott could not fathom.[3] Scott mistrusted the missionary spirit which

[1] The best biography is J. G. Lockhart (Scott's son-in-law), *The Life of Sir Walter Scott, Bart.*, 2 vols., 1836-8, frequently reprinted, which should however be read in conjunction with H. J. C. Grierson, *Sir Walter Scott, Bart. : A new Life, supplementary to, and corrective of, Lockhart's Biography*, 1928, and Hesketh Pearson, *Walter Scott : His Life and Personality*, 1954. John Buchan (Lord Tweedsmuir), *Sir Walter Scott*, 1932, contains the best criticism ; cp. also Edwin Muir, *Scott and Scotland : The Predicament of Scottish Writers*, 1936 ; J. A. L. Fraser, *Scott and Stevenson*, 1929. See also Scott's *Journal*, ed. J. G. Tait, 3 vols., 1939-50 ; *Letters*, ed. H. J. C. Grierson, 12 vols., 1932-7 ; *Short Stories*, ed. Lord David Cecil, World's Classics, 1934 ; and J. C. Corson, *A Bibliography of Sir Walter Scott, 1797-1940*, 1943.

[2] Here we should, however, except the tale of "The Highland Widow."

[3] Cp. *Old Mortality* ; *The Heart of Midlothian*.

raises banners and seeks to question traditional judgments ; if he had any mission of his own, it was to reconcile warring factions, Scots and English, Lowland and Highland, to bring out the best in both sides, and to " amuse " his readers. Scott grew up in Hume's Edinburgh, and its enlightened atmosphere is reflected in many of his own characteristic traits, such as his habitual emphasis on common sense, his mistrust of enthusiasm, his gentlemanly reticence, his impartial preference for the middle course, his desire to benefit society not by revealing the good, but rather by showing how it may be reached. In *Old Mortality*, the rival suitors of Edith Bellenden are a *moderate* Covenanter (Morton) and a *moderate* Episcopalian (Lord Evandale) ; and there is a fine touch of irony when, in *The Antiquary*, Edie Ochiltree, a Presbyterian beggar, is haughtily rejected by his Episcopalian and Roman Catholic brethren. Perhaps Scott's own early disappointment in love had made him withdraw into a private world of imagination as a means of avoiding any painful searching of the heart,[4] except in his *Journal*, which does contain " what the heart whispers to itself in secret." [5] His marriage shows passion controlled by duty, and his wife never entered into his inner life. When obliged to write a love-scene, Scott is always painfully self-conscious, and it is only in delineating the minor characters in his novels that he can really let himself go. This might well help to explain why Scott's was essentially a dual mind in which a sober judgment acted as a check on a powerful imagination, and usually prevented him from abandoning himself whole-heartedly to his romance.

So far we have been drawing the picture of a writer who was incapable of intimacy or introspection, and seems even to have deserved Carlyle's sarcastic criticism that he drew his characters from the skin inwards, never getting near the heart of them ; a writer who also followed in the wake of Hume and the North Britons, and (if only in his own German studies and imitations) was true to their European outlook.

In turning to Scott's positive achievement it is not enough to say that his mind was like a " mighty cauldron " out of which came up provosts and poachers, burgesses and bandsters, doctors and drovers (Buchan) ; that his vivid and immense imagination allowed the author to *see* whole stories, past like present ; that he discovered in history, and in the Highlands, themes for novels peopled with the

[4] Cp. Edwin Muir, *Essays on Literature and Society*, pp. 64 ff.

[5] Hazlitt missed this quality in Scott's novels.

products of an incredibly fertile imagination; that he gave colour and life to the past by interweaving it with real persons and events of his own experience; or that his creative power was unparalleled, evoking incidents, settings, characters both pathetic and comic, intensely romantic and shrewdly realistic. Most of that might still be said even if his work were solely a glittering historical pageant, full of dazzling but superficial portraiture and antiquarian "auld nick-nackets"—and indeed that is the impression left in the mind by his novels of English and European history, which are, in general, those best known outside Scotland (*Ivanhoe*, *Kenilworth*, *Quentin Durward*). To Scott, however, history was more than an antiquarian interest or "Gothick" fashion. He viewed human nature against the background of the historic past, and tried to interpret it in terms of a man's own family's, church's and nation's traditions. According to his own statements, Scott's purpose was "to throw some light on the manners of Scotland as they were, and to contrast them, occasionally, with those of the present day . . . ," to recreate "scenes in which our ancestors thought deeply, acted fiercely, and died desperately . . ."; he was interested to know "how Fletcher of Salton spoke, how Graham of Claverhouse danced, what were the jewels worn by the famous Duchess of Lauderdale," and was "fond of sketches of the society which has passed away."[6] What is the purpose of this insistence on a past society, its manners and ways of thinking? The answer is contained in the judge's comment at the end of "The two Drovers," in which the crime that has been committed is viewed as a consequence of the fact that men act "in ignorance of each other's prejudices." The same conception of tragedy is implicit in many of his novels and stories, from *Waverley* to "The Highland Widow." What interests Scott in history, and in man, is the clash of different traditions, or the clash of an individual with a tradition, and the Scottish background affords numerous examples.

Man, to Scott, is no chance being, but a part of the organic life of the community, and he makes us see how the actions and fates of men are moulded by their society and its history. In *The Heart of Midlothian*, the religious passions surviving from the seventeenth century, the effects of the Union of 1707, the situation arising out of the Porteous Riot of 1736, national character and prejudices, and

[6] See *Chronicles of the Canongate*, chs. v ("Mr Croftangry settles in the Canongate") and vii ("Mrs Baliol assists Croftangry in his Literary Speculations"), and "My Aunt Margaret's Mirror," designed for the same collection, but published in *The Keepsake*, 1828.

contemporary social conditions, all go to determine the situation in which Jeanie Deans has to act. On every page of *The Antiquary* we are made to realise how the present state of society is conditioned by its own historic past; the pent-up passions of *The Bride of Lammermoor* (1819) are only possible against the background of the forfeitures of 1689 and under the shadow of the Jacobite threat. Far from being merely background figures, the Malignants and Covenanters in "Wandering Willie's Tale" [7] are essential to the atmosphere in which alone the story is possible. Nor is Scott's history dead or of purely academic interest: it still moves in his own time as a living force which shapes the lives of the people. In Scotland historical forces and traditions die hard, and four or five generations after the Edinburgh Tolbooth was pulled down you can still see Edinburgh folk spitting or stamping on the stones marking the place where the door of this prison, "the heart of Midlothian," once was. Scott tries to communicate a sense that the spirit of another age is active in our present lives, and his greatest novels are those which deal with the recent past or some two or three generations before. In *Old Mortality* (1816) Scott took his first step into a more distant past, but one that was (and is) still furiously alive, the time of the Covenanters; even so, he uses a stepping-stone in his titular hero, Old Mortality, a wandering mason who went round repairing the tombstones of the Covenanters towards the end of the eighteenth century. No man was better equipped than Walter Scott to sense the influence of the past, for none was steeped more deeply in his country's chronicles, balladry, traditions, and antiquities—or in the poetry of its Makars. Characters in his novels often repeat the proverbial sayings traditionally associated with certain great events in Scottish history—such as the assertion, quoted in *Rob Roy* (1817), that a Campbell has been at the bottom of every Scottish treason. Like Chancellor Seafield on signing the Act of Union, Caleb, the faithful servant in *The Bride of Lammermoor*, and the dying man in *Old Mortality*, both make reference to the "end of an auld sang"; in *The Antiquary*, Edie Ochiltree's prayer "Let death spare the green corn and take the ripe" echoes Richard Cameron's prayer in the fatal battle of Ayrsmoss; and when one of the spectres in "Wandering Willie's Tale" repeats the Earl of Douglas's saying that "It's ill speaking between a fou man and a fasting," Steenie, though only a crofter, recognises it as such

[7] Contained in *Redgauntlet* (1824), Letter X

and therefore interprets it as ill-omened. Since Scott had a singularly retentive memory, this clearly was quite deliberate. It was in fact a way of drawing attention to constantly recurrent historic patterns.

Sir Walter's Scottish novels thus have this advantage over his English and Continental ones that they are not satisfied with a pageant but give depth by depicting the formative power of history. But the difference goes deeper. As he pondered the words and deeds of past generations of Scotsmen, as they still were at work in the doing and thinking of his countrymen, it was not only the voice of the greatest and most brilliant historical figures that spoke to him, but that, too, of the common people. He is far less often concerned with the history of his people as it appears in history books than as it still lived on in their folk memory and so still conditioned their outlook and even influenced their actions. This is (as Lady Gregory termed it in her own plays) folk-history, and therefore it must be conventional. In his English and Continental novels, such great historical figures as Louis XI, Leicester, Elizabeth, are usually the outstanding characters ; his great Scottish novels, however, are dominated by such heroes of folk tradition as Old Mortality, Rob Roy, the Porteous mob, Jeanie Deans, or the ballad-like lover in *The Bride of Lammermoor*. Scott was, indeed, the first great writer who fully appreciated the importance of the common people in history, and many of his most remarkable characters are simple folk—tramps, crofters, farmers, advocates, burgesses, bonnet-lairds, and so forth. In this he was only striking a note that has often been heard in Scottish literature, from Barbour and Henryson, who asserted the dignity of the husbandman and the labourer, to Neil M. Gunn and the modern writers who understand by history the forces which shape the life of the common people. Among the moderns, this interest in the common people may arise out of political conviction, or out of the contemporary emphasis on social and economic history ; in the Tory Walter Scott it arose out of his own deep and implicit confidence in the common man. If we wish fully to appreciate this, we must examine the structure, characters, language, and content of the novels.

Structure is, admittedly, the weakest point in most of Scott's novels. In fact, *Old Mortality*, *The Bride of Lammermoor*, *Quentin Durward*, and the main part of *Waverley*, have all the strength of construction that could be desired. Yet it is true that most of the stories end anyhow, and that chance plays an excessive part in the development of the plot. Scott often fails to prepare the way for later developments in the story, and tries to make up for it by tardy and sometimes rather perfunctory explanations. He lacks a strong sense of proportion, and puts in too much padding, which John Buchan—unconvincingly to me—tries to explain away as providing a necessary relaxation of tension. We must however remember the conditions in which Scott wrote, and had to write, his novels : the earlier parts often had to go to press before the end was even conceived. His age, moreover, had more leisure and more patience than we have. Then we must consider the state of the English novel as Scott found it (Buchan, ch. vi). Finally, Scott's own temperament had little patience with technicalities—instead he offers a mass of life bubbling with energy. What if the winding-up of *Rob Roy* is painful ? After the feast we have had, surely we can forego the coffee ! For indeed it is a sumptuous feast.

In *Chronicles of the Canongate* Scott says of his narrator, Mrs Bethune Baliol, that she dismissed circumstantial place, time, etc., which only make a tale cold and languid, " bringing forward, dwelling upon, and illustrating, those incidents and characters which give point and interest to the story." Incidents and characters ! Each of the novels has a number of magnificent scenes, unforgettable highlights, each of which stands out like a brilliant jewel against the foil of a duller setting. These great moments are presented with consummate skill, and for each in turn the stage is carefully set.[8] The splendour of the novels is thus essentially episodic, and Scott's mind seems instinctively to have leapt from one brilliant episode to the next. In this insistence on the dramatic episode instead of structure Scott is in line with the Scottish genius, and essentially the same attitude is revealed in his miscellaneous prose writings (for example, the Introduction to *Rob Roy*), and in his assumption that a metrical romance must necessarily be episodic and rhapsodic (review of Southey's *Amadis of Gaul*). In his short stories, he is free to concentrate on a single incident, and they are masterpieces of construction.

Fully to appreciate the excellence of a short story like " Wandering Willie's Tale," or of the great episodes in the novels, we must examine their characters. We can dismiss in a few words Scott's ostensible protagonists, who resemble (as John Buchan noted) a wheel-hub,

[8] See A. W. Verrall, " The Prose of Walter Scott," in *Collected Literary Essays, classical and modern*, 1913. Verrall investigates Meg Merrilies' denunciation of Bertram of Ellangowan in *Guy Mannering*.

which shows little movement, but yet controls the furious revolution of the circumference. The very fact that they are so colourless allows the author to make them move freely from one of the contending parties to the other. And by taking an English hero for such a novel as *Guy Mannering*, Scott gets a chance to explain and interpret the Scottish background.

Scott's " protagonists " are often insipid. Who exactly was Lovel, or Edith Bellenden ? In which of the novels does Francis Osbaldistone occur ? Some of the protagonists stand out better : Claverhouse (*Old Mortality*), the Antiquary, and perhaps Diana Vernon (*Rob Roy*). But there is no mistaking or forgetting Edie Ochiltree, Jeanie Deans, Andrew Fairservice, Cuddie Headrigg, Meg Merrilies, Elspeth Mucklebackit, Bailie Nicol Jarvie, and a whole gallery of boldly delineated figures from among the common people. Their lives have an austere dignity and are governed, not by sophisticated thoughts and theories, but (like the Porteous Mob) by single-minded purposes and by such deep, elemental, and essentially simple passions, emotions and sentiments, as grief, devotion, savage fidelity and a generous hatred of injustice. Though these may not be the deepest wells of life, Scott shows a wide and warm sympathy with human nature. And while the high-life characters in Scott's novels have (as he himself points out in the Introduction to *The Antiquary*) " that general polish which assimilates to each other the manners of different nations," his crofters, bonnet-lairds, burgesses, gangrels, and outcasts are emotionally less inhibited and can express themselves in stronger and more powerful language. Consequently Scott can let himself go over them and need not be self-conscious as he is over his high-life characters. They are more truly representative of their background, and are a product of certain material and historical conditions. Their lives and doings show more palpably the impact of history and traditions ; they are of the main stream of the life of the nation, with which those of gentler birth tend to lose touch when assuming " that general polish."

There is a technical reason, too, why low-life characters in Scott's novels are real flesh and blood and the others often mere shadows. Scott does not analyse, he has a direct, unanalytical manner and lets the characters reveal themselves ; he enters into them and *re-enacts* their experiences. This is what Scott learnt from popular story-tellers, and explains why in some respects he is so like Barbour or " Blind Harry." Scott does not observe his characters and then record their actions and speech ; he *identifies* himself with them. He was aware of this himself. Old Mortality, he says, had so penetrated into the spirit of the Covenanters that he spoke as if he had witnessed all. Wandering Willie says :

> " [I have] heard their communing so often tauld ower, that I almost think I was there myself, though I couldna be born at the time." (In fact, Allan, my companion mimicked, with a good deal of humour, the flattering, conciliating tone of the tenant's address, and the hypocritical melancholy of the laird's reply. . . .)[9]

The crucial scene of the tale is then rendered as pure dramatic reincarnation. The superb power of " Wandering Willie's Tale " lies mainly in the fact that it is told in character, with all the terse directness and conciseness implied. The Scotsman's delight in telling a story dramatically, almost acting the different parts, is excellently brought out in Andrew Fairservice and Bailie Nicol Jarvie.[10] Scott knows the importance of dramatic dialogue for his type of art, and each novel contains long passages of pure dramatic vision. In *The Bride of Lammermoor* he defends his use of dialogue against the method of the painter, as literature is directed towards the ear.

For these reasons Scott is truest to character in the case of his crofters and common people, as their speech is the most inherently dramatic. It is true that he also invented a conventional language for great figures which is simple and dignified, and which escapes the inhibitions of the Richardsonian tradition ; Claverhouse's speech on death is for instance, a masterpiece of style.[11] But on occasion Scott's genteel English style can become highly embarrassing, as in *Rob Roy*, where telling in the first person heightens the banality, and his " Gaelic " style as a rule is altogether too Ossianic. But with his Scots speech he enters his characters and makes them live : witness how the entrance of Andrew Fairservice brings pace, drama, raciness, and graphic imagination into some of the most stilted writing that Scott had ever done.

Whenever Scott allows his Scottish low-life characters to express themselves in their own way, their speech has many of the qualities characteristic of the Scottish genius. Though Scott is liable at times

[9] This trick of speaking in character in highly characteristic of Scots speech. According to James Hogg (*Domestic Manners of Sir Walter Scott* [1834], 1909, pp. 82 f.), Scott had the same gift.

[10] *Rob Roy* ; see especially ch. xiv.

[11] See *Old Mortality*, ch. xxxiv (" ' You would hardly believe,' said Claverhouse . . .").

to exaggerate the " humour " of such a character as Andrew Fairservice (especially in the later part of *Rob Roy*), or to overdo the habit of talking in metaphors drawn from the speaker's trade or religious persuasion, his Scots in general has nothing stereotyped about it. Most of those who speak it view life with a shrewd scepticism which refuses to take things at face value : often we hear the ominous " I hae kend . . . "

> " *His* honour !—I hae kend the day when less wad ser'd him, the oe of a Campvere Skipper ! "[12]

Sharp realism punctures mere oratory, and there is no room for nonsense.[13] Though Scott's folk can rise to the highest peaks of feeling and expression in their great moments, they are reticent and grimly tight-lipped about them in everyday life, and praise or love is uttered grudgingly. They often express their meaning not so much by direct statement, as by suggestion, or merely by sucking in their cheeks. Their humour tends to be dry and grim, and their reluctance to spoil their own jokes by laughing at them is characteristically Scottish—as also their headstrong obstinacy, and the cautious shrewdness which often prompts them to answer one question by asking another.[14] They have a keen sense of the dramatic which (for " nippin and scartin's Scots fowk's wooin ") leads them to flyte their best friends (the Antiquary and Sir Arthur Wardour) ; and, though one cannot help noticing that much of the most violent invective in Scott's novels is contained in the sermonising of such staunch Presbyterians as Old Mause and Habakkuk Mucklewrath,[15] the language used on these occasions has all the pungency of the traditional flytings. Many of them show the fervid Scottish delight in arguing—with themselves if no other opponent is available—and their devotions are full of it. The speech of his simple folk has the Scots richness of sensuous impressions, graphic images, and vivid comparisons which, quite as daring as those in traditional Scots proverbs, or in the Authorised Version itself, have all the direct simplicity and flavour of everyday Scots speech :

> ' [An idea] came on her mind like a sun-blink on a strong sea.'

[12] See *The Heart of Midlothian*, ch. xviii.

[13] Cp. *The Antiquary*, ch. v.

[14] Cp. above, p. 84, n. 17.

[15] Cp. Hamish Hendry's poem " Saunders MacSiccar " (in *Scottish Verse 1851-1951*, ed. D. C. C. Young, 1952) : " ' The kirks noo,' quo Saunders, ' hae tint a' their flyting . . . ' " Of course that implies a change of vocabulary : the abomination of " backbiting " has given way to the no less heinous sin of " backsliding."

'I have seen his pen gang as fast ower the paper, as ever it did ower the water when it was in the grey goose's wing.'[16]

'Thae pleasant and quiet lang streaks o' moonlight that are lying sae still on the floor o' this auld kirk, and glancing through the great pillars and stanchions o' the carved windows, and just dancing like on the leaves o' the dark ivy as the breath o' wind shakes it.'[17]

'Let that flee [fly] stick in the wa', when the dirt's dry it will rub out.'

'They were ower auld cats to draw that strae afore them.'

'A hadden tongue makes a slabbered mouth.'[18]

If the style of "Wandering Willie's Tale" is so outstanding, it is because the speaker is conceived as terse, tight-lipped, shrewd, realistic, suggestive, and inclined to understatement, and the tale is told in character. In moments like this Scott develops an intensity that is not satisfied with an appearance, but tries to get inside, behind it.

The Scots dialogue is the highlight of Walter Scott's style. It is not used as a vulgar tongue : in the author's youth it was a cultivated language, and his Mrs Bethune Baliol speaks Scots not as a broad vulgar dialect, but as it had been spoken at the ancient Court. Scott rarely tries to indicate origin or milieu by the dialect ; in their sublime moments his characters speak a language that has just a tinge of Scottish flavour and a strong element of pulpit language.[19] Scott relies little on quaint dialectal spellings, but more on the rich vivid idioms, the pregnant and suggestive simplicities, the apt and pithy force, the subtle humour, the bold comparisons, and above all the rhythm, of Scots speech. Far from being a more vulgar form of expression, Scots thus assumes a semi-poetic quality by its undercurrent of rhythm and submerged music. The vernacular, to Scott, is the language of the heart, and his Scots passages are fraught with a higher significance and strike at the very core of feeling[20] ; and in moments of deepest feeling, the suggestive terseness of Scots enables him to be more sharply realistic and supremely articulate.

If we follow this line of thought to its logical conclusion, we shall

[16] See *The Heart of Midlothian*, chs. xxii, xl.

[17] See *The Antiquary*, ch. xxi.

[18] See *Rob Roy*, chs. xxiii, xxxiii, xxvii ; the first of these proverbial Scots sayings had been used *verbatim* by T. Smollett (*The Reprisal*, 1790, I.II), and in a shortened form by Scott himself (*Waverley* ch. lxxi) ; see *S.N.D.*, *s.v.* flee.

[19] That Scott did this consciously is revealed in *Rob Roy*, ch. xxxv.

[20] Cp. Verrall (above, n. 8), p. 257.

be in a position to understand the significance of the best of Scott's novels. He has often been criticised for lacking depth and a vision of life, but many of his *Scottish* novels do have a " consecrating power," especially the more contemporary ones like *The Heart of Midlothian* or *The Antiquary*, where the attention of the author is not so deeply concerned with an historical conflict as it sometimes is in others. Here he shows sureness of touch, and a deep sense of the tragic fatality of human life, of a kind that can help others to understand themselves.[21] His Scottish characters now and again say things of a more than individual significance : a Meg Merrilies, an Andrew Fairservice, an Elspeth Mucklebackit, an Edie Ochiltree, a Jeanie Deans will utter a voice that comes not only out of themselves, or even out of the Scots people, but speaks for all humanity to all humanity. The Antiquary may dabble with the surface of history, and occupy himself with the inessentials of the past—but Edie Ochiltree is part and parcel of the past, its lore, or its tradition, and draws life from its reality. Edie is of the people, the source of all humanity, and in him accumulates all the wisdom and knowledge of the folk among whom he wanders. Call him a beggar, a sorcerer, a bard or a sage—essentially, he is *man*, and in him is summed up the past of the people that Scott wants to recreate. With the shrewd commonsense of the people he is imperturbable as the rocks, and so goes his determined way.[22] Edie embodies such fundamental and essentially simple virtues as honesty, loyalty, discretion, abiding faith. With the simplest of words he propounds a philosophy of life that a lord envies [23] ; nobody could speak more directly to the heart in standing up for his country,[24] or better express the majesty of death and the vanity of worldly possessions, than this old beggar : trapped by the tide while trying to rescue the laird, who offers him riches if he is saved, Edie replies :

> " Our riches will soon be equal," said the beggar, looking out upon the strife of the waters—" they are sae already ; for I hae nae land, and you would give your fair bounds and barony for a square yard of rock that would be dry for twal hours." [25]

" I have heard higher sentiments," Scott says, " from the lips of poor uneducated men and women. . . . than I ever yet met with out of

[21] Cp. " The Highland Widow " and " The two Drovers," both in *Chronicles of the Canongate*.

[22] Towards the end, he becomes, however, too much of a *deus ex machina*.

[23] Cp. *The Antiquary*, ch. xxviii.

[24] Cp. ch. xliv.

[25] Ch. vii.

the pages of the Bible." [26] And Edie Ochiltree is only one of the common folk whom Scott endowed with the poetical and rhythmical voice of the prophet. There are, in the same novel, Elspeth Mucklebackit and her son, the fisherman, whose words interpret life to us. There is old blind Bessie Maclure, who has lost her husband and two sons for the Covenanters' cause, but shelters the wounded enemy officer—" I wot I had nae divine command to shed blood, and to save it was baith like a woman and like a Christian." [27] Or take Jeanie Deans before the Queen, awkward, shy, yet taking her heart in both her hands, and rising to grand eloquence in her appeal that contains all that matters in life :

> " Alas ! it is not when we sleep soft and wake merrily ourselves that we think on other people's sufferings. Our hearts are waxed light within us then, and we are for righting our ain wrangs and fighting our ain battles. But when the hour of trouble comes to the mind or to the body—and seldom may it visit your leddyship—and when the hour of death comes that comes to high and low—lang and late may it be yours—Oh, my leddy, then it isna what we hae dune for oursells, but what we hae dune for ithers, that we think on maist pleasantly. And the thought that ye hae intervened to spare the puir thing's life will be sweeter in that hour, come when it may, than if a word of your mouth could hang the haill Porteous mob at the tail of ae tow." [28]

Oracular sayings come often from the mouth of such sybil-like figures as Meg Merrilies, the half-crazy gipsy who presides over the action like fate ; Habakkuk Mucklewrath, the Covenanter who lost his reason in prison and whose voice arises like a sombre prophecy ;[29] the three old " cummers " in *The Bride of Lammermoor* ; the half-witted Peter Peebles in *Redgauntlet* ; Madge Wildfire in *The Heart of Midlothian.* These key scenes are invariably written in a powerful rhythm and with a command of sound-sequences that show Scott as a verbal artist, a poet, of the highest quality. It is here, and in the interspersed lyrics from the mouths of the same people, that Scott rises to sublime height.

The lyrics are sometimes snatches from folk songs or ballads, sometimes original—but who could tell the difference between Elspeth's " Red Harlaw " and a genuine ballad ? These songs are

[26] Lockhart, *Life*, VOL. VI, pp. 60 f.
[27] See *Old Mortality*, ch. xlii.
[28] See *The Heart of Midlothian*, ch. xxxvii.
[29] Cp. *Old Mortality*, ch. xxxiv.

always thematic, especially in *The Bride of Lammermoor*, but they do more than strike the mood of the tale : they touch us with a sense of the mystery of life and death, elevate us into a sphere of purer being, or cast the shadow of another world over the brightness of youth :

Look not thou on beauty's charming,
Sit thou still when kings are arming,
Taste not when the wine-cup glistens,
Speak not when the people listens,
Stop thine ear against the singer,
From the red gold keep thy finger ;
Vacant heart, and hand, and eye,
Easy live and quiet die.[30]

This expresses something that cannot be said in other words ; we seem to have crossed the threshold into another world. And the same is true of Madge Wildfire's wild song :

Proud Maisie is in the wood,
 Walking so early ;
Sweet Robin sits on the bush,
 Singing so rarely. . . .[31]

At other times, the Scottish characters are a kind of chorus, or help to provide a background for enthusiasms and idealisms : the three old cummers at the funeral ; the town gossips in *The Antiquary* ; Cuddie in *Old Mortality*, a voice of peasant common sense and moderation, with his feet on the ground. The Falstaff-like figure of Andrew Fairservice expresses the prejudices, obstinacy, and slyness of the Scots crofter, on the Union or on the whore of Rome sitting on her seven hills (" as if ane wasna enough for her auld hinder end "), on the justification of smuggling, or on religion and the Sabbath. With his recognition of the good effects of the Union, and his distaste of " the pridefu' Edinburgh folk," Bailie Nicol Jarvie, Andrew's counterpart, has more of the sober shrewdness and the clannish loyalty of the Glasgow businessman.

How much Scott the story-teller owed to his early contacts with the common people is seen in his treatment of the supernatural, which has the same kind of structural importance in Scott's novels as the prophecies of such sybils as Elspeth Mucklebackit or Meg Merrilies. As a man of the age of Hume, Scott felt ill at ease with dreams, superstitions, visions, and when obliged to express his own views about

[30] See *The Bride of Lammermoor*, ch. iii. [31] See *The Heart of Midlothian*, ch. xl.

such matters, he can be painfully self-conscious about them, both in his novels and his verse romances. But when he is concerned with the supernatural as an object of popular belief, and as a factor in the life of the common people, he regains his sureness of touch, and gives it precisely the same matter-of-factness as in the ballads. Though, ostensibly, it is just the sort of supernatural story which would most strongly have appealed to a " Gothick " taste, " Wandering Willie's Tale " differs from most examples of Gothick literature in being in many respects so like a genuine folk-story. The Devil appears in the guise of a mysterious stranger—" one that, though I have been sair miscaa'd in the world, am the only hand for helping my freends " ; and in Hell the dead Laird sits drinking with Lauderdale, Rothes, Dalyell, Bluidie Mackenzie, Claverhouse, and many others long execrated in popular tradition as the persecutors of the Covenanters. The existence of the supernatural is taken completely for granted, it is part of the folk's view of life, and to the narrator all these grim figures are every inch as real as Steenie himself and the new Laird. Together with the fact that the dead Laird's prophecy does not come true, some of Wandering Willie's own admissions point, indeed, to a perfectly natural explanation : " Indeed, ye'll no hinder some to threap, that it was nane o' the Auld Enemy that Dougal and my gudesire saw . . . , but only that wanchancy creature [the Laird's ape] capering on the coffin." But Willie himself firmly believes in the supernatural character of the events which he narrates ; and, throughout, Scott's manipulation of the supernatural, as Willie sees it, is so assured that the reader is half willing to accept Willie's own account of the matter as, for the time being, far more plausible. The brooding sense of fate which colours the narrative is closely akin to that expressed by J. M. Synge in *Riders to the Sea*, and is nourished by similar fateful symbols ; it comes out still more strongly in *The Bride of Lammermoor*, especially in the masterly little scene where the " spaewife " hints at the supernatural knowledge that she has received from " a sure hand." [32]

Scott's novels have a significance which is greatly enhanced by certain features of style that arise directly out of Scots speech. The speech of Edie Ochiltree and all the rest of them is full of bold comparisons which seem tacitly to bring man into harmony with nature, both animate and inanimate—and with his own mysterious destiny. But still more striking is Scott's masterly use of dramatic contrast to

[32] Ch. xxiii.

heighten the pitch of tragic pathos. " Glad and proud," raves Auld Mause in her exalted fanaticism, " and sorry and humbled am I, a' in ane and the same instant, to see my bairn ganging to testify for the truth gloriously " : " Whisht, whisht, mither ! ," Cuddie retorts, " I like nane o' your sermons that end in a psalm at the Grassmarket." [33] Scott had, in fact, a strong and poignant sense of anticlimax that he may have learnt from Shakespeare. In *The Antiquary*, pathos is intensified when from deep grief we are brought back to earth by the reminder that drink is essential at a funeral. Again and again, it is the plain folk in Scott's novels who enrich the meaning of the story by thus emphasising the necessity of this return to the reality of common daily life. " And what would you have me to do," gruffly exclaims the grief-stricken fisherman in *The Antiquary* when asked how he can bring himself, on the day of the funeral, to repair the boat that has killed his son, " unless I wanted to see four children starve, because ane is drowned ? . . . She maun be mended though again' the morning tide—that's a thing o' necessity." This is the same realistic acceptance of fate that we find in the ballads at their best.

It has often been said of Burns and Fergusson that like Antaeus they derived their strength from contact with the earth. This is quite as true of Scott. As our analysis has shown, Scott usually is greatest when most Scottish : and to the qualities already mentioned must also be added such characteristically Scottish traits as his shrewd, level-headed realism (for, as John Buchan remarked, Scott's " eyes were not so dazzled by the tapestry on the walls as to miss the cobwebs in the corner ") [34] ; his strong interest in character ; the vigour which he is capable of putting into such crowd scenes as those in his account of the Porteous Riots ; and that fundamental clannishness which enables him to combine an almost exaggerated respect for any hereditary chief with an unwavering conviction of the worth and dignity of the meanest of his clansfolk. The touch of fantasy and exaggeration with which so many of the Scottish characters in his novels are drawn, and the demoniac streak which runs through not a few of them—for example, the Redgauntlets, Meg Merrilies, and Fergus MacIvor—likewise have many parallels in traditional Scots literature.

[33] See *Old Mortality*, ch. xxxv. The Grassmarket was the scene of many Edinburgh executions, including those of the Covenanters.

[34] Buchan (above, n. 1), p. 248.

" A kail-blaid, or a colliflower," says Andrew Fairservice, " glances sae glegly by moonlight, it's like a leddy in her diamonds." He is by no means the only character in Scott's novels in whom we find the same intense concentration on minute sensuous detail, the same trick of combining two images so that one of them is charged with additional vitality, the same poetic vision, as in the Makars themselves. But Scott was the first Scottish writer who endowed *landscape* with a life of its own, to the extent of making it one of the protagonists in his novels—an example that was followed not only by Emily Brontë and Thomas Hardy, but especially by many modern Scottish, Welsh, and Irish novelists, from Stevenson to Neil M. Gunn, Leslie Mitchell (" Lewis Grassic Gibbon "), Liam O'Flaherty, and Rhys Davies. Scott himself had deep roots in the Scottish scene, and the elaborate word pictures in which he presents it to us have so much descriptive power that, for example, Old Edinburgh, as he describes it in *The Heart of Midlothian*, or the cliff where, in *The Antiquary*, Edie hastens to meet the laird, are almost as real to us as anything that we have seen with our own eyes. We are made, above all, to feel the magic spell that the sight of heather or a desolate moor cast over Scott ; and Rob Roy's exclamation, " But the heather that I have trod upon when living, must bloom over me when I am dead—my heart would sink, and my arm would shrink and wither like fern in the frost, were I to lose sight of my native hills," recalls Scott's own statement that he would die if he could not see heather at least once a year. Landscape, in Scott's novels, is much more than a mere background : it is itself a formative influence, and in *The Bride of Lammermoor* it becomes a protagonist like Egdon Heath in Thomas Hardy's *Return of the Native* (Buchan).

Scott had an exceptionally powerful memory, and it is difficult to say how many of these features came from a knowledge of older Scottish poetry, or straight out of his knowledge of the people. I am inclined to believe that they came mainly from the latter, for much in Scott (as in all Scots literature) is attributable to *oral tradition* : we have seen this in Scott's whole way of telling a story, and we are now going to see it in the strong impact of the ballads on his work. When Scott turned more intently to the oral tradition of his people and collected its balladry in *Minstrelsy of the Scottish Border* (2 vols., 1802 ; 3 vols., 1803), this helped him to find his own genius and to overcome the influence of the German *Sturm und Drang*. The influence of the ballads is perhaps most obvious in the short stories and in *The*

Bride of Lammermoor (in all of which, incidentally, he foregoes his usual moral) : but it is when Scott used Scots speech to give depth to his novels that it brings forth its noblest fruit. These great moments are charged with the same stern passions, and have the same grim simplicity, the same elemental fatalism, the same unrelieved tragic intensity, as the ballads themselves. Just as, in the ballad, Graeme kills Bewick against his will, so, for reasons of honour, Scott's Highland Drover is bound to kill his friend, even though there is no hatred between them ; and both meet their fate with the same courageous resignation : after the storm of pent-up passion, the Drover's words " he was a pretty man " are fraught with love, sorrow, and tragic irony. Here, at any rate, Scott's narrative often is terse indeed, and has all the dramatic speed and direct brevity of the ballads themselves. The use of repetitions, echoes, pairs, alliteration, parallelisms, antitheses, and so forth, is economical, yet at the same time inescapable : it is chiefly from the cumulative effect of all of these, which give, for example, " Wandering Willie's Tale " or the curse of Meg Merrilies their ballad-like atmosphere, that such moments derive their intensity. As in "Jock o' the Side," common sense asserts itself at the very moment of highest pathos. Scott's use of symbols, omens and the supernatural, is strongly reminiscent of the ballads ; and, as in them, such a place as the parting of the ways in *Old Mortality*, may mysteriously be fraught with destiny. Insistence on place-names and local connexions is not, it is true, a common feature of ballads in general, but it is frequent in the Scottish Border ballads, and still more so in many Scots folk-songs and poems of the seventeenth and eighteenth centuries. This fits in with the Scots linguistic habit of particularising, and helps to give a heightened sense of reality. Scott exploited the emotional value of place-names and their associations to the full, and he also understood the powerful, almost hypnotic effect of resounding names (as in the curse of Meg Merrilies). The influence of the ballads is seen, however, at its most powerful in Scott's use of spoken Scots in such passages as these :

> ' Hist ! ' he said—' I hear a distant noise.'
> ' It is the rushing of the brook over the pebbles,' said one.
> ' It is the sough of the wind among the bracken,' said another.
> ' It is the galloping of horse,' said Morton to himself . . ., ' God grant they may come as my deliverers ! ' [35]

[35] *Old Mortality*, ch. xxxiii.

'But this warld winna last lang, and it will be time to sharp the maiden [guillotine] for shearing o' craigs [necks] and thrapples [throats]. I hope to see the auld rusty lass linking at a bluidy harst [harvest] again.'[36]

'Laith, laith was the lass—(Sybil Knockwinnock they ca'd her that tauld me the tale)—laith, laith was she to gae into the match . . .' [37]

To the width of outlook that he inherited from Hume and the North Britons, Scott thus added a depth derived from national tradition ; and if his had not been far and away the most comprehensive spirit in the whole field of Scottish literature, he could not possibly have achieved such a large measure of success in his self-appointed task of reconciling Highland and Lowland, Scots and English.

[36] *Rob Roy*, ch. xxix. [37] *The Antiquary*, ch. xxiv.

VIII

Backwash: The Nineteenth Century

1. The Emigrants

BURNS AND SCOTT had put Scotland back on the international map, and for some time to come they gave added impetus to the efforts—for the most part comparatively feeble—of a whole host of imitators. But, if only because they themselves had their eyes fixed on the past, even Burns and Scott could not stem the stream of people taking the road southwards. The nineteenth century moved at a tremendous pace as it followed its adventurous path of industrialisation, "progress," expansion, emancipation. Even on the spiritual plane, a distinctively Scottish utterance seemed increasingly difficult—and was it indeed necessary? Thanks to Scott, Scotsmen were more readily accepted in the South, and took over an increasing share in the life of Britain and the British Empire. Why should not Scottish writers, too, prefer to raise their voice in the larger concert of Great Britain—especially after the disintegration of the school of criticism associated with *Blackwood's Magazine* and the *Edinburgh Review*? Lockhart himself went to London, which seemed more and more the centre for a professional writer.

During the nineteenth century, most of the work of the Anglo-Scots was so inextricably woven into the general pattern of British culture that it is largely a waste of time to go looking for traces of Scottish blood in Thomas Hood, Thomas Campbell, Ruskin, Macaulay, Kipling, William Archer, Francis Thompson. Still, we must not entirely ignore certain salient peculiarities. The Anglo-Scots have been, in general, an unruly element, inclined to disregard established English conventions; and it would perhaps help to simplify the pattern of Victorian literary history if Robert Browning's "alleged Scottish descent" could be demonstrated.[1] This is not meant to suggest that the Scots were innovators—at home they were traditional

[1] Cp. D. C. C. Young, *Scottish Verse 1851-1951* (1952), p. xx; and Hogg's *Private Memoirs and Confessions of a justified Sinner*, Cresset Library (1947), p. xii, where André Gide points out that the same theme recurs in Browning's "Johannes Agricola." As we have seen. dramatic lyric and monologue is of frequent occurrence in Scots poetry.

enough—but rather that as outsiders they did not readily fall in with English modes of thought and expression, and could therefore the more easily reach out towards German transcendentalism or see London as a City of Dreadful Night. Secondly, the fact that they came, in general, from poorer homes than many, perhaps most, of their English brethren, helps to explain the extreme radicalism which (like Hood) so many of them displayed both in Scotland itself, and also in London. Finally, critics sometimes point to a peculiar quality in the language of these Scoto-English writers : thus Osbert Burdett points out that Carlyle spoke Scots and " came to Greek and Latin, to German and Italian without the stamp of an English of his own " [2] ; and T. S. Eliot suggests that Byron was like a foreigner who wrote English as a dead or dying language, adding nothing to the language, its sounds or meanings.[3]

When all is said, we shall not finally arrive at a full understanding of the work of Byron, Carlyle, Davidson, or Thomson, until we have considered *certain aspects* of it in the light of Scottish tradition. BYRON said,

> But I am half a Scot by birth, and bred
> A whole one, and my heart flies to my head ; [4]

and T. S. Eliot has shown how essentially Scottish he is.[5] He points to Byron's peculiar diabolism and to the delight it gave him to pose as a damned creature, with evidence provided. Byron's double role, as an individual isolated from and superior to other men because of his innate daring evil, and as a naturally good and generous nature distorted by the crimes of humanity against himself, almost suggests a split personality. (This is a point we shall have to take up again in the course of this chapter). Eliot explains this attitude from the background of a " country ruined by religion, and taking religion more seriously than England " ; it is a " perversion of the Calvinist faith " of its ancestors. We might add, as another case in point, the

[2] *The two Carlyles* (1930), p. 214.

[3] " Byron," in *From Anne to Victoria*, ed. Bonamy Dobrée (1937), pp. 601-19. In *Scottish Literature* (1919), pp. 281 ff., G. Gregory Smith makes a similar statement about Stevenson.

[4] *Don Juan*, Canto X, st. xvii.

[5] In " Byron " (above, n. 3). See also E. Lovall, *His very Self and Voice* (1955), the latest biography. Byron's lines " So we'll go no more a roving " are taken from " The jolly Beggar " (attributed to James V), a ballad which must have been current in the North-East of Scotland, where Byron spent his childhood : a version was picked up in Aberdeenshire in the early twentieth century (G. Greig, *Last Leaves of traditional Ballads and Ballad Airs*, ed. A. Keith, 1925).

intent and unconventional probing into the question as to what is evil in *Cain* and other plays. But T. S. Eliot's main point is " that Byron's satire upon English society, in the latter part of *Don Juan*, is something for which I can find no parallel in English literature " (p. 617), and the dedication of *Don Juan* to Southey " is not English satire at all ; it is really a flyting and closer in feeling and intention to the satire of Dunbar " (p. 618). His vices and virtues, Eliot concludes, are not those of English poetry, " and his own vices seem to have twin virtues that closely resemble them." We are reminded of the deliberate changes from one level of style to another in the Makars, or the epistles of Burns in a more sophisticated garb. Byron's violent libertarianism was less uncommon in Scotland than in England. It is not only because Byron was ostracised by English society on moral grounds that he has been less popular as a writer in England than on the Continent.

If Byron's " Scottishness " has to be discovered, THOMAS CARLYLE'S (1795-1881) is patent ; he looks at John Bull as one not of his own kin, and he often goes out of his way to quote Scottish examples (*Past and Present*, 1843). However, it is the man rather than the work that is " Scottish." His Calvinist inheritance, his peasant blood, his grudging adjustment with the world as he finds it, the gap between the Scottish cottage and the English city parlour, and the nineteenth-century decline of dogma—these all go to shape a character whose Scottish features stand out in high relief. His insistence on liberty and independence has the touchiness of one formerly an underdog. In grim humour he resembles Barbour, even Henryson (though he lacks Henryson's poise). Beneath the gruffness there is, however, the same underlying tenderness ; and if we do not take this Scottish contrast of angularity and tenderness into account we will never fathom Carlyle's seemingly disconcerting relationship with his wife, Jane Welsh. As a true Lowlander Carlyle knows the value of silence, and when confronted by feelings, is apt to approach them purely as elements in an intellectual problem, and as materials for a good argument. This has been attributed to Carlyle's Calvinism ; for though he was not a believing Christian, Carlyle was indeed in many respects a Calvinist, who maintained the same gospel of work, and displayed precisely the same dogmatic assurance, the same controversial acerbity, as the most Calvinistic of his Covenanting forebears. Osbert Burdett maintains that in *Sartor Resartus* Carlyle argues and expostulates as if he still had not been finally convinced by his own teaching : but he misses one point here. As Hogg reminds us in *The Confessions of a justified Sinner*, Bible-reading and prayer alone are not enough for a true Scotsman : to get full spiritual satisfaction out of religion, he must have somebody to argue with. The same passionate delight in argument had appeared in Scots literature long before Calvin ; and Carlyle's violent assertion and denunciation must undoubtedly be seen in a much longer perspective.

Though unusual in English literature, the mixture of the serious and the grotesque that is found in so much of Carlyle's work has close parallels in that of many Scots authors—even though he may never have read their writings. Carlyle's English critics have seen in him an unusually gifted phrasemaker, and have marvelled at the vividness, descriptive power, and graphic pictorial intensity of which his strange English is capable. Yet, as we know, these characteristics are highly developed in Scots speech. Often, too, Carlyle flashes together two images so that one of them is charged with additional reality.[6] The wilful comparisons in *Past and Present*, the contrasts in *Sartor Resartus*, are carried to the same grotesque extremes of logic as in the traditional flytings ; and though in most respects both morality and style are purely his own, Carlyle's use of echo and alliteration—sometimes for emphasis, sometimes for ludicrous effect—also recalls the flytings. In *Sartor Resartus* we have the same uncomfortable feeling as in *The Cherrie and the Slae* that we do not know how far the author is from mock seriousness ; witness the names, the German-English, the remarks on methodical, metaphysical Germany, and indeed the whole philosophy of clothes. " Our professor, whether he have humour himself or not, manifests a certain feeling of the Ludicrous, a sly observance. . . . " But, like Dunbar, Carlyle joins the apparently unjoinable and proceeds from the grotesque to serious metaphysics—and back again. In his satires, there is snarling and jesting at the same time.

John Davidson (1857-1909) has been understood as a symbolic representative of the Scottish writer in the nineteenth century.[7] Brought up in Greenock in a home which derived its fervent Calvinism from a secession of the second or third degree, he fails to achieve a

[6] Cp. G. D. Brown (below, pp. 267 f.).

[7] His verse is contained in *Fleet Street Eclogues* (1893), *Ballads and Songs* (1894), *New Ballads* (1897) and *The last Ballad* (1899).

satisfactory relationship with his environment, rebels after experience of life in Glasgow, cuts himself adrift, and finds his way to London, the " dusksome cell where men go mad." He belongs to an *avant-garde* abandoning itself to the *Zeitgeist* and to Nietzsche, seeks " to cope with new ideas through the medium of English," but fails (Douglas Young), and seals his failure by drowning himself in the Channel. But Davidson deserves better study than this, both as a poet in his own right and as a potent influence on the young C. M. Grieve (" Hugh MacDiarmid ").

The literary influences which shaped Davidson's work were those of *fin-de-siècle* London : Pater and Oxford and the " Rhymers' Club " ; Baudelaire and Verlaine, and Impressionism—not *entirely* unlike the kind of impressionism that we have seen in much earlier Scottish poetry—with a touch of Nietzsche and Ibsen. But the decisive influences were Scottish, and *un*literary ; the map of his mind was determined by his Scottish environment, inheritance, and principles, by his cultural and social roots in his native community, and by the pressure of Calvinism, the only chamber that his father kept open in his own wide intellect. All this is evident from " A Ballad in blank Verse of the Making of a Poet " :

> For this was in the North, where Time stands still
> and Change holds holiday, where Old and New
> welter upon the border of the world,
> and savage faith works woe.

But Davidson cannot stand still, nor placidly take things for granted. His whole work (except some of his fine lyrics) arises out of a clash with this rock-like stability where " Time stands still." The poet worries his soul and brain trying to answer the question of God, I, creed, truth, science ; this is neither the fervour of the mystic, nor the scientific negation of the atheist, nor the listening to his soul of a believer. Davidson tries to figure out his problem, to fight it out with himself. " God is an artist, not an artisan " ; after creating Man, the mind of the world, He left His creation in man's hand and did not tinker with it. But the truth is, even if you do not believe in God, " that God himself believes in you "—the very opposite of Calvinism.[8]

But fighting it out with himself also means a dramatic tension, and the " split personality " crops up again. Davidson often personifies

[8] " Queen Elizabeth's Day," in *Fleet Street Eclogues*.

different moods or tempers within himself as different beings, especially in "Thirty Bob a Week," where the revolutionary and the man trusting in his thirty shillings a week "ride me like a double-seated bike." I am also inclined to regard the dramatic situation in *Fleet Street Eclogues* as fundamentally the dramatisation of a conflict in Davidson's own mind: in his soul, the poet, the dedicated journalist, and the man sneering at journalism were at war with one another.

The importance of these points is heightened by some close parallels with an older fellow-exile, JAMES THOMSON the younger (1834-82).[9] He found himself in a similar predicament, wrestled intently and furiously with questions of sin and guilt, tried to get beneath surfaces, tormented his soul with "why's," and temporarily hoped to find answers in Shelley, Novalis,[10] and Heine. His life appears as full of similar dramatic contrasts as those in Davidson's breast, and he repeatedly sees himself as two separate personalities, as in *The City of Dreadful Night*:

I was twain,
Two selves distinct that cannot join again;
One stood apart and knew but could not stir. . . .[11]

[9] *Poetical Works*, ed. B. Dobell (1895).
[10] Hence his pseudonym B.V. (= "Bysche Vonalis").
[11] 1870-74; IV (similarly VIII).

2. The Stay-at-homes

What of the Scottish scene? In the early decades of the century, during Scott's lifetime, there was some remarkable activity: there was an interest in ballads and folk poetry, and Scott himself had created a public for Scottish novels and historical poems. The Scottish background was now ripe for exploitation, as in the three novels of Susan Ferrier (1772-1834), in which an occasional secondary character is all that "gets across" to a modern reader. But it helped also to create the climate for two writers whose best work was wholly independent, even revolutionary for Scotland, namely James Hogg and John Galt.

In a century when poets in Scotland tried to pose as untaught ploughmen in false emulation of Burns, JAMES HOGG (1770-1835), the "Ettrick Shepherd," was a genuine rural bard without schooling.[1] But while the horizon of the others was limited to the but-and-ben or, possibly, the public house, Hogg's achievement was not confined to his rural poems and tales of fairies and warlocks: he penned skilful parodies in *The Poetic Mirror*; in *Blackwood's Magazine* we find his hand in the remarkable satire of the "Chaldee Ms," which shocked Edinburgh so much that it had to be discontinued; in the same *Magazine* he was the moving spirit in John Wilson's *Noctes Ambrosianae*, whether true to life or not; and above all, he left the unique *Private Memoirs and Confessions of a justified Sinner*.

Hogg was certainly untaught, and the spark of his genius only glows through clouds of coarseness. But it would not be true to say that he wrote in ignorance of the Scottish tradition.[2] He was steeped in the ballad lore and folk tales of his Border hills, and his mother was one of the best ballad-singers. Hogg himself helped to collect

[1] His poetry is contained in *Scottish Pastorals, Poems and Songs* (1801), *The Queen's Wake* (1813), *The Pilgrims of the Sun* (1815), *Mador of the Moor* (1816), *Queen Hynde* (1824), and *Songs* (1831). See also *Selected Poems of James Hogg*, ed. J. W. Oliver, Saltire Classics, 1940. His prose includes *The Brownie of Bodsbeck* (1818) and *The private Memoirs and Confessions of a justified Sinner* (1824; Cresset Library, 1947, with introduction by André Gide).

[2] Cp. E. C. Batho, *The Ettrick Shepherd* (1927); and see also D. Carswell, *Sir Walter: a four-part Study in Biography* (1930), pp. 175 ff.

ballads, and occasionally re-arranged them; ballad lines or echoes mark many of his poems (" O mother, mother, make my bed . . ."; " Oh, came ye ower by the Yoke-burn Ford . . ."). His poems of the supernatural are best when he keeps away from the Gothick and presents his tale in the matter-of-fact, comment-less style of the ballads, with their dramatic presentation, understatement, and suggestive symbols (" the beer that was never browin, . . . ane wee, wee man "). It is just because it has these characteristics that " Kilmeny " is one of the finest poems of the supernatural in Scottish or English literature, and in the unique " Witch of Fife " daft absurdity is raised to the pitch of sublimity: yet the fact remains that Hogg could award the prize of the contest in *The Queen's Wake* to a Gothick horror-story!

As anybody will see if he compares " The Aged Widow's Lament " with Mickle's " Sailor's Wife," Hogg's work also shows traces of the influence of the eighteenth-century Scots popular vernacular poems. According to the inscription on the monument which stands at the head of St Mary's Loch, not far from Tibby Shiel's Inn, Hogg " taught the wandering wind to sing." [3] The claim is not unjustified; for indeed there is all the singing and soaring of the bird in Hogg's " Skylark," and his book of popular *Songs* (1831) has helped to keep his name alive. For the Highland Society of London, Hogg collected, translated, and arranged *Jacobite Relics*,[4] a contact with the Gaelic tradition which also left traces in his work. A number of his songs [5] have the soft cadences of Gaelic rhymes; and " Lock the Door, Lariston," [6] with its hidden rhymes, alliteration, and anticipations, comes closer to the Gaelic delight in sounds than any other poem in Scots or English in centuries. Then, of course, Hogg was inspired by Burns, as witness " The Author's Address to his auld Dog Hector " or " The auld Man's Fareweel to his wee House."

Hogg's knowledge of earlier Scots poetry was fragmentary, but not narrow, and we find some surprising traces, such as his use of the *a b a b* : *b c b c* stanza for grave reflexion. There is a touch of the " ballads of impossibilities," [7] and of grotesque exaggeration, especially in the riotous absurdity of " The Village of Balmaquhapple " (ll. 1 ff.):

[3] Quoted from *The Queen's Wake*, *ad fin.*

[4] 2 vols., 1819-21.

[5] *E.g.* " Bonnie Prince Charlie," " McLean's Welcome," and " Donald McGillavry," in *Selected Poems* (above, n. 1), pp. 45, 47 f., 48 f.

[6] In *Selected Poems*, pp. 43 f.

[7] Cp. " Birniebouzle " and " The Lass o' Carlisle," in *Selected Poems*, pp. 55 f., 60.

D'ye ken the big village of Balmaquhapple,
The great muckle village of Balmaquhapple ?
'Tis steeped in iniquity up to the [a]thrapple, [a] *wind-pipe*
An' what's to become o' poor Balmaquhapple ? [8]

The description of the Queen in *The Queen's Wake* is full of the old Scots delight in shimmering colour effects, and Hogg is a master of the old Scots trick of sketching in the scene with a few quick strokes of the pencil :

The [a]reek o' the cot hung over the plain, [a] *smoke*
Like a little wee cloud in the world its lane.[9]

More often, however, we sense the deliberate touch of Coleridge :

. . . as spotless as the morning snaw.

It was probably from Coleridge that Hogg learnt the technique of rhythmical variation : the main body of " Kilmeny " has the same anapaestic gallop as *Christabel*, but such a couplet as

The land of vision it would seem,
A still, an everlasting dream [10]

is purely in iambics, and has not one syllable too many ; its lingering cadence is deeply expressive of calm and wondering reflexion.

Thus Hogg was no mere follower in the wake of Walter Scott, and there is more in his poems and tales than merely dross and arrogance. And this brings us to *The Private Memoirs and Confessions of a justified Sinner*,[11] his one really remarkable achievement. Nothing in Hogg's other work—not even " The Village of Balmaquhapple "—helps to prepare our minds for this astonishing study of religious fanaticism—or for the direct and economical simplicity of the language in which Scots folk speech is often combined with Hebrew rhetoric :

' I will lay the strongholds of sin and Satan as flat before my face as the dung that is spread out to fatten the land.' [12]

It is amazing that a book like this could lie forgotten on the back

[8] In *Selected Poems*, pp. 49 f.

[9] " Kilmeny " (*Selected Poems*, p. 7).

[10] *Op. cit.* (*Selected Poems*, p. 8).

[11] Above, n. 1. References below are to the Cresset Library edn. (1947).

[12] P. 14. And cp. p. 111 : " ' May he be a two-edged weapon in Thy hand and a spear coming out of Thy mouth to destroy, and overcome, and pass over ; and may the enemies of Thy Church fall down before him, and be as dung to fat the land ! ' "

shelves almost till André Gide took it up. But it needed our experience of totalitarian thinking to recognise the greatness and the horror of the book. We can fully appreciate the significance of Robert's conviction that " the elect of God would be happier, and purer, were the wicked and unbelievers all cut off from troubling and misleading them," and can no longer derive much comfort from the supposed Editor's concluding suggestion [13] that Robert *may* only have been " a religious maniac, who wrote and wrote about a deluded creature, till he arrived at that height of madness that he believed himself the very object whom he had been all along describing."

The action begins about 1704-5, and it concerns two brothers. The elder, George, is a true son of his worldly father, a laird and gentleman ; but the younger, Robert, is of doubtful legitimacy and is brought up by his fanatical mother, and by her spiritual adviser, the Rev. Mr Wringhim, who together indoctrinate him with their own narrowly Calvinistic principles, from which he draws the antinomian conclusion that as an " elect and justified person " he cannot sin, and consequently that, no matter how wicked it may seem, nothing that he does can really be sinful once he has been accepted by the Lord. The story is told twice, first in an objective " Editor's Narrative," [14] and secondly in the longer " Private Memoirs and Confessions " [15] of the younger brother. Hence arises a sustained contrast between theme and variation, substance and shadow, objective and subjective reality. This raises the agonising question : Is there any such thing as objective reality—or is everything subjective ? " If you and I believe that we see a person, why, we do see him." [16] And indeed it is terrifying to see how different an appearance the same action presents in each of the two versions, and how subtly the mind works to create its own reality :

> I will not deny that my own immediate impressions of this affair in some degree differed from this statement. But this is precisely as my illustrious friend described it to be afterwards, and I can rely implicitly on his information, as . . . he could have no motive for saying what was not the positive truth.[17]

This " friend " is the Devil ; and what distinguishes him is that he always presses Robert's antinomianism to its extreme logical

[13] Cp. p. 154. [14] Pp. 5 ff. [15] Pp. 89 ff. [16] P. 78.
[17] P. 155. For another account of the matter, cp. pp. 65 ff.

conclusions. It is he who succeeds in persuading Robert that there is enough merit in the blood of Christ to annihilate all his sins, however atrocious, and that, since everything is pre-ordained, the " sins " of the elect are among the instruments by which God's purposes are fulfilled. Purely by reasoning along such ostensibly orthodox lines as these, he forces Robert to admit that even perjury or murdering his own brother is justified in terms of a cause which transcends blood-relationships. He has an uncanny gift of entering into the " conceptions and feelings " of others, and it gives a reader of today goose-flesh to see how he worms his way into Robert's mind and creates in it an illusory reality which receives impulses from outside, but is at best a distorted and purely subjective reflexion of the real external world ; and we are left wondering which is real, the external fact, or the distorted image of it in Robert's mind. A good example is the subjective impression in the haze, the light effects in the mist, and the fairy web of water drops on the hat in the critical scene on Arthur's Seat.[18] This impression is actually received by George, and though even he is occasionally subject to hallucinations, it is meant, probably, to represent the response of an essentially healthy mind to the stimulus of external nature. Still, even he tends to create his own subjective version of reality from the elements of sensuous perception. (We shall henceforward call this process " animism " or " pan-demonism.")

Nor is this all—the dualism between inner and outer reality leads Robert to conceive of himself as two people : he looks from outside and sees his " apparition "[19] ; " I have two souls . . . , the one being all unconscious of what the other performs."[20] Was Stevenson acquainted with the *Confessions of a justified Sinner* when he wrote *Dr Jekyll and Mr Hyde*? At any rate, the frequency, in Scottish literature, of " theme and variation," duality, split personality,[21] demands an explanation, which at best can only be tentative.

Several recurrent traits of the Scottish tradition may perhaps have gone to produce this phenomenon. One is the intense pre-occupation with character,[22] with which is linked a relentless curiosity, an insatiable desire to enter into other people's minds. The Scot usually is not satisfied with outward appearances ; he worries what

[18] Pp. 37-8. [19] Pp. 139 ff. [20] P. 174.

[21] Cp. Byron, Davidson, James Thomson the younger. Dunbar, too, has been described as a split personality (by Rachel A. Taylor).

[22] Evidenced by the Scots trick of speaking in character ; in telling a story, a Scotsman always *acts* his tale.

may be behind the surface. Then there is the subjective impressionism so characteristic of Scots and Gaelic poetry (Henryson, Dunbar, Hume, Montgomerie, etc.), from which arises a tendency to create one's own subjective vision of reality. The same thing can be seen from different angles, as a whole series of variations on a single theme. From the beginning, Scots poetry showed a combination of two or more seemingly irreconcilable qualities : of high pathos and everyday realism, of stark tragedy and grim humour, of high seriousness and grotesquerie, of tenderness and sarcasm. With their effortless transition from mood to mood, and their frequent change of level, such apparently diverse poems as " Colkelbie's Sow " and the mock elegies all express essentially the same attitude. This emotional and intellectual dualism—the " Caledonian Antisyzygy," as Gregory Smith called it —*may* possibly have been reinforced by the schizophrenic tendencies of a nation which came to use one language to express thought, another to express feeling. It *may* also have been hardened by the stern intellectual discipline of Calvinism ; and, as the impact of the Reformation gradually wore off, people *may* have become increasingly conscious of the latent emotional and moral dualism implicit in the overt contradiction between the Scottish Sabbath and the Scottish Saturday (or Friday) night. Yet it would clearly be wrong to explain the underlying dualism simply, or even chiefly, in terms of them. At any rate, the problem of a strangely subjective vision of reality is dominant in much of modern Scottish literature.

John Galt (1779-1839) [23] was sorely neglected in his own century. At a time when Scottish literature was still wallowing in the romantic past or already retiring to the kailyard, Galt kept his eyes fixed realistically on the present and on the changes which, in his own lifetime, radically transformed Scottish social life. His *Annals of the Parish* (1821) and *The Provost* (1822) are companion-pieces : they give a picture of the cultural, social, economic changes and improvements in the life of the people over a lifetime, the one recorded by the minister of a village parish, the other by a councillor and provost of a burgh. Galt's ambition had been to create a Scottish *Vicar of Wakefield*, but he went much farther and achieved something completely

[23] See J. W. Aberdein, *John Galt* (1936), and some of the John Galt Lectures in *Papers of the Greenock Philosophical Society*, *e.g.* W. M. Brownie, *John Galt : Social Historian* (1951) ; W. Croft Dickinson, *John Galt : " The Provost " and the Burgh* (1954).

different. His minister is not a gentleman living in a vicarage, but a man whose profession is the ministry, who lives in his work and in his congregation. He writes to testify anent the great changes that have happened in his day and generation,[24] and consequently all historic events are seen in the village perspective, as they influence the daily life of people : agrarian changes and traffic improvements, the problem of smuggling and the intrusion of town fashions, the first tea-kettle, the cotton mill and all the resultant change of social patterns, are more real than wars in America and revolutions in France. The latter assume importance only by their impact on the people : in the weavers' town, a bookseller makes his appearance to satisfy the workers' curiosity about the new ideas, and church discipline, alas, relaxes after that. This is realistic contemporary folk history in which man is seen as a social being.

This realistic, almost psychological, approach enables Galt to draw individual characters who are no mere personifications of vices and virtues, but real people, with their own oddities and peculiarities. Galt really enters into the mind of his minister or provost and, as a result, we, too, see with their eyes and judge as they do. Galt is not satisfied with a façade, but is intent on getting behind it. What the minister and the provost tell us about themselves is subtly supplemented by what they do and by how they justify it. In seeking to convince himself of his own righteousness, each unfolds a highly disciplined train of arguments, and in *The Provost*, especially, it is fascinating to see how public happens eventually to coincide with private interest.

Story-telling so truly in character produces the same highly subjective vision of reality already mentioned [25] : the historic events in the two books are the same, but they are seen differently and have different effects. The Provost, lacking the humanity of the minister, is narrower in outlook, but deeper, more devious in his psychological meanderings, and of course more urbane. He focuses our attention on changes in the administration of the burgh which are less obvious than those which occur in the parish, and are brought about by subtler means than overt parliamentary or burghal acts of legislation.

The *Annals of the Parish* and *The Provost* are rather character studies than novels ; *The Entail* (1822) is Galt's best effort to translate his

[24] *Annals of the Parish*, ch. 2.

[25] Cp. James Park in a letter to Galt dated 14 Feb. 1812 : " You write from the very peculiar associations of your own mind, instead of attending to those general associations which are common to the bulk of mankind " (see *The Literary Life and Miscellanies of John Galt*, 3 vols., Edinburgh 1834, VOL. I, pp. 131-2).

own ideas of recent or contemporary social changes into the form of genuine fiction. The rest of his novels are outstanding only in parts (for example the beginning of *Sir Andrew Wylie*), but Galt lacked structural craftsmanship and had not enough patience for a plot. But a word must be said about his language. " It is true," Galt said, " that in polite companies a Scotsman is prohibited, by the imputation of vulgarity, from using the common language of the country, in which he expresses himself with most ease and vivacity, and, clothed in which, his earliest and most distinctive impressions always arise to his own mind. He uses a species of translation, which checks the versatility of fancy, and restrains the genuine and spontaneous flow of his conceptions." [26] The *Annals* and *The Provost* are essentially monologues, and like Galt's dialogue in general are Scots in syntax, idiom, grammar, and pronunciation, with an occasional Gaelic undertone (" I know not what was in it," *i.e.* what was the matter, going to happen). In his other novels, even the narrative and contemplative passages have a liberal sprinkling of Scots words, which often convey a special touch of intimacy or tenderness, robust vigour or pictorial vividness, shrewd humour or comic extravagance: " A carle that daunered about the doors wi' his hands in his pouches, and took them out at meal-time " ; " his een . . . are like gowans in a May morning, and his laugh's as blithe as the lilt o' the linty " (*Sir Andrew Wylie*).

John Galt's sensitive awareness of *contemporary* social and economic changes was a new gift to Scottish literature, and his insight into contemporary Scottish life went much deeper even than Fergusson's. But the nineteenth century did not realise the gift. When D. M. Moir (" Delta ") dedicated *Mansie Wauch* to Galt, he may have believed he was writing in the same vein, but instead of social changes we find only " a good few uncos " and other quaint incidents that befell the tailor of Dalkeith. They are broadly caricatured in " couthie " style, and even where a certain cultural importance might be felt, as in the case of the first playhouse, this leads ultimately to clownishness. In Scotland, as elsewhere, the nineteenth century was a time

[26] Essay on " John Wilson," in *Scottish descriptive Poems*, ed. John Leyden, 1803. Cp. the Postscript to *Ringan Gilhaize*, where Galt maintains that there is " such an idiomatic difference " between Scots and English that " very good Scotch might be couched in the purest English terms, and without the employment of a single Scotch word," and that the style of *The Provost* has consequently been censured " as being neither Scotch nor English —not Scotch, because the words are English—and not English, because the forms of speech are Scottish."

of violent changes. Ever-sprawling Glasgow had more spindles than Lancashire and built its huge shipyards ; the tragic Highland clearances changed the structure of a whole society—but apart from a few political songs the present only speaks in an occasional short poem like Alexander Smith's " Glasgow," which expresses the sad and stern beauty of the capital of the Clyde, the fiery stream of blinding ore, and says " yes " to the city. Of all the major Scottish events of the nineteenth century, the only one that finds its way into literature is, characteristically enough, the Disruption of 1843, when the Free Church seceded from the Church of Scotland. This is the background to Hugh Miller's *My Schools and Schoolmasters* and especially to William Alexander's *Johnny Gibb of Gushetneuk* (1871), an honest and realistic series of sketches of landward places in the North-East that repeats Galt on a narrower scale. The focus of interest, for these country-folk, is the question of patronage and the Free Kirk, but in the bygoing we see real life develop around us, or get some idea how the introduction of some new thing like guano is brought about. The language, the Buchan dialect, is more seriously Scots than Galt's, and we feel that Alexander needs the Scots words to render exactly what he means.

Apart from this, the less said about the two generations after Scott the better. The shadow of Burns and Scott had fallen across the path, and minor spirits were content to move inside it. Burns had summed up a tradition, but since little was added to it, it rapidly became an exhausted stereotype. There are some few good songs, mostly by gentle ladies (Dorothea Maria Ogilvy of Clova, " The weary spinnin o't "), one or two readable local poets (" J. B. Selkirk," = James B. Brown), a few echoes of Gaelic, but more caricature. Otherwise, whisky and weaver bodies and bairnies and nostalgia and sentimentality, all gloriously " successful." The *Poetic Gems* of the Great William McGonagall, Poet and Tragedian, and shabbiest of public-house rhymesters, are still reprinted almost every year ; and their continuing popularity would indeed be an interesting problem for a psychiatrist to study. It is not rock-bottom that we touch here, that would suggest something solid ; with him, poetry is irretrievably sunk in mire.

The novel fared little better. To look at village or small-town life sixty years before provided so much heartfelt satisfaction. George Macdonald (1824-1905) is better remembered today for his sermons and sayings, his myths and mysticism,[27] than for his sentimental

[27] See *George Macdonald, an Anthology*, ed. C. S. Lewis, 1946.

best-sellers that exploited the Scottish provincial background. At the end, there is the " Kailyard School " of the close of the century.[28] Taken in themselves, James Matthew Barrie's *Auld Licht Idylls* (1888) and *A Window in Thrums* (1889) are not bad, with their humorous presentation of rough exterior and soft heart in a little self-contained world ; they are one-sided, it is true, but there is observation and skill, and genuine humour. But expanded into novels, and mass-produced by countless imitators, these stories have a sickening sentimentality and quaintness. One cannot help feeling that here is a commercial exploitation of a cheap whimsicality about bairnies and heroes in homespun. But the Rev. John Watson (" Ian Maclaren ") and Samuel Rutherford Crockett still have their successors after the First World War in J. L. Waugh, J. J. Bell, and others. Whatever their merit, they have nothing to add to the Scottish literary tradition.

The tradition seemed really to have come to an end, and not with a bang, but a whimper. As seen in, say, 1880, there seemed no future for a distinct Scottish utterance in poetry or prose. Those who had something to say catered (whatever the disadvantages) for the British public : those who did not catered for provincial quaintness and tartan-hungry holidaymakers ; and in their case the sweeter (and sicklier), the better.

[28] For a recent study, see G. Blake, *Barrie and the Kailyard School*, 1951.—" Kailyard School, from ' kail-yard,' a cabbage patch such as is commonly attached to a cottage, a term applied to writers of a recent class of fiction, describing, with much use of the vernacular, common life in Scotland. . . ." (*Oxford Companion to English Literature*).

Part III

Another Spring ?

IX

Heaving Again: From Stevenson to World War One

1. Prose

DISTINCTIVELY Scottish literature as such had foundered in a bog, or seemed at best to have been relegated to the kailyard, the bothie, and the Burns Night Supper. Yet again the tide turned, almost miraculously, and again it was by a conscious return to the native tradition. But ROBERT LOUIS STEVENSON (1850-94),[1] the Ramsay of the late nineteenth century, was less of a propagandist, and much more of an artist, than his eighteenth-century predecessor.

Stevenson has a place of his own in English literature, and even in the *fin-de-siècle* cross-currents of world literature. Yet his work was thoroughly Scottish, and it cannot be fully appreciated apart from its Scottish background. Stevenson himself was well aware of this, as witness "The Foreigner at Home" (1882) [2] and his feeling of kinship with Robert Fergusson.

We are not concerned here with Stevenson the stylist, the "sedulous ape" who was so intent on finding the correct word that he "came to literature with too many words and two few insights" (Daiches). This was part of his European background. But the preoccupation with style as a fastidious taste—with intricate forms, echoes and

[1] There are several editions of Stevenson's collected works. References in this chapter are to the Edinburgh Edition, i.e. *The Works of R. L. Stevenson* (Romances, 8 vols. ; Travels and Excursions, 3 vols. ; South Sea Tales, 2 vols, ; Tales and Fantasies, 3 vols. ; Biography, 1 vol. ; Correspondence, 1 vol. ; History, 1 vol. ; Drama, in collaboration with W. E. Henley, 1 vol. ; Poetry, 1 vol. ; Miscellanies, 3 vols. ; Appendix, 1 vol.), London 1895-8. See also *The Letters of Robert Louis Stevenson to his Family and his Friends*, ed. S. Colvin, 2 vols., London 1899. The best study is D. Daiches, *Robert Louis Stevenson*, London 1947. For biography, see J. A. Steuart, *R.L.S.*, 2 vols., London 1924, and J. C. Furmas, *Voyage to Windward*, London 1952.

[2] In *Memories and Portraits* (Miscellanies, VOL. 1), pp. 89 ff.

alliteration, with the dance of sounds and meanings, with word-painting, and with possibilities of variation and counterpoint—all this represents a mood frequent enough in older Scots poetry and is strongly reminiscent of the way in which Dunbar especially is apt to subordinate thought to meter.

Stevenson's debt to Walter Scott is obvious, but one thing ought to arrest us here. Why are "Thrawn Janet" (1881) [3] and the beginning of Black Andie's "Tale of Tod Lapraik" [4] so much less successful than "Wandering Willie's Tale"? Stevenson had perhaps a finer command of the vernacular than Scott himself, more conscious knowledge of "the kindly Scots tongue, that set a value on affectionate words." [5] But in "Thrawn Janet" the style is often too literary, with a scattering of folk idioms tacked on to it, almost as if it was a translation of Stevenson's English style Scotticised; and, as a result, we the readers are unable to visualise the speaker by whom it is told. Why is it that a Scots tale needs a sharply portrayed character to tell it? Is it only the effect of a tradition in which Scots prose had almost exclusively been used for dialogue? Or is it because the Scots way of speaking is so dramatic that it requires a speaker behind it? Stevenson himself said that the English speak with less interest and conviction, while the Scot puts his whole personality into it and "will give you the best of himself." [6] Is there any such thing as an absolute, detached prose in Scots? Is it, indeed, possible?

That Stevenson was fully alive to the essentially dramatic character of spoken Scots is shown by his own description of the shepherd in "Pastoral" (1887): "When he narrated, the scene was before you." [7] Perhaps his finest dialogue is the highly dramatic scene between father and son in *Weir of Hermiston*, where "the Scots words [of the father] seem to hiss with scorn, making Archie's elegant English seem artificial and effeminate" [8]; the rendering of the vowel qualities of "I'm nearer v*oa*miting, though, than you would fancy," [9] and the final "just try to be less of an *ee*diot," [10] heighten the emotional effect and

[3] In *The Merry Men and other Tales* (Tales and Fantasies, VOL. IV), pp. 244 ff.

[4] In *Catriona* (1892: Romances, VOL. V), pp. 169 ff.

[5] *The Master of Ballantrae* (1889: Romances, VOL. VI), p. 104. Cp. "The Foreigner at Home," in *Memories and Portraits* (above, n. 2), pp. 91-2.

[6] "The Foreigner at Home": *Memories and Portraits, loc. cit.*

[7] *Memories and Portraits* (above, n. 2), p. 148; cp. with this Scott's introductory remarks about "Wandering Willie's Tale" in *Redgauntlet.*

[8] Daiches (above, n. 1), p. 121; *Weir of Hermiston* (1896: Romances, VOL. VII), pp. 170-6.

[9] *Op. cit.*, p. 175; my italics.

[10] *Op. cit.*, p. 176; my italics.

emphasise the contrast. Never had spoken Scots been used to more artistic purpose. For Stevenson, " the dramatic artist " lay, he tells us, " dormant or only half awake in most human beings " [11]; often, too, his own strength lies in getting inside a person's mind. Quite the best thing in *The Master of Ballantrae* is the dramatic monologue at the beginning in which Ephraim Mackellar (through whose eyes we see the story) explains what has gone before. [12] The result of this essentially dramatic approach is, once more, a subjective version of reality, similar to that which Scots poets have always handled with such sureness of touch. The tense atmosphere of *Weir of Hermiston* is due partly to the readiness with which, in her jealousy, Old Kirstie enters into the two young lovers' minds : " Now she was reincarnated in her niece, and now in Archie. Now she saw through the girl's eyes. . . . " [13]

In his determination to enter into his characters, Stevenson seizes on, and recreates, the sensuous impressions which they receive, together with the images, metaphors and comparisons which the impressions themselves evoke in their minds. In his early tales, the general effect is apt (in a way typical of nineteenth-century " decadent literature ") to be unduly conceited : but even in them—for example, the evocation, in *The Master of Ballantrae*, of intense cold—there are flashes of a virtuosity which rivals that of Dunbar or Gavin Douglas at their most subjective ; and in the novels of his maturity, this impressionism is finally subordinated to the overall artistic purpose. As they accumulate, the minute impressions and images are built up into a vivid and coherent picture of reality. As it exists only in the mind, it is not a static picture, but one that changes with the character's prevailing mood. Sometimes, as in " Pastoral," the images evoked in the mind are finally so far removed from any external reality that they are projections of the mind itself ; [14] and this self-created reality may become a strong agent in the fate of men. When Archie sees young Kirstie on the moor, and is now dealing " in serious matters of life and death," [15] we are presented with so many sensuous details of colour, shape, touch, that the landscape seems to be alive with meaning. The beginning of the last chapter brings this to a climax and crisis :

[11] *Op. cit.*, p. 246.
[12] *The Master of Ballantrae* (above, n. 5), pp. 1 ff.
[13] *Weir of Hermiston* (above, n. 8), pp. 275-6.
[14] In *Memories and Portraits* (above, n. 2), pp. 144 ff.
[15] *Weir of Hermiston* (above, n. 8), p. 244.

> . . . The Hags were in shadow. But still, through the gate of the Slap, the sun shot a last arrow, which sped far and straight across the surface of the moss, here and there touching and shining on a tussock, and lighted at length on a gravestone and the small figure awaiting him there. The emptiness and solitude of the great moors seemed to be concentred there, and Kirstie pointed out by that finger of sunshine for the only inhabitant. His first glimpse of her was thus excruciatingly sad, like a glimpse of a world from which all light, comfort, and society were on the point of vanishing. And the next moment . . . the whole face of nature smiled upon him in her smile of welcome. Archie's slow pace was quickened ; his legs hasted to her though his heart was hanging back.[16]

This is only apparently objective. The subjective perception has taken on a vivid life of its own, and the landscape is an actor in the tragedy in the same way as in *The Bride of Lammermoor*, or as Egdon Heath in *The Return of the Native*.[17]

Oddly enough, subjective impressionism of an unusual intensity is again combined with a pronounced interest in split personality. In *Kidnapped*, Captain Hoseason "was two men, and left the better one behind as soon as he set foot on board his vessel."[18] In *The Master of Ballantrae*, we are concerned with the same kind of mind-conditioning as in Hogg's *Confessions of a justified Sinner*. And in *Dr Jekyll and Mr Hyde* (1886)[19] the last trace of the objectivity of the ego seems to have vanished ; here the duplicity of life is accentuated by the clash between a respectable social façade and secret indulgence in a life of pleasure.

Stevenson's artistic conception of the novel grew with his psychological insight, and the rather vague theory expounded in "Pastoral" and other essays in *Memories and Portraits* provides a rough-and-ready yardstick by which we can measure its rate of growth. Shepherding is, he remarks, "a trade . . . in which we have all had ancestors employed, so that on a hint of it ancestral memories revive . . . ;

[16] *Op. cit.*, pp. 283.

[17] Cp. Thomas Hardy's method in *The Return of the Native* : "When she looked down sideways . . . she became pretty, and even handsome, particularly that in the action her features caught slantwise the rays of the strongly coloured sun, which *made transparencies of her eyelids and nostrils*, and *set fire on her lips*." The description of Egdon Heath at the beginning of the novel is also a fine example. Hardy was consciously expressing the spirit of a landscape which had been the meeting-place of Celt, Roman and Saxon. Was he aware that his animistic interpretation of it might seem to have had its origins in Celtic tradition ?

[18] *Kidnapped* (1886 : Romances, VOL. IV), p. 51.

[19] In Tales and Fantasies, VOL. III, pp. 1 ff.

and when I hear with a particular thrill of things that I have never done or seen, it is one of that innumerable army of my ancestors rejoicing in past deeds." [20] And as for novels, they " begin to touch . . . the gross mass of mankind, when they leave off to speak of parlours and shades of manner and still-born niceties of motive, and begin to deal with fighting, sailoring, adventure, death or childbirth ; and thus ancient out-door crafts and occupations, whether Mr Hardy wields the shepherd's crook or Count Tolstoi swings the scythe, lift romance into a near neighbourhood with epic." [21] Add to this the intangible inheritance of Scotland—her streams and their sound and colour, her sea, shipwrecks, heathery mountains, hunted Covenanters, songs and Border ballads, and the fibres of the legend of her history [22] —and you have all the ingredients of that almost mystical belief in the impact of ancestral or inherited experience on our lives which is the keynote of the best twentieth-century Scots fiction. " These aged things have on them the dew of man's morning ; they lie near . . . the trunk and aboriginal taproot of the race." [23]

In *Treasure Island* (1882) [24] and the other early romances this conviction is hardly more than a vague notion designed to justify the escape into the realm of adventure. *Kidnapped* (1886) [25] begins in the same vein, and the clash between the Lowland Covenanting and the Highland Jacobite traditions is at first rather superficial. But the hero, David Balfour, has the name of one of Stevenson's own forefathers. The Jacobite events become a set of symbols of much that is picturesque and tragic in Scottish history. After the Appin Murder the story takes on a deeper meaning. It also assumes a topographical interest that helps to explain the historical emotions and conflicts ; various incidents fill in the picture of the Highland situation, and David's reflexions raise the events to moral significance. We feel we are up against one of the vital issues in Scottish life and values. But this level is not maintained, and Alan Breck's behaviour during the flight rather heightens the staginess of his character.

There is less escape and adventure in the early parts of *The Master of Ballantrae* (1888),[26] with its Lowland background and sombre and

[20] " Pastoral " : *Memories and Portraits* (above, n. 2), pp. 151-2.

[21] *Ibid.*

[22] See " The Foreigner at Home " : *op. cit.*, pp. 96 ff.

[23] " Pastoral " : *op. cit.*, p. 152.

[24] Romances, VOL. I.

[25] Above, n. 18.

[26] Above, n. 5.

fatalistic ballad atmosphere. Life may be less colourful here, but it is "a richer and sadder phenomenon" (Daiches), and Stevenson shows a deeper and more adult insight. As told by the dour, home-spun Ephraim Mackellar, the story is subtler and closer-woven: but after having come close to human tragedy Stevenson shies away from it, and off he goes on a series of fantastic overseas adventures.

Achievement came to Stevenson only in *Weir of Hermiston* (1896),[27] the novel which he wrote on his deathbed. It is a fragment, but like the *Hildebrandslied* it contains all that matters—in fact, one cannot help wondering whether further chapters might not have impaired that touch of perfection. The *diabolus ex machina*, Frank Innes, already makes us feel uncomfortable. The hero is Archie Weir, son of Lord Hermiston, the Lord Justice Clerk, a hanger of Radicals, whose forebears had been fighting under Claverhouse; behind his mother's tremulous delicacy and sentimental piety there lie generations of Border reivers and Covenanters. The place: a spot in the heath where Claverhouse shot a praying weaver. Long-forgotten tales?

"For that is the mark of the Scot of all classes: that he stands in an attitude towards the past unthinkable to Englishmen, and remembers and cherishes the memory of his forebears, good or bad; and there burns alive in him a sense of identity with the dead even to the twentieth generation."[28] Not that Stevenson's doctrine of heredity is either mystical or metaphysical. The history and traditions of the Border reivers and the Covenanters have themselves a psychological impact which is direct and immediate. "The power of ancestry on the character is not limited to the inheritance of cells. If I buy ancestors by the gross from the benevolence of Lyon King of Arms, my grandson (if he is Scottish) will feel a quickening emulation of their deeds."[29] The impressionable boy whose mother's tales of the Covenanters have given him a horror of persecution suffers the agony of hearing the mob revile his father as himself a "persecutor."[30] The conflicting strains of paternal and maternal inheritance are unevenly mated and we foresee a violent solution. In his analysis of the complex of forces—historical, hereditary, and psychological—which determine human relations and reactions, Stevenson weaves thread after thread into his rich tissue of crime and passion, history and heredity, till

[27] Above, n. 8.
[28] *Weir of Hermiston* (above, n. 8), p. 198.
[29] *Op. cit.*, p. 199.
[30] *Op. cit.*, pp. 138-9.

the life of the Borders (and Edinburgh) becomes a continuous pattern which stretches from the time of the ballads almost to the present day. The main action is laid in or about 1814, but on to the social background against which it takes place Stevenson deliberately projects the manners of a generation or so earlier, thus enhancing the continuity of Border tradition, and striking its essential keynote—namely the tragic fatalism of the ballads. Old Kirstie's tales of the Elliots, the mother's family,[31] are full of this spirit, and give many disturbing glimpses of the hidden passions that lie so deep in the quietest and most ordinary people.

Here, too, Stevenson's evocation of the ballads is very deliberate: "It was at a graceless face that he asked mercy" strays in from "Johnie Armstrang"; and, as Stevenson comments, "some century earlier the last of the minstrels might have fashioned the last of the ballads out of that Homeric fight and chase."[32] The foreboding of doom thus evoked in our mind gets further nourishment from the popular belief that the weaver's grave on the moor is an unchancy place.

Weir of Hermiston has been called a ballad in prose, but at the same time it has elements of the folk tale, with proverbial sayings and bits of traditional lore. Though the word "I" occurs rarely, it is told in the first person singular. This establishes the intimacy required and sets the key for an inexorable pattern of all life that reaches back deeper even than the ballads:

> 'Folk have dee'd sinsyne [since then] and been buried, and are forgotten, and bairns been born and got merrit and got bairns o' their ain. Sinsyne woods have been plantit, and have grawn up and are bonny trees . . . ; and auld estates have changed hands, and there have been wars and rumours of wars on the face of the earth. . . . But, Mr. Erchie, do ye no' think that I have mind o' it a' still? . . . Do ye no' think that I have mind of the bonny simmer days, the lang miles o' the bluid-red heather, the cryin' o' the whaups [curlews], and the lad and the lassie that was trysted? Do ye no' think that I mind how the hilly sweetness ran about my hairt?'[33]

Stevenson brought more—much more—to Scottish fiction than style, a feeling for words, and the ability to create scenes and atmosphere. He cross-bred the traditional ballad and folk-tale with a

[31] *Op. cit.*, pp. 198-205.
[32] *Op. cit.*, p. 199.
[33] *Op. cit.*, p. 280.

literary tradition which laid most emphasis on style, structure, psychological insight and total effect—two strands that had been separate for ages. His gift was too great for his immediate successors, who sought rather to follow the path indicated by Alan Breck, or, like John Buchan, were satisfied with the shadow of Walter Scott. But within half a dozen years from the appearance of *Weir of Hermiston* the course of the Scottish novel was changed violently by GEORGE DOUGLAS BROWN (1869-1902).

The House with the green Shutters (1901), Brown's masterpiece,[34] was practically the first Scottish novel since Galt which dealt with nineteenth-century Scottish life as it really was; to do this, and to get away from the sentimentalism of the Kailyard, it had to be sharply, almost brutally realistic. Its harshness was doubtless accentuated by the fact that Brown was an illegitimate child, and was morbidly sensitive to the resultant social stigma.

The forces which work together to bring about the tragedy of John Gourlay—his own dourness, the small-town social environment, and (according to Brown) his son's excessive imagination—are all unmistakably Scottish, and Brown's presentation of the story marks the culmination of what we have seen to be a specifically Scottish style. For these reasons, *The House with the green Shutters* is pre-eminently a "Scottish Tragedy." But this statement does not preclude "foreign" influences, for true culture avoids inbreeding. Brown loved Greek drama, and in structure his novel is closely modelled on the great Aeschylean tragedies. It is clear, too, that he was profoundly influenced by nineteenth-century French psychological naturalism, and by that of Turgenev, his favourite Russian author.

John Gourlay's tragedy arises out of the power of a character like his "to poison the mind of a community"; and the more he poisons it, the more forces of hate and vice are set free. Thus, in the last analysis, his doom and that of his house originate—as Aristotle requires—entirely in his own character. Gourlay is a man of small-farming ancestry—brave, headstrong, a man of one idea, doggedly individualistic, and essentially stupid—whose sole ambition, fitly symbolised by the house with the green shutters that he has planted on top of Babrie Hill, is to increase his own commercial power. By sheer dourness

[34] *The House with the green Shutters* appeared under the pen-name George Douglas. Brown's other works include a number of stories and sketches, published under various pseudonyms; none of them are of any importance. J. Veitch, *George Douglas Brown* (1952) completely supersedes the older biography by C. Lennox (1903). Refs. below to *The House with the green Shutters* are to the 1st edn. (London 1902; repr. 1905).

and brute force of character, he has achieved a monopoly of the carrying trade around Barbie, and all that goes with it: but to this one aim he has even sacrificed his family, and his neglected wife has become a slut whose shiftlessness is a constant source of irritation to her methodical husband. Gourlay is both socially and intellectually inferior to the "bodies" or leading men of Barbie, the small Scottish town in which he lives, and tries, in his desire for revenge, to crush them by sheer demoniac force of personality. United in their impotent hatred of Gourlay, they rally round a rising business competitor of his whose up-to-date methods undermine Gourlay's monopoly; and, unable to negotiate a single bend of the road, the steam-roller of Gourlay's energy hurries him on to his destruction.

Brown originally conceived the novel as a counterblast against Kailyard fiction, and himself tells us that he intended in it "to show up the Scot malignant." Later he came to feel that there was perhaps "too much black for the white," and his picture of Barbie is indeed a gloomy one.[35] It is a society which lacks leadership—whether of laird or minister, provost or schoolmaster—and in which spite is the great leveller. "The Scot," Brown says, "is an individualist," and (for only a mere outward shell of Presbyterianism is left) "his religion alone is enough to make him so. . . ." From it "he gets the grit that tells"—fortunately for him, because the "keen spirit of competition" which also results from it breeds in turn a ferocious belittlement of rivals which is at its most virulent in a small town like Barbie, where the "nestie bodies" are always probing the question "Where'll *he* be off till, at this hour of the day?" and where such local news as that "Jock Goudie has won the C.B." is likely to provoke the retort: "Oo-ooh I ken *him* fine. His grannie keepit a sweetie-shop in Strathbungo."[36] Such a society is the soil where a tyranny like Gourlay's can grow. Gourlay is in this respect no match for the bodies, whose malicious innuendo reaches its climax when, one day, he is obliged to travel with them in the brake to Skeighan.[37] The contrast here between the "suave enveloping greatness of the world" and the pettiness and cruelty of the "human pismires" travelling together is in the best Scottish vein.[38]

But *The House with the green Shutters* is much more than a *genre*

[35] Cp. J. Speirs, *The Scots literary Tradition*, London 1940, pp. 161 ff.

[36] *The House with the green Shutters*, pp. 41-2; cp. p. 35.

[37] *Op. cit.*, pp. 154 ff.

[38] *Op. cit.*, p. 159.

study of Scottish life and character: it is a tragedy which transcends its own time and setting. Young John Gourlay is a weakling, "cursed with an imagination in excess of his brains," and "with impressions which he couldn't intellectualise." [39] Old Gourlay despises him; but stung by the malice of the bodies, and not to be outdone by his successful rival, he decides, though at enormous sacrifices, to send him on from secondary school to college. The more his own star declines, the more desperately he pins his hope on the education of his son; to deepen the gulf into which they are going to be hurled, John wins a prize by his vivid imagination—but then succumbs wholly to his weakness, drink, and is finally expelled. Now we feel sympathy with old Gourlay, who at least has stood up to everything, without flinching. "Hitherto, then, he was invulnerable—so he reasoned. It was his son's disgrace that gave the men he had trodden under foot the first weapon they could use against him," and allowed them "to get their knife into him at last." [40] His son had disgraced the House with the green Shutters, and he resolves to break his spirit, and "send him slinking away *animo castrato*." [41] In its sheer horror, this scene has a superb magnificence.

Finally, the son, drunk and like an animal at bay, murders his father by striking him on the head with a poker (which has skilfully been introduced into the narrative almost at the beginning of the story). Barbie accepts Mrs Gourlay's explanation that her husband "fell from the top o' the ladder and struck his brow on the muckle fender": but Gourlay's eyes, like furies, haunt the son day and night till he takes poison. He is followed in death by the penniless mother and sister. Both had hugged death as a relief for years, the one from the effects of a blow by old Gourlay, the other from those of pneumonia, and neither had been able to find a way to the hardened hearts of the others; but before crossing the threshold of rest, the mother reads a chapter from the Bible, "Though I speak with the tongues of men and of angels, and have not charity, I am become as sounding brass, or a tinkling cymbal." Charity—that is the gospel that Barbie needs. And the Barbie bodies "gazed with blanched faces at the House with the green Shutters, sitting dark there and terrible, beneath the radiant arch of the dawn."

To elevate the tragedy above time and surrounding, the events are

[39] *Op. cit.*, pp. 161, 172.
[40] *Op. cit.*, pp. 268 f.
[41] *Op. cit.*, p. 273.

made representative: by a very potent symbolism, till " the house was himself: there was no division between them " ; by indefinite plurals (" bowed old men stood in front of their doorways ") ; by the chorus of the bodies, a composite actor providing the moral environment and the eye through which to see the central character ; by echoes of Biblical and other styles [42] that seem to include all ages of the past, in much the same way as T. S. Eliot was later to adopt. All this creates a ballad-like atmosphere of impending doom that is relentless in its impact on our soul.

What does Brown mean when he suggests that young John Gourlay's excessive imagination, the factor that actually precipitates the catastrophe, is specifically Scottish? It is no mere question of an oversensitive boy brought up in uncongenial surroundings, in a society without culture. John lives by impressions ; they spring to life in his mind, and the pictures which they create are his reality. We are given the key to this phenomenon in ch. xvii,[43] in which young John's Edinburgh friends discuss the strange Scots knack of phrase-making. Though Englishmen think that Carlyle was unique in this respect, " every other Scots peasant has the gift." As a case in point, one of them repeats a sentence he once heard said: " The thumb-mark of his Maker was wet in the clay of him." Another wonders " what's the cause of that extraordinary vividness in the speech of the Scotch peasantry " ; and John's answer is that " ' It comes from a power of seeing things vividly inside your mind . . . seeing them so vivid that you see the likeness between them. When Bauldy Johnston said ' the thumb mark of his Maker was wet in the clay of him,' he *saw* the print of a thumb in wet clay, and he *saw* the Almighty making a man out of mud . . .—so Bauldy flashed the two ideas together and the metaphor sprang ! ' " [44]

In a letter to Meldrum,[45] Brown remarks that the peasants of his country " not merely see what they say, they *say* it so that you see

[42] Cp. the beginning of ch. xiv (*op. cit.*, p. 141) : " In those days it came to pass . . . even James, the red-haired one, with the squint in his eye. . . . Whereupon Gourlay . . . And it also came to pass that James, the son of James the Grocer took many prizes. . . . Whereat there were ructions in the House of Gourlay." Similarly, chs. xvi (p. 165), which begins in the vein of verse romance, and xvii (p. 174), which begins with the fiction of a letter which " has fallen into the hands of the patient chronicler." These deliberate variations in style are very remarkable, and in some degree foreshadow the well-known sequence of English styles in Joyce's *Ulysses*.

[43] *The House with the green Shutters*, pp. 174 ff.

[44] *Op. cit.*, pp. 182, 183.

[45] See Veitch (above, n. 34), pp. 94 f.

it also. . . . But it is not only the outer and external phrase they can give the visual picture of; they can pierce behind the trappings and paint character by one dynamic word." [46] And it was from his own father that Brown got most of the phrases discussed by young John's Edinburgh circle. Throughout the novel, Gourlay senior coins many such phrases. Young John has the gift, too, but it is his fate that he has also "inherited his mother's nervous senses with his father's lack of wit," [47] and he escapes into a private world of vivid mental pictures which he can only express when drink loosens his inhibitions. In a lucky moment this wins him the class essay prize, but his professor warns him that unless he learns to subject his imagination to the control of intellect (or, as he puts it, philosophy), it will not be a blessing but a curse.[48] In such a home as the House with the green Shutters, no intellectual development is possible, and the curse is inevitably fulfilled.

The same dominant trait ruled Brown's own artistic vision and determined his style. Brown's vision is a culmination of the subjectivism and animism that we have seen developing through the centuries. "A shaft of golden light, aswarm with motes, slanted in the quietness." His style is full of such images, and in it are summed up (but all with sharper focus) Dunbar's quick flashes and comparisons, Alexander Hume's detached impressions, the uncanny subjectivism of *The Confessions of a justified Sinner*, and the vivid impressionism and assiduous accumulation of minute sensuous detail so characteristic of Gaelic poetry. With its "gaspy little sentences," all joined together by *and*, just "as if a number of impressions had seized the writer's mind," John's prize-winning essay unconsciously reproduces much in Gaelic language and literature.[49] Brown enters into the minds of old Gourlay and his son and lets them reveal themselves so that they are seen both from outside and in. The resulting subjective picture thus built up of numerous apparently objective details has an intense reality of its own, which makes possible scenes of great dramatic intensity (such as the beginning), and is itself alive, changing, taking part in the action as if possessed by so many demons: "What he saw, it possessed him, not he it." In the culminating scene between father and son,[50] everything that the narrator mentions itself takes part in the action: the silence, the ticking, the tinkling glasses on the

[46] This would be a good definition of, say, Burns's treatment of abstract ideas.

[47] *The House with the green Shutters*, p. 57.

[48] *Op. cit.*, p. 195.

[49] *Ibid.* Brown was himself a native of Ayrshire.

[50] *Op. cit.*, pp. 272 ff.

tray, the wild-beast snarl leaping at times through the moaning intensity, the insinuating, pursuing " Eh ? " Or, in a later scene, the helpless mother mechanically sewing with too long stitches, puckering the hem : " Vacantly she tried to smooth them out, stroking them over in her hand, constantly stroking and to no purpose." [51] With this subjectivism, we accept " the voice from beyond the world " with which the mother reads the Bible chapter of charity.

Yet another important development which occurs in the novel of this period is that the voice of the Highlands begins to be heard as never before in Scots or English. It can faintly be discerned in the poetry of Thomas Aird, who uses assonance and alliteration in its soft Gaelic form in " St Mary's Well," and in the *Verses* (1893) of Sheriff Alexander Nicolson, himself a Skyeman, whose English reflects a Celtic imagination, and is full of Gaelic syntax, idiom, and traditional poetic images.

The first voice widely hailed as Celtic was not genuine. The work of William Sharp (" Fiona Macleod," 1856-1905) is Ossianic in its " slow, solemn, soundless rhythm " and melancholy landscapes ; Pre-Raphaelite or even *fin-de-siècle* in its heavy-scented sensuousness and surfeit of word-painting ; Yeatsian in its shadowy Celtic twilight, mystical mythology, and assumed mutual pervasiveness of man, nature, and the other-world.[52] Of course, rich sensuous images, subjective vision, and superstition are a feature of Gaelic speech, lore and poetry ; but where Gaelic has the brilliant light of enamel, and a sharp or even grotesque vision, " Fiona Macleod " is shadowy, languid, nostalgic, mystical. This may be a perfectly legitimate poetic attitude, but it is not Celtic ; and his drooping, lily-white Mountain Lovers are altogether too late-Victorian.

Sharp's failure was due partly to the fact that he had to invent an idiom capable of expressing a soul that had not previously expressed itself in English. A verbal translation of a common-place metaphor from one language into another gives it an unaccustomed quaintness : " schwerfällig " is everyday German for " clumsy," but the word-for-word translation " heavy-falling " would have an oddly archaic

[51] *Op. cit.*, p. 351.

[52] Under his own name, *e.g.* in *Songs and Poems, old and new* (1909), Sharp merely echoed the various conventional lines of nineteenth-century romanticism. Under his pseudonym, *e.g.* in *The human Inheritance* (1882), he propounded, long before Yeats, a pagan mysticism embracing all creatures which expressed his own longing for a world of shadows. It seems however to have been Yeats who first gave this its characteristically " Celtic " twist.

ring about it. Gaelic is rich in such metaphors, and too many verbal translations give it a false picturesqueness. As long as there is genuine vision behind Sharp's images (as in " the rowan berries . . . kissed into flame by the sun "), they come off; and when he forgets his lyrical Celtic Twilight, and feels dramatic tension, he often achieves a direct, highly subjective perception of minute details that is genuinely Gaelic. So, in *The Mountain Lovers* (1895), when the body is found and brought home, " his weather-brown face had become deep red, and about his moist brow a haze of midges hovered." That is Gaelic impressionism at its most exact, much better than " the sunflood falling upon him in gold waves out of the west." And it would be hard to better such a Highland picture as this : " At the far end a heat-haze obscured mountain-flank, and bracken slope, and birk-shaw—all save the extreme summits of the hills, purple-grey shadows against the gleaming sky."

Was NEIL MUNRO (1864-1930) more successful than William Sharp? [53] He dealt with the past only, stopping short of the middle of the nineteenth century; a Stevenson of the Highlands, with sometimes a suspicion of Alan Breck about him. There is some escapism in his historical adventure stories; but taken together his romances are meant to draw a picture of the past that has created the present : from the changing times when, in the seventeenth century, the Marquis of Argyll brought Covenanters from Ayr to teach the arts of peace and commerce,[54] to the period after the Napoleonic wars with " the last of the old Highland burgh life and the raw beginnings of the new," when the new merchant class steps into the shoes of the old Highland gentry.[55] But frequently these historico-social problems are hardly more than a backdrop for adventure. Munro's most serious effort in historical fiction is *The New Road* (1914). Again adventures predominate, but adventures that are only possible in the peculiar topographical and historical situation of the time between the Jacobite risings of 1715 and 1745, when General Wade was building his roads. There is a genuine effort to understand the Gael in terms of his country, of his tradition of story, *ceilidh* and poetry, of his history, of the indelible vestiges of the past where his race trod. But the old order is in transition, it has become shallow, bragging,

[53] See H. Wernitz, *Neil Munro und die nationale Kulturbewegung im modernen Schottland*, Neue Deutsche Forschungen (1937); *The Works of Neil Munro*, Inveraray Ed., 1935.

[54] Cp. *John Splendid* (1898).

[55] Cp. *Gilian the Dreamer* (1899).

a sham. The " new road " may be a shame, a blot in the landscape, sore on the feet, but it has become necessary, and will in time be venerable. The road, the path of the merchant—who at the same time takes vengeance on the clans of the North for their hostility—is the old Gael's grave, but it must bring modern ways of life to the Highlands, a thing the Romans failed to achieve. With its changes of the pattern of life the Road is the way of Argyll, Munro's native Argyll where, he says, Highland and Lowland influence combined to create a national outlook higher than clan loyalties. Munro recognises the tragedy of " the old, darling, foolish Highlands in us " : the old stupid stories of the ceilidh, the lure of the hills, the constant complaint of the sea. All this comes out in a pibroch.[56] The pipes, if played by a master, make you listen back to your forefathers, make you " ken the colour of Fingal's hair, and see the moon-glint on the hook of the Druids." They evoke all the old associations, " when the wild men in their red tartan came over hill and moor ; the tune with the river in it, the fast river and the courageous." [57] The lost pibroch that the old piper plays is a symbol which sums up the whole history of the Gaeltacht from the conquest to the massacre of Glencoe, from Loch Duich to the Highland emigration ; for when the lost pibroch of the broken clans is played it makes them crave for something they cannot name and puts them on the open road. Munro could have dealt with the fate of the modern Gael, but he never did. And he wrote his excellent modern humorous tales of *Para Handy* under the pseudonym " Hugh Foulis."

We recognise the genuine Gaelic tradition when Munro describes a landscape or setting [58] : the same detailed mosaic of intimate observation of localities in close personal relation to himself as in Alexander MacDonald or in Duncan McIntyre, down to the names of different grasses found in a special place. This is part of the clannish localism, and Munro's heroes never leave Inveraray on Loch Fyne for long. The close intensity in seeing, hearing, feeling, smelling the many small things creates not " *a* landscape," but " *his* landscape," and there is little room for reflexion. This is animism

[56] See *The lost Pibroch and other Stories* (1896).

[57] It struck me, while I was in Scotland, how closely most pibrochs resemble the traditional Gaelic songs—when these are sung in the traditional manner, not by a concert-hall singer : they have the same relationship of unstressed notes and rhythms, the same insistence on the stresses. And most of the pipers seem to have inherited the traditional pride of the old *filidh*.

[58] Cp. *John Splendid*, ch. x or p. 11.

or " pan-demonism " of a different quality from the Lowland writers. There is, for one thing, a conscious delight in sensuous pleasures, a play with them ; for another, it is more highly subjective and impulsive, and the mind works more vividly on the impressions it receives from the outside world [59] : poking the fire " made the boy and the man and the timbers and bunks dance and shake in the world between light and shadow." [60] " His body [in shooting] . . .—all but an eye and a shoulder." [61] Familiar objects are frequently personified, which after all is but an echo of the Gaelic tongue (" the joists held scarred arms to heaven "). Munro's language has a strong undercurrent of Gaelic, its short unconnected sentences, its rhythm, its syntax and idiom, its substantival character, its images, and a vocabulary of Gaelic and Scots origin : in one sentence you find " corri, brae, smooring, to lapper, bairn, quirky, joist."

In Munro, the subjective vision is part of the Gael's outstanding ability to see an imagined scene vividly in his mind. His characters are frequently setting a stage (don't call it acting), and on that stage there springs to life what they will, or might do, till " I could scarcely say myself when a passion of mine is real or fancied now." This also means acting the role of the other persons on that stage, penetrating into their personalities. " I put myself in his place, and felt the skin of myself in his place, and felt the skin of my back pimpling. . . . " [62] This explains why a Highlander cannot say " no " if it might hurt a friend, and why certain taboos must be kept, even if it means telling tales. Munro knows the " blight and rot " of this softness, but this insight enables him to create characters that are not mapped out for all to see in a few lines, souls that have secrets from themselves, an indistinct longing. Perhaps we have here something of the finer, deeper, more intangible aspirations of the Gael ; not only the swashbuckling heroism and pride of Alan Breck, but the world of the imagination behind it that yet has a thousand contacts with reality.

[59] In his autobiographical *Two Years* (1930), the Irish novelist Liam O'Flaherty expresses a very similar attitude : " The visible world and the movements of men upon it have both become completely absorbed by my imagination, which has gone farther than reality to create its needed harmony and only looks out upon reality with a frown, and seizes upon its various aspects with remote and critical interest, merely to imagine harmony more vividly by contrast with disappointing reality " (p. 116). I do not mean to imply that this is an inherited Celtic characteristic, still less that it is a Celtic monopoly, but that it is a tradition which has grown up in countries of an originally Celtic population.

[60] *Gilian the Dreamer.*

[61] *John Splendid.*

[62] Both these quotations from *John Splendid.*

It comes out like a flash in a sentence like that of Para Handy, the west-country captain : " We ask people civilly to do a job, if they don't we do't ourselves, and that's the way to vex them "—do we not hear the *fili* who wins by suffering ?

J. MacDougall Hay, a fellow-Argyllman from Tarbert on Loch Fyne, dedicated his one novel *Gillespie* (1914) to Neil Munro, but it is a more courageous effort to deal with contemporary life in the West. The novel is much more in the vein of *The House with the green Shutters* and takes over much from Brown. The object is the same, to show how one ruthless character (he is of Lowland origin) can poison the mind of a small town, but finally falls a victim to the hatred he has engendered, " for whatsoever a man soweth, that also shall he reap." The fate that is fulfilled through his own family, the over-sensitive boy Eoghan, the symbolism, the chorus of the female gossips, all recall Brown's novel, and *Gillespie* looks at first like *The House with the green Shutters* on a lower artistic level ; with the repetitions in the first half we ask ourselves if the novel was not revised before printing. But once Hay has got his story under way, his grip tightens, and we soon see that he is doing more than Brown. The curious time schedule of the different chapters is not a picking up of forgotten threads, but like the movement of themes or counterpoint in a piece of music. It is theme with variation again, to catch the course of true events in different consciousnesses, minds, moods. For Hay is not a man of one situation like Brown ; the life that surges in his novel is richer, more subtle. While Barbie only existed in its hostility against Gourlay, " Brieston " has a life of its own that is not always so predictable, and it consists of the whole community. Therefore Hay succeeds better than Brown in one respect, namely that Gillespie's malice is in its outcome an insult to God's universe. Hay also reaches farther back and sees man not only as a social being starting from scratch ; to him comes a dim, ancestral voice : " We are driven by something deep within us that we have got from our ancestors, to do strange things that were allowed in their age, but are unlawful now," in the same way as the wild geese are " borne along by the ' something deep ' within them." Almost an echo of Stevenson. The psychological handling of superstition and dreams may not always be successful, but is an important motif in the symphony.

The symphonic nature of the novel shapes its style. On the one hand we have the minute observation leading to intentness with all the subjective vision and pan-demonism. But this tense style is reserved for essential moments. It is strange how many of these " demonic " moments are bound up with the sea : the sea watching " with fixed glassy eyes," the sea and the herring-fishers, the men going out to fish (" it was in their blood to listen"), the storm, the sweeping for the dead bodies in the gloaming : " In the heart of the glowing sky pain was seated." The vision here is even more subjective than Brown's, one stage removed from reality, and of finer suggestion. The intentness can border on obsession, as when the grandfather takes down the signboard with the dagger, or Eoghan is maddened by his mother's excesses.

But this is only in a dramatic climax of the symphony, in the active moments when an inner reality is projected outward. Many episodes have no logical connexion with the story as a whole, they are semi-independent pictures which, taken together, form a general impression in our mind. It is the Gaelic sentence structure on a large scale,[63] with a series of episodes strung together without conjunction, which creates what I might venture to call an " impressionistic structure." It is curiously akin to the style developed by the inter-war group of Irish writers from Cork—Daniel Corkery, Sean O'Faolain, Frank O'Connor. It is the passive counterpart of demonism, yet has the same reality of its own creation. Instead of projective energy there is receptive feeling, and the Highlanders of Munro and Hay are able to enjoy a feeling and, in special moments, to express it ; there is nothing here of the tight-lipped emotions of, say, Violet Jacob's *Tales of my own Countryside* from the East coast.

[63] See above, pp. 190, 268, 272.

2. Poetry

In poetry, the tide did not turn so perceptibly as in fiction, but turn it did. Stevenson was a " poet " only in some of his verses, and then often on a minor scale.[1] But he did bring a new vision to Scottish poetry ; he made it reach out again towards the meaning of life, the place of man, sophistication (" A Portrait "), while yet remaining distinctively Scottish. Most significantly, he showed a new respect for poetry in Scots and dared step outside the shadow of Burns. To Stevenson, Scots was no dialect, and in the preface to *Underwoods* he explains how his Scots is made up from the language of all parts, " not caring if it hailed from Lauderdale or Angus, from the Mearns or Galloway ; if I had ever heard a good word, I used it without shame." This is almost the " Synthetic Scots " of the modern school, but it is also the method of the Makars and Burns.

It is worth comparing two or three Scots poems from *Underwoods* with one or two poems in English from *Songs of Travel.* In " The Maker to Posterity," the Scots tongue helps the poet to be precise, concrete, not abstract. The poem is very direct and sharply focused, with nothing flabby or vague. The shrewdness of Scots prevents theatrical pathos and views things realistically and without pretence. There is intellectual depth, crystallised in sharp pictures kept very much in the foreground of the mind. But each of these pictures is only a crystal in which something of eternity is caught. What we are given in " A Mile an' a Bittock " is a sharp scene of three young men seeing each other home in the moonlight. No sentimentality, no " hameliness," but bare statement :

> The clocks were chappin' in house an' ha',
> It blew the stars as clear 's could be.

But what we receive is the idea of youth and its fervour, and it is the very bareness of the sharp outlines, and the " My lads, ye'll mind " in the final stanza, that communicate this deeper meaning.

Take, as a poem in English, " In the Highlands." The effect is largely achieved by a virtuosity in handling the metrical form ; the stanza runs $aab : ccb_5$, but by a pause the *b*-verses are broken up into two lines, one of six, one of three syllables. Still there is no additional rhyme or syllable. This in itself slows down the rhythm,

[1] The only critical edition is *Collected Poems of R. L. Stevenson*, ed. J. Adam Smith, 1952.

and is enhanced by words in the short line suggesting calm and eternity: "Quiet eyes," "Broods and dies," "Bright with sward," "Lamp-bestarred," "Quiet breath," "Life and death." This brings out the idea of the poem: there is true sensuous delight in the Highland environment, with its million tints, birds, flowers, grasses, cheerful people—but the essence is the eternal, primeval tranquillity:

> Lo! for there, among the flowers and grasses,
> Only the mightier movement sounds and passes;
> Only winds and rivers,
> Life and death.

This is certainly what one feels when seeing the West and North Highlands (though I wonder whether it is what a Highlander feels). A flight like this had not been tried in Scots poetry since Dunbar or Alexander Scott. Could Stevenson have written this in Scots? Its whole movement is opposite to that of all his Scots poems; it wings its way outwards, towards abstraction, towards "life and death." Of course, one might object that Stevenson could not well write a poem about the Highlands in Lowland Scots. But we have the same in the English poem "To S. R. Crockett," and there is nothing at all to even suggest a similar flight in his Scots poems. For Stevenson, at any rate, the associations of Scots seem to have been too strongly bound up with concreteness.

Some minor voices besides Stevenson's indicate a similar awareness of the deplorable parochialism of existing Scottish verse. In some of his poems, Andrew Lang tried to suggest more than meets the eye; in some of his, George Macdonald strove to rid Scots of sentimental dross. J. Logie Robertson ("Hugh Haliburton") picked up Ramsay's pastoral translations and wrote *Horace in Homespun*, a widening of scope, but too homespun; his *Ochil Idylls* (1891) have a tinge of the Kailyard, while his more serious poems were graced with English. But there is an effort here and there to rise above the intellectual level of the proverb and to deal with modern life. Logie Robertson recognised the self-limitation of Scots poetry by imitating Burns, and he raised the cry "back to Dunbar," both in his chapter on "Our earlier Burns" (In *In Scottish Fields*, 1890), and in the poem "To William Dunbar" (*Ochil Idylls*): "thou finer spirit," "with thee I tread the city ways," "mysteries of life and death," "our secret care still speakest thou."

The example of Stevenson and Logie Robertson slowly bore fruit.

John Buchan (1875-1940; *Poems Scots and English*, 1917) translated Theocritus, still too kailyairdily; but it is worth noting that practically all his nature poems (1911-17) are in Scots, while his English verse reads like exercises in a foreign language.

The stronghold of Scots poetry in the first decades of this century was the North-East, with its granite qualities. In this older school of modern poets we find a new assurance and poetic artistry, and even though the themes are mostly traditional—the village and the old way of life, the nostalgia of the exile, the graveyard and the kirk, past youth and history—they are handled creatively. Mary Stuart, in Marion Angus's "Alas! Poor Queen," has no old-fashioned sentimentality, but, rather, a modern sharpness not unlike that of T. S. Eliot's "Portrait of a Lady."

Charles Murray (1864-1941; *Hamewith*, 1900) [2] has least of this modern spirit, and most Burns-stanzas. From his new home in the Transvaal he remembered the Scottish village community and recalled its representative types, "The Packman," "The Lettergae," "The Antiquary," usually with an unsentimental sharpness. There are some serious notes, too, as in "Hame," of the glen in the Highlands with the croft whose roof is now caved in—just a hint of the clearances. Murray has a power of suggestion which sometimes enables him to paint a genuinely evocative picture or mood,[3] and his nostalgic poems express genuine feeling.[4] His "Virgil" and "Horace in Scots" show signs of a widening of scope, and as a whole his work holds out the promise of a return to deeper things. Murray's Scots, treasured in exile, is the most consistent.

In the poems of Violet Jacob (1863-1946) [5] there are, indeed, a few kelpies, and a few shepherds and their lasses. In the main, however, she strikes out in a new direction. She is less concerned with village life than with the individual and with his secret inner life, against a village background, and shows a delicate touch in dealing with his repressed emotions; strong feelings give "The Jaud" its depth, and humanity replaces conventional sentiment even in her Jacobite lyrics.[6] Though in the end she may shy away from hard facts, and

[2] Other volumes: *A Sough o' War* (1917) and *In the country Places* (1922).

[3] *E.g.* "The Hint o' Hairst [harvest]."

[4] *E.g.* "Hamewith [homewards]," "The Alien," "Scotland our Mither."

[5] *Songs of Angus* (1915); *More Songs of Angus* (1918); *Bonnie Joann* (1922); *Two new Poems* (1924); *Northern Lights* (1927). See also *The Scottish Poems of Violet Jacob*, Saltire Classics, 1944, which contains a good representative selection.

[6] *E.g.* "Cairneyside."

though the background is rural, she does try to give it a more universal meaning.[7] She is loath to see the old order disappear, but she is not whimsical about it. Scots helps her, as it did Stevenson, to be precise, even harsh, as in the fine study of " Pride " ; there is proud love of the North-East bareness and hardness and haar.

Marion Angus (1866-1946) [8] carries us over the threshold of World War I, for only then did she take up poetry seriously, and her mature work already contains anticipations of the modern Scots school. The most important development in her poetry is that the individual becomes still more fully emancipated, and is seen not as a member of society but as an individual. This important Romantic phenomenon had not previously appeared in Scottish poetry, and is here done with the delicate hand of a woman. Marion Angus seems to go one step beyond Violet Jacob. She often sees a sensitive girl in a dramatic situation and sounds the soul whose love must go unfulfilled. There is much serious matter in her verse, combined with the exact observation that Scots encourages, as the solemn meditation of " The Tinker's Road " or the hint of tragedy in " The Fiddler," with its three stanzas of wooing, of childbed, of a derelict home where the heather creeps back. This indicates the strongest influence on Marion Angus's poetry, that of the ballads with their starkness, symbols, hinted situations, echoes ; we hear the ballads in the " barley bread " and " elder wine " and lost love. As a woman, Marion Angus does not take up the action of the ballad, but the moment of reflexion, and this gives a fresh note. If she seems rather to belong to the older school, it is because of her elf-poems, her frequent conventional themes—even if presented in a highly personal vision—and the cobwebs of regret spun over most of her poetry : regret of lost youth, lost love, lost ideals. This dream of old and faded figures takes her away from real life and makes her fondle the past.

In the older school we can also include J. Pittendrigh MacGillivray (1856-1938) and Helen Burness Cruickshank (1896). With the latter, however, we step over the line of demarcation into the modern period and become conscious of the influence of C. M. Grieve (" Hugh MacDiarmid "). Her Scots has a power of abstraction absent for generations (" The Ponnage [pontage, ferrying point] "), and " Spring

[7] Cp. " The lang Road."

[8] *The Lilt and other Poems* (1922) ; *The Tinker's Road* (1924) ; *Sun and Candlelight* (1927) ; *The Turn of the Day* (1931) ; *Lost Country* (1937). See also *Selected Poems*, ed. M. Lindsay, with personal memoir by Helen B. Cruickshank, Edinburgh 1950.

in the Mearns" is symbolic: burning the whins makes new life spring from the ashes.

Among these four, regarded severally, only Marion Angus seems a poet worthy of a place in the history of Scottish literature in her own right. But regarded as a group, they foreshadow the coming of the Scottish Renaissance. Their work is predominantly rural, and there is much traditional matter in it; but they have stopped handling this matter in clichés, and develop it creatively. It is a heritage, not a convention. Remarkably enough, the Scots poems of Violet Jacob and Marion Angus had most depth, and this is an important step towards the claim that Scots still has poetic validity: even in the twentieth century it can be used to higher purposes than Kailyard or parochial satires or bothie humour. In retrospect, the generation of the beginning of this century looks as if it were struggling to cast a skin that had grown too tight, as if it were aware of self-imposed limitations, and were getting ready for something greater, more daring, to come.

X

Breakers : The Scottish Renaissance

I. The Modern Makars

By arousing interest in the rights of small nations, the First World War helped to stimulate the revival of national consciousness already foreshadowed in the Scottish poetry of the first two decades of the present century. True, it was not until 1934 that C. M. Grieve was to exclaim :

Was it for little Belgium's sake
Sae mony thoosand Scotsmen dee'd ?
And never ane for Scotland, [a]fegs ! *[a] forsooth !*
Wi' twenty thoosand times mair need ! [1]

It was, however, in 1920 that Sir Alexander Gray (1882) [2] published the first of several volumes containing Scots translations of German songs by, among others, Heine, and Scots versions of many German and Danish ballads. This was more than another Horace in homespun : it was a deliberate attempt to use Scots for the expression of European meanings—if only those of the past—and Sir Alexander was mining a vein that suited the Scottish genius. By aiming so high, even if he could not go all the way with those who spoke of a " Scots language," he succeeded in making his North-East Scots more flexible and in increasing its powers of expression. His own poems are rural, with much of the ballad mood, and perhaps not " modern " ; but they have been hammered into a fine hardness and at their best (as in " Grief ") are timeless. They breathe the spirit of the bare muirs of his home, and are (as in " Scotland ") a genuine expression of the tenderness which lies behind the granite of the North-East. His humour has shed all traces of whimsicality, and, though he sees men against the background of a community, he is chiefly concerned with them as individuals.

[1] " Towards a new Scotland," III, in *Stony Limits and Scots unbound*, 1st combined edn., 1956, p. 76.

[2] *Songs and Ballads, chiefly from Heine* (1920) ; *Any Man's Life* (1924) ; *Poems* (1925) ; *Gossip* (1928) ; *Songs from Heine* (1928) ; *Arrows* (German ballads and Folk-songs, 1932) ; *Sir Halewin* (1949) ; *Four-and-forty* (Danish ballads, 1954) ; *Selected Poems* (1948).

Lewis Spence (1874-1955) [3] widened the scope even more. He was aware that what Scots poetry required was intellectualism and subtlety, and a fuller canon of expression. With this in view, he experimented (sometimes not altogether seriously) with the style and language of the Makars, and in his artificial Scots recaptured something of their intellectual quality : like them, he also leant heavily on consonantal alliteration, and even achieved a certain emotional sophistication.[4] Yet he did not wholly abandon himself to the past ; and in some of his poems he raises the question of man's origin, nature, or age-old heritage.[5]

The man who really put Scottish poetry back on the map of Europe was, however, CHRISTOPHER MURRAY GRIEVE (" HUGH MACDIARMID," 1892).[6] In addition to true poetic genius, he had (and still has) all the tenacity and fighting spirit of a true Borderer ; and though the latter may, of recent years, sometimes have run away with the former, no other Scottish writer of the twentieth century has done half so much for Scottish literature as he has. Grieve has always wanted Scotland once more to take part in the concert of Europe, as she did in the time of the Makars (Back to Dunbar !). He is convinced that Scotland still has an important part to play in the " parallelogram of forces," and he envisages a Scotland that takes freely from other nations, and freely gives back in her turn. Scotland's contacts with other nations must, however, be direct contacts, and must not be mediated by England, because, he insists, the spirit of English is alien to that of Scottish culture. There is indeed a profound difference of attitude between the contemporary Scots Renaissance inaugurated by Grieve and the vernacular revival of the eighteenth century, with its defensive isolationism. Grieve prays he'll

never be
Cut aff and self-sufficient,

[3] *The Phoenix* (1924) ; *Plumes of Time* (1926) ; *Weirds and Vanities* (1927) ; *Collected Works* (1952).

[4] *E.g.* " The Queen's Bath-house, Holyrood " ; " Portrait of Mary Stuart, Holyrood."

[5] *E.g.* " The Carse " ; " The Prows o' Reekie."

[6] Poetry : *Sangschaw* (1925) ; *Penny Wheep* [small beer] (1926) ; *A drunk Man looks at the Thistle* (1926 ; 2nd edn., with good introduction by D. Daiches, 1953 ; repr. 1956) ; *To Circumjack Cencrastus* (1930) ; *First Hymn to Lenin* (1931) ; *Scots unbound* (1932) ; *Stony Limits* (1934) ; *Second Hymn to Lenin* (1935) ; *A Kist o' Whistles* (1948) ; *In Memoriam James Joyce* (1955) ; *Selected Poems* (1944) ; *Stony limits and Scots unbound*, 1st combined edn. 1956. See also the following prose works : *Lucky Poet* (autobiographical study, containing much unpublished poetry, 1943) ; *At the Sign of the Thistle* (1933) ; *Scottish Eccentrics* (1936) ; *Albyn, or the Future of Scotland* (1927).

and, like modern English poetry, his works contain a wealth of echoes ranging from Nietzsche to T. S. Eliot (" it's a Scottish name "), and from Spengler to Dostoevski (who can teach Scotland " to be hersel ").[7]

As a poet, Grieve is " tyauvin' wi' this root-hewn Scottis soul." Pondering on his Thistle, Grieve's Drunk Man exclaims :

> I canna feel it has to dae wi' me
> Mair than a composite diagram o'
> Cross-sections o' my forebears' organs.

And yet, he goes on,

> . . . like bindweed through my clay it's run
> And a' my folks'—it's queer to see't unroll.
> My ain soul looks me in the face, as 'twere,
> And mair than my ain soul—my nation's soul ! [8]

He is in search of Scotland's essential instincts, the beast, often deemed extinct, which yet lies lurking in every breast.[9] But this is not enough, for, says the Drunk Man, whatever Scotland is to him,

> He canna Scotland see wha yet
> Canna see the Infinite,
> And Scotland in true scale to it.[10]

Grieve's message is one that is meant " to reach the general mind," [11] and Scotland is simply the doorway through which alone he can enter the cosmos. He is no provincial writing about his kailyard, but an obstinate mystic who brings man, and Scotland, face to face with the universe, with the mysteries of life, death, man, God, the past, and the future. The true Romantic achievement has at last reached Scotland. But instead of Romantic emotionalism, there is a hard intellectual clarity. And since each generation has to express its own creed in terms of its own actual experience, Grieve's imagery is chiefly taken from an industrial, metropolitan world.

The Scottish soul, Grieve feels, cannot adequately be expressed in English, but only in Scots or Gaelic ; though he sees the ultimate root in Gaelic, his own tongue is Scots. But if Scots is to be the medium of a poetry that can reach the stars, it must undergo development, for

[7] *A drunk Man looks at the Thistle*, 3rd edn. (1956), henceforth cited as *Drunk Man*, pp. 6, 13, 15, 28.

[8] *Op. cit.*, p. 13.

[9] Cp. " Gairmscoile," in *Penny Wheep*, pp. 64 ff.

[10] *Drunk Man*, p. 90.

[11] *Op. cit.*, p. 89.

having been restricted so long to mere sentimental " hameliness," it is of poor intellectual quality, and entirely lacks the upper strata of vocabulary. Grieve therefore revives old Scots words with no precise equivalent in present-day English, and also borrows freely from Gaelic and other sources. This " synthetic Scots " (Denis Saurat), or " plastic Scots " (Douglas Young), goes farther than Burns's or Stevenson's mixture of dialects, it repeats the serious effort of Gavin Douglas to make Scots a language capable of dealing with any matter.

In his first volumes Grieve gave Scottish literature a new type of lyric, in which sentiment is given a painful twist, and (in the words of one of his later poems) even the " little white Rose of Scotland . . . smells sharp and sweet—and breaks the heart." Though highly personal (and, at the same time, characteristically modern), this juxtaposition of opposites also stands in the direct line of Scots tradition :

> To pit in a concrete abstraction
> My country's contrair qualities,
> And mak' a unity o' these.[12]

This insistence on the contrast of extremes—harsh and tender, solemn and grotesque, exterior and interior, " Love wi' a scunner in't "[13]—which is so pronounced in earlier Scots poetry, is also an essential element in Grieve's lyrics. More than anything else, it enables him to evoke the awe we feel when confronted with the universe. He brings to perfection the direct, concise utterance so frequent in Scottish poetry, and by placing objects in a cold light and stripping them of all ephemeral details, he creates images of startling intensity which makes us see these objects in their full implication : " Earth, the bare auld stane . . . White as a mammoth's bane," " the warl' like an eemis stane."[14] And the poem called " Perfect "[15] is simply a sharp and accurate representation of a pigeon's skull :

> . . . twin domes, like bubbles of thin bone,
> Almost transparent, where the brain had been,
> That fixed the tilt of the wings.

With their intensity of vision, these early lyrics of Grieve's have

[12] *Drunk Man*, p. 72.
[13] " Scunner," in *Penny Wheep*, p. 46.
[14] " Au clair de la lune : III (The Man in the Moon)," and " The Eemis-stane [*i.e.* The Rocking-stone]," in *Sangschaw*, pp. 16, 23.
[15] *Selected Poems*, p. 20.

much in common with the poetry of the older Yeats. Far from being mere effusions of sentiment they have a delicate and sharply intellectual approach,[16] and are truly singable; many of them have been set to music by Grieve's teacher, Francis George Scott, whose accompaniments often stress the contrasts by telling the story from the other point of view, thus providing an ideal complement. Their success is largely due to the Scottish "power of seeing things vividly inside your mind . . . and flashing the two ideas together,"[17] as when Grieve flashes together a rainbow and the look of a friend dying:

Ae [a]weet forenicht i' the [b]yow-trummle   [a] *wet* [b] lit. *ewe-tremble*
I saw yon [a]antrin thing,   [a] *unusual*
A [a]watergaw wi' its [b]chitterin' licht   [a] *indistinct rainbow* [b] *shivering*
Ayont the [a]on-ding;   [a] *downpour*
An I thocht o' the last wild look ye [a]gied   [a] *gave*
Afore ye dee'd!

There was nae [a]reek i' the [b]laverock's hoose   [a] *smoke* [b] *lark's*
That nicht—and nane i' mine;
But I hae thocht o' that foolish licht
Ever [a]sin' syne;   [a] *since then*
An' I think that mebbe at last I ken
What your look meant then.[18]

As usual, this creates a highly subjective vision of reality,[19] which in Grieve's poetry sometimes assumed metaphysical dimensions:

Lay haud o' my hert and feel
Fountains [a]outloupin' the [b]starns   [a] lit. *outjumping* [b] *stars*
Or see the Universe reel
Set [a]gaen' by my [b]eident harns.[20]   [a] *going* [b] *busy brains*

Grieve's lyrics may be the best-known part of his work, but his most important poem, and the test of his belief that Scots poetry can be made to express anything under the stars, is *A drunk Man looks at the Thistle* (1926). This rhapsodic testament contains all the intellectual substance a poem can possibly have, and ranges from the commonplace to the most abstract thinking, "The Warld and

[16] *E.g.* "The frightened Bride," *op. cit.*, p. 9.

[17] See above, p. 267.

[18] "The Watergaw," in *Sangschaw*, p. 2. A note in the Glossary explains that the "yow-trummle" is the cold weather that often comes in July just at the time when the sheep are sheared.

[19] *E.g.* "The diseased Salmon," *op. cit.*, p. 40.

[20] *Drunk Man*, p. 19.

Life and Daith, Heaven, Hell ana'." [21] It is not only a synthesis of culture and politics, of metaphysical speculation and social flyting, for here the poet reaches highest and tries to

join issue wi' the Will
That raised the Wheel and spins it still.[22]

What am I? How am I related to the Universe? Those are fundamentally his questions, and he tries to answer them by deliberately creating a "Caledonian antisyzygy." Together with the grotesque incongruity of the extremes which he asserts, the abrupt changes of mood have the effect of ousting and abolishing all existing boundaries of thought and of creating, in their stead, a new and self-willed relevancy. The poem is another, deeper *Don Juan*—for indeed Grieve has something Byronic about him, but without Byron's pose. His fate is to see and feel deeper than other men. "Aye, this is Calvary," he exclaims—

to bear
Your cross wi'in you frae the seed
And feel it grow by slow degrees
Until it rends your flesh apairt.[23]

To find his way the poet must first plunge into chaos and find his footing there. The agony is foreshadowed in poems like "I heard Christ sing" and the "Ballad of the Five Senses," [24] where the poet recognises it as his task to see the world as God felt when He made it.

But why a Drunk Man and a Thistle? It is a counter-part of the medieval dream-allegory about the rose. Grieve's thistle is not only Scotland's national badge, it is also an exemplification of his own precept "to be yoursel'"—and, at the same time, a singularly expressive symbol of the Scottish soul, of modern man, and of himself:

O for a root in some untroubled soil,
Some cauld soil 'yont this fevered warld,
That 'ud draw darkness frae a virgin source,
And send it slow and easefu' through my veins,
Release the tension o' my grisly leafs,
Withdraw my endless spikes,
Move coonter to the force in me that hauds
Me raxed and rigid and ridiculous. . . . [25]

[21] *Op. cit.*, p. 12. [22] *Op. cit.*, p. 89. [23] *Op. cit.*, p. 59.
[24] *Sangschaw*, pp. 5 ff., 43 ff. [25] *Drunk Man*, p. 77.

Like young John Gourlay in *The House with the green Shutters*, Grieve's Drunk Man has a heightened power of seeing things in pictures and flashing together symbols and associations that are not obviously related to one another—much as in dreams—so as to reveal how much they really have in common. The drunkenness permits abrupt transitions and changes of mood, another way of reducing symptoms to a common denominator. This raises the ultimate questions: is life reality or a dream? And what is man?

> Am I a thingum mebbe that is kept
> Preserved in spirit in a [a]muckle bottle? [26] *[a] big*

Moreover, the Drunk Man has the right kind of obstinacy that is not just pugnacity, but seems to carry logic to impossible extremes. The moonlight is "fickle" enough to give "a different life to't"; it

> owre clear defines
> The thistle's shrill cantankerous lines, [27]

and distorts the perspective just enough to make things take on a new life.

But there is still more to this fiction of the drunk man looking at the thistle. It allows Grieve to use Scots dramatically, to let the man speak in character; the dramatic way of speaking is preserved everywhere. The accent is that of conversation, and any deviation achieves violent emphasis:

> And owre the kailyaird-wa' Dunbar they've flung.[28]

This keeps the concrete picture sharply focused in the forefront of the mind, with enormous concentration. There is no real abstraction here: the abstract is seen through the crystal of the concrete picture in which it is embodied, and it always has its "objective correlative" in the concrete world. The same is true of "Wheelrig." [29] Grieve works in the very centre of what seems to me the true Scots idiom, with all its sharpness, visualisation, dramatisation. This does not mean that Scots is necessarily a limited language, incapable of expressing abstract ideas: it means that, like every language, Scots has its own genuine idiom, and that this is how it expresses abstract ideas—as indeed the *Drunk Man* shows. And, once again, as with Stevenson's "Thrawn Janet," there seems to be no question of any "absolute Scots."

[26] *Op. cit.*, p. 11.
[27] *Op. cit.*, p. 68.
[28] *Op. cit.*, p. 28.
[29] *Sangschaw*, p. 30.

In subsequent years Grieve seems to have lost touch with this central Scots idiom. With its stronger Gaelic and international appeals, *To Circumjack Cencrastus* (1930) fails partly because the Celtic symbol of the Snake of Wisdom with its tail in its mouth is not visualised so concretely as the Thistle, partly because the poet has neglected the dramatic aspect and personal vision of Scots, and lastly because the preacher is taking over from the poet. The snake of wisdom—and wisdom more and more obsesses him. For, since then, Grieve has been mainly concerned with putting across ideas, especially a highly personal dogma of Communism ("In workin' out mankind's great synthesis"). Instead of himself writing his type of poem, he writes, often in English, long verse treatises on the type of poetry he wants to see ; some of these are in *Lucky Poet*, and there are fine passages in each of them, but the whole is all too prosy. William Soutar may well have had Grieve in mind when he wrote "Wait for the Hour : To a Poet" : "to curb the fretful brain and trust the blood." The real spirit flashes up now and again. "The seamless Garment" has the real Scots vision, with the eye dead sharp on the picture that is to be projected into the outer world. By making us *see* something, "Cattle Show"[30] achieves more than all his long prose poems, and the four lines of "The Skeleton of the Future"[31] communicate, purely by sensuous imagery, a suggestion of eternity by which, whatever his politics, no reader can fail to be carried away. His most recent work, *In Memoriam James Joyce : From a Vision of World Language* (1955) shows Grieve striving for a world literature in Goethe's sense, but one that should be fertilised by James Joyce's revolutionary achievement ; this world-wide vision of the present and future problems of East and West may be universal in appeal and spirit, but is none the less Scottish in temperament : like Barbour's, or Henryson's, or Carlyle's, Grieve's headstrong personality will not leave his subject alone, but will break in again and again in angry comment.

Though Grieve's own genius is highly original, his points of contact with the Scottish tradition, especially with Dunbar and Alexander Scott, are unmistakable : his flyting spirit ; his use of the grotesque, which is made to serve the vision,[32] and of alliteration

[30] *Stony Limits and Scots unbound* (above, n. 1), p. 84.

[31] At Lenin's tomb ; *op. cit.*, p. 2.

[32] Cp. "Au clair de la lune : IV (The Huntress and her Dogs)" and "Crowdieknowe," in *Sangschaw*, pp. 17, 21 f.

(especially in moments of anger), sound-painting, echoes, word-variation.[33] In the lyrical insets of the *Drunk Man* we find folk-song rhythms, and in parts of *Circumjack Cencrastus* Grieve even succeeds in making the Burns-stanza carry a serious meaning. But there is no narrow Scottishness : he can claim kinship with Villon or Skelton, Yeats or Rilke, and European echoes are manifold.

Christopher Murray Grieve has left his indelible mark on Scottish poetry, and his efforts alone give us the right to speak of a Scots Renaissance ; his *Scots unbound* was a book to make disciples. The old post-Burnsian school of ploughboy poets still has a large following. But modern Scottish poetry has none the less opened its windows to let in fresh air and light, and has created a fresher intellectual atmosphere in which its poets seriously try to get to grips with the deepest human problems. It is no longer men as members of village communities, but Man and the immensities of destiny, death, and eternity that are the theme of poetry. There is a realisation that instead of trifling with superficialities, modern psychology requires a new evaluation of the really crucial questions ; and the question that lies at the root of much contemporary Scottish poetry is that of our own deepest nature. With all its sophisticated intellectual cosmopolitanism, the answer is no less Scottish than in earlier ages. " Who am I ? " is soon translated into " Who are we ? " and this is answered in various ways. In some respects, twentieth-century Scottish poetry is more representative than for many generations, for the voice of the Gaeltacht makes itself heard, in Gaelic, English, and Scots, directly or indirectly (as in Norman McCaig,[34] whose imagery reflects a Gaelic background). Never since the time of the Makars had the Gaelic and the Scots stream of Scottish culture been so close to each other, on the way to a confluence. In all the major poets we find a strain of the Scottish tradition, not as imitation, but as a living development ; even in " Embro to the Ploy," a modern " Christis Kirk " by R. G. Sutherland (" Robert Garioch "),[35] in which the traditional pattern is followed closely, the picture of the crowds that flock to Edinburgh for the Festival has a metropolitan spirit that is almost entirely new.

There are some other phenomena that seem to indicate a greater

[33] Cp. " Water Music," in *Scots unbound and other Poems*, 1st edn., pp. 5 ff.

[34] *The far Cry* (1943) ; *The inward Eye* (1946) ; *Riding Lights* (1955) ; *The Sinai Sort* (1957).

[35] *Seventeen Poems for Sixpence* (with Gaelic poems by Somhairle Maclean, 1940) ; *Chuckie Stanes for the Cairn* (1949) ; *The Masque of Edinburgh* (1954). As a poet, Sutherland has a certain affinity with Robert Fergusson, as is evident in " Embro to the Ploy."

awareness to the needs of an all-embracing Scottish culture,[36] though sometimes as yet it is a promise rather than an achievement. Mention must be made of the Saltire Society, whose aim it is to promote all aspects of Scottish culture ; and above all, there is the outstanding achievement of the great Scottish composer Francis George Scott (1880), one of the great song-writers of the world, who translates the Scottish poetic tradition over into music.[37]

A question that sometimes seems to split Scottish poetry from top to bottom is that of language. Is Scots a language? Is it alone genuinely expressive of Scottish feeling? Or is it confined to the simpler aspects of experience—especially childhood? In his lyrics, and in the *Drunk Man*, C. M. Grieve had restored its dignity, largely by making it once more an adult language capable of expressing human experience in general.

William Soutar (1898-1943),[38] the only other important poet of Grieve's own generation who wrote Scots as well as English, presents a somewhat different picture. He was an invalid, who was not only confined to his room, but knew that he was a dying man, and with enormous courage still wrote poetry. His thoughts,

> unwittingly,
> Wing forth from the blood's edge.[39]

At the immensity of the universe, the mystery of life and death, he feels a childlike wonder. "Touch not," he exclaims, "with irreverent hands," the dust that may have been the walls of Zion, Nineveh or Troy, the Queen of Sheba, or King Solomon.[40] As with so many mystics, his insight springs from a delight in sensuous beauty, often from a nature miniature ; there are some remarkable transformations of things seen into brilliant imagery, for example "drops of liquid light which fall from air," hedges "made of glass," and leaves so

[36] See *Some Scottish Arts*, ed. J. M. Reid, Saltire Society, 1951.

[37] Scott's music is full of the true Scots dramatic idiom, psychological insight, and tension of extremes—the last often between melody and accompaniment, sentiment being counterpointed by satire, solemnity by irreverence. Though proposterous extravagance is combined with an eldritch delight in pricking the bubble of pomposity, and a witty sense of form that sometimes is carried to excess, there is also a deep underlying tenderness.

[38] *Gleanings by an Undergraduate* (1923) ; *Conflict* (1931) ; *Seeds in the Wind : Poems in Scots for Children* (1933, repr. 1943) ; *The solitary Way* (1934) ; *Brief Words* (1935) ; *Poems in Scots* (1935) ; *A Handful of Earth* (1936) ; *Riddles in Scots* (1937) ; *In the Time of Tyrants* (1939) ; *But the Earth abideth* (1943) ; *The expectant Silence* (1944) ; *Collected Poems*, ed. "Hugh MacDiarmid" (1948). See also *Diaries of a dying Man*, ed. A. Scott (1954).

[39] "Reverie," in *A Handful of Earth*, p. 22.

[40] "Dust," in *A Handful of Earth*, p. 11.

white in the sunshine that " over snow I hear : *cuckoo.*" [41] It is this concentration on an image that gives depth to the mystery of expectant life.[42] Consequently Soutar prefers short, pure, set forms like miniatures, of which the simplicity is intensified by echoes of early folk rhythms (not only in his bairn rhymes) and the ballad. According to his *Diaries,* Soutar rated the ballads as the highest achievement of Scottish poetry, higher than Burns or Dunbar ; and in a note in *But the Earth abideth* he asserts his belief that the qualities of the ballad are the most appropriate for our time if we seek " to outline the background of universal law against which the compulsions of war reveal their obedience to necessity." *But the Earth abideth* is not simply, however, an echo or imitation of the ballads : it has the same suggestiveness, the same dramatic courage in face of fate, but the method is sublter and aims at greater validity, at the formulation of a law. Take the following extracts[43] :

And are these black and broken stones
Communing with the skies . . . ?

The dead are walking everywhere
Wearing the world for shroud.

Beauty is shaded by our grief,
Our dust is on the bloom :
With the returning of the leaf
Our thoughts of blood come home.

There is always one line that suggests a ballad, but the next has an abstraction, a general sweep and intellectuality totally absent from the ballads. Here modern thought reaches out from the facts to grasp a law :

There is a shape of humankind
Still to be recognised.

From every battlefield comes a murdered man, without name,

He is a man of common earth
Born from a common grave.

[41] " A sunny Shower " and " Summer Snow," in *A Handful of Earth,* pp. 32, 36.
[42] Cp. " Advent," in *A Handful of Earth,* p. 12.
[43] See *But the Earth abideth,* pp. 9, 13, 14, 17.

He is bone of our bone, carries the heritage in his hands, his sires raging in the wood, Cain's curse and Abel's wound :

> Brother since time began . . .
> . . . that he is everyman.[44]

But this is in Soutar's English verse. His poems in Scots have nothing of this union of traditional forms with modern complex thought, nothing of the general sweep. They are frequently more traditional, full of diablerie and grotesque humour. But they are more direct in their expression, keenly individual, and less in danger of becoming vaguely conventional. They keep the concrete picture sharp, and the vision is sometimes more dynamic, apter to see nature as a protagonist.[45] With their passion and haunting intensity, his ballads in Scots keep closer to the traditional form, but they lack the relevance to our modern world. Their personal feeling would put them side by side with Sir Alexander Gray's " timeless " poems. Instead of complex thought, we sometimes are dangerously near the level of a proverb.[46] In some poems,[47] we feel the trembling of the veil, but we do not advance beyond the threshold of the inner chamber of mystery.[48]

To Soutar, the associations of Scots seem to be too strongly personal and concrete for his mystic flight : and one wonders whether he could have generalised in Scots as he did in " Recollection of first Love " : [49]

> I have known women fonder far
> Than you, more fair, more kind ;
> Women whose passionate faces are
> Flowers in the mind.

And still, it is in one of the Scots poems, his " Song " with the refrain " Gang doun wi a sang, gang doun," that Soutar achieves his highest poetry : here, for once, under the impact of his own fate, Soutar combines the range and reverberation of his English poems with the intent visualisation of his Scots :

[44] *Op. cit.*, pp. 61, 62.

[45] *E.g.* " The Gowk [cuckoo]," in *Poems in Scots*, p. 15.

[46] *E.g.* " Content," in *Collected Poems*, p. 416.

[47] *E.g.* " The Makar," in *Collected Poems* p. 448. ; " The Thocht," in *Collected Poems*, p. 33. ; and " The lanely Müne," in *Seeds in the Wind*, p. 29.

[48] *E.g.* " The Sea Shell," in *Seeds in the Wind*, p. 55.

[49] *Conflict*, p. 35.

Whaur yon broken [a]brig [b]hings owre ; — [a] *bridge* [b] *hangs*
Whaur yon water maks nae soun' ;
Babylon blaws by in [a]stour : — [a] *wind-blown dust*
[a]Gang doun wi a sang, gang doun. — [a] *go*

Deep, [a]owre deep, for onie [b]drouth : — [a] *over*, i.e. *too* [b] *thirst*
Wan eneuch an ye wud droun ;
[a]Saut, or [b]seelfu', for the mouth ; — [a] *salt* [b] *pleasant*
Gang doun wi a sang, gang doun.

Babylon blaws by in stour
Whaur yon water maks nae soun' :
Darkness is your only door ;
Gang doun wi a sang, gang doun.[50]

In its second phase, the Scots Renaissance has produced several poets who have shown increased confidence in a modern literary Scots (or " Lallans " [51] as it is now sometimes called). Sydney Goodsir Smith, Douglas Young, Alexander Scott and their contemporaries not only write Scots more concisely and consistently : they sometimes use it for expository as well as purely poetical purposes, and have adopted a new orthography in which Scots is no longer spelt as if it were a dialect of English—" o, aa, singan," etc., being substituted for " o', a', singin' (part.)," etc. And they use Scots to express all human experience.

SYDNEY GOODSIR SMITH (1915) [52] is, after Grieve himself, the most important living poet who writes Scots. In his best lyrics, which have a passionate but strictly controlled intensity, he reduces experience to its essentials, cutting out every word that is not vital to it, and stripping off the outward crust of sentiment until he comes to the fiery core that lies at the heart of it.[53] He is heavily indebted to the Scots tradition of direct statement,[54] and draws much of his vocabulary from the Scots poetry of earlier centuries. Not that he is by any

[50] *Poems in Scots*, p. 56.

[51] *I.e.* " Lowland speech."

[52] *Skail Wind* (1941) ; *The Wanderer* (1943) ; *The Deevil's Waltz* (1946) ; *Under the Eildon Tree* (1948 ; repr. 1954) ; *So late into the Night* (1952); *Cokkils* (1953) ; *Orpheus and Eurydice* (1955) ; *Omens* (1956) ; *Selected Poems* (Saltire Society, 1947). His most important prose work in *Carotid Cornucopius* (1947).

[53] Cp. " The Mandrake Hert," and " Defeat o the Hert," in *So late into the Night*, pp. 26, 56.

[54] Cp. " Prolegomenon," in *The Deevil's Waltz*, pp. 9 f., esp. the stanza beginning " For want o luve we live on hate." (A better text of this poem will be found in *The Faber Book of Twentieth-century Verse*, edd. J. Heath-Stubbs and D. Wright (1953), pp. 310 ff.)

means an antiquarian. He sees the present as the result of the past: Flodden and Culloden are part of the whole huge historical process which also led to the invasion of Poland; Wallace and Villon are in a sense the ancestors of Pushkin. But far from being thirled to the past, Smith can declare:

> We luik til the kenless dawn aheid.[55]

Though he does not often imitate their verse forms, the Makars have taught him many of the secrets of their own sophisticated verse music. His poetry is full of the exultation of the singing voice, but he also knows the hardness of an enamelled surface.[56] His song "*Lenta la neve fiocca, fiocca, fiocca*" [57] shows some of the same delight in word-patterns, as such, that we have seen in the poems of Alexander Scott and of the later Makars, but owing to its evocation of the movement of the snowflakes it has more poetic integrity than was customary in the older Makars:

> Slaw, dear, slaw the white flakes [a]faa, [a] *fall*
> Slaw the snaw,
> O white it faas. . . .

He develops the Scottish tradition by bringing it into relation with our modern life. His own poetry is full of echoes of the ballads, songs, the Makars, the spirit of carnival wildness; and in elaborating its huge nexus of associations, he has invented a mythology which provides a framework for such major works as *Carotid Cornucopius*, *Under the Eildon Tree*, and *Colickie Meg* (a still unpublished comic drama), and also for such individual pieces as "The Deevil's Waltz" with its echo of Dunbar's Mahoun, "The Birks in November," "In a Time of Deepest Wanhope" with its refrain "*timor mortis non conturbat me*," [58] and "Quhar art thou gane, my luf Euridices?" [59] In artistic outlook he is fairly close to the old Makars, but not in the feelings with which he contemplates the problem of modern man's place in the universe: "Godlike, speiran, miscontentit Man" surveying "his riven legacie." [60] For Smith can also claim kinship with Baudelaire or Racine, Aristophanes or Juvenal, Ezra Pound or T. S.

[55] "To the Shades of Yeats," in *The Deevil's Waltz*, pp. 37 f.
[56] Cp. the "Hymn of Luve til Venus Queen," in *The Deevil's Waltz*, pp. 27 f.
[57] *Selected Poems*, p. 13.
[58] *The Deevil's Waltz*, pp. 9, 15, 20.
[59] See *Under the Eildon Tree*, 2nd edn., pp. 33 ff.
[60] "The Viaduct," in *The Deevil's Waltz*, p. 32.

Eliot, and sometimes gains his perspective by bringing the Scots outlook into relationship with classical and Celtic mythology.

But, above all, Smith's lyrics are concerned with life as we live it, not with a world of dreams. There is modern psychological insight in the statement that

> A demon bydes in the breist [a]in dern — [a] *in hiding*
> That's neither saul nor mynd nor hert . . .[61]

His poems express an unflinching acceptance of experience, which, as we know, is not all roses. There are moments of unspeakable bliss, when the eye is blinded with tears of joy and he turns out of the window to see the

> [a]Sclate roofs like siller — [a] *slate*
> [a]Schire-bleezan yon morn.[62] — [a] *bright-blazing*

But there also is defeat, which we must accept, as in "Defeat o the Hert"[63]; or an impotent feeling of helplessness against impersonal forces as in "Largo."[64] This poem comes straight out of the heart of the Scottish tradition: it has a sharply focused picture in the foreground, the last boat fishing from this shore, and through this picture the poet sees the inevitable course:

> And never the clock rins back,
> The free days are owre;
> The warld shrinks, we luik
> Mair t'our maisters ilka hour—
> Whan yon [a]lane boat I see — [a] *lonely*
> Daith and rebellion [a]blinn ma [b]ee! — [a] *blind* [b] *eye*

More and more, however, Smith has turned away from these "wechtier maitters" and now finds his true inspiration in modern love-poetry: "you are my subject anerlie." *Under the Eildon Tree* (1948) is perhaps the best modern love-poem; it is a cycle of twenty-four "elegies," in which the poet laments the loves of Orpheus and Eurydice, Dido and Aeneas, Burns and Highland Mary. On the underlying foundation provided by the Scottish myth of Thomas the Rhymer, all are presented as variations on a single theme, and the

[61] "Saagin," in *So late into the Night*, p. 12.

[62] "For my newborn Son," in *Selected Poems*, p. 6 (At this moment of intense emotion, the poet is looking out of the window; only Henryson shows similar mastery here).

[63] *So late into the Night*, p. 56. [64] *The Deevil's Waltz*, p. 33.

mood ranges from consuming devotion to the casual encounter with " the hure o Reekie—I got her i the Black Bull . . . Gin I mynd richt, in Leith Street." [65] Why these rants? Perhaps only because

Bards hae sung o' lesser luves
  Than I o thee,
O, my great follie and my [a]granderie, — [a] *grandeur*
That nane kens but [a]anerlie thee.[66] — [a] *only*

There is much besides, for the poet of *Under the Eildon Tree* is another drunk man looking at a thistle. From his love, Smith reaches out to everything under the stars, to a full experience of life. Like T. S. Eliot or Ezra Pound, Smith has enriched the texture of this poem by weaving into it a whole host of associations with world literature, and especially with Scottish poetry. The more one recognises these echoes and their implications, the deeper one's comprehension of the poem as a whole. Smith does not wear his heart upon his sleeve: rather, he brings to perfection the characteristically Scottish habits of understatement, of contrasting harshness and tenderness,[67] and of putting a sharp edge on feeling. Yet the feeling shines through every movement, and the eye that turns away beholds the sensuous splendour of a mystery in simple everyday incidents. Love, to Smith, is not merely a personal emotion; still less is it merely a sentiment. He sees it in a modern essentially metropolitan setting:

I [a]loe ma luve in a lamplit bar — [a] *love*
Braw on a wuiden stool,
Her knees cocked up and her [a]neb doun — [a] *nose*
[a]Slorpan a pint o [b]yill.[68] — [a] *swilling* [b] *ale*

Above all, love is a complex and very subtle experience: at once carnal, emotional and spiritual, rational and irrational. It is an experience in which thought heightens feeling, and feeling intensifies thought. As Smith is well aware, love's different aspects do not fit together perfectly; and in his admission [69]

That [a]ahint the bravadie — [a] *behind*
This hert is near spent

[65] *Under the Eildon Tree*, 2nd edn., pp. 37 ff.

[66] *Op. cit.*, p. 11.

[67] Cp. *op. cit.*, p. 13: " Biggit wi bluid and greit [weeping] —And your damned flichterie!"

[68] " Five blye Sangs for Marion: IV," in *The Deevil's Waltz*, p. 25.

[69] *Under the Eildon Tree*, p. 24.

there is the suggestion of unresolved pain and struggle which goes much deeper than any in the love-poetry of earlier generations. The first stanza of " The Scaur " is perhaps only the age-old sigh for a love that might heal the " braird [burgeoning] " of an old scar ; but the second reflects a knowledge of modern psychology which endows it with fresh meaning and so intensifies the pain :

Whan thochts rin free
[a]Reid-wud lik wolves. . . .[70] — [a] *mad*

Though in some ways the " sang-quair " entitled " Reasoun an the Hert " [71] resembles the love-poems of Mark Alexander Boyd, Alexander Scott, Dunbar, and though its dramatic contrast is characteristically Scottish, the depth that Smith achieves in it is unprecedented :

Hert, ma hert, [a]forgae — [a] *forgo*
This [a]dirlin o ma saul, — [a] *drilling*
Ye [a]steer ma deeps til a reel o flame — [a] *stir*
Lik a smashed coal.[72]

Here we have authentic passion, and even a sense of physical violence, expressed in modern imagery which rises out of today's awareness of the hidden depth of the soul : but the feeling itself and the artistic method used in expressing it are both characteristically Scottish.

DOUGLAS YOUNG (1913) [73] shows none of this passion, none of this emotional violence. He is a classical scholar who lectures in Greek at St Andrews University, and his verse is characterised by a technical and intellectual mastery which enables him to compress all that need be said about love into four lines :

Gie aa, and aa comes back
  Wi mair nor aa.
[a]Hain ocht, and ye'll hae nocht, — [a] *keep back*
  Aa flees awa.[74]

[70] *The Deevil's Waltz*, p. 22. Cp. Sorley Maclean, " Coin is Madaidhean-allaidh [Dogs and Wolves]," in *Scottish Verse 1851-1951*, ed. D. C. C. Young, 1952. (Maclean speaks of his " unborn poems " as " bloody-tongued lean dogs and wolves ").

[71] *Op. cit.*, pp. 13 ff.

[72] " III. Reasoun an the Hert," *op. cit.*, p. 14.

[73] *Auntran Blads* (= *Occasional Pages*, 1943) ; *A Braird o' Thristles* (= *A Crop of Thistles*, 1947). *Selected Poems*, Saltire Society (1950).

[74] " Luve," in *A Braird o Thristles*, henceforth cited as *Thristles*, p. 17.

Still, even he is aware of the irrational in man, as shown by the panic which he feels in killing a bat (which alights on Vol. III of Farnell's *Pindar*), and in the shuddering agony of guilt which he feels afterwards.[75] Many of his poems are really dramatic monologues. This is what makes Young's Scots—or " Lallans," as he prefers to call it—so convincing, and in " Sabbath i the Mearns " [76] we can almost see the prosy old farmer sententiously wagging his head as he speaks. Though it might easily have been merely another bucolic piece, this austere poem about the " auld-farrant fermer-fowk " of the Mearns, who " dinna muckle fash theirsels wi ither fowks' concerns," shows real psychological insight, and more than a hint of hidden depth in its historical evocations. Like most of Young's poems, it seizes one of those moments in which the round of common life brushes the circumference of a larger circle, and man has a sense of contact with something greater than what he sees in front of him. The same sense of the intangible is also evoked in Young's best lyric, " For a Wife in Jizzen [childbed]," [77] with its suggestion of the mysteries of life and death that only women and mothers know :

> [a]Dern frae aa men — [a] *hide*
> The [a]ferlies ye ha seen. — [a] *wonders*

Young has the same " power of seeing things vividly " in his mind,[78] and he often combines it with understatement in a manner that is strongly reminiscent of Henryson. There is also a touch of Henryson in the delight that he takes in sensuous experience, and in his sense of humour. In late nineteenth and early twentieth-century Scottish literature, humour had been so heavily overloaded with whimsical sentimentality that most serious writers had shied away from it ; but it is not the least of Young's achievements that he has given true Scottish humour a new lease of life in poetry. With the help of the ballad convention's " braid letter " and its " neist but barely three," he pokes fun at second sight, and his own humour has some of the traditional grimness which laughs at the sight of a body chopped in two.[79] His poetry shows signs of the influence of the ballads also in

[75] " August Night," in *Auntran Blads*, pp. 31 f. [76] *Op. cit.*, p. 27.

[77] *Thristles*, p. 7.

[78] See above, pp. 267, 284.

[79] Cp. " Ice-flumes owregie their Lades [Glaciers give up their loads]," and " Duncan the Joiner," in *Thristles*, pp. 12 f., 20 f.

its frequent alliteration; and his "Bairn-music"[80] contains echoes of traditional nursery rhymes and folk-songs.

Young is both a poet and a cultural fighter, but even his political satires or lyrics are genuine poetry; "Last Lauch" is essentially a poem, and polemical only by implication:

> The Minister said it wad [a]dee, — [a] *die*
> The cypress [a]buss I plantit . . . — [a] *bush*
>
> It's growan stark and [a]heich, — [a] *high*
> Derk and straucht and sinister,
> Kirkyairdie-like and [a]dreich. — [a] *dreary*
> But whaur's the Minister?[81]

Young has published Scots verse translations of Gaelic poems by Sorley Maclean and George Campbell Hay,[82] and of poems in a dozen other languages old and new. He has also written verses of his own (not always so good) in several foreign languages. Though there is something Goliardic in it, all this is also reminiscent of the Scots humanists of the sixteenth century, and it betokens a genuine effort to establish cross-relations with other cultures.

The impact of contemporary European literature is strongest, however, in the work of the Orcadian Edwin Muir (1887),[83] critic and poet, and protagonist of a Scottish literature in English. After welcoming the Scots Renaissance, he became more and more convinced that Scots was inadequate for high intellectual purposes, that it represented the world of childhood, and that all its adult qualities were lost with its status as an independent language.[84] Muir is, in some respects, a descendant of the North Britons of the eighteenth century, who were more at home in Europe than in England. As it roves through the whole field of European or universal culture, his mind establishes direct contact with Heine, Nietzsche, Kafka, Rilke, Hölderlin, Galsworthy, Dostoevski, Shaw, Joyce, Hoffmannstal, Lawrence, psycho-analysis, the pessimism of the thirties. But Muir differs from the North Britons in that he enters the field of European

[80] *Op. cit.*, p. 19. [81] *Op. cit.*, p. 15. [82] See below, pp. 305 ff.

[83] Poetry: *First Poems* (1925); *Chorus of the newly Dead* (1926); *Variations on a Time Theme* (1934); *Journeys and Places* (1937); *The narrow Place* (1943); *The Voyage* (1946); *The Labyrinth* (1949); *Collected Poems 1921-51* (a selection, 1952). Criticism: *Latitudes* (1924); *Scott and Scotland* (1936); *Literature and Society* (1948); etc. See also *The Story and the Fable* (1940), and *An Autobiography* (its complement, 1954).

[84] *Scott and Scotland.*

thought only in order to bring it into relation with his own experience and with the society in which he lives. His *Autobiography* shows us his mind, and his art, developing as he sifts the currents of European thought and gradually finds ways of expressing the mind of the society to which he belongs. The contact which he establishes with the thought of the world outside Scotland, and outside England too, causes a re-orientation of Muir's attitude towards the Scottish heritage —and especially towards Scottish Calvinism. He envisages a Scotland which belongs to the European concert of nations, but is not painfully and self-consciously Scottish. Though it often seems to be near the surface, the word " Scottish " does not often occur in the *Autobiography*, and, as J. C. Hall points out in *Collected Poems*, Muir's poetry and preoccupations " have more in common with European, than with specifically English, ways of thought."

Muir's poetry, though somewhat marmorean, is of high intellectual and spiritual quality. He is a metaphysical absorbed in trying to solve the ultimate problem of man, the enigma of his deepest being. As a man deeply steeped in modern thought, Muir sees the answer in terms of psycho-analysis, and especially of the archetypal world and the racial subconsciousness. What is man, whence coming, where going, how living with others? The problem must be solved by the mind within the mind. The experience of his first seven years, his Orcadian childhood, moulded his mind and character, and was unconsciously to furnish much of the imagery of his poems. " Our first intuition of the world expands into vaster and vaster images, creating a myth which we act almost without knowing it."[85] That is why Muir ultimately relates everything to a Scottish (or rather an Orcadian) society. Lambing, sowing, slaughtering are part of the ritual of the life-cycle; this lifts the killing to an entirely different plane. It was in Orkney, where the lives of living men are transformed into legends, that Muir, as a boy, got his conception of life on two planes. This is for him an essential way of seeing: often, as in " The Little General,"[86] he describes the outward appearance of historic events in terms of heraldry; and their Orkney laird's annual shooting expedition becomes a " pious ritual of faith," " weaving a wordless tale where all were gathered," a " perennial emblem painted on the shield."[87]

[85] *An Autobiography*, p. 48. [86] In *The narrow Place*, *C.P.* p. 81.

[87] Cp. too, the heraldic horses in *Variations on a Time Theme*; and the description of man's history as " the great non-stop heraldic show " in " The Recurrence," or the heraldic ground of " The Grove," in *Collected Poems* (henceforth cited as *C.P.*), pp. 73 f., 78 f.

Muir's *First Poems* communicate a sense of this mysterious ritual, and in them we already find unpitying Time trapping and betraying Beauty. In *Variations on a Time Theme*, we already discern, behind the heraldry of outward appearances, something of the road we are travelling: our thought runs far ahead, beyond the horizon, but our horses, inherited "from regions dreadful past all knowledge," pace on unperturbed, and we sit in the old old saddles where untold generations (and wild beasts) have sat. This preoccupation with man's journey increases in Muir's poetry: if I could retrace my steps, Charlemagne and Augustine would live their lives backward, the whole world would revert to primeval times. Time goes on, but the past is ever-present in me, in eternity. Muir dives into the ancestral past to find the drowned original of the soul of man; he puts the question "Where was I ere I came to man?" [88] We are only the latest stage in a journey whose earlier stages we dimly divine and carry in ourselves. Can we be free of the bondage that determines our way? If we could eradicate Memory, and so unmake our present state, we should only lose "our kingdom's crown" and revert to Nothingness.[89] The history of man is not, as Nietzsche said, a circle, a wheel [90]; that is only the outward show. It is a journey of which we carry, in our myths, a knowledge of the places through which our ancestors have passed. We may now be living in the light, but we know that once "there was no road except the smothering grove." [91] The road leads on, there is no return, no standing still, even; and though we feel that we have lost it, there is only this one road.[92] The climax of recognition comes in "The Journey Back" [93]:

> Seek the beginnings, learn from whence you came . . .
>
> Through countless wanderings,
> Hastenings, lingerings,
> From far I come,
> And pass from place to place
> In a sleep-wandering pace
> To seek my home. . . .

[88] Cp. "The Fall" and "Then," in *C.P.*, pp. 48 ff., 69.
[89] Cp. "The unattained Place," in *C.P.*, pp. 59 ff.
[90] Cp. "The Recurrence," in *C.P.*, pp. 73 f.
[91] See "The Grove," in *C.P.*, pp. 78 f.
[92] Cp. "The Way" and "The Return," in *C.P.*, pp. 138, 139.
[93] In *The Labyrinth*, *C.P.*, pp. 141 ff.

Here, too, is the final answer (already foreshadowed in " The Fall ") :

For once I was all
That you can name, a child, a woman, a flower.

In poetry such as Edwin Muir's, the main requirement is integrity and sincerity of thought. But to create poetry, and not a psychological treatise, the poet must be able to project his thought into a vision, an image complete with all its essential characteristics, and to hold this vision focused in the reader's eye. In his better poems, Muir succeeds superbly. His *Autobiography* reveals the means, the faculties growing in the boy. The boy's thoughts, as formed by his farm surroundings and by the language of these people on the threshold of the ritual, grasp the fleeting impression and see it in its essentials. He fixes in his mind " the fan-shaped cast of grain " in sowing. The Scots way of speaking helps him to flash pictures together and create a highly subjective reality, as in " A small, tomato-red sun, like a jelly-fish floating in the sky, appeared and disappeared as the air grew thicker or finer." [94] As I have so often emphasised, this highly subjective way of seeing things is inherent in Scots, but Muir carries it over into English, and this enables him to penetrate the outward realities—eating and drinking, the heraldic non-stop show—and to visualise the truth that lies hidden underneath. Muir's way of expressing his abstract thought in concrete images has something essentially Scottish about it. Though he has gone deep into the English metaphysical poets of the seventeenth century, he keeps his purpose before his eyes and does not allow himself to be sidetracked into mere conceits.

Among other contemporary Scottish poets who write English, mention must at least be made of GEORGE BRUCE (1909),[95] who gives yet another answer to the question " What made us ? " His " English " is, in its own way, quite as Scottish as any Lallans. Its music is totally unlike that of Southern English : its consonants are much more prominent, and it is firmer and much more distinctly articulated. It is hard as the rocky foreshores of Bruce's home—Fraserburgh and the North-East, the granite knuckle that Scotland thrusts out into the sea—and its austerity matches the bareness of the " stone ribs of earth " whipped bare by the sea-wind over the fields.[96] And just as the softer parts of the rocks have been washed out by the waves,

[94] *An Autobiography*, p. 96.
[95] *Sea Talk* (1944) ; *Selected Poems* (Saltire Society, 1947).
[96] *Sea Talk*, pp. 20 f.

so has Bruce's English been reduced to its bare bones: even the copulative verb is often eliminated.[97] This is a general modern trend, but in Bruce it is the effect of his North-Eastern environment. He feels, too, that this cold rocky coast, rebutting the sea's violence, and "yielding to history nothing," is a "fit monument for our time."[98] His rhythms recall the battering of the waves on the rocks, or sometimes an easterly gale. Though it lacks the conventional beauty of flowers, graceful lines, and softness, the coast of the North-East is full of strength and will; and Bruce achieves a sense of beauty by means of the intense concentration with which he (and his characters) regard the things that interest them—like the boys intent on catching fish

> Inches long only, and quicksilver,
> But pink beneath the dorsal fin
> Moving with superb locomotion.[99]

Like a sculptor—Bruce has written on sculpture and addresses some of his poems to a sculptor—he chisels the essence of life out of his hard material. To the question what made man as he is in the North-East, Bruce gives his own answer. It is "A Land without Myth," without the shades of deep valleys or misty high mountains:

> Here the shadow's length is man, or the tree
> That is his, or the house he has built.[100]

It is not so much myths, a historic past, or even biological heredity that has made him what he is: rather the characters of generations of men have been determined by that impersonal force, the sea hammering against the rocks for ages. In this respect, Bruce is a mystic who sees all his own ancestral past embodied in himself, an ancestral past created by the impact of these impersonal forces:

> This which I write now
> Was written years ago
> Before my birth
> In the features of my father.
> It was stamped
> In the rock formations
> West of my hometown.
> Not I write

[97] *E.g.* "Inheritance," quoted below, p. 302 f.
[98] "Kinnaird Head," in *Sea Talk*, p. 15.
[99] "Boys among Rock Pools," in *Sea Talk*, p. 14.
[100] *Sea Talk*, p. 18.

But, perhaps, William Bruce,
Cooper . . .

And his words are merely

. . . the paint
Smeared upon
The inarticulate,

The salt crusted sea-boot
The red-eyed mackerel,
The plate shining with herring,
And many men,

Seamen and craftsmen and curers,
And behind them
The protest of hundreds of years,
The sea obstinate against the land.[101]

This is the reason why so many of Bruce's poems turn around youth, the period which is fullest of the echoes of the ancestral past; it flashes upon the boy in some impression fixed in the mind. The sea, to Bruce, is a mystic force—not a merely physical force, nor a romantic or pantheistic power. It is the force that comes closest to God.[102]

[101] "Inheritance," in *Sea Talk*, p. 10.

[102] It would be fascinating to study the role played by the sea in Scottish literature—Scots, Gaelic and English. It is amazing, in such a country, how many of its poets do not mention the sea at all (*e.g.* Burns, who lived quite close to it). It is amazing, too, that until well on in the eighteenth century it was chiefly the Dutch who fished off the Scottish coast (in 1750, 2 Scottish as against 150 Dutch vessels were fishing off the East Coast: and according to P. F. Anson, "Sea Fisheries," in *Scotland*, ed. Meikle, pp. 68-9, the Dutch had for two centuries "an almost complete monopoly of the herring industry," and even later the Scots were "inshore fishermen," not venturing far from land in their small, undecked vessels). Welsh poetry neglects the sea altogether, but Gaelic poetry regards the sea as the pathway to a distant wonderland (see "Sea Thoughts of two Races," in *T.L.S.* for 7 Aug. 1930), and delights in its sensuous beauty as seen from the shore, but views it with the terror of a land-dweller (K. H. Jackson, *Studies in early Celtic nature Poetry*, 1935, pp. 91 ff., and NOS. VI, XXII, XVII, XXXIII-V; only XXXII reflects the fascination of the sea with all its terrors). Iain Lòm thinks of the sea as always having the upper hand. Alexander MacDonald's "Iorram Cuain" and *Birlinn Chlann Raghnaill* are often described as great sea-poetry; and they certainly contain fine pictures of the tempestuous sea and much minute nautical detail. Yet they express the attitude of those who cross the sea, that hostile force, only because they needs must; and in both it is with a sigh of relief that the seafarers land, once more to sleep quietly in their beds, and take food and drink unstinted. In Scots, Barbour has one fine sea-voyage (III.690-720), but according to Mackenzie it is historically unfounded, and is perhaps borrowed from somewhere else; otherwise only the English have sea-going boats. *Wallace* and Douglas' *Eneados* display a considerable knowledge of seafaring, and each has several fine sea-passages. But except in these (and in some of the ballads), the sea is scarcely mentioned in Scots poetry until

And of all men, it is the fisherman, with his calm acceptance of the sea as it is, his assurance and his almost mystic skill, who is able to touch the mystery :

> He carries out from within something of the dark
> Concealed by heavy curtain . . .

Sometimes he seems part of this impersonal force, rather than one of us :

> The road takes him from us.
> Now the pier is his, now the tide.[103]

George Bruce's men are closely integrated with their own organic community. Under the impact of such a force, isolation is not possible ; nor can the poet himself write in a vacuum. But in one important respect this conception of man integrated with his community is quite different from the merely communal aspect of man in former periods. There is a very strong individuality, a personal emotional force behind the poems ; man is an individual as well as a communal being. Bruce achieves this largely by his half personal, half impersonal hero (" he," " the short man ") ; yet these experiences spring from specific moments of his personal life, are expressed in very personal symbols (such as the curtain half way up the stairs) and seen in flashes of very personal and momentary observation. This fixes a moment in eternity,[104] which is often expressed in the old Scots device of the contrast between smallness—as of the crab—and the vast impersonal force behind it.[105]

Side by side with the Lowland Scots Renaissance, there has been a renaissance of Gaelic poetry, and one of the most striking developments in modern Scottish poetry has been a rapprochement between

---

the eighteenth century. William Falconer, the author of *The Shipwreck* (1762), was an unwilling sailor. Scott does not have much to say about the sea ; but Stevenson used it as a fitting background for adventure. The sea plays a demonic role in J. MacDougall Hay's *Gillespie* (see above, pp. 273 f.) ; and in the works of Neil Gunn, Paterson and George Bruce, the sea has become an essential aspect of experience in modern Scottish literature. Even so, its attitude is one of passive acceptance of the sea as one of Fate's forces (cp. the similar Irish attitude in J. M. Synge's *Riders to the Sea*), not the glad acceptance of it as a path to glory which is found in Scandinavian poetry. The whole question needs further study.

[103] " The Fisherman," in *Sea Talk*, p. 26.

[104] Cp. " The Curtain " and " A Departure," *op. cit.*, pp. 12, 34.

[105] Cp. " Sea Talk," *op. cit.*, pp. 19 ff.

Gael and Lowland Scot in literature. The voice of the Highlands and Islands is raised in the Gaelic poems of Sorley Maclean (Somhairle Mac GhillEathain) and Derick Thomson (Ruaraidh MacThomais), and in the Gaelic, English and Scots verse of George Campbell Hay (Deorsa Caimbeal Hay). It is also unmistakable in the English poems of Joseph Macleod (" Adam Drinan ") [106] and Norman McCaig.

George Campbell Hay (1915),[107] the son of John MacDougall Hay from Tarbert, and, like Douglas Young, a classical scholar, has written some very musical verse which has been worthily set to music by Francis George Scott and Mrs Oliver Brown. His Gaelic poems follow the poetical tradition of that language, but perhaps with greater economy in the use of words.[108] We find the same approach to a poem, the same artistic vision and style in his verse in English, and here for the first time the genuine voice of the Gael can be heard in poetry outside Gaelic. His poems are knit much more closely in consonantal pattern and vowel harmonies than is usual in English poetry :

> Leaving those men, whose hearts
> are hearths that have no fire . . . [109]

The expression is largely substantival (" they had the fishing for school and learning ") and the syntax often Gaelic. But Hay has invented an idiom that just suggests enough of the Gaelic expressiveness and subtlety without overdoing it. His sentences are often impressions put side by side without grammatical connexion, the elements of a metaphor juxtaposed ; yet they imply a logical variation of his theme, as in this impression of a fishing boat at sea :

> Rain from windward, sharp and blinding ;
> Sweet to hear my darling tramping
> On her way, the seas unminding,
> Swinging forefoot wounding, stamping.[110]

Or in this glimpse of Ireland as seen from the sea :

> Branches rocking, waves of shadow, all the trees
> Becked and swung in Glennan to the singing breeze.[111]

[106] Poetry : *The Cove* (1940) ; *Men of the Rocks* (1942). Poetic plays : *Women of the happy Island* (1941) ; *The Ghosts of the Strath* (1943).

[107] *Wind on Loch Fyne* (Scots, English and Gaelic, 1948) ; *Fuaran Sléibh* (Gaelic, 1948) ; *O na ceithir Airdean* (Gaelic, 1952)

[108] " Ceithir Gaothan na h-Albann," in *Fuaran Sléibh*, p. 33.

[109] " Kintyre," in *Wind on Loch Fyne*, p. 2.

[110] " Ardlamont," *op. cit.*, p. 3.

[111] " The Kerry Shore," *op. cit.*, p. 7.

This is coupled with a vivid sensuousness, a delight in the pictures that are suggested by the outer world, yet are of the poet's own making, and have much animation :

Listenan tae the [a]burns [b]gang doon— [a] *torrents* [b] *go*
Listenan tae the wund in the [a]*rashes*— [a] *rushes*
Watchan Autumn doon the [a]braes, [a] *hillsides*
A [a]spate o gowd amang the bracken. [a] *flood of gold*

Watch him rinn alang the glen—
Listenan tae the wund in the rashes—
Edge the bramble leaves wi bluid,
Kendle fire on [a]rowan branches.[112] [a] *mountain ash*

His whole " Scots Arcadia " is of such images and imaginings ; even its place-names are " like the sounding sea " and " sweet to the mouth." [113] As often in Gaelic poetry, the structure of most of Hay's poems has no climax : he turns his object round and round, finding new facets in it, presenting metaphor after metaphor to give it a new meaning :

Little you heed, or care to change with changes,
To go like a broken branch in the grip of a torrent.[114]

When all aspects are exhausted, the circle is closed, like the Celtic snake of wisdom with its tail in its mouth. The description of the waves in " The Kerry Shore " [115] could be from a bardic poem :

Waves green-sided, bright, white-crested
Glittered gay.

A poem to a boat like " Seaker, Reaper " [116] reads like some Gaelic song to a sword, with its reproduction of sounds and exhaustion of epithets, and its presentation of the boat as a sensitive living being that would " whiten the world's watter." It is remarkable that these Gaelic traits are usually more distinct in his English than in his Lallans poems ; the latter tend to have more emphasis and substance. It may be doubted whether Hay could have expressed in Scots the same subtle sensitivity as in the Fisherman, who is put to work on

[112] " Scots Arcadia," *op. cit.*, pp. 2 f.
[113] " Kintyre," *op. cit.*, p. 2.
[114] " To a Loch Fyne Fisherman," *op. cit.*, p. 5.
[115] Above, n. 111.
[116] *Wind on Loch Fyne*, pp. 34 ff.

the roads as " unemployed " while on the Loch the herring shoals wander :

> Along the shore the [a]solans strike, [a] *gannets*
> And rise, and strike again in spray,
> And I myself, and all my like,
> Can curse our fate and look away.[117]

The expression by way of picture, yes ; but the delight in it against his own will? Or the looking away at such a moment?[118] This seems to me distinctly a West Coast attitude. Perhaps Hay's finest lyric—it almost sings itself—is " The old Fisherman " with the refrain " My dancing days for fishing are over."[119] Many of the Gaelic features are here, and to get the full value of the sounds one must read it like a Gaelic poem, dwelling on the stresses and letting the consonants after a short stress swing out to their full :

> The éyes that would gáze in the sún wáver.

Then the poem assumes the music of a pibroch.

But we must not regard Hay merely as a Gaelic voice ; he is a poet in his own right. In his early lyrics, he can so purify an emotion that it soars to heaven ; but he can also relate it with a deeper insight into life, a deeper awareness of the forces that have gone to man's making : wind, sea—all have gone to mould him.[120] Even in his earlier poems, Hay's awareness of the irony of fate gives him occasionally a twinge of pain. Wartime experience intensified these painful feelings, and in the wild, metaphysical speculations of " *Esta Selva selvaggia* "[121] his agony finds its bitterest expression :

> Yesterday ? We saw it die
> Among the shellbursts in the sky . . .
>
> Man, violent against his will
> Tore himself open, looked his fill
> And saw ; and he is shuddering still.

[117] " The Fisherman speaks," *op. cit.*, p. 10.

[118] The impulse which here causes Hay to look away is of course quite different from that which causes Henryson to turn his eye away from grief in *T.Cr.*, and S. G. Smith to look out of the window in " For my newborn Son " !

[119] *Wind on Loch Fyne*, p. 12. There is a fine setting by F. G. Scott. " My dancing days " is a Gaelic-English expression, and Hay had heard a Loch Fyne fisherman say the words that form the refrain.

[120] *E.g.* " The Fisherman," in *Wind on Loch Fyne*, p. 15.

[121] *Op. cit.*, pp. 20 ff.

SORLEY MACLEAN (SOMHAIRLE MAC GHILLEATHAIN, 1911)[122] is a less traditional Gaelic poet, and his poems have from the beginning a new economy of language, and more intellectual substance than most earlier Gaelic poetry. In his love songs, personal hopes and fears are closely and almost metaphysically integrated with socialism and with Europe's cry of agony (" gaoir na h-Eòrpa ") during the Spanish Civil War. His Calvary is a backroom of poverty in Edinburgh and the slums of Glasgow.[123] Maclean has published English prose translations of many of his poems ; many of them have also been translated into Scots verse by Douglas Young (in *Auntran Blads*), R. G. Sutherland (" Robert Garioch "), J. M. Russell, Sydney Goodsir Smith, Dugald MacColl, and the Rev. John Mackechnie. Most of these verse translations, however, do not give an authentic idea of the originals ; despite their many points of contact, the idioms of Scots and Gaelic poetry are too different for that. A study of the divergences will reveal much of the difference of characters of Gaelic and Scots expression.

In translation, the hard enamelling and sharp transparent clarity of the Gaelic tends to be replaced by a few broad strokes of the brush. As a case in point, here is the last stanza of *Dàin do Eimhir*, XLIII :

> Agus air creachainn chéin fhàsmhor
> chinn blàthmhor craobh nan teud,
> 'na meangach duillich t'aodann,
> mo chiall is aogas reuil.[124]

[And on a [a]mountain-peak, [b]distant, [c]overgrown, — [a] *creachainn,* [b] *chéin* [c] *fhàsmhor*
grew, [a]full of blossom, the Tree of Harp-strings, — [a] *blàthmhor*
among its leafy branches your face—
[a]my reason and likeness of a star.] — [a] *mo chiall*

And here is Young's rendering :

> The tree o strings was blawan bonnie
> Owre far awa on a growthy cairn,
> Among its [a]fullyerie your face, — [a] *foliage*
> My reason, and a semblance o a [a]stern.[125] — [a] *star*

[122] *Dàin do Eimhir agus Dàin eile* (*Songs to Eimhir and other songs*, 1943) ; and jointly with R. G. Sutherland (" Robert Garioch "), *Seventeen Poems for Sixpence* (1940). Some of Maclean's best work, esp. *An Cuilithionn* (*The Cuillin*), remains substantially unpublished ; some portions of *An Cuilithionn* have however appeared in *Lines*, 7 (Jan. 1955), pp. 7 ff.

[123] " Calbharaigh " (*Dàin eile*, II), in *Dàin do Eimhir*, pp. 54, 101.

[124] *Dàin do Eimhir*, pp. 36, 100.

[125] *Auntran Blads*, pp, 12-13.

Maclean's Gaelic stanza embodies a pattern of rhyme, assonance, and alliteration that binds it all tightly together in a unity that cannot adequately be carried over into Scots, in which Young's purely decorative alliterations (" blawan bonnie," " fullyerie your face," " semblance of a stern ") at most serve to unify each a single phrase. Unlike some of the older bards, who often allowed metre to get the upper hand, Maclean keeps his sentence firmly under control. The metrical pattern has all its traditional intricacy, but in all its wanderings the sense traces out to its conclusion one unbroken and inherently logical line, meandering like a Pictish snake ; at no point is it possible to stop or break or take off. In accordance with a general European convention, Young's stanza, however, contains two movements, one rising, the other falling. The loss of Maclean's cogent integration of images and associations also detracts from the total effect ; and even if " tree of strings " and " fullyerie " were not separated, in Young's version, by more than a full line, Young's stanza would not have the same indissoluble unity as Maclean's. With its intellectual clarity, Maclean's terse Gaelic has no room for such vaguely evocative expressions as Young's " blawan bonnie " or " owre far," and the Scots terms by which Young translates them do not adequately render the precision of the Gaelic words *creachainn* (the bare summit slopes of a mountain), *teud* (harp strings), *mo chiall* (my object of thought, object of all my thought). Young's are not the only Scots verse translations of Maclean's poetry in which the Scots, though sometimes pithier, is less subtle in emphasis and less specific than the original Gaelic. Often, too, the Scots has a grimness of humour, a sententious tone, closer to the spirit of Thomas Carlyle than to anything in the original.

Just because of these differences the increasing contacts between Gaelic and other contemporary Scottish poetry have been mutually advantageous. It is perhaps owing to them that Scottish is of tougher intellectual fibre than modern Irish Gaelic poetry ; and in the past (unless I am mistaken in thinking that the flashes of vision which occur so frequently in Scots speech are largely attributable to centuries of contact between Scots and Gaelic) they have greatly enriched and intensified the imagery of Scottish poetry. They seem also to hold out the hope that Scottish culture may have, in future, a much broader basis.

This ramble through modern Scottish poetry cannot hope to be either definitive, or comprehensive. Many poets have had to be left out, some of them as good as (or perhaps better than) one or two of those whose poetry we have discussed. Nothing has been said about Alexander Scott (1920) [126] with his hard brilliance and contemporary relevance, of William Jeffrey (1894-1946) [127] with his rhapsodic modern rhythms, his metaphysics; of the "apocalyptic" poets W. S. Graham (1917),[128] J. F. Hendry,[129] and Hamish Henderson [130]; of Norman McCaig, of A. D. Mackie,[131] of Tom Scott, Maurice Lindsay,[132] and a number of others. I have not made it my aim to give an exhaustive account of contemporary Scottish poetry, but rather to illustrate the persistence and development, in our own times, of the Scots poetic tradition; and I hope that I have succeeded in showing that whether they write Scots, Gaelic, or some kind of English, contemporary Scottish poets have developed a variety of idioms all having a specifically Scottish flavour and able to express (so far as Scottish can be distinguished from British and international) the thoughts, feelings, and emotions of the Scottish mind. I personally am convinced that both Scots and English verse have come to stay in Scotland for some time at least; not because the one could not express what the other can—Grieve and Smith, Muir and Bruce are evidence enough—but because *one* poet cannot express in Scots what he can in English, and *vice versa.* In Scotland, Scots and English poetry are really cousins, though they sometimes take too literally a Scottish proverb that we have already quoted: "Scarting and biting is the Scots folk's wooing."

[126] *The latest in Elegies* (1949). *Selected Poems* (Saltire Society, 1950).

[127] See his *Selected Poems,* ed. A. Scott (1951).

[128] *Cage without Grievance* (1942); *The seven Journeys* (1944); *The Nightfishing* (1945); *Second Poems: The white Threshold* (1949).

[129] *The bombed Happiness* (1941); *The orchestral Mountain* (1943).

[130] *Elegies for the Dead in Cyrenaica* (1948).

[131] *Poems in two Tongues* (1928); *Sing a Song for Scotland* (1944).

[132] *No Crown for Laughter* (1943); *The Enemies of Love* (1946); *Hurlygush* (1948); *At the Wood's Edge* (1950); *Ode for St Andrew's Night* (1950). *Selected Poems* (Saltire Society, 1947).

2. Scottish Drama

Not until the twentieth century was there anything that can properly be called a Scottish theatre or a Scottish tradition of drama. During the late Middle Ages, Scotland seems to have had its own popular mysteries, morality plays, and pageants, but perhaps not so many of them as other countries. An Aberdeen mystery play called *The haly Blude* belongs to the middle of the fifteenth century, and Dunbar mentions an historical pageant of Bruce and the Stewarts with which the same city welcomed James IV some sixty years later.[1] Gavin Douglas is said to have written " Comoedias," and, as Dunbar again bears witness, pageants were frequently presented at the court of James IV. In the next generation, Sir David Lyndsay staged a pageant to welcome James V's Queen ; and in " The Entertainment," written when Charles I visited Edinburgh in 1633, even Drummond of Hawthornden lent his pen to a similar purpose.

" The Droichis [Dwarf's] Part," sometimes attributed to Dunbar,[2] suggests that there were popular performances as well, and we know that there were Robin Hood plays that had to be forbidden. The Reformation at first made full use of the stage as a platform of attack. We have already discussed Lyndsay's *Satire of the Thrie Estaitis*. James Wedderburn, of the *Gude and Godlie Ballatis*, is said to have written several tragedies against the corruption of the old Church, and it is because of one of them that he had to flee the country ; we know that his play on *John the Baptist* was performed in his native town Dundee. Every town in Scotland had similar plays,[3] which even John Knox attended, against Catholic tyranny ; and as an exile in France George Buchanan wrote Latin plays on Jephthah and John the Baptist, and translated Euripides.

Soon, however, the Kirk set its face against the enjoyment of such worldly entertainment as the Robin Hood plays. In 1575 the General Assembly went further and banned " clerk-plays or comedies based upon the canonical scriptures " : but as long as it remained at Edinburgh, the Court continued to favour the theatre. Mary of

[1] 64. " To Aberdein " (in Dunbar's *Poems*, ed. MACKENZIE, pp. 137 ff.), ll. 33 ff.

[2] BANN., VOL. II, pp. 315 ff. ; 86. " The Manere of the Crying of ane Playe," in Dunbar's *Poems*, ed. MACKENZIE, pp. 170 ff.

[3] See the introduction to *Gude and Godlie Ballatis*, ed. A. F. Mitchell, S.T.S., 1897.

Guise saw a Latin drama in 1567, and the Regent Moray a play by Robert Sempill the following year ; while English players performed in Edinburgh and Aberdeen, though four kirk sessions pronounced their ban, in 1594, 1599, and 1601. The Court was the home of *Philotus*, a romantic comedy in strophic verse sometimes attributed to James VI, and of the Senecan *Monarchick Tragedies* of Sir William Alexander, Earl of Stirling. But with the removal of the Court, the curtain drops for good. During the next hundred years, we do find a few Scottish playwrights writing an occasional drama and putting it on in London, but none of any importance (unless we can regard Ben Jonson as a Scotsman) : Sir Thomas St Serfe (Sydserf), David Crawfurd, Catherine Trotter (*alias* Cockburn), James Thomson. *The Assembly* (*c.* 1700, printed 1722 ; perhaps by Archibald Pitcairne) is one of the very few such plays that has a Scottish setting or even a single Scottish character.

Later in the eighteenth century, as we have seen, Allan Ramsay gained a bridgehead for the drama in Edinburgh itself. True, his ecclesiastical opponents succeeded in their attempt to have his theatre closed down : but by appealing to the taste of the countryfolk, the pastoral charm of *The Gentle Shepherd* adventitiously, and in the long run, promoted interest in drama. The somewhat rhetorical Gothicism of John Home's *Douglas* (1755) also appealed strongly to contemporary taste, but as a minister of the Church of Scotland, it was brave of him to have it staged in Edinburgh, and in fact he had to resign his ministry. The dream of a theatre haunted many later Scottish writers. Burns dreamt it ; the nineteenth century saw the (sometimes embarrassingly) unsuccessful dramatic attempts of Walter Scott, Hogg, Galt, Stevenson, John Davidson, William Sharp (" Fiona Macleod "). Sometimes the dream took a more tangible shape. Byron's *Cain* has a thematic importance for Scottish twentieth-century drama ; and Joanna Bailie's plays might have been a starting point for a Scottish theatre. It was a Scotsman, William Archer, who helped to introduce Ibsen into the English theatre. And James Matthew Barrie (1860-1937) was the first really outstanding playwright of Scottish birth. As is obvious in *Peter Pan*, *The Admirable Crichton*, *Mary Rose*, or *Dear Brutus*, Barrie's plays must rather be regarded as a contribution —certainly a fine one—to English rather than to Scottish drama ; and for this reason they lie outside our present scope.

Though there is no Scottish tradition of drama, there is much that is intensely dramatic in Scottish literature (and history) : the flytings, the ballads, the dramatic monologues. Perhaps no other European literature is intrinsically so dramatic. We have seen how Scottish poets are accustomed to enter into the minds of their characters and to see the world from their point of view ; we have seen, too, that the Scots tongue, with its trick of speaking in character, is itself inherently dramatic. Yet there is no Scottish drama. This is usually explained as simply a consequence of Presbyterianism. But I wonder whether that is the whole story. Scottish literature has many dramatic qualities : but has it yet seen that combination of sustained effort with selective discipline and unity of vision which alone would have taken these qualities and made great drama out of them ? Perhaps it is not out of place to recollect that Scottish Gaelic, with its many similarities of theme and *genre*, never developed a drama, and that Ireland and Wales have only done so since the Celtic Revival of modern times. Even today the drama is the weakest branch of the tree of modern Scottish literature, and its future growth and shape is not yet recognisable. Drama requires the fulfilment of so many material conditions—adequate finance, buildings and stage equipment, a public, a critical spirit, and a habit of theatre-going—that it takes much longer to mature than most forms of literature. Even then it will not flourish unless it has a sufficiently receptive public and actors capable of " putting it across." Fundamentally, drama is a communal art : it speaks from a platform to the community, and about the community's problems. In the last analysis, therefore, everything depends on the relationship between actors and audience, and in his one-act comedy *Choosing a Play* [4] Neil M. Gunn puts his finger on a sore spot when he points out that the reader of a novel has plenty of opportunities of correcting any misinterpretation that the reader may have made, but that once the audience has laughed, a play will be labelled a comedy and judged accordingly.

The impetus for the emergence of a Scottish drama came from the repertory movement, and especially from the early efforts and achievements of Dublin's Abbey Theatre. The influence of the Abbey Theatre, and of the Irish drama which it helped to foster, was most obvious in the Glasgow Repertory Theatre before the first war, but it has continued in subtler ways long after that. It is palpable in the two plays that may be said to have started the turn towards the larger possibilities of the native theme, John Brandane's *The Glen is mine*

[4] *In Scottish one-act Plays*, ed. J. Macnair Reid (1935). It is revealing to compare this with what has been said about sculpture (above, p. 188, n. 17).

and Gordon Bottomley's *Gruach*, both produced by the young Scottish National Theatre Society early in 1923, at the Athenæum, Glasgow. The Scottish National Players have since then produced some six dozen new Scottish plays. The most promising asset of the drama in Scotland today is the amateur Scottish Community Drama Association, of which Gordon Bottomley had been Honorary President. It has grown to some 750 clubs and 2200 individual members, and its annual National Festival (its twenty-third was in 1955), with preliminary, divisional, and final rounds, makes the drama an essential element in the life of the community, chiefly in rural areas. Its libraries, holiday courses, and publications elevate drama above the level of the circus, and for the first time in half a millennium the drama is becoming a living force in Scotland. Among the theatres that devote themselves to drama as a form of art instead of cheap entertainment mention must be made of the Gateway, Edinburgh ; the Glasgow Citizens' Theatre (1943) ; the Dundee Repertory Theatre ; the Perth Theatre ; the Pitlochry Festival Theatre ; and the Edinburgh International Festival, with its revival of historic Scottish dramas,[5] and its occasional commissioning of a modern Scottish play.[6] The attitude of the Kirk, too, has changed : ministers act as adjudicators ; the Gateway is sponsored by the Church of Scotland ; and the very Assembly Hall has been opened, not only to Lyndsay's *Satyre of the Thrie Estaitis*—to which the Kirk may well have felt itself indebted—but also to other plays.[7] Still, to a visitor from the Continent Scottish theatre and drama seem far from secure, and the recent dissolution of a well-known Scottish repertory company [8] is a sign of alarm. And how successful has the theatre movement been in creating a Scottish drama ?

Modern Scottish drama inevitably comprises much romantic history, clan warfare, and ballad matter, much kailyard, much but-and-ben, much superficial comedy of manners, and many adaptations of novels. In order to show how much effort has been made to penetrate to the spiritual centre of the community, its beliefs, tenets, and attitudes—which, after all, is really the beginning and end of drama—I propose here to single out three contemporary Scottish playwrights for special consideration, namely John MacIntyre (" John

[5] *E.g.* Lyndsay's *Thrie Estaitis* ; Ramsay's *Gentle Shepherd* ; Home's *Douglas*.

[6] *E.g.* O. H. Mavor (" James Bridie "), *The Queen's Comedy* ; Eric Linklater, *The Atom Doctor*.

[7] *E.g.* Thornton Wilder, *A Life in the Sun* (1955).

[8] The Wilson Barrett Company, 1955.

Brandane "), Gordon Bottomley, and O. H. Mavor (" James Bridie "). This means that I shall have to ignore much experimental work that has been done by some of the younger Scottish playwrights (Robert Kemp,[9] Alexander Scott,[10] Ewan MacColl, William Douglas Home,[11] Joe Corrie) and by the main protagonists of plays in Lallans [12] (Robert Maclellan,[13] Alexander Reid [14]) and in Gaelic (Hector MacIver).[15]

The plays of DR JOHN MACINTYRE (" JOHN BRANDANE," 1869-1947) mark the point when Scottish drama was leaving the initial stage of imitation. As a Western Islander he could not quite escape the shadow of Alan Breck,[16] or at least John Splendid,[17] and the example of the Anglo-Irish theatre was always before his eyes. But while the Gaelicised language of the latter often merely strikes an attitude, the Gaelic undertones of MacIntyre's Scots or English are genuine. His language is of a harder quality, shows better observation (" And isn't it Morag herself that is in it ? "), and, though suggestion might sometimes have been better than completeness, catches the true idiom. *The Glen is mine* is certainly his finest play. Though it was a happy idea to use a well-known pibroch to sound the theme, MacIntyre does not labour the point ; he just strikes the chords of half-conscious longings. The play touches upon the problem of life in the Highlands : is it to be the old healthy way with deer and sheep and heather (and getting up at three of a cold morning and wearing yourself out carrying loads), or progress and science and industrialisation (and money-grubbing and another Glasgow slum) ? The complications solve themselves too easily, in fact they almost vanish ; that is a pity,

[9] Author of *Henrietta, M.D.* ; *The other dear Charmer* (Burns and Clarinda) ; *Let Wives tak Tent* (translated from Molière) ; and various other comedies and radio plays. It was he who adapted *The Thrie Estaitis* (1949, in *The Scots Review*) and *The Gentle Shepherd* for the Edinburgh Festival.

[10] Author of *Right Royal* (received Arts Council Award and Trophy of the Scottish Community Drama Association, 1950) ; etc.

[11] Author of *The Chiltern Hundreds* ; *Now Barrabbas* ; etc.

[12] It is still too early to determine the value of contemporary plays in Scots (which must be distinguished from dialect plays in the old sense) : but after hearing, *e.g.* Reid's Lallans play *The World's Wonder*, one feels that in English it could not have had the same sharpness and relevancy ; its comedy is shot through with serious meaning, its feelings have a harsh edge to them, and it is owing to these essentially Scottish characteristics that when necessary it attains a higher level without solemnity. The graphic, intensely damatic character of Scots speech should give Lallans drama a fine opportunity.

[13] *Jeddart's Justice* ; *Toom Byres* ; *The Laird of Torwatletie* ; *Jamie the Saxt.*

[14] *The World's Wonder* ; *The Lass wi' the muckle Mou'.*

[15] Most of his Gaelic plays have been for radio.

[16] Cp. *The Lifting* (1925).

[17] Cp. *The Glen is mine* (1923, printed 1925).

for the problem is there : it recurs at short intervals in the correspondence columns of *The Scotsman.* But the figure of Angus, the crofter, is a fine study of a Gaelic character.

The second performance that started the Scottish theatre movement on its uphill path was that of *Gruach* in March 1923. Though born in Yorkshire, GORDON BOTTOMLEY (1874-1948) [18] was Scottish on his mother's side, and in the later stages of his career consciously tried to foster a Scottish drama. As a poet, he had fallen under the combined influence of Rossetti's dreamy sensualism and of the early Yeats. In his early poetry and verse plays he turned to Celtic and Northern legend,[19] and touched Scottish history only through Shakespeare (Gruach is Lady Macbeth on the first step of her ambitious career). When Gordon Bottomley first visited Scotland to see *Gruach* performed by the Scottish National Theatre Society he felt that he belonged to his mother's home : " This is my place : I am part of it and belong to it." It was not only that Bottomley turned for inspiration almost exclusively to the Scottish past, worked predominantly with Scottish amateurs, or in later plays sometimes used the vernacular : as he grew older, he wove a closer and closer texture of historical, local, cultural allusions, and so created a canvas on which he could depict the essential facts of life as he saw them. He too puts the question what man is, and the answer that he gives is a very personal one :

> Mortals are other than they know :
> Memories fashioned them long ago.

The recurring memories that shape men are the basic theme of all his plays. Most of them centre around some deed or crime of passion —in which Scottish history with its ballads and clan loyalties is rich enough—but a crime that carries some element of redemption in it : some love in the killing hate, repentance before the deed was cold. These unresolved passions of evil mingled with good tendencies are unseen forces that draw the participants, or later generations, to the place of perpetration by some " miracle of sympathy " ; longings, tenderness reach out like disembodied hands. The persons do not know why they have to come, but their known or half-known memories drive them to the place where the deed finds expiation by its element

[18] See *Poems and Plays* (1953), and other volumes mentioned below.
[19] *King Lear's Wife and other Plays* (1920) ; *Gruach and Britain's Daughter* (1921).

of virtue. Personal hatreds are bridged, and the bridge passes through the sphere of eternity, years, hundreds of years after the event. What was " knit by fear and tragedy " is at last knit by love, and the guilt is cancelled. The obsessing problem of guilt and expiation, good and evil, strikes a keynote in Scottish drama from Byron to O. H. Mavor.

Bottomley, we see, was not concerned with individual events, or with fate as such, but with events and fate as factors determining the actions of subsequent generations. To express this he needed a form of drama that could deal with more than everyday life. He found it in Yeats's discovery of a stylised chamber-play using poetry, movement, dance, masks, and the simplified symbolism, as Yeats had developed them from the old Japanese Nō plays. Like Yeats or Masefield, Bottomley aimed at the kind of dramatic poetry that can be performed in any large room. His *Scenes and Plays* (1929) were written for Oxford recitals and for the Scottish Association for the Speaking of Verse, and it was Bottomley who started the Choric Speaking Movement. The early pieces which marked his progress towards a new verse drama were more often lyrical, or narrative with lyrical insets, than dramatic ; they were, in fact, poetry for recitation. But with his *Lyric Plays* (1932) and *Choric Plays* (1939) Bottomley achieved genuine dramatic intensity in this new form.

Bottomley was no mere imitator in the form of chamber-drama. He took over the stylisation of movement, the chorus, and the idea of the curtain bearers, but he developed this, sometimes introducing a living curtain. He used the chorus in a subtler way than Yeats ; not only as a chorus of waves, winds, or the snow, not only as comment, but as an inner voice, as an expression of a character's conscience. In his later plays, the Scots used by the chorus—in " The Bower of Wandel " a Border shepherd and his daughters, in " The White Widow " a few fishwives—is sharply realistic, which makes the chorus itself seem more relevant and is associated (as in " Marsaili's Weeping ") with the intensification of a personal (and Scottish) note of harshness that is reminiscent of C. M. Grieve's " love wi' a scunner in't." [20] Finally, and above all, it is chiefly by means of the chorus that Bottomley establishes his different time-levels, and shows how the old

[20] This also entailed a resuscitation of the true fatalistic spirit of the ballads (cp. " The White Widow," about Mary Stuart ; first performed at Aberdeen, 1936) ; Bottomley had formerly used ballad motifs to express his own lyrical mood, or, sometimes, " Celtic twilight."

memories fashion our lives. Here he is completely independent of Yeats, and this form is his own ; more than in Yeats, it is essential to the idea that has to be expressed.

Bottomley himself compared his plays to string quartets : " a chamber drama to set beside our most precious heritage of chamber-music." [21] Dr O. H. Mavor (" James Bridie," 1888-1951),[22] on the other hand, wrote for the full limelight of a big stage. Though his name was usually connected with the London West End theatres, many of his plays were performed by Scottish amateur or professional companies, such as the Perth Repertory Theatre, the Edinburgh Lyceum, the Lyric Theatre, Glasgow ; and Mavor was the moving spirit behind the Glasgow Citizens' Theatre. All his plays have a highly cultivated and sophisticated wit, and an intellectual restlessness, that give them considerable depth. It is wit of a very delicate fibre, and there are so many layers of meaning, like the folds of a delicate veil or lace, that clumsy fingers would only tear them should they try to separate them. There is much more in it than meets the eye, much subtle questioning of values, much strict searching of the heart. All this is characteristically Scottish, and Mavor grows more obstinately Scottish with every play. He cannot take things for granted, or at their face value, and make the best of it Like so many Scottish writers, he *worries* about good and evil, sin and righteousness, charity and faith, courage and goodwill ; they are not simple formulas, but terribly mixed up, and it is not easy at all to unravel the good. Mavor's uneasy, worrying, self-torturing mind is always trying to get behind the surface. He flares up at the complacency of people who " know " what is good, what evil : as black and white is necessary to make a print recognisable, so " we cannot perceive the Universe except as a pattern of reciprocating opposites." [23] This is a note that is heard in Byron's *Cain*, and, more faintly, Gordon Bottomley sounds it too. True, it is also struck by Irish and Welsh [24] playwrights,

[21] *Scenes and Plays* (1929), Note.

[22] See esp. *The Anatomist and other Plays* (incl. *Tobias and the Angel* ; *The amazed Evangelist*), 1931 ; *Colonel Wotherspoon and other Plays* (incl. *What it is to be young* ; *The dancing Bear* ; *The Girl who did not want to go to Kuala Lumpur*), 1934 ; *The King of Nowhere and other Plays* (incl. *Babes in the Wood* ; *The last Trump*), 1938 ; *Susannah and the Elders and other Plays* (incl. *What say they ?* ; *The golden Legend of Shults* ; *The Kitchen Comedy*), 1940 ; *Plays for plain People* (incl. *Lancelot* ; *Holy Island* ; *Mr Bolfry* ; *Jonah 3* ; *The Sign of the Prophet Jonah* ; *The Dragon and the Dove*), 1944.

[23] *Mr Bolfry.*

[24] *E.g.* Richard Hughes ; and H. A. Jones, who worries about saints and sinners.

but in Scotland, common though it may be, it seems to have been heightened and intensified by Presbyterianism—and by the Calvinist intellectual tradition.

Much of Mavor's work is really a clash with Presbyterianism, not in the narrower sense of fighting out problems of Scottish importance, but in its wider implications. His comedies are not problem plays: what Bridie has to say is delivered with so much wit and enjoyable humour that we sometimes are not conscious of the fine barbs he leaves in the wound, but only of a general tenderness to the touch. The issue of Presbyterianism is dealt with directly in *What say they?*, a devious satire on the plight of a creative mind involved in the atmosphere of surface respectability and outbreaks of rectorial hooliganism in a very Presbyterian Scottish university; it is the subject of *The golden Legend of Shults* (1939) and *Mr Bolfry* (1943). The latter play is laid in a "Wee Free" (U.F. Church) parish in the Western Highlands, the most strictly Sabbatarian part of Britain. (An English Sunday is a roaring feast in comparison.) The visitors from London—Scots and English—are deeply disgusted with this "narrow-mindedness" and totalitarian clerical interference, but in discussing this with the minister they are easily bested by his superior arguments, and grudgingly admit that after all it was Calvin who invented modern democracy. But when the visitors raise the Devil in the person of the black-coated Mr Bolfry, the picture changes. As in Milton, Goethe, Blake, Hogg, and Burns, he is a proud and educated Devil, and the minister finds himself usually in agreement with Mr Bolfry in his logic against his irreverent visitors: the Devil is really the rationalist nature of Calvinism! It is only when the minister forgets his rationalist logic and relies on blind, purely irrational faith that he worsts the Devil.

The De'il still has his familiar attraction for Scottish writers. He appears again in Mavor's last, perhaps his finest play, *The Baikie Charivari, or The seven Prophets* (1952, printed 1953). This is a combination of the Punch and Judy legend with that of Pontius Pilate (a traditional one), and James Pounce-Pellot's middle name is MacArthur. But above all it is Mavor's variation of Goethe's *Faust*—you need a fist for a punch—from the Prologue to the Walpurgisnacht. Pounce-Pellot aspires to perfection as an administrator, an artist, a thinker. Mephistopheles is a minister, who thinks he is worshipping God, but in fact is hearing the voice of the De'il, who wants to shake Pellot's Spiritual Pride. The play is on two levels—real life in prose, the idea behind it in some kind of verse—and ends with Pellot slaying the cocksure seven prophets : politician, anarchist, aristocrat, artist, minister, publisher, psycho-analyst. Then he asks the De'il :

P.-P. Can I wait for time ?
DE'IL. I dinna ken.
P.-P. . . . I've killed all those fools who pretended to know . . . the soothsayers littered about the stage . . . I must jest again and await my reply.

Elsewhere, Mavor deals indirectly with Presbyterianism. Jonah [25] is another " Calvinist " who has put down dancing, secular songs, images, sacred places, and who is in vain warned by the whale that he need not assume that God always keeps him informed of His most secret purposes. The priest who is one of the party to civilise the Holy Island [26] at the time of King Lot of Orkney, finally recognises that the Lord had taught his disciples first the alphabet, then the mysteries, while we have not learned the alphabet, and do not know how to live in peace with our neighbour, but yet claim to understand the mysteries. But of course his Church will have none of that.

Mavor knew that his moral idiom and his delight in theological argument were both characteristically Scottish,[27] and his characters like to argue especially about momentous subjects which they " thoroughly understand "—such as the Creation, or the nature of dreams [28]—or merely for the sake of argument.[29] His plays are all thoroughly modern, for though some of them purport to deal with Biblical or Apocryphal subjects,[30] and others are based on Arthurian legends,[31] all are concerned with problems of contemporary life, society (the English gentleman), and civilisation. Why this " disguise "? Mavor maintained that there are not many really original stories. By taking a few of the oldest and best-known, looking at them from new angles, seeking out new meanings, and devising new variations of them, he tried to elicit new responses. It is theme and variation

[25] *Jonah and the Whale* (1932) ; rewritten as a radio play, *The Sign of the Prophet Jonah* (1942), and as *Jonah 3* (1942).

[26] *Holy Island* (1942).

[27] Cp. the preface to *Susannah and the Elders* (1940).

[28] *Jonah and the Whale.*

[29] *E.g.* esp. *Susannah and the Elders.*

[30] E.g. *Tobias and the Angel* (1930) ; *Susannah and the Elders* (1937) ; *Jonah and the Whale* (1932, 1942) ; *The Dragon and the Dove* (1942) ; etc.

[31] *Holy Isle* (1942) ; *Lancelot* (1944).

all over again, and the comparison with music would also suggest the many overtones to be heard with the basic melody. Like so many Scottish writers of the past and present, Mavor deliberately assumed a subjective point of view : " truth has as many faces as a nightmare," and according to him you have to find and *create* your own truth.[32] By presenting the story of *Susannah and the Elders* as seen by the Elders, who cannot tell how they slid into this baffling business, he creates an authentically tragic atmosphere. *The Golden Legend of Shults* is not a problem play about " what makes a crook," but a human story seen from the point of view of the " crook," whom people just will not let alone.

Was it because he had had a Scottish education that Mavor was so fond of Biblical analogies ? Whether it was or not, he used them for a specially Scottish purpose, for by projecting the problem of modern Anglo-Scottish tensions back into a Biblical past, he gave it a new look, and also endowed it with universal significance. In their dealings with their captors (or hosts) the Assyrians, Mavor's Hebrews show the defensive self-consciousness typical of national minorities (" We lost our homes because we were much fonder of talking and arguing and quarrelling than of fighting to defend them ") ; and though the Assyrianised among them consider the Assyrians as perfectly humane and sympathetic, the militant Hebrews have a very different tale to tell.[33] The detrimental effect of social, national, and racial tension, resentment, and prejudice is, of course, one of the commonest themes of all contemporary Western literature : but Mavor displays a heightened awareness of such tensions which presumably reflects his own experience as a Scotsman whose nationality is, in the modern world, a psychological problem to him. Signs of something similar can be discerned in much current American literature, but (perhaps understandably) it is not nearly so highly developed in contemporary French, German, or English literature.

In reading Mavor's plays, one is reminded, at first sight, of George Bernard Shaw's. But the similarity is only superficial. Mavor's plays cannot be mapped out so logically as Shaw's, and have no social purpose, but pose the question " who knows the heart of a man and what moves in that darkness ? " [34] With his anachronistic historical plays, his proof by paradox, his outrageous audacity, Shaw's

[32] Cp. *Lancelot* ; *Jonah and the Whale.*

[33] *Susannah and the Elders.*

[34] *Op. cit.*

was certainly a kindred spirit. But Mavor was more fanciful, and at the same time far more sensitive. He traces more of a pattern in delicate lines, and his themes and their variations allow for different layers of fun and seriousness, with overtones of mingled irony and extravaganza. His combination of extreme contrasts, the mischievous twinkle that he gives in moments of seriousness, and the depth behind his fun, are echoes of a characteristically Scottish idiom that runs, as we have seen, all through the Scottish literature of the past. Though Mavor does not ultimately have so much depth as C. M. Grieve, his plays have much less in common with Shaw's than with *A drunk Man looks at the Thistle*, and time may well show that for the first time drama achieved in them a specifically Scottish form.

3. The Modern Novel

If Scottish drama has hardly gone beyond a promise, modern Scottish fiction can hold its own beside poetry. It shows a new sense of responsibility, and the contrast with the nineteenth century is manifest. Then, the dominant attitude was one of escape into the vanished (and largely imaginary) Scotland of popular romance. Now, its eyes are open to contemporary life and social conditions. Not however as a backwash of international realism or naturalism : in the best representatives we shall find a style that is peculiarly Scottish and springs from the soil of the Scottish tradition.

For the first time, too, the city becomes the field of Scottish fiction. Not so much Edinburgh, which sits so stiffly on its seven hills,[1] as Glasgow : sprawling, sooty, ugly, slummy—yes ; but Scotland's largest and busiest city, the beating heart of the common people, the city where the present age was forged, the Glasgow of the docks, the shipyards, the Glasgow of iron and steel and unemployment, of the passions of the " fitba' mad " populace—and of the big heart. Glasgow is the titular subject of Alexander McArthur's *No Mean City* (1936). It is the setting of Dot Allan's novels of lower-middle-class family life (*The Deans*, 1929), of industrial strife (*Hunger March*, 1931), and of the shipbuilding industry (*Deepening River*, 1932). Glasgow life is also the background of John Cockburn's *Tenement* (1926) and George Woden's *Mungo* (1932), of F. J. Niven's (and J. J. Bell's) novels, and (on a more psychological level) of Edwin Muir's *Poor Tom* (1932). Victorian Glasgow figures in Guy McCrone's trilogy *Wax Fruit*. Best known of all are the novels of George Blake (*b.* 1893).[2] His finest achievement, *The Shipbuilders*, is more than a social novel of the depression years in the shipyards. When the loss of inherited craftsmanship is painted as " a glory, a passion . . . in decay," it is a question of something much more valuable than mere local colour. The novel tries to get beneath the surface to answer

[1] *E.g.* Campbell Nairne, *One Stair up*, 1932 ; Fred Urquhart, *The Ferret was Abraham's Daughter*, 1949.

[2] *Mince Collop Close*, 1923 ; *The wild Men*, 1925 ; *Young Malcolm*, 1926 ; *Paper Money*, 1928 ; *The Seas between*, 1930 ; *Returned empty*, 1931 ; *Sea Tangle*, 1932 ; *Rest and be thankful*, 1934 ; *The Shipbuilders*, 1935 ; *David and Joanna*, 1936 ; *Down to the Sea*, 1937 ; *Late Harvest*, 1938 ; *Path to Glory*, and *The Piper's Tune*, 1950.

modern Scotland's besetting problem: "What are we?"[3] Again and again it spotlights the differences between Scots and English, and emphasises the contrast between the outward decency, and respectability of the Anglified upper middle class and the crude vehemence of the passions expressed by the explosive consonants of native Scots speech. The riveter dourly sticks it out in Glasgow, but the manager, with his Oxford education and his English wife, escapes, however reluctantly, into the old comfortable certainties of life in the English home counties—almost, in itself, another Scottish tragedy. With the traditionally subjective vision of Scots writers the novel now takes easily to a mild form of "stream of consciousness."[4] But George Blake does not take over his form ready-made; he adds to it a typically Scottish delight in sensuous impressions, and the delicate touches by which he sketches in the world of outward reality suffice to keep subjectivism firmly under control.

The historical novel, once the mainstay of Scottish fiction, has undergone a remarkable transformation. Especially in the ten or fifteen years after the First World War, we do still find Jacobite novels, romances of Mary, Queen of Scots, or Montrose. Even in these the escapist tendency is less pronounced. *The Bull Calves* (1947), Naomi Mitchison's Jacobite novel about her own Haldane ancestors in Gleneagles in 1747, is a serious attempt to recreate history as the people then must have seen it; the ultimate object is to determine the common denominator of Scotland's two national traditions, the Lowland and the Highland.

Other contemporary Scottish novels reveal a new attitude towards the "clearances," the crucial event in the history of the Highlands during the nineteenth century, and still a burning issue in the hearts of many Highland crofters. Among the novels which grapple with it are *The Albanach* (1932) and *And the Cock crew* (1945), by Tom MacDonald ("Fionn MacColla"); *Campbell of Duisk* (1933), by Robert Craig; and, above all, *Butcher's Broom* (1934), by Neil M. Gunn. These novelists do not approach the clearances primarily as a means of creating a picture of past history, but as the buried root of contemporary Highland difficulties, and as the immediate cause of the crofting problem that the present generation is desperately trying to solve. History is here regarded as the matrix of the present.

[3] A question also very much in the foreground in Bruce Marshall, *The uncertain Glory* (1935), and *Father Malachi's Miracle* (1931).

[4] Cp. Sir Compton Mackenzie, *Sinister Street*, 2 vols., 1913-14.

It is only in our own generation that most Scots novelists seem to have recognised that Scott's best novels are those in which he does not confine himself to historical pageantry, but rather shows how the past shapes our lives : but these three novelists have none of Scott's romanticism, and far from envisaging the past as exerting a vague general influence, they represent it as something which has a direct impact on the daily life of their own generation. Moreover, they lay much more emphasis on past folk-experience as a factor in shaping the present than on the part played by the outstanding personalities who figure so prominently in historical text-books. In *Butcher's Broom*, the clearances are represented as the climax of a social revolution, or rather as an outcome of the disintegration of clan society ; for Neil Gunn is not interested in the exploits and achievements of kings, generals and statesmen, but in folk-life, and folk-history. This attitude is widespread in modern Scots fiction ; perhaps it is a projection of the old Scots egalitarian spirit.[5]

At first sight, this emphasis on folk-history might be dismissed as merely another instance of the modern tendency to see history from the social and economic side. But there is far more to it than that. Neil Gunn makes himself the spokesman of the old Gaelic way of life, a strongly communal life in the polity of the clan. The history of his own folk has taught him that whenever a man of genius of " humble origin," a man of the folk, aspired to a background more propitious to " the free exercise of their finer gifts of recognition," he not only failed, but was bound to fail " because the greater the genius the more certain the failure of finding the desired background where it was looked for." " If kings and nobles and millionaires did not especially attract Kenn, he believed it was because he had no particular need of them, not out of pride, inverted or otherwise, but simply because all the more subtle elements of human intuitions, the sap and health of life, came naturally out of his heritage from the folk." [6] And similarly : " ' You have the folk idea strong in you.' ' That may come out of our past, for we were a fairly communal folk until we were thoroughly debauched by predatory chiefs and the like. A feeling lingers that the poor have always been wronged. It goes pretty deep . . .'." [7] In both quotations, the behaviour of the chiefs during

[5] Other cases in point are Neil M. Gunn, *The lost Glen* (1932) ; and Ian Macpherson, *Pride in the Valley* and *Land of our Fathers* (1933).

[6] *Highland River*, 1937, p. 297.

[7] *Op. cit.*, p. 310.

the clearances is a test-case. We have seen signs of a similar attitude in the Scottish literature of earlier periods. Modern Anglo-Irish literature is full of it, and it has evidently increased with the emergence of the Celtic writer.

The role of the past in Neil Gunn's work will be fully discussed later. Here we must for a moment consider the rather different turn that an interest in the past took in Eric Linklater's *The Men of Ness: The Saga of Thorlief Coalbiter's Sons* (1932), and in Neil Gunn's *Sun Circle* (1933), a saga of the struggles of the native Gaels or Picts with the invading Northmen. Neither is really an historical novel: rather they are both groping towards a mythology of the events which made the forefathers of their race. This is especially true of *Sun Circle*, which deals, as it were, with the intersection of the mythological age, Druidism, Christianity, and the worship of Odin. This harking back to the primordial beginnings of the race strikes a keynote for modern Scottish fiction, in which the dim ages of history often throw their shadow across the path of modern man. Man is no longer seen as a being living on the level of the present; he carries his ancestors on his back, and whether he realises it or not his values and reactions are largely determined by his ancestral past. When Linklater wrote a novel of contemporary life he called it a saga (*White-Maa's Saga*, 1929), and in Gunn's whole work the age-old past can never be isolated from the present. In J. Leslie Mitchell's trilogy *A Scots Quair* the standing stones of Blaweary symbolise the survival of the past in the present, and a circle is closed when these standing stones erected by their dim ancestors become the memorial of the war that hastened the final disintegration of the crofting community.

There is something else that is revealed by works like *The Men of Ness* and *Sun Circle*. For centuries Scottish literature and culture had been the product of Edinburgh, the Lowlands, and the Border. In the twentieth century, however, there is a greater decentralisation: we see the emergence of the Highlands, the Western Isles, the extreme North where Gael and Pict and Norseman met, and of the Orkneys with their Norse past. For the first time Scottish literature presents a picture of complexity, with all the component parts and widely differing traditions contributing to and enriching Scottish culture. Perhaps the three most outstanding contemporary Scottish novelists are Neil M. Gunn, from Caithness, J. Leslie Mitchell ("Lewis Grassic Gibbon") from the Mearns of the North-East, and Eric Linklater, from Orkney; and even though some of my readers may not agree with me in placing them so high, or in that order of merit, they will serve to illustrate many of the different facets presented by the contemporary tradition of Scots fiction.[8]

Eric Linklater (1897) [9] returned to Scotland and the Orkneys largely under the influence of Scottish nationalism and of the incipient Renaissance. His plots sometimes revolve about these modern Scottish movements, which Linklater however sees, not as a reflexion of any mere parish-pump isolationism, but rather as part of the burning problems confronting the younger generation of the inter-war period. In several passages, he speaks of the lure of the soil, and confesses the dream of returning to the Orkneys to breed cattle ; his native island and the sea often symbolise purity and cleanness as against the perversion and misery of the cities. Orkney is for him a place to which he can return broken-winged to gather new strength, for there he apprehends the continuity of life from of old ; and life there is thirled to the racial past by means of all sorts of links—mysterious, mythological, irrational, scientific, and psychological. There are the brochs [10] and the sea, and man's life appears as a saga.[11] Linklater feels a pagan delight in that roaring mother-goddess, the sea round the islands ; and, as so often, the sea is endowed with its own mysterious quasi-demonic qualities. The finest passages in Linklater's novels are those fascinating, captivating Orkney sea-pictuers. In them, he shows all the old Scottish delight in precise sensuous impressions, comparisons, metaphors : " Like a flock of sheep in the morning,

[8] Apart from the novels and novelists already mentioned, one must at least enumerate : (1) Among his many other works, Sir Compton Mackenzie's humorous Highland tales (*The Monarch of the Glen*, 1941 ; *Keep the Home Guard turning*, 1943 ; *Whisky galore*, 1947 ; *Hunting the Fairies*, 1949 ; *The rival Monster*, 1952 ; *Ben Nevis goes east*, 1954 ; *Rockets galore*, 1957), in which the humour is always related to specifically Scottish questions, problems and associations, and shows fine insight ; (2) Neil Paterson (*b.* 1915), *Behold Thy Daughter* (1950), which gives an interesting picture of mid-nineteenth-century social and cultural developments in the North-East, with its herring industry ; (3) Fred Urquhart's stories (*The Clouds are big with Mercy* ; *I fell for a Sailor* ; *The last G.I. Bride wore Tartan* ; *Selected Stories*), and novels (*Time will knit* ; *The Ferret was Abraham's Daughter*, 1949 ; *Jezebel's Dust*, 1951) ; and (4) G. Scott-Moncrieff, *Café Bar* (1932) ; *Tinker's Wind* (1933), *Death's bright Shadow* (1948).

[9] *Poet's Pub*, 1929 ; *White-Maa's Saga*, 1929 ; *Juan in America*, 1931 ; *The Men of Ness*, 1932 ; *Magnus Merriman*, 1934 ; *Ripeness is all*, 1935 ; *Juan in China*, 1937 ; *The Wind on the Moon*, 1944 ; *Private Angelo*, 1946 ; *Sealskin Trousers*, 1947 ; *Mr Byculla*, 1950 ; *Laxdale Hall*, 1951 ; *The House of Gair*, 1953. See also *The Man on my Back* (autobiography), 1941.

[10] Prehistoric drystone fortifications, scattered over the North of Scotland and the Northern Isles, of problematic age and origin.

[11] Cp. *White-Maa's Saga*. (" White-maa " is an Orcadian term for the herring-gull, and is used as a nickname for the hero because of the poise and stoop with which he hits).

gently moving in a mist whose fringes are pale gold and briar-pink, Margaret's words travelled with a deceptive grace : but examine them coolly and they were nothing more than butcher's sheep." [12]

And Linklater does examine them coolly, which produces his outstanding characteristic—that slight yet unmistakable flavour of the grotesque which gives relish not only to the *Juan* novels, but to all his writing. *Juan in China* is inscribed with a Byronesque motto which ends with the verse : " I *will not* sketch your world exactly as it goes." *Juan in China* and *Juan in America* have both been misinterpreted as travel books where to find an elucidation of Oriental or American phenomena ; but Linklater is chiefly concerned to hold up a different (and largely imaginary) pattern of life in order to reveal certain ludicrous aspects of British and Western life. His grotesque distortions of history are like a stereoscope : once focus the lenses, and the picture suddenly makes sense. This he achieves by means of the old Scots trick of antithetical juxtaposition : the bar resembles an altar, the drinking an act of ritual. " To relish the unusual, the grotesque and the heteroclite was one of [Juan's] more notable faculties." [13] This characteristic runs through the whole of Linklater's work. Yet it is so elusive that one cannot easily put one's fingers on it. It is not the grotesquerie of (say) Rabelais or Smollett. The events depicted are perfectly normal, but the comparisons which they suggest in Linklater's own mind have the effect of slightly distorting the original image, which thus acquires a certain colouring of the grotesque. The brassière that Magnus's mistress has left behind suggests " grape-skins discarded on the rim of a plate. Its wistful abatement produced in Magnus a corresponding collapse, and now he perceived in his defiant sonnet something that resembled, not a soldier's plume, but a mental brassière, a lace bandage for a sagging mind." [14] At different levels of consciousness, these subtle distortions serve a strictly artistic purpose, and in laying one of these transparent images on top of another, but slightly out of place, Linklater reveals all sorts of unexpected colours, patterns, connexions, and combinations. If modern town life [15] appears as a kind of puppet-show with the pawnbroker giving lessons in wisdom and with Time in a particoloured cap banging his pig's bladder unnoticed on the face of the

[12] *Magnus Merriman*, 1934, p. 22.

[13] *Juan in China*, 1937, p. 119.

[14] *Magnus Merriman*, p. 33.

[15] It is noticeable that this grotesque element is less pronounced in Linklater's Orcadian scenes.

actors [16]—don't we start wondering about customary values? The students in *White-Maa's Saga* "played chess with words for queens and bishops, and ideas for common pawns" [17] and this is exactly Linklater's own game.

Linklater's stereoscopic distortions are often brought about by the characters viewing ordinary things when under the influence of drink. The question of drink in Scottish literature would be a fascinating and rewarding study, both in the older period when it seems part of a hilarious rebelliousness, and in recent centuries when it has often narrowed down to an occasional revolt against, or escape from, kirk discipline and bourgeois respectability.[18] Linklater's novels would be a revealing starting-point. Drink here is not so much a vice, nor an escape or stimulant, but a gateway to a new kind of world that provides distortion, new perspectives, and surprising insights. Though it has less purpose, the idea here is similar to that of *A drunk Man looks at the Thistle.* By holding his discrepant impressions side by side, Linklater creates the picture of an apparently unfamiliar world. In such moments (and also, not necessarily in connexion with drink, in his crowd scenes) we behold the wild fantastic dance of grotesque figures similar to those in "Christis Kirk," "The Dance of the sevin deidly Synnis," or "The jolly Beggars," and the outrageous fun of "The twa mariit Wemen" is never far off. This wild mocking at set forms of life has pagan violence behind it. I do not know of any other country in which is found a similar attitude to drink: but when Magnus Merriman speaks of this violent Scotland with its hard drinking as a country worth living in and refashioning, it reminds me at once of several Scottish acquaintances, poets and others, whose attitude is here summed up.[19]

The question of "reality" arises yet again in Linklater's work. Unlike George Douglas Brown and others, he does not "create" his own reality, and only an occasional sea-picture shows traces of "animism." Yet what we are shown is not strictly an objective reality, either. Often (as in his account of the prosperous Sabiston

[16] Cp. *Juan in China,* in which we find "Time's wingèd chariot changing gear."

[17] Pp. 63 f.

[18] Cp. Neil M. Gunn. *Whisky and Scotland,* 1935.

[19] In "Caraid agus Namhaid an Uisge-bheatha" (see his *Songs,* ed. W. Matheson, S.G.T.S., pp. 28 ff.), Iain MacCodrum mentions it as one of the *delights* of drinking that one of his companions may be blind drunk, another talking nonsense, and a third weeping. I have never heard of anybody else who took the same detached pleasure in these aspects of drinking!

family in *White-Maa's Saga*), Linklater goes off at a tangent, and—especially in *Juan* and *Magnus Merriman*—the total effect is that of a world which, though recognisable enough in outline, is essentially unfamiliar. The method by which he achieves this total impression is that which G. D. Brown considered characteristic of the Scottish mind, and it is one which runs, as we ourselves have seen, through the whole Scottish literature : namely the flashing together of different pictures of vivid sensuousness to produce a new compound image highly charged with meaning—actual or metaphorical. It is because the pictures thus flashed together are themselves so incongruous that the final effect has its characteristic flavour of the grotesque—as when the lobster blushes the more for the scarlet vulgarity of the tomatoes and the shameless white nakedness of the egg next to it. And though the images themselves are modern, all the essential ingredients of Linklater's grotesque irony are in fact purely traditional.

In his trilogy *A Scots Quair*, J. LESLIE MITCHELL (" LEWIS GRASSIC GIBBON," 1901-35) [20] produced the most ambitious single effort in Scottish fiction. The story moves on three distinct levels : personal, social, and mythical. On the purely personal level, it is the life story of Chris Guthrie, a crofter's daughter, who is pulled hither and thither between love and hate of the land, and of English and Scottish culture, but ultimately decides in favour of Scotland and the land. On the social level, the first of the three novels of Mitchell's *Scots Quair* deals with the breakdown of the crofting system after the artificial boom of the war ; the second with the disintegration of small-town society, which it represents as a consequence of lack of understanding and co-operation between the crofters and the working classes ; and the third (which is sometimes doctrinaire, and artistically inferior to the other two) with the fermentation in the city and the resultant upsurge of socialism and communism.

The trilogy only achieves its meaning on the third level. The personal and the social history are part of a larger, mythological cycle. All is change, nothing endures but the land, while the forms of social organisation are blown away like chaff. " Oh, once she had seen in these parks, she remembered, the truth, and the only truth that

[20] *A Scots Quair*, which comprises *Sunset Song* (1932), *Cloud Howe* (1933), and *Grey Granite* (1934), was first published as a trilogy in 1946, and reset and reprinted in 1950. Refs. below are to the 1950 edn. Mitchell's other writings (mostly published under his own name) are of no consequence from our present point of view.

there was, that only the sky and the seasons endured, slow in their change, the cry of the rain, the whistle of the whins on a winter night under the sailing edge of the moon." [21] What remains is the age-old link with the past, our dim ancestors. Not only with those who created the present form of social organisation in the Middle Ages, but more potently with our deepest roots in the time before history began. The standing stones on the hill in the Mearns, the flints of the primeval hunters before kings and culture and classes perverted the natural disposition of man. We must regain these essential, innate, unspoilt roots of life before we are able to find a way out. Chris's son Ewan, later a Communist, wonders " how the people had lived in those times." His stepfather, Robert Colquohoun, the minister of Segget, tells how " the hunters had roamed those hills, naked and bright, in a Golden Age, without fear or hope or hate or love, living high in the race of the wind and the race of life, mating as simple as beasts or birds, dying with a like keen simpleness." [22] And to Chris herself it seems that " the dead old gods that once were worshipped in the circles of stones, christianity [*sic*], socialism, nationalism—all—Clouds that swept through the Howe of the world, with men that took them for gods : just clouds, they passed and finished, dissolved and were done, nothing endured but the seeker himself, him and the everlasting Hills." [23] So it is that Chris, the woman becomes, more and more, " Chris Caledonia," [24] Scotland herself.[25] Coming from the land, she first marries a Highland crofter, then a minister, and finally a common man who is also an occasional poet. But she must be herself. And while her son Ewan starts on a Communist hunger march to London to ring in the new order, she goes back to the cottage where she was born. Here she sees that " Change, who ruled the earth . . ., Change whose face she'd once feared to see, whose right hand was Death and whose left hand Life, might be stayed by none of the dreams of men, love, hate, compassion, anger or pity, gods or devils or wild crying to the sky."[26]

If Mitchell's *Scots Quair* succeeds on this mythological plane (and many will probably agree with me that it does), that is largely because the whole story is told subjectively. Unlike most other novelists,

[21] *Cloud Howe*, henceforth cited as *C.H.*, p. 13.
[22] *C.H.*, p. 89.
[23] Ibid.
[24] *C.H.*, p. 104.
[25] *C.H.*, p. 79.
[26] *Grey Granite*, cited below as *G.G.*, p. 144.

Mitchell does not present an " objective " picture of outer reality ; instead, we are given the picture of reality as created in the mind of his characters. This, however, has nothing to do with the *parole intérieure* of the modern European or American novel. For we do not consistently view reality through the mind of one character, but are constantly flitting in and out of different minds—and often we do not even know whose thinking or monologue we are following. Often it is a vague " they of the village," and what this style presupposes is a kind of communal mind ; the total effect of this is a reality that is *both* subjective and communal. This is the culmination of the inherently dramatic character of Scots, for all the time somebody is imagined to be speaking—or letting his thinking become audible—though his identity may not be specified. One consequence of this dramatisation of the ego and its mind is the peculiar fact—which we have seen, for instance, in Hogg or Galt or Munro—that a person can view himself as " you " ; another is the intense animism or demonism that colours the resultant subjective vision of reality. Different images are flashed together, " dead " things are animated (" snow stroked the window with quiet soft fingers "), and the whole landscape, the whole environs become a living impersonation, an active force. There is always the moor round the standing stones ; [27] " it was Time himself she had seen, haunting their tracks with unstaying feet " ; [28] after a bout of religious melancholy, Robert comes " seeking her, sad and sorry for the queer, black beast that rode his mind in those haunted hours " ; [29] Chris is overcome by a renewed desire for motherhood, but suddenly remembers her first husband, killed in the war, and later recalls how she " had set her teeth fast after that, for an age, the thunder of that sea cut off by a wall, as she herself was, by a wall of fire " ; [30] and one frosty morning she sees how " the path opened out through the ragged fringe of the moor that came peering and sniffling down at Segget as a draggled cat at a dish out of doors, all the country-side begirdled with hills and their companions the moors that crept and slept and yawned in the sun, watching the Howe at its work below." [31] All this clearly is what we have called animism, made to serve the trilogy's essentially mythological purpose.

[27] The parallel with Egdon Heath in Hardy's *Return of the Native*, elsewhere general, is here specific.

[28] *C.H.*, p. 13.

[29] *C.H.*, p. 19.

[30] *C.H.*, p. 65.

[31] *C.H.*, p. 105.

As we are always listening to one speaker or another, the story is told throughout in Scots [32]—but, according to the character who is imagined to be speaking, with a varying degree of modification by the English (or pseudo-English) that has long been taught in Scottish schools. Mitchell's narrative style has consequently a transitional character, and perhaps for that reason it has received much adverse criticism. Yet it has the same music, the same cadences,[33] the same dramatic intensity, the same way of presenting abstract thought in terms of a concrete picture, the same grotesque distortion as a first step towards creating one's own reality, as the spoken Scots of earlier periods. It also contains occasional traces of Gaelic sentence structure : " They left the road and went into the wood and were presently tackling the chave [toil] of the slopes, sharp and tart the whiff of the broom, crackling underheel the old year's whins." [34] As the story flows on through the minds of the speakers, we gradually begin to recognise it for what it is—namely Scotland's modern folk speech transformed into a literary language which perhaps lacks polish, but has all the vitality of folk imagination. Mitchell's *Scots Quair* was perhaps the first major Scottish work of fiction in which any kind of Scots was used throughout for narrative as well as dialogue—that is to say, as a first-order language. And with all its crudities, his Scots is by far the most promising attempt that has yet been made towards the creation of a modern Scots prose.

It seems to me, however, that modern Scottish fiction reaches its highest peak in the novels of NEIL M. GUNN (1891),[35] so far the only Scottish novelist whose work in some measure embodies all the ideals of the Scots Renaissance. On the surface, Gunn seems chiefly or even exclusively concerned to mirror the way of life followed by crofting and fishing communities of Caithness and Sutherland. But

[32] Mitchell does not, however, use dialectal spelling.

[33] According to Ivor Brown, in his introduction, Mitchell's aim was " ' to mould the English language into the rhythms and cadences of Scots spoken speech'," but his voice is " the voice of Scotland itself."

[34] *G.G.*, p. 111. Cp. *Sunset Song*, p. 180, where Chris's first husband recalls the peewits of his native Mearns : " ' Bonny they're flying this night in Kinraddie, and Chris sleeping there, and all the Howe happed in mist '."

[35] *The grey Coast*, 1926 ; *Hidden Doors* (stories, 1929) ; *Morning Tide*, 1931 ; *The lost Glen*, 1932 ; *Sun Circle*, 1933 ; *Butcher's Broom*, 1934 ; *Highland River*, 1937 ; *Wild Geese overhead*, 1939 ; *Second Sight*, 1940 ; *The silver Darlings*, 1941 ; *Young Art and Old Hector*, 1942 ; *The Serpent*, 1943 ; *The green Isle of the great Deep*, 1944 ; *The Key of the Chest*, 1946 ; *The drinking Well*, 1947 ; *The Shadow*, 1948 ; *The lost Chart*, 1949 ; *The white Hour* (stories), 1950 ; *The Well at the World's End*, 1951 ; *Bloodhunt*, 1952.

Gunn is rarely satisfied with what meets the eye. He is well aware that each individual lives his life on many different levels at once, and Gunn shows the same insistent urge as many previous Scottish writers, not only to come very close to his object, but to probe beneath the surface and if possible to get right inside it. Consider his dialogue. Often it is not merely a communication, an exchange of opinions and information, but the words are often only the ripple on the surface which betrays thoughts or feelings that lie beneath ; and there is much " searching innuendo," much stealthy manœuvring, as each of the speakers in turn probes the other's mind, and tries first to draw him on and ultimately to drive him into a blind corner. Doubtless this reflects an essential feature of Scots conversation, with its laconic remarks and the deliberation with which it chooses each individual word.

Consequently the real life is that which is lived inside the mind. It gets its vivid signals through all the senses—and Gunn's writing is full of such wonderfully poetic impressions of the outside world, as, for example, " the hiss-hiss of the milk muffled now by the froth coming through the silence." [36] But these innumerable minute impressions have no objective value, they are only the elements out of which the mind creates its own reality. This has a life of its own ; the object is no longer a dead thing but a living creation : the thing itself is alive. Therefore Gunn can paint the force of the silence through which one cannot break, when one just cannot find a word no matter how much depends on it ; a silence that one experiences as a force, a black madness choking one. Or the moment when one just cannot bring oneself " to the point of considering any action in its bearing on " somebody else. And the final outcome is " a merging sense of oneness with the elements about " one.

Gunn achieves this typically animistic effect by essentially the same method as G. D. Brown, namely by the sheer subjective intensity with which he visualises his objects inside his mind, and also by flashing together the vivid mental pictures so formed : " The silence became so audible that Jeems heard the chuckle that was Tullach's dark smile." [37] Gunn's animism has a consciously Gaelic undertone.

[36] *The grey Coast*, p. 24.

[37] *Op. cit.*, p. 259. Other examples from *The grey Coast* : " The picture became very vivid. He saw himself . . . " ; " So vivid was the visualisation that Ivor's fingers closed involuntarily on a stone." And from *Highland River* : " Unless Kenn saw a thing he could never with certainty remember it " ; " so vividly in the dark could Kenn see a rabbit or a fox that he could put his hand on it."

The Gaelic basis of Gunn's style is apparent in the rhythms, sentence-structure and idioms [38] of the dialogue, and also, though less obviously, of the narrative. Many of the similes (for example, " the haze on the mountains was like the smoke-bloom on ripe blaeberries " [39]) are clearly of Gaelic derivation ; and Gaelic is for him the unique expression of the working of his people's mind. It is " a tongue and a rhythm that were not merely countless centuries old, but had been born out of the earth on which they starved and feasted." [40] It has " phrases that snare the heart with a hair," names that evoke " each kind of man with an astonishing, almost laughable magic." A man may say in greeting, " ' It's the fine day that's in it,' as though he were setting the day in the hollow of the world so that they might with courteous detachment regard it." [41] All this is essentially animistic; and it is precisely to this holding of a thing within arm's length and regarding it with " the eyes and the mind fastened upon it " that the intensity of Gunn's own vision is due.[42] Nor is there anything vaguely sentimental about his attitude to the old tongue. In describing a *ceilidh* he shows how an almost poetic way of expression is handed down together with all the traditional lore and wisdom, and in his account of a proverb-match we can recognise the essence of his own dialogue. The speech of his people is full of imaginative comparisons ; they " revelled in this sort of invention, for it was born naturally out of their love of the ancient tales of their race, of proverbs, of impromptu satirical verses, of song-choruses, of witty sayings and divinations. They relished the finer turns with a far keener appreciation than they relished differences in food or drink and shelter." [43] Gunn's own prose is full of pagan animism (" the moor waited, silent and flat "), and in translating abstract into concrete often personifies it : " His spirit crept out again, its tender feelers searching the desk beside him." [44] From this it is only a short step to the seeing of life in terms of an allegory : " In the centre of this gloom was the fire, and sitting round it, their knees drawn together, their heads stooped,

[38] *E.g.* " You are so " ; " after all the rain there's been in it " ; " I have heard him tell that story in a way that would take half the night and you interested and laughing " ; and Gunn's use of prepositions.

[39] *Butcher's Broom*, p. 350. The way of dividing the spectrum that lies behind the colour-adjectives used in Gaelic requires for exactness, some such comparison.

[40] *Butcher's Broom*, p. 293.

[41] *Op. cit.*, p. 13.

[42] His characters frequently watch themselves mentally.

[43] *Butcher's Broom*, p. 287.

[44] *Highland River*, p. 41.

were the old woman, like fate, the young woman, like love, and the small boy with the swallow of life in his hand." [45]

Thus we are brought face to face with the purpose behind Gunn's style. He is not interested in chance happenings ; he is looking for the pattern of life, the underlying ritual, the myth. In itself, the experience of the individual is of little interest, unless it has a relevance for all life, for the life of the race, so that the writer can say " Here is destiny ! " When, at the end of *Butcher's Broom*, the old knowing woman comes back to gather herbs near the home from which she and hers have been evicted in the Clearances, Gunn sees in her " the human mother carrying on her ancient solitary business with the earth, talking good and familiar sense with boulder and flower and rock, and now and then following a root below the surface ; in easy accord, the communion sensible and so full of natural understanding that silence might extend into eternal silence, for wind and sun to play upon." And in *Highland River*, even in hunting the salmon as it pursues its pilgrimage between light and darkness back to the source of its life, Kenn himself is making a similar journey back to the source of his own life.

But where is this source? What is the law, the ritual, the driving force by which man is governed in tracing the pattern of his life? This is the key question of modern literature. Ernest Hemingway, the American, answered it by going back to the elemental, primitive, instinctive values. Neil Gunn, the Scot and Gael, answers it in terms of man's ancestral past, in terms of the primordial ages before the dawn of history. In order to understand this, one has to see Sutherland and Caithness, the far North, where the strange mountains that rise so abruptly out of the lonely moors give nature itself a primordial appearance.

Far from being either romantic or sentimental, Gunn's vision of history and prehistory is at once scientific and mystical. He knows how profoundly man is affected by his environment—and how profoundly he affects it ; he knows, too, how close man can grow to the things by which he is surrounded. Here speaks the Gael, with all that fervent loyalty to his native glen which made the Clearances so tragic. Man is at one with all his ancestors, he carries his racial past in him ; especially in a woman, " all the history of her people is writ on her face." But to have this importance, history must be the history of the folk, not history as contained in school books. Gunn's

[45] *Butcher's Broom*, p. 31.

mind quickens when he stands before the traces of his real ancestors, who left the brochs behind them : " If he could recapture this he would recapture . . . the old primordial goodness of life, . . . its moments of absolute ecstacy." Therefore man must find his source : " It is a far cry to the golden age, to the blue smoke of the heather fire and the scent of the primrose ! Our river took a wrong turning somewhere. But we haven't forgotten the source. . . . Who knows what's waiting me there ? " [46]

As he broods on the old dark potent ways, Gunn sees man as in the last analysis a product of the processes that went to the making of the race itself, and " ancestral " is sometimes almost identical with " atavistic." Why does the heart beat higher in hunting, in fishing? Isn't it everywhere in Scottish literature? Why is the soul searched by the cry of the pee-wit and curlew? What is it that allures us in the scent of the heather fire or the primrose, if not some ancestral instinct? The frenzy a boy feels when burning dry whin in spring is an age-old tribal urge, and darkness, " mythic light," holds man with primordial powers : " In this darkness of the world identity is lost and time becomes one with the monstrous beginnings of life, which legend recreates in such beings as centaur or water kelpie." [47] And beyond that is the sea, a mystic and cleansing force, the uncertain sea, older than myth itself.

" The monstrous beginnings of life." The " blind " instinctive urges that make us act as we do, are older even than our ancestors. Gunn the scientist is keenly aware of man's pre-human heredity, and his conception of it as a living force is similar to Edwin Muir's. The boy Kenn muses on his fight with the salmon : " No wonder Kenn was inclined to fall into a state of abstraction, where story and meaning ran into a silver glimmer, or dropped out of sight altogether, dropped, perhaps, upon some ' continental ledge ' of the mind, whence, through aeons back beyond reckoning, it had emerged upon the beaches, the rivers, and finally upon the dry land." [48] That is why Gunn so frequently takes a boy, or a woman, as the central figure : in them the myth of life with its primordial urges is strongest.

But Neil Gunn does not merely hark back to the historic or the primeval, prehuman past ; nor is he a provincial. Our ancestral heritage, our native environment is the gate through which we enter

[46] *Highland River*, p. 168.
[47] *Butcher's Broom*, pp. 297 f.
[48] *Highland River*, p. 43.

life. To understand ourselves we must know how we reached this gate. But at a gate the main question is, " Where do we go from here ? " More than any other Scottish writer Neil Gunn is " modern "; he always strives to relate the past to the present, and in doing so he uses the past to provide symbols which could express the contemporary issues with which he is ultimately concerned. " In fact if a Scot is interested in dialectical materialism or proletarian humanism, it seems to me he should study the old system in order to find out how the new system would be likely to work amongst his kind. It might help him at least to get rid of his more idealistic wind." [49] *The green Isle of the great Deep* might be called a fantasia, a dream-allegory put to new purpose. It moves on many different levels and is almost a poem. On one level, it is concerned with totalitarianism (and with all the correlated issues of freedom, order, " brain-washing," psychological research into the mind of man, civilisation, culture, science, war, mathematics), and has a dispassionate clarity that one would hardly have believed possible in a novel written during the Second World War when these issues were at stake. But this discussion does not take place in a vacuum. The universe is presented in terms familiar to the Celtic mind, and the clue that finally supplies a solution is the purely Gaelic symbol of the hazelnuts of knowledge that have fallen into the river of life, and been eaten by the salmon of wisdom. Though knowledge has been divorced from wisdom, the legend, in Gunn's eyes, contains a remedy ; for whereas modern civilisation has destroyed the unity even of a child's mind—where the myth of life should be strongest—young Art the Highlander is still an integrated personality, a complete boy. This recognition includes a revaluation of " primitive " patterns of culture, and of Gaeldom, and it provides the key for Gunn's set of symbols.

My own favourite among Neil Gunn's novels is *Highland River* (with *Silver Darlings* second). Outwardly the plot is simply the story of Kenn's search for the source of the Highland river where he was born ; but the action is only a gateway to Gunn's interpretation of life, of the modern world, of the heritage of man.

The Highland river becomes the river of life to Kenn at the age of nine, when, one early dawn, he discovers an enormous salmon in the pool. Irrational, primal fear comes upon him : " Out of that noiseless world in the grey of the morning all his ancestors came at

[49] *Op. cit.*, p. 311.

him," and he simply must catch this salmon. Man ancestral has met man modern. The mysterious force that makes the fish seek the source of the river enters Kenn's breast, and he too feels a compulsion to follow the traces of his ancestors. First, he makes the lower part of the river, the realm of man, his own ; then he conquers the middle part, the strath with its darkness and ancestral memories. And finally, after the war and a career as a scientist, Kenn finds the way from the habitation of man by the sea to the source in the moor, where he discovers what man has lost. And he also finds his own soul : "I am the Pict. . . . He was a solitary. That was his destiny." But this is only a framework, and only beginning and end have their fixed place in time. At any moment, the shadow of the dim past may fall across Kenn's path, or the hand reach for the stars. This novel—or is it a prose poem ?—comprises the whole complexity of life : science, Shakespeare, Nietzsche, Kepler—but mirrored in a perfect crystal. We divine the real history of mankind and the myth of life, from men of daring, from fishers and explorers to the modern scientist, while politicians, clerks, generals are what the river carries with it. *Highland River* also contains Gunn's style and vision at their best.

It is fitting to end this survey of the Scottish tradition in literature with Neil Gunn. More clearly even than C. M. Grieve he embodies the aims of the Scottish Renaissance. All his strength, his vision, his style come from his people, from the Scottish tradition, from the Gaelic past, but he applies them to the crucial questions of our time. What he has to say is a concern of all men. Scottish literature here is national, yet knows no national limitations.

General Bibliography

This selective bibliography contains works of general reference, and is merely supplementary to the detailed bibliographical information provided in the footnotes. For general works on Gaelic poetry, see p. 185, nn. 1-2. Most of the Scots texts cited from Barbour to Fergusson, though not all, have now appeared in the Scottish Text Society (S.T.S.), several of the Gaelic texts cited in the Scottish Gaelic Text Society (S.G.T.S.). Some anthologies are included in this general list.

BROWN, P. HUME. *A Short History of Scotland*, 1908 : rev. edn. by H. W. Meikle, 1951.

—— *Early Travellers in Scotland*, 1891.

—— *History of Scotland*, 3 vols. 1911.

—— *Scotland before 1700, from Contemporary Documents*, 1893.

BUCHAN, JOHN. *The Northern Muse*, anthology, 1931.

CHAMBERS, E. K. *English Literature at the Close of the Middle Ages*, Oxford History of English Literature, 1945.

COCHRAN-PATRICK, R. W. *Medieval Scotland*, 1892.

Edinburgh Essays on Scots Literature, being a Course of Lectures delivered at the University of Edinburgh, with pref. by H. J. C. Grierson, 1933.

EYRE-TODD, GEORGE. *Medieval Scottish Poetry; Scottish Poetry of the Sixteenth Century; Scottish Poetry of the Seventeenth Century; Scottish Poetry of the Eighteenth Century;* anthologies, 1892 ff.

FERGUSSON, JAMES. *The Green Garden*, anthology, 1946.

FINLAY, IAN. *Scotland*, 1945.

GEDDIE, W. A. *A Bibliography of Middle Scots Prose*, S.T.S., 1912.

GRANT, I. F. *The Social and Economic Development of Scotland before 1603*, 1930.

—— *Everyday Life in Old Scotland*, 1931-2.

GRAY, M. M. *Scottish Poetry from Barbour to James VI*, anthology, 1935.

GRIEVE, C. M. See " MACDIARMID, HUGH."

HENDERSON, T. F. *Scottish Vernacular Literature*, 1898 ; 3rd edn., 1910.

KINSLEY, J. See *Scottish Poetry*.

LAURIE, H. *Scottish Thought in its National Development*, 1902.

LEWIS, C. S. *English Literature in the Sixteenth Century, excluding Drama*, Oxford History of English Literature, 1954.

LINDSAY, M. *Modern Scottish Poetry, An Anthology of the Scottish Renaissance, 1920-45* (cf. also *Poetry Scotland*, ed. M. Lindsay, semi-annual anthology, 1943-9).

" MacDiarmid, Hugh " [C. M. Grieve]. *The Golden Treasury of Scottish Poetry*, anthology, 1940.

Mackenzie, A. Mure. *An Historical Survey of Scottish Literature to 1714*, 1933.

Mackie, R. L. *A Book of Scottish Verse*, anthology, World's Classics, 1934.

Metcalfe, W. M. *Specimens of Scottish Literature, 1325-1835*, anthology, 1913.

Millar, J. H. *A Literary History of Scotland*, 1903.

—— *Scottish Prose of the Seventeenth and Eighteenth Centuries*, 1912.

Muir, E. *Essays on Literature and Society*, 1949.

—— *Scott and Scotland: The Predicament of the Scottish Writer*, 1936.

Oliver, J. W. See Smith, J. C.

Power, W. *Literature and Oatmeal*, 1935.

Rait, R. S. *History of Scotland*, 1914.

Ramsay, M. P. *Calvin and Art*, 1938.

Reid, J. M. *Modern Scottish Literature*, Saltire Society, 1945. See also *Some Scottish Arts*.

Scotland: A Description of Scotland and Scottish Life, ed. H. W. Meikle, 1947 ; repr. 1955.

Scottish Poetry: A Critical Survey, ed. J. Kinsley, 1955.

Smith, G. Gregory. *Scottish Literature: Character and Influence*, 1919.

—— *Specimens of Middle Scots*, 1902.

—— *The Transition Period*, 1927.

Smith, J. C., and J. W. Oliver. *A Scots Anthology*, 1949.

Smith, S. G. *A Short Introduction to Scottish Literature*, 1951.

Some Scottish Arts, ed. J. M. Reid, Saltire Society, 1951.

Speirs, J. *The Scots Literary Tradition*, 1940.

Thomson, G. M. *A Short History of Scotland*, 1930.

Veitch, J. *The Feeling for Nature in Scottish Poetry*, 2 vols., 1887.

—— *The History and Poetry of the Scottish Border*, 1893.

Watt, L. Maclean. *Scottish Life and Poetry*, 1912.

Wood, H. Harvey. *Scottish Literature*, 1952.

Young, D. C. C. *Scottish Verse, 1851-1951*, anthology, 1952.

Index

O

P

Q

R